CHRISTIAN
PERSPECTIVES
ON
SOCIOLOGY

D1044565

CHRISTIAN
PERSPECTIVES
ON
SOCIOLOGY

Stephen A. Grunlan &
Milton Reimer, Editors

ZONDERVAN
PUBLISHING HOUSE OF THE ZONDERVAN CORPORATION
GRAND RAPIDS, MICHIGAN 49506

CHRISTIAN PERSPECTIVES ON SOCIOLOGY
Copyright © 1982 by The Zondervan Corporation
Grand Rapids, Michigan

Library of Congress in Publication Data
Main entry under title:

Christian perspectives on sociology.

    Bibliography: p.
    Includes index.
    1.   Sociology, Christian—Addresses, essays,
lectures.   I.   Grunlan, Stephen A.   II.   Reimer, Milton K.
BT738.C475   301   81-23135
ISBN 0-310-36331-4   AACR2

This edition February 1982

Edited by John Danielson and Edward Viening

Designed by Martha Bentley

Printed in the United States of America

093680

CONTENTS

PREFACE

Both of us have been teaching sociology on the undergraduate level at Christian colleges for several years. While teaching sociology we have used what we felt were the best introductory texts on the market. However, these texts were produced for the secular market and have been at best neutral and at times antagonistic to Christian concerns. Therefore, for the past few years we have felt a need for a reader that would give a Christian perspective to the discipline as a whole, as well as to specific subareas within the discipline. In discussions with some of our colleagues, we sensed that they saw a similar need.

After some research and discussion it seemed that the best approach was to produce a collection of essays dealing with the various subfields of sociology. To accomplish this we decided to recruit from various Christian colleges Christian sociologists who would address the subfields in which they were most competent.

Our contributors represent a broad range of theological and sociological perspectives. The common denominator for all of them is a commitment to sociology as a discipline and a commitment to integrating the discipline with their Christian faith. Although our contributors represent various theological traditions, they all are committed to the lordship of Jesus Christ and the infallibility of the Bible as the divine rule for Christian faith and practice.

The contributors were not given a strict outline to follow, but rather were supplied with the basic purpose of the volume and general stylistic guidelines. Each essay was critiqued by another contributor and revised in line with the recommendations made. As editors we have attempted to allow the authors' ideas to stand with as few editorial changes as possible. Not all of the contributors have agreed with each other, nor have we always agreed with the contributors; however, we believe that an honest exchange of ideas within an evangelical perspective is healthy. Education should stimulate thought and debate rather than just indoctrinate.

The reader may agree with some of the contributors and disagree with others. It is our hope that the reader, whether agreeing or disagreeing, will be stimulated to integrate his or her Christian world view with a sociological perspective. It is also our hope that the reader will catch a glimpse of the potential contributions that sociology can make to the furtherance of the gospel of Jesus Christ and the growth of His church. The discussion questions at the end of each chapter are designed to help the reader think through some of these issues.

This collection has been written so that it may either be used by itself in the classroom, supplemented by lecture material, or used as a supplement to a standard text. While the volume is capable of standing by itself, it would make an excellent supplement to a standard introductory sociology textbook.

We would like to thank our wives and families for their cooperation and patience during this project. We also want to thank Carol Anderson for coordinating the typing and Linda Lenz, Jane Whipple, and Sally Yoder for their typing of the edited manuscript. We would also like to thank sociology students Bonnie Bowers, Steve Hill, Sue Ostigaard, Peggy Shoop, Arlys Walter, and Jay Williams for their help in compiling references.

Bible quotations are from the New International Version, unless otherwise stated.

Stephen A. Grunlan
Milton K. Reimer

CHRISTIAN PERSPECTIVES ON SOCIOLOGY

1

MILTON K. REIMER
St. Paul Bible College,
Minnesota

THE STUDY OF SOCIOLOGY: AN INTRODUCTION

"Sociology is a growing industry. Each year larger numbers of people start courses in sociology, either as a main subject for a degree, or as a component of a course in education, social work, or industry" (Lyon, 1976:7). This condition obviously has implications for the Christian community, which is increasingly committed to providing a total education for its members. Christian youth are studying sociology—along with other related social sciences—and are confronted with views and data that frequently appear hostile to a biblical perspective of humanity and society.

Appearance, however, is often inadequate in its portrayal of reality, and it is my view that valid sociological data (or raw facts) are not inherently hostile to a biblical perspective. Indeed, as Holmes (1977) declares in the title *All Truth Is God's Truth*, the Christian must assume the ultimate coherence of sociological data with biblical truth. It is in the area of interpretation and perspective that the Christian may differ from and disagree with the non-Christian sociologist.

SOCIOLOGY DEFINED

Sociology has been variously defined as "the scientific study of human social behavior" (Perry and Perry, 1979:4), "the systematic study of the development structure, interaction and collective behavior of organized groups of human beings" (Horton and Hunt, 1976:3), "the study of those aspects of human life that result from our being members of society" (Denisoff and Wahrman, 1979:9), "the application of scientific methods of inquiry to the puzzles of social life" (Boughey, 1978:3), and "the study of the agreements that people make, organize, teach, break and change" (Babbie, 1977:11).

These definitions vary according to each author's perspective and intended purpose, but in most cases they emphasize two main components: that sociology deals with society and social interaction, and that it relies on the scientific method to pursue its goals. These emphases are significant, not only because they identify sociology as a social science, but also because they distinguish it from the other social sciences such as economics, geography, and psychology.

Of all the social sciences, psychology shares the most common features with sociology. The line of demarcation between where psychology ends and sociology begins is blurred; hence a course such as social psychology is often taught in both the psychology and sociology departments of the same university. The simple difference betwen the two areas is that psychology deals with the individual, while sociology deals with the group. But society is composed of individuals, and no one person functions in complete isolation from his or her social environment.

There is, of course, some overlapping among the social sciences because all are concerned with the various aspects of human behavior. In fact, when sociology first emerged as a distinct social science, it was conceived to be the "queen of sciences." All knowledge related to human behavior was to be integrated in this discipline. Sociological pioneers such as Auguste Comte, Herbert Spencer, and Lester Ward were essentially social philosophers who concentrated on the "grand system of theory" (Horton and Hunt, 1976:17). They were concerned with the development of all-encompassing philosophical explanations rather than the collection of data to support their theories.

The emergence of sociology as a distinct discipline was predicated on its strong scientific orientation. In order to compete with the long-established disciplines such as history, law, and political science, it was necessary that sociology have a recognized and legitimate area of study not yet covered by other disciplines. The direction that this necessity imposed on sociology, coupled with the Comtian heritage of positivism,[1] was to make it increasingly scientific in nature. This scientific development of the discipline became"increasingly apparent in the twenties and consummated in the dominance of an empiricism heavily weighted with methods of research and 'systems analysis' by the end of the thirties" (Hansen and Gerstl, 1967:11). Sociology has in recent decades been dominated by a "movement toward methodological sophistification in both statistical techniques and conceptual systems" (Hansen and Gerstl, 1967:11).[2]

From the foregoing discussion three things are obvious: (1) sociology is not a static discipline; (2) it does tend to reflect the tempo of the times; and (3) it lays claim to being a full-fledged social science.[3]

SOCIOLOGY, SCIENCE, AND METHOD

Because sociology makes strong claims to being a social science and consequently uses the scientific method as its tool to arrive at

---

[1]Positivism, or logical positivism, holds that valid knowledge can come only from directly testable experimentation and not from personal experience. Comte serves as a direct link between sociology and positivism because he first coined the word *sociology* and also pioneered in the development of positivism as a philosophy.

[2]Not all sociologists are so statistically oriented. For example, Jacques Ellul, a French sociologist and author of the insightful and incisive work *The Technological Society,* has little use for this exclusive orientation. And Peter Berger (1963:11–12) notes that although statistics may be necessary at times and can provide some necessary data for the sociologist, it is not the whole orientation of the discipline. Indeed, it is but a small part of it; the use of statistics is to sociology what making nasty smells in test tubes is to chemistry.

[3]Many introductory sociology texts place a strong emphasis on the scientific nature of the discipline. There is, however, a growing awareness among sociologists of nonscientific dimension to the discipine (Boughey, 1978:215–26).

truth, it is necessary to define both science and the scientific method. In the early history of thought, science and knowledge were essentially synonymous terms. Later, especially during the period known as the scientific revolution, science emerged as a very special kind of knowledge. Science as a branch of knowledge must be precise and deal with facts, or truth, systematically arranged and clearly defined. Further, science assumes that there is order in the universe as well as regular patterns and rules that can be discovered and understood.

The source of truth has been debated and discussed for as long as there has been recorded history. Several of the main sources are (1) intuition, (2) authority, (3) tradition, and (4) common sense (Horton and Hunt, 1976: 3–7). Each of these has served a useful purpose in the accumulation of human knowledge. Logic—a fifth, nonscientific source—should be added. The ancient Greek philosophers (as well as some more modern ones) arrived at some rather profound insights and knowledge regarding humankind and their world purely on the basis of logic.

Science, however, suggested a totally novel approach to truth. In fact, the scientific methodology is so much a part of science itself that the two are essentially synonymous. To arrive at truth via the scientific method several important steps must be followed. First, the problem must be stated in precise terms. It must be carefully defined and delineated in the form of a hypothesis. This hypothesis, in turn, must be tested or verified, *but not necessarily proven true.*[4]

The second step is to collect data. As far as possible all data relevant to the hypothesis are gathered for analysis. The third step is to analyze the data and determine their significance to the problem. Depending on the sophistication of the project, various possible statistical designs may be employed to determine the significance.

The final step is to draw conclusions from the data and to deter-

---

[4]Given the idea of scientific truth as discussed below, the usual procedure in science is to use the null hypothesis, that is, the hypothesis stated in negative terms. Science supposedly can only prove things false, not true. This position raises some serious philosophical questions, for if we cannot recognize truth, only error, how can we be sure that the error is not, in fact, truth?

mine the extent of their support of the hypothesis. When this is done one more thing remains—the verification of the research. To insure against false conclusions and erroneous findings, the projects must be repeated under the same conditions and with the same results.

Several references have been made to *truth*, and it is important to understand some distinctions that are made in the use of that term and how it is perceived. There are three questions we need to ask. The first is, Is truth objective or subjective? This question assumes that our standard of truth generally is either internal or external. Objective truth is truth that can be verified by criteria outside of the person seeking it. On the other hand, subjective truth needs no external verification and simply meets one's own personal standard. Scientific truth is objective.

A second question regarding truth that is relative to this discussion is, Is it tentative or final? Final truth is a closed case and needs no further examination. Tentative truth, however, is simply the current state of human understanding. There is always the possibility that further insights and new information will change current knowledge. Scientific truth, above all else, is tentative. There are no final answers to scientific questions, and the most hallowed theories of science are subject to modification if and when new data are brought to bear on the problem.

A third and final question that may be raised is, Is truth relative or absolute? This philosophical question is somewhat less relevant to the present discussion than the previous two issues. Believers in truth as relative insist that there are no final, absolute answers. Truth along with everything else is in a state of continuous change. Those who believe that there is absolute truth search for it, although it may be difficult to arrive ultimately at truth.

Scientific truth may be perceived as being either relative or absolute, depending on the scientist's personal world view. Neither of these positions is inherently either proscience or antiscience, and it is perfectly compatible with science to believe that there is absolute truth but that our present view of a problem represents a tentative understanding of the truth related to it.

Sociology as a science is committed to the use of the scientific method that most other sciences scrupulously use. But because it is a *social* science, sociology cannot be as accurate and exact as the physical sciences. Social action is not as predictable as the physical universe; and unless one holds to absolute determinism, human will and freedom preclude *ultimate* scientific understanding and prediction of social action.

But sociologists can proceed with meaningful investigations. Given the scientific tools and recognizing the limits of the discipline, they can observe, do content analysis, engage in survey research, use case studies, and conduct controlled experiments as they gather objective data for further analysis.[5]

Before leaving the area of science, two additional items need some further consideration. The first item is that of scientism. Scientism, according to *Webster's Third New International Dictionary* is "a thesis that the methods of the natural sciences should be used in all areas of investigation including philosophy, the humanities and the social sciences; a belief that only such methods can fruitfully be used in the pursuit of knowledge." Thus scientism is an ideology—a world view—that assumes all other approaches to truth are useless if not worse. In fact, scientism affirms that no knowledge other than scientific knowledge exists, according to Robert Fischer, who quotes Holton as saying, "Scientism divides all thought into two categories—up-to-date scientific knowledge and nonsense" (1971:44).

The difference between science and scientism must be clearly understood. It is not necessary to believe in scientism to be either a scientist or to study the physical or social sciences. The scientist, like any other human being, goes to work with a set of assumptions and presuppositions—a world view—that affects his perspective of the scientific data. But "the practice of science is not limited to persons who adhere to any particular world view" (Fischer, 1971:104).

The second item has already been introduced in the discussion

---

[5]Berelson and Steiner (1964:16–17) have summarized the criteria by which the social sciences can conduct meaningful and *scientific* investigations: (1) the procedures are publicly knowable and known, (2) the definitions are clear and precise, (3) the investigation is objective and unbiased, (4) the findings are reproducible, (5) the procedure is organized and cumulative, and (6) the purpose is to explain, to understand, and to predict.

of the first—the assumptions and presuppositions of science.[6] One of the often-repeated claims of science is that it is objective, and scientists will normally attempt to do their research in this frame of reference. But it is impossible for any person to be completely objective. Our presuppositions, according to Schaeffer, form a grid through which we see the world. They also provide a basis for our values, and these in turn determine our behavior and our decisions (1976:19–20).

C. A. Coulson, an Oxford mathematician and scientist, states emphatically that

> science is full of presuppositions—it is true that these may be derived from some earlier metaphysic, but they have been adopted and, like most presuppositions, their existence is frequently not recognized even by those most affected by them. In this case the presuppositions are such as to carry science, properly understood, into the realm of religion (1958:75).

It is important for every student of science, whether physical or social science, to spend time examining the presuppositions and assumptions basic to the material presented. The author of the text, the professor in the classroom and lab, and the resource materials made available to the students all come permeated with assumptions and presuppositions. This is not in itself a bad situation. The tragedy comes with the belief that science is totally objective while, let us say, religion is the opposite. Again Coulson speaks plainly: "The greater part of our schoolboy's acceptance of science and rejection of religion springs from his unexamined belief that science accepts no presuppositions, and therefore must be superior to a Christianity which is overloaded with them. Yet this view is wholly wrong" (1958:72).

SOCIOLOGICAL ASSUMPTIONS AND PERSPECTIVES

Having seen that science in general cannot claim to be totally objective or free from assumptions and presuppositions, we now observe that sociology as a social science is bound by the same limitations. Most sociologists will admit to some assumptions and

---

[6]In chapter 2 the author provides a treatment of the assumptions of science from another perspective. Although there appears to be considerable overlapping of materials, the reader is encouraged to note the differences in approach and emphasis in each author's treatment.

will state them for clear recognition. Duberman and Hartjen identify three major assumptions: (1) "that there are patterns and order in social life," (2) "that people cannot become human unless they interact with human beings," and (3) "that humans differ from other animals in that they possess culture " (1979:5–6).[7]

A few additional assumptions must be identified that surface frequently in the study of sociology and that are rather widely accepted in secular[8] sociology. The first of these assumptions is that all things are relative in society. Lyon (1976:13) refers to this as "the tendency of sociology to relativize." Certain social values, beliefs, and norms are simply the expression of that society, and one set is as good as another. Granted, a sociologist does not *have* to hold these assumptions, but the predominant view within the discipline is that there are no absolute social guidelines (see chap. 3 for a discussion of cultural relativism).

Closely related to this assumption is another one: that nothing is sacred and that every human act is the open domain of sociological inquiry. On the one hand this leads to what Peter Berger calls the "debunking motif," in which the so-called myths of society are exposed for what they are by sociologists who have the final scientific answers. On the other hand it may lead the sociologist into an ethical dilemma of using surreptitious means to obtain data that otherwise might be unavailable.[9] (Ethical issues related to social research will be discussed in chap. 2.)

The presuppositions and assumptions held by sociologists form the subconscious grid through which the data passes and that determines to some degree its interpretation. There are, however, several sociological perspectives or theoretical frameworks that

---

[7]Note that these assumptions are in turn based on further assumptions. For example, (2) assumes that the unborn child, or for that matter, the newly born infant, is not yet a human being (see chapter 2 for some additional assumptions of science). It should also be noted that not everyone will accept these statements as assumptions.

[8]See footnote 13 on page 21.

[9]An example of this is the Tearoom studies conducted by Laud Humphrey. In this study of homosexual behavior in public restrooms, the researcher posed as a lookout for the men and in only a few instances did he reveal his real purpose. Almost all his research was done surreptitiously (Perry and Perry, 1979:21).

constitute the primary ways sociologists explain human interaction and social organization.

The first of these to serve as a grand theory was the evolutionary model. The early sociologists were especially enamored with the then current findings of Darwin, so they easily adapted a biological model to explain the workings of sociology. As the full implications of social Darwinianism gradually dawned on sociologists, they began searching for alternative theories.[10]

Sociologists traditionally have held to one of the following models: the functional model, the conflict theory, and the symbolic-interaction model. The functional model takes its cue from biology. As a living organism has many parts with varying functions, with each part fulfilling an essential role to keep the whole alive, so society consists of separate parts—numerous social systems and groups—that maintain the whole. When all parts function properly and cooperate with each other, society is healthy. If any part breaks down, society suffers.

This model appears to be quite compatible with a Christian perspective. The Bible often uses the human body as an illustration of the interdependence and function of the Christian community (Eph. 4:16). When one member suffers, the whole body suffers. When one part fails to function properly, the entire body is negatively affected by the failure. Thus the Christian community affects society as a whole.

The view of the conflict theory is just the opposite of the functional model. Adherents of this theory see society as a system made up of competing parts and groups. The tension resulting from such competition may sometimes be disruptive and temporarily destructive, but in the end the results will be beneficial and positive. This theory fits easily into the Marxian view of history and society.

Although this theory appears to have a more limited application from the Christian perspective, it is still informative and instructive. Conflict is a fact of life, and some conflict is at times necessary and even beneficial in the Christian context. Biblical conflict is

---

[10]In theory, social Darwinianism supported the idea of the superiority of certain races, and it also implied that an inferior genetic quality produced poor and underprivileged people.

between good and evil, and Jesus Himself said, "I did not come to bring peace, but a sword" (Matt. 10:34).[11]

Symbolic interaction is the third major model. As the term implies, sociologists who hold to this theory believe that the basis for society is in the interaction among individuals in everyday life. Such interaction occurs either verbally or nonverbally and usually in small groups. Effective communication becomes the key to the orderly maintenance of societal structure. People create and share symbols and behave in predictable patterns in order to ensure that others will do the same in return.

It is not desirable to identify any of these various models as *the* Christian model. The Christian needs to learn from all the possible perspectives and carefully develop an integrated Christian view.

SOCIOLOGY AND CHRISTIAN BELIEFS

At this juncture it becomes important to focus directly on the implications of the Christian faith for the study of sociology. Some of these have been alluded to already; others will be specifically dealt with in this section.

To begin with, it needs to be stated that while the authority of the Bible must be respected, it is not a Christian sociology that is advocated. The discipline of sociology is in itself neutral and descriptive, not normative. What is advocated are Christian sociologists[12] and a Christian perspective of sociological data. This requires the subordination of the discipline to the authority of the Scriptures. This is not to say that the Bible is a textbook on sociology; it is not. But when it speaks on topics that have implications for sociology, it takes precedence over secular authority. Furthermore the Bible does lay down norms for human behavior that the Christian sociologist must take into account.

A second implication that arises from seeking a Christian perspective in sociology is that Christian assumptions that have their source in Scripture must be carefully identified and must become

---

[11]It needs to be pointed out that some Christian sociologists see the conflict model as quite compatible with their Christian perspective.

[12]It is not merely sociologists who are Christians that I am advocating. There is a profound difference between the two. The Christian sociologist integrates his faith into the study of the discipline, while the other is first of all a sociologist who happens to be a Christian by religious identity.

the grid through which the data passes. Again, this does not presuppose a single interpretation for all data. Christian sociologists may well disagree on the meaning of events and trends, but even in their disagreements they have a common reference point—the Word of God.

Because sociology is primarily concerned with the behavior of human beings in a social environment, one of the first questions to be raised in relation to Christian belief is, What is the essence of human nature? The answer to this question is ultimately the starting point for two very divergent sociological perspectives. Also, it has profound implications for current social issues and concerns. Cosgrove states this clearly in relation to psychology, but his comments have equal significance to the study of sociology: "It is especially important to clarify our understanding of the nature of man because our view of human nature affects critical issues of society, such as capital punishment, abortion, and biological and psychological engineering, to name a few" (1977:12).

The secular sociologist[13] is almost always committed to a random/chance-evolutionary view of humanity. From this view it follows that a person *becomes* human as a result of socialization (Horton and Hunt, 1976:88). Also, through socialization a person *becomes* either a man or a woman; a person *becomes* oriented either toward the opposite sex or to his own sex.

The Christian, however, is compelled to begin with a biblical view of human nature. God created humans in His own image, and the reflection of God's image continues in all people regardless of age, sex, skin color, or moral condition. The child does not *become* human when he or she begins to assimilate the cultural patterns of environment. Rather, the child *is* human by virtue of God's creative act (Gen. 1:26–27).

Part of the question concerning human nature has to do with its inherent sinfulness. Secular social scientists (the term social sci-

---

[13]By *secular* this author means a view that essentially omits God. In the classical definition of this term, secular meant the removal from ecclesiastical control, but not necessarily nonreligious. In modern parlance the term is commonly used to distinguish between that which includes a notion of God and that from which such a notion has been removed. Hence secular has come to mean godless.

entist rather than sociologist is used here to include the entire social science field) generally assume a neutral moral condition for people and their behavior. Humanistic social scientists see human beings as basically good. While people may have some bad qualities, they will tend to do the best when left to themselves. Human nature is good—or at least neutral—and therefore it should be encouraged rather than suppressed (Cosgrove and Mallory, 1977:26). This view goes along with the secular sociological idea that it is never appropriate to pass judgment on any social behavior, no matter how bizarre or deviant. It often further follows that no person need assume any moral guilt for any behavior.

The behaviorist is equally adamant regarding the neutrality of human nature. After all, if a person is strictly the product of his or her environment, then it is the environment that must take the blame for behavior, not the person.

The Christian view of human nature takes into account both good and evil in the person. Cosgrove states:

> Succinctly, the Christian view explains that man aspires to good because he is created in God's image, but it is impossible for man not to "sin" because he is born alienated from God, and thus is self-centered at birth. Consequently, life is a struggle to become other-centered. This Christian view of man offers an explanation for much that is paradoxical about man's nature (Cosgrove and Mallory, 1977:27).

Sin, too, represents a notion that needs attention. According to Lyon, the Christian will recognize that people in society are sinful and that many of the expressions of society may indeed be the result of sin. Secular sociologists will not usually admit this, but they will bring their own assumptions into their studies— assumptions regarding the innate neutrality or goodness of people and of the nonexistence of universal or absolute norms (1976: 65–66). When viewed from the secularist perspective, social deviance is simply an alternative lifestyle and carries with it no moral responsibility or guilt.

Not all secular social scientists have abandoned the notion of sin. Karl Menninger states that for the past fifty years social scientists (he refers here specifically to psychologists) have persistently attempted to annihilate the "sin" concept. And, as he sees it, they have been quite successful. Those who continued to articulate their belief in sin became fewer and fewer in number, and in any case were no longer heard above the "cheers of the new psychologists" (1973:46). According to Menninger, however, there is a need to revive the concept of sin. Sociological terms such as crime, delinquency, and deviance do not adequately cover such human behavior as immorality, unethical behavior, and wrongdoing. The concept of sin is needed to deal with the moral aspects of human behavior.

It is not likely that Menninger represents a major movement among secular social scientists to reintroduce the concept of sin to the discipline. Sin carries with it too many implications regarding moral responsibility to a divine authority. Such moral responsibility is incompatible with either the humanist or the behaviorist position. But Menninger's position does throw doubt on the generally accepted notion of human neutrality and/or innate goodness.[14]

In the final analysis the acceptance or rejection of the assumptions underlying any belief system is related to choice and the individual will. "If any man is willing to do His will, he shall know of the teaching, whether it is of God, or *whether* I speak from Myself" (John 7:17 NASB). Once the will is exercised to make the choice in favor of Christian assumptions, the person finds ample support for his or her perspective.

Conversely, the person who rejects Christian assumptions does so, not because of overwhelming evidence against them, but because of a personal preference for the logical consequences of those assumptions. Aldous Huxley gives a clear and honest expression of this point:

> I had motives for not wanting the world to have a meaning; consequently assumed that it had none, and was able without any difficulty to find satisfying reasons for this assumption. . . . The philosopher who finds no meaning in the world is not concerned exclusively with a problem in pure metaphysics; he is also concerned to prove that there is no valid reason why he personally should not do as he wants to do, or why his friends should not seize political power and govern in the way that they find most advantageous to themselves. . . . For myself, as, no doubt, for most of my contemporaries, the philosophy of meaninglessness was essentially an instrument of liber-

---

[14]It must be noted here that Menninger's view of sin is not necessarily consistent with the biblical notion. But to have a respected member of a social science profession raise the issue is in itself significant.

ation. The liberation we desired was simultaneously liberation from a certain political and economic system and liberation from a certain system of morality. We objected to the morality because it interfered with our sexual freedom; we objected to the political and economic system because it was unjust. The supporters of those systems claimed that in some way they embodied meaning (a Christian meaning, they insisted) of the world. There was one admirably simple method of confuting these people and at the same time justifying ourselves in our political and erotic revolt; we would deny that the world had any meaning whatever (1937:270–73).

THE STUDY OF SOCIOLOGY

In the preceding pages an attempt has been made to define sociology, to identify its scope and its concerns, and to point out specifically some of those areas that impinge directly on the Christian's faith. What still remains to be dealt with is a justification for the study of the discipline by the Christian.

In the first place, the same general reasons that support the study of sociology by secular students hold for the Christian as well. A study of sociology will give the student a handle on some of the concepts and terms that sociologists use and without which their data are often incomprehensible. These concepts and terms provide a useful vehicle for conveying ideas and insights of the society about us.

But more important than terms and concepts are the data that sociologists have researched. These data provide insights into human relationships that may prove very valuable. Invariably students can make applications of the theoretical data to their own experiences and gain added understanding of their own personal and corporate lives. For the Christian, this should provide further knowledge about one of the most important aspects of the world. In order for a person to function effectively as a Christian, it is necessary that he or she understand how to become a viable part of human society. After all, Jesus called His followers the "salt of the earth" (Matt. 5:13), which certainly means that He expected them to permeate their society. As John Scanzoni states: "One benefit for the Christian student in studying sociology . . . is to give him new perspectives on the social orders. In turn, this should drive him to the Bible to discover for himself what it really says (or does not say) about human relationships of all sorts and on all levels" (Smith, 1972:129).

The areas of concern for the Christian in our present society are almost limitless including the expected roles of men, women, and children; the changing nature of the family and the home; and changing values and views regarding sex, divorce, abortion, race, singleness, working and career mothers, discipline, and capital punishment. These and many other areas challenge the Christian student of sociology to sort out the cultural (and therefore relative) expectations from biblical imperatives.

Although sociology and social work are not synonymous, and the concept of sociology as a pure, objective discipline does not impose on its students a mandate to right the wrongs of society, yet the Christian must move from an awareness of need to an attempt at remedial action. The discipline may not mandate it, but the Word of God does: "Anyone, then, who knows the good he ought to do and doesn't do it, sins" (James 4:17).

It is impossible to conceive of a vocation that a Christian might pursue in which a knowledge of sociological concepts and data would not be beneficial. Indeed, just being a member of society makes such an understanding important.

But there are some specific items that can serve as examples of the application of sociology to Christian understanding. First, there is a sense in which a better and more complete idea of God can be achieved through a study of His creation. After all, the human being is created in God's image; therefore a study of that image should teach the Christian about the Creator. Grunlan and Mayers describe this point well:

> Because man is the apex of God's creation, it is in the study of man that we can learn of God. . . .
>
> As we study man as a social being, as well as a spiritual being, we learn more about God, because man is created in the image of God. In fact, God in the Bible shows us what He is like by using illustrations from various human social relationships of the family and compares Himself to a father (Matt. 5:45) and a mother (Isa. 66:13). He uses the social relationships in the legal system and compares Himself to a judge (Rev. 18:8) and a lawyer (1 John 2:1). God uses the economic system and compares Himself to the owner of a vineyard who goes out and hires laborers (Matt. 20:1–16). As we can see, God uses human social relationships to reveal Himself to man. As we study human social relationships, we can understand God better. Man, the social creature, as well as the spiritual creature, is created in God's image; so as we study man . . . we learn more about God (1979:268–69).

25

And second, an understanding of sociological terms and tools can be used to analyze and gain insights into the whole Christian community. The organized church as a social institution becomes more understandable when studied sociologically. Such problems as conflict and competition, urban, suburban, and rural shifts and movements, and racial and cultural confrontations within the church and its wider ministry all yield to new insights when applying sociological techniques. (See Engel and Norton, 1975, and Engel, 1977, for a treatment of techniques and strategies for effective analysis of the church and its mission.)

It must be remembered, however, as stated earlier in the chapter, that in the final analysis it is not the Scriptures that must yield to the discipline of sociology. Rather, the discipline must yield to the Scriptures. The neutral tools can be very helpful, provided the fundamental assumptions remain biblical.

CONCLUSION

In this chapter an attempt has been made to lay a basis for the Christian student to study sociology. This introduction is obviously not an exhaustive treatment, but should provide some focus and suggest some direction for the Christian student to pursue. After this will come a look at the hard questions, the moral dilemmas, and the countless implications.

Given the complexity of the subject matter of sociology, it is especially necessary that Christian students draw on the one profound resource at their disposal—the Holy Spirit. He is the Spirit of truth and will teach us all things (John 14:17, 26). If, indeed, all truth is God's truth, then the Christian student can consult his or her Teacher for a Christian perspective of sociological data.

DISCUSSION QUESTIONS

1. Does sociology qualify as a science in the same sense that biology or physics does? Why? Why not?
2. If science is the search for truth and God's Word is true, what should be the relationship between science and Scripture?
3. What assumptions and presuppositions do Christians bring with them when they engage in scientific research?

4. What is your reaction to the statement in this chapter that sociology is a neutral discipline?
5. What values do you see for Christians in the study of sociology?

SUGGESTED READING

Peter L. Berger, *Invitation to Sociology* (New York: Anchor Books, 1963). An excellent introduction to sociological thinking. A secular view, but one that deals accurately with the issues.

Mark P. Cosgrove, *The Essence of Human Nature* (Grand Rapids: Zondervan, 1977). Written for the psychology student but giving a clear definition of the nature of the human being from a Christian perspective.

C. A. Coulson, *Science and Christian Belief* (New York: Fontana Books, 1958). An excellent treatment on the nature and limitations of science by an Oxford professor of mathematics.

David Lyon, *Christians and Sociology* (Downers Grove, Ill.: Inter-Varsity, 1976). A clear Christian overview of the role and limitations of the discipline of sociology.

2

PAUL V. JOHNSON
Bethel College,
Minnesota

RESEARCH METHODOLOGY IN SOCIOLOGY

"The littlest science is sociology—the study of social behavior. That it is little, no one can doubt. That it is a science may raise some question" (Mazur, 1968). Such a statement may not be acceptable to an individual who has devoted his life to the study of sociology. It is enough to make beginning college students question the real value or importance of the study. Hopefully, the above quotation will make students think about the nature of science and its relationship to sociology.

As late twentieth-century members of a technologically advanced and urban-oriented society, Westerners are science oriented. Science has become extremely important to everyone, even to those who don't consider themselves to be scientists. They believe in science and give science and scientists a very high status—one might even say they sometimes worship science and things scientific.

Why all this emphasis on scientific proof? What is so special about knowing something scientifically as opposed to knowing something nonscientifically? What makes science so important in today's society?

These kinds of questions and others will receive attention in this chapter. The focus will be on some of the things that most textbooks take for granted but seldom present to students. Some of the assumptions that science offers about our world will be examined. The discussions may raise some questions regarding the importance given to science. An attempt will be made to give credit in those areas where science has allowed the advance of knowledge; however, some of the operations of the scientific method will be questioned. The relationship of one's Christian faith to the process of science will also be examined. It is hoped that students will thus be exposed to a wider view of science than they usually can obtain in an introductory text.

In a more practical vein, the discussion will include various ethical problems that face persons participating in scientific social research. These ethical questions will not be screened just for social researchers who are also Christians, but questions of interest to all social researchers will be handled.

Finally an effort will be made to explain how the particular brand of science used by sociologists can be helpful in the local church. An examination will be made of some of the useful and needed things that an introductory sociology student can do with social research skills to assist in the ministry of a church.

SOCIOLOGY AS SCIENCE

The term *science* has come to mean many different things within our culture. If the reader will remember that the term as used in this chapter refers to a method, and will dismiss from mind other commonly encountered meanings, it should be possible for him or her to understand the chapter more clearly.

Kenneth R. Hoover (1976:4–6) identifies some "distractions" that are simply ways of thinking about science and that confuse the issue. For example, he suggests that science is often used as a synonym for technology. Thus moon landings have been captioned "Science Marches On." However, technology is the application of science to various tasks, and it should not be thought of as synonymous with science.

Another distraction is the view that science is some specific body of knowledge. Thus it is very misleading to say that "science tells us that stress on the job is damaging." Actually science doesn't tell us anything, for the information comes from people using scientific procedures to obtain data. Science, then, is not some cut-and-dried body of knowledge that is ours for the taking; instead, it is a way of approaching our world. It is involved with deciding how questions are formulated and answered. Its concern is to help people obtain reliable answers to the important questions that face them.

A final distraction is the view that science can be practiced only by persons who call themselves scientists and that one has to be a part of this elite group in order to use scientific methods. That this view is untrue can be seen in the fact that many individuals who would never describe themselves as scientists use various forms of the scientific method in simply going about their everyday activities. Thus the professional scientist does not have a corner on the practice of science. Certainly, the trained professional practices science with more precision than the man or woman on the street, but the basic principles of science are available to anyone to use.

In order to identify a person as a scientist or an academic discipline as scientific, it is necessary to look at the procedures used by the person or discipline in attempting to understand the world. Is the *scientific method* used? If so, the person or discipline can be called scientific.

The scientific method has two major components—the empirical or research component, and the rational or theoretical component. In the research component, data are collected and analyzed; usually this is thought of as the scientific component. However, the theoretical area that draws the research findings into a coherent whole is no less a part of the scientific method. Later we will look at some of the specific aspects of the research component as it is applied to sociology. First, however, it is important to highlight some of the basic assumptions that science makes in order that the research component can be better understood.

ASSUMPTIONS OF SCIENCE[1]

It is my contention that the major reason many people view science as the best, most informed, and most reliable way of

---

[1]See chapter 1 for an additional treatment of this topic.

knowing about our world is that they do not closely examine and evaluate the basic assumptions on which science is based. Such an evaluation would make people less prone to accept anything solely because it was scientific. The list of three assumptions to be given here is by no means exhaustive; hopefully, however, the items mentioned will give some additional information with which to evaluate the concept of science.

1. *The assumption that the world is a closed, self-contained system in which there are ordered, patterned, and recurrent themes.* The crucial concept in this assumption is that of system. Viewing the world as a system allows people to picture it as a large whole made up of many individual parts. All of these individual parts work together in an interdependent fashion to make up the whole. A change in any of these parts results in repercussions throughout the system. A closed, self-contained system implies that everything needed for its operation is contained within it. Any change that may occur results from forces operative within the closed boundaries of the system.

It is believed that in a closed and self-contained system, any change within the system is caused by a change somewhere else in the system. Much as a pebble dropped into a pond sends ripples to all parts of the pond, so a change in one part of the world system is thought to cause things throughout the system to change. An important aspect of the system theory is that every change supposedly is caused by a previous change elsewhere in the system.

When this cause-effect relationship within a system is carried to its logical extreme, it leads to the idea that everything that happens within the system is according to a pattern or ultimate order. Behind this assumption is the idea that everything has a cause and anyone who looks long enough will be able to identify it. Within this perspective nothing ever just happens. Everything fits into the overall pattern within the system.

2. *The assumption that sensory data are the best, if not the only, usable data.* This assumption leads to science's demand for empirically observable data. It is thought that data obtained through the use of the senses are free from subjective interpretation, outside biasing forces, and other contaminants. It is obvious, however, that sensory data are also subject to forces that can distort, a fact

confirmed by Solomon Asch's (1956) experiments in which subjects were asked to do something as simple as to indicate which of
three lines was the longest. We must reject the common idea that
sensory data are factual and that their use will produce objective
and true knowledge. Those things that are determined via the
senses are influenced by other subjective things such as how one
happens to feel at any particular time. Reliance on sensory data is a
weakness of the scientific method, and it is imperative for us to see
that such empirical data are not totally objective.

3. *The assumption that the ultimate goal of science is the ability to
predict and control.* Because science assumes that the system is
patterned and ordered, it is thought to be possible to predict
which will happen in any particular situation if all the variables
involved can be identified and their relationships determined.
Experiments have shown that once the relationship among variables is known, it is often possible for a scientist to manipulate
one or more of those variables and thereby control what happens
in that particular situation.

However, a problem may arise in applying those same characteristics of the natural sciences to the study of human beings. This
is because a human seems to be so much less predictable and/or
controllable than a chemical in a test tube. Science accepts the
parallels between the study of chemicals and the study of human
behavior even though these parallels appear to be somewhat
strained. Moreover, science attempts to study the behavior of
human beings according to the same procedures it uses to study
the behavior of chemicals in chemical reactions.

What are the implications of these assumptions of science for
the study of human beings? One implication is that if these assumptions are held too rigorously, humans become depersonalized. Humans become objects of study rather than subjects of
study. Humanity becomes an *it*. People become nothing more
than a result of prior causes within a closed system. Furthermore
humans are not free but instead are subject to the other components of the system of which they are just parts.

But an even more serious implication of these assumptions is
that if humans are not free to act on their own behalf, they also are
not responsible. They will always be able to refer back to something else within the system and say it caused them to do what

they did. Thus they can claim they are not responsible for their own actions. This, then, is the heart of the objection to a deterministic view of humanity.

This view of humanity that arises from the assumptions of science stands in contrast to the biblical view. The biblical view is that each person is a willing, choosing, and volitional being. Each person is a creature of meaning who is self-conscious and self-aware, not merely a responder to his or her environment. The effect of the assumptions of science is a tendency to devalue humans and place them in the same category with chemical reactions and forms of animal life. We believe that it is important to specify how people are influenced by the social forces around them, but, for the above reasons, feel it is dangerous to give social determinism this much explanatory value.

SCIENCE AS A VALUE-FREE ENTERPRISE

One final characteristic of science—that it supposedly is value-free—warrants special attention. Most introductory textbooks dealing with the concepts of science or the characteristics of scientists specify that the ideal scientist is capable of doing his or her work without letting personal values interfere with scientific endeavors. Value-free sociology embodies the attitude that sociologists must develop their theories and do their research in an unbiased manner. In addition, value-free sociologists refrain from promoting any particular ideological perspective in the course of doing their professional work.

Max Weber, among the most influential of all sociologists throughout history, is credited with stressing the need for this kind of neutrality by sociologists. Weber stated, "An empirical science cannot tell anyone what he *should* do—but rather what he *can* do" (Friedrichs, 1970:80). Weber also put down any prophetic role for the sociologist, saying, "It is not the gift of grace of seers and prophets dispensing sacred values and revelations, for whenever the man of science introduces his personal value judgment, a full understanding of the facts ceases" (80).

George Lundberg (1947), an American sociologist of the 1940s and 1950s, wrote a classic work entitled *Can Science Save Us?* in which he affirmatively answered the question he posed. Like Weber, he stressed the need for a value-free sociology. He stressed

33

that judging the value of any particular activity is not a part of a sociologist's responsibilities.

While Weber's and Lundberg's position on value-free sociology has been dealt with briefly, it is apparent that both believed it is possible for sociology to be done in a value-free environment. However, I cannot accept this last conclusion. No scientist—natural, physical, or social—can place his or her values totally outside of what he or she happens to be studying at any given point in time. We are what our values dictate, and to believe that we can put our personal values on a back burner, so to speak, while studying a particular research problem is fallacious. Our personal values influence every aspect of the basic research model and determine to a large extent what is done and how it will be done.

An example may help clarify this point. Suppose that a social researcher was employed on a research project studying the issue of abortion. Suppose also that the researcher's personal value system, which was developed over several years of life, places a high premium on human life, even in fetal form. Could the researcher justifiably claim to be able to divorce himself or herself from personal values so as to objectively view the issues involved with abortion? I think not. The only honest course of action would be to refuse to work on the project because personal values related to the topic in question would interfere with objective research.

Scientists, like all other humans, are influenced greatly by the values they hold. It is expecting too much to assume that such values can be compartmentalized and held in limbo during the course of a research project. Although science must attempt to be objective, it is simply expecting too much to stress total value neutrality as the ultimate goal.

Probably the person who has done as much as anyone to identify the reasons why science cannot be value free is Thomas Kuhn. In a classic work entitled *The Structure of Scientific Revolutions,* Kuhn (1962) shatters many of the concepts that one may hold about science. He presents an alternative view that highlights the extent to which science is influenced by many factors of the social context in which it occurs.

George Ritzer (1975:2–3) has specified some of the major premises of Kuhn's perspective on science. Kuhn based his view on a myth that he says developed over a long period of time. The myth deals with how science develops. It implies that science advances in a cumulative manner through slow and steady increments of knowledge. In other words the myth views science as continually progressing toward ever-increasing amounts of truth.

Kuhn challenges such a belief and blames the authors of science textbooks for continuing the myth by only reporting the current state of knowledge within any particular scientific area. Textbook authors usually give little or no attention to the failures, changes of directions, or blind alleys that scientists met along the way while working in their areas of specialization. Also, textbook authors often omit some of the confusion that may have existed in a particular area of science in order not to make that whole area look confused or disorganized.

For Kuhn, this idea of accumulation of knowledge is truly a myth that must be replaced by the reality of scientific revolution. Science is better characterized by revolution than by accumulation of knowledge, for if one takes a careful and honest look at history, the revolutionary processes through which science has come will be evident.

To help the introductory student understand Kuhn's important argument, the specific phases through which he says science proceeds will be highlighted. I am indebted to my colleague, Thomas Correll, who in a team teaching endeavor developed the chart on the following page as a means of explaining Kuhn's perspective.

Kuhn believes that at any point in time science is dominated by a specific way of looking at the world. He refers to this way of looking at the world as a "paradigm." Kuhn simply means there are major assumptions, concepts, and propositions that tend to dominate science at any given point in time. As Kuhn begins his discussion of the revolutionary process through which science passes, he refers to the stage of "normal science." It is within this phase that scientists work and expand the current paradigm, whatever it happens to be. Using the major assumptions, concepts, and propositions of the paradigm, scientists attempt to solve the various research problems that emerge. In this phase everything appears to be in a state of equilibrium, and it is this phase about which most textbook authors write.

After scientists have worked for a period of time within the

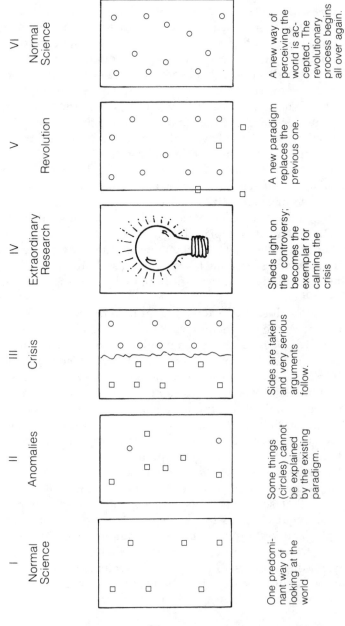

Kuhn's Phases of Scientific Progression

I	II	III	IV	V	VI
Normal Science	Anomalies	Crisis	Extraordinary Research	Revolution	Normal Science
One predominant way of looking at the world	Some things (circles) cannot be explained by the existing paradigm.	Sides are taken and very serious arguments follow.	Sheds light on the controversy; becomes the exemplar for calming the crisis	A new paradigm replaces the previous one.	A new way of perceiving the world is accepted. The revolutionary process begins all over again.

normal science phase, they invariably will come up with anomalies, or things that cannot be explained by the existing paradigm. Several different things can be done with such anomalies, including the alternative of glossing over them or simply concluding that they are not that important anyway. Other scientists, however, will not be so easily dissuaded; they will pursue an anomaly that the current paradigm cannot explain. An unexplained anomaly may cause some scientists to question the value of the entire paradigm. However, a paradigm usually will continue to dominate the ways scientists think.

If the anomalies are serious enough, and many times they are, the crisis phase is entered. At this point scientists actually take up sides and argue. The debate concerns the strengths of the current paradigm that cannot explain the anomalies as opposed to a new paradigm that has been offered and that can explain the anomalies. This period can become a very uncomfortable one as scientists from the two sides oppose and attack one another. Neither side is able to convince the other that the paradigm for which they are arguing is the best way of understanding the world.

In order to resolve this standoff, there must be forthcoming a piece of research that is scientifically acceptable to both sides. Such a piece of extraordinary research, if it can be done, will have the effect of clearing the air and resolving the conflict involved. The research becomes an examplar and is often referred to in the subsequent year as *the* piece of research that gave the important and much-needed answer.

Depending on the findings of this extraordinary piece of research, the initial paradigm is returned to and the original anomalies evaluated as unimportant, or the original paradigm is replaced by a new one that explains the anomalies. When the previously reigning paradigm is overthrown and replaced by a new one, a true revolution has occurred.

Once the revolution takes place, most scientists accept the new paradigm and begin to use it to solve the problems they encounter (see Diagram VI of "Kuhn's Phases of Scientific Progression"). It will be apparent to the reader that this new period of "normal science" is yet another phase in beginning the revolutionary cycle of science all over again.

Kuhn's major contribution in offering this model of science is that he shows how seemingly far-removed processes influence science. Being able to secure funding in order to follow up on an anomaly, deciding what to do with a particular finding that does not agree with what one's research director already *believes* to be true, and politically blackballing the research of a group on the opposite side during the crisis phase are all aspects of the scientific research process that are often neglected in a discussion of science. A scientist's personal values and code of ethics become very important in these instances. If the beginning student is aware of this process through which science progresses, he or she will be much better prepared to understand how scientific discoveries have reached their current status.

Finally, it should also be stressed here that the discussion of Kuhn's view of science has been somewhat simplified in order to make it understandable. The idea that each scientific discipline has but one dominant paradigm at any given point in time is misleading, for most disciplines may have several paradigms that are vying for dominance. (Three of these paradigms in sociology are discussed in chap. 1.)

ETHICAL ISSUES IN SOCIAL RESEARCH

Almost all of the professional societies representing various academic disciplines (for example, the American Sociological Association, American Psychological Association, American Anthropological Association, and National Association of Social Workers) believe that doing research according to a set of specified ethical principles is important. Each organization publishes a code of ethics relevant to the kinds of research done within its discipline. An examination of these different publications reveals that they all deal with areas of concern common to these disciplines. Common areas, for which there are standards, include relationships with the individuals studied, responsibility to the public or consumers of the proposed research, responsibility to students, and responsibility to sponsors. The codes of ethics that have been developed are not only for the researcher who is a Christian but for all researchers. It is not expected that Christians will follow the codes of ethics more rigorously than will non-Christians, but rather it is expected that *all* researchers will follow the codes of ethics developed for their particular social science discipline. However, the researcher who is a Christian should be more aware of and willing to work under the restrictions of such codes of ethics simply because of the value structure that accompanies the Christian's perspective.

The student may be surprised to know that there are ethical considerations in doing social research at *every* step of the research process. A good social scientist will take those considerations into account as the research is being done. In the following paragraphs some of the main areas will be highlighted where the Christian researcher and the secular researcher need to pay special attention to ethical considerations.

The subject of study in any of the social sciences is human beings or some aspect of their behavior. Since this is so, I believe that the most basic ethical consideration for the researcher in this field is to determine his or her value of human life. This statement has important implications. If the researcher puts a high value on human subjects, there will be several things the researcher will and will not do. Researchers may be tempted to take advantage of human subjects in one way or another simply to get the proposed research completed. However, researchers—especially Christian researchers—must take care at all times to honor the value of subjects as human beings whom God loves. It is especially easy in some forms of research where the human subject is never really encountered in a personal, eyeball-to-eyeball fashion by the researcher to take advantage of that subject and do things that would not be done if there were closer relationships between researcher and subject. Regardless of how personal or impersonal the contact is with subjects during the course of the research, researchers must continuously remind themselves that they are working with human beings who have individual personal value.

There are many specific areas where ethics become involved in the process of carrying out a piece of social research; however, only a few of them will be mentioned here. The ones discussed are considered to be of special importance for the beginning researcher.

The first area involving serious ethical questions is in the use of deceit or deception, a very common practice in many forms of research. It is unfortunate that many research projects involve deceit. The deceit may be in telling the subjects in a research project only part of the truth. More serious is the use of an untruth to get individuals to participate. Whenever this is done, the individual suffers harm, the extent of which depends on the untruth circulated and the person involved; potentially, the results can be disastrous. In addition to harming the respondent, this form of unethical behavior also hurts the entire profession of social research. Social researchers depend greatly on the willingness of individuals to participate in various types of studies. If individuals find that researchers are taking advantage of them through deceptive practices, they may never again agree to participate in any form of social research. The result will be that social research in general receives a bad reputation.

A related deceptive procedure involves withholding from the participant the true nature of the research. Often a researcher thinks that if people find out what the research will be used for, they will not participate. As a result a cover story is often developed that does not include all the truth regarding how the research will be used. Also, if the subject later finds out that he has been deceived, he will never participate again. This sort of unacceptable behavior on the part of researchers may lead to the need for every researcher to obtain a document of consent from each respondent indicating that he or she will participate in the research. Such a requirement would cause much additional paperwork. One of the reasons it would come into being is that past researchers have taken advantage of individuals in collecting data.

Another form of deception may occur during the observation of people who do not realize they are part of a research project. The mere observation of people is not unethical in itself. This type of research is most frequently done in a participant observation situation where the researcher simply observes the behavior of subjects under certain circumstances or in response to certain stimuli that are presented. The potential problem here involves what the researcher does to influence the behavior of those he is observing. If the observer is only doing something like observing crowd behavior at a hockey game when a goal is scored, there is no problem with deception. The ethical question arises when the stimulus that causes the behavior to be observed is potentially harmful. For example, to pretend to suffer a heart attack in order to see how people will respond would be deceptive behavior, and such an act is definitely questionable on ethical grounds.

A final area where deception is often practiced is in the presentation of one's findings. Many beginning social researchers have the idea that the hypothesis they are testing in their research must be supported; and if it is not, they consider their research to be a failure. Under this kind of mental pressure, the temptation to tamper with data or results becomes extremely strong. The true measure of a research project lies not in whether the hypothesis was supported, but in how the entire research project was done. Keeping the right perspective on research may minimize such temptations.

Probably the social research tool known as statistics provides the easiest means for deceiving the consumers of one's research. Darrell Huff's (1954) well-known and often-cited book *How to Lie With Statistics* provides several suggestions on how to deceive readers through the use or abuse of various statistical procedures. If a researcher uses statistical techniques to alter what the data are really saying, that person is obviously violating important ethical principles.

A second general set of ethical considerations involves the treatment of subjects as human beings. The consent of persons who participate as subjects in social research should be obtained. When asked, some may decline to participate, and these should be excused from participating. Too often, especially in classroom settings where a teacher has authority over students, or in a work situation where an employer has authority over employees, it is common for people to be forced against their will to participate in various forms of social research. It cannot be stressed too strongly that respondents need to be willing participants in order for this ethical question to be satisfied. The researcher should be skeptical of including people who are either very hesitant to participate or very demanding that they be allowed to participate, for both of these groups would tend to bias the results in one way or another.

An ethical issue that falls into the category of respect for research subjects has to do with the privacy of individuals and the right of an individual researcher to invade that privacy. The invasion may take several forms, some of which appear to be more damaging than others, but all of which can cause a degree of harm. Even the

41

act of sending a questionnaire through the mail to ask some personal questions of the respondent constitutes an invasion of privacy. Probably the most serious invasions involve pestering subjects to complete an interview, following an individual to observe behavior, or continually calling over the telephone to ask the individual to participate in the research. Researchers must respect the privacy of respondents and allow them to decide in a natural and unpressured way if they will or will not participate.

Another ethical question associated with respect for persons involves what the subject is required to do as part of the research. Stanley Milgram's (1963) study of obedience is a classic example of research subjects being asked to do some things to other individuals that they did not wish to do (for example, give another person an electric shock). Even under experimental conditions where subjects are later told that they did not actually administer a shock, the emotional and psychological effects of such behavior linger long after the research has been completed. Research subjects have been asked to cheat, lie, steal, and do other things that may act to diminish their self-respect, all in the name of social research. However, such requests that involve taking advantage of the subject are assuredly unethical.

A final ethical question to be dealt with here also falls under the category of respect for persons. It involves the question, What responsibility does the researcher have to the subject once the research has been completed? Of course, the answer to this question depends a great deal on the specific kind of research being done. In most forms of research the subject is forgotten after he or she has served the purpose. In forms of research where the researcher and the subject are never in any face-to-face contact, it is especially easy for the researcher to totally forget about what the subject has done to contribute to the research process. Subjects who have given of their time and energy to carefully complete a long and sometimes complicated questionnaire are often totally forgotten once the completed questionnaire has safely arrived in the research office. It is these people who should be cared for, informed of the findings of the research, and sincerely thanked for their participation in the research.

To conclude this discussion of the ethical questions involved in doing social research, it is important to underscore the fact that at *every* point of the research model there are ethical questions and moral dilemmas that the researcher must resolve. All researchers are responsible for their decisions in these areas; however, the Christian researcher is even further motivated to exercise extreme caution and wisdom in these areas where one may so easily be tempted to violate basic ethical values in an attempt to do better research.

PRACTICAL APPLICATIONS OF SOCIAL RESEARCH IN CHURCH AND OTHER MINISTRIES

The beginning student of sociology, having just been exposed to the research process for the first time, may well question the practical payoff in this scientific process of doing research. Because questions have been raised about the assumptions on which it is based and because some of the ethical pitfalls that may occur along the way have been highlighted, the student may wonder where the positive product of social research can be found.

It seems reasonable that the church is an excellent place for a student of social research to contribute his or her skills to the glory of God. As rather complex organizations, most local churches have a need for some individuals trained in planning, designing, and carrying out social research within the contexts of their ministries. Let us now see where an aspiring social researcher who wants to put skills to work for some practical good can focus time and energy.

Churches, like other social organizations, have a great need for information about themselves and their environment. Social science researchers can help provide such information. For example, a local church should have on hand a file of information so that the skills and needs of specific members can be determined quickly whenever the need for such information presents itself. A church should have on record each member's address, size of family, major reasons for joining this particular church, particular skills that might be useful in the ministry of the church, special needs as a result of illness, age, or special handicap, and any other information that the church leaders feel would be useful, whether in ministering to the person or in helping the person minister to others. Even a beginning social researcher could take the responsibility for drafting a survey questionnaire to be given to every current church member and then to every new member as part of their being welcomed into the congregation. Such a draft should be shared with the minister and other lay leaders, both for refining the questions that are included and for adding any other questions that might be needed. By studying this information the church leaders will get a much more accurate and complete picture of the congregation.

Not only is it important to keep an information file about each church member, but it is helpful to have descriptive data on the various programs of the church. Such information as the number of persons involved with a particular program, the costs to operate such programs, and other records involving these programs can be invaluable in presenting an accurate picture of what the church actually does. If this type of information were studied, many congregations could improve their programs.

A major mistake made by many churches is that they remain virtually unknowledgeable about their environment. Many are truly an island in the midst of the sea and really do not know what is going on outside the perimeter of their lot. For example, how many churches have begun a ministry to singles without ever knowing the number of single persons who live in their community? Or how many churches engage in serious planning for the future without ever consulting population trends, political developments, or economic factors that will influence their congregation? Again, it is the social researcher who can assume the responsibility for obtaining some of this information that is so helpful when planning for the future. All the actual work need by no means be done by the researcher, for much of the information has been collected already. It is simply a matter of the researcher knowing how to go about retrieving the data from city or county agencies. The researcher who has had exposure in the use of census data and other existing data and documents can often easily acquire the information needed for intelligent planning in the local church.

A social researcher could also provide an invaluable service to a local church by developing a way to evaluate some of its programs to see if they really are doing what they are intended to do. Falling under the category of evaluation research, this involves taking a particular program, finding out what the goals for that program are, and then determining if the current program is meeting those goals. If every program of a church were periodically subjected to this kind of evaluation, the church could revolutionize its ministry. Gone would be programs that exist only because they have always existed; in their place would be programs that actually meet the needs of members. The evaluation of existing programs can be a difficult task if some older members insist that "we've always done it that way." However, there is no more important area in which the social researcher can contribute his skills to furthering the ministry of the local congregation.

The above are only a few of the ways in which social researchers can use their skills within a church or other form of ministry. There are any number of specific things that persons skilled in the art of doing social research can do. Different needs will be found in different ministries. Wherever information such as statistical data, opinion surveys, attitude surveys, or responses to specific items on a questionnaire are needed, the social researcher can be of help. When situations arise that make decisions necessary, the researcher can supply accurate, up-to-date information on which to base those decisions. This is where social researchers can contribute their skills to the mission of the church.

CONCLUSION

As an academic discipline sociology attempts to contribute to the advancement of knowledge through the two facets of advancing theories and conducting research. In this chapter some of the things have been discussed that come into play in conducting research in the social sciences. Although some serious shortcomings of the assumptions of science were noted, it is important to realize that social science research tries to follow the positive aspects of the scientific method. The work of research involves many ethical dilemmas that often are totally unexpected by the beginning researcher unless he or she has thought through all of the many places where they might crop up. Hopefully the ones presented will at least help prepare the beginning researcher and stimulate further thought in this important area. Finally, an attempt was made to indicate some of the many places where the social researcher can use his or her skills for God's glory in a church or other place of ministry. The highest value of research in the social sciences is seen when that research serves some practical and useful purpose in better understanding the world in which we live. The satisfaction of making such a contribution through social science research is in many instances motivation enough to continually strive for a practical application of one's skills in the area of social research.

DISCUSSION QUESTIONS

1. What do you see as the relationship between human behavior and environmental and social forces?
2. How does the discussion of science in chapter 1 relate to the discussion in this chapter?
3. Do you believe there are areas of human behavior a Christian sociologist ethically should not study? Why? Why not?
4. Do you believe deception in social research is ever justified? Why? Why not?
5. To what extent should a local church utilize social research?

SUGGESTED READING

Earl R. Babbie, *The Practice of Social Research* (Belmont, Calif.: Wadsworth, 1979). A comprehensive and well-written text that covers every major area of the social research process. Highly readable and well liked by most students.

Darrel Huff, *How to Lie With Statistics* (New York: Norton, 1954). A widely known work that warns the reader of possible ways in which statistics can be used for deceptive purposes.

Malcolm A. Jeeves, *The Scientific Enterprise and Christian Faith* (Downers Grove, Ill.: Inter-Varsity, 1969). A book based on a conference in which thirty-six scientists discussed the relationship between science and the Christian faith. The book develops a biblical view of the relationship of God to His creation and explains some of the key concepts in modern science and their relationship to Christian beliefs.

Thomas S. Kuhn, *The Structure of Scientific Revolutions* (Chicago: University of Chicago Press, 1962). A classic work that challenges our traditionally held views of science and how science developed throughout history. This book has been found to be a stimulus to work by many authors in the philosophy of science.

George Ritzer, *Sociology: A Multiple Paradigm Science* (Boston: Allyn and Bacon, 1975). A book based in part on Kuhn's *The Structure of Scientific Revolutions* in which Kuhn's paradigmatic view of science is applied to sociology.

3

STEPHEN A. GRUNLAN
St. Paul Bible College,
Minnesota

BIBLICAL AUTHORITY AND CULTURAL RELATIVITY

In studying sociology one soon discovers that sociologists use a specialized vocabulary. Part of this vocabulary makes use of words common to everyday speech. However, in order to facilitate communication with their colleagues, sociologists give these words specific definitions that often differ from everyday use. One such word is *culture.* Culture in everyday speech may refer to the way of life of a people, to so-called civilized societies, to good breeding, or to the appreciation of good manners and the arts and other things categorized as the finer things of life. While in everyday usage one might speak of those who attend the opera and art exhibits, and who maintain a certain lifestyle, as having culture, the sociologist sees all persons as having culture.

The classical definition given by the pioneer British anthropologist Sir Edward Tylor states that culture is "that complex whole which includes knowledge, belief, art, morals, law, custom, and any other capabilities and habits acquired by man as a member of society" (1871:1). Many sociology textbooks speak of culture as learned and shared (Horton and Hunt, 1976:46; Federico, 1979:33; Broom and Selznick, 1977:56; DeFleur et al.,

1969:99; Babbie, 1977:77; Dressler and Willis, 1976:33). By drawing on Tylor's definition and the concepts of learned and shared, the following definition of culture can be developed: culture is the learned and shared attitudes, values, and ways of behaving of the members of a society.

Some sociologists distinguish between material and nonmaterial culture. Nonmaterial culture consists of the attitudes, values, and patterns of behavior. Material culture consists of the artifacts created by the members of the culture.

Both Tylor's definition of culture and the one presented above make use of the word *society*. Surveying the definitions of society in leading sociology texts, one finds two concepts common to all of them, namely, territory and culture. Using these two concepts, one may define society as a self-perpetuating group who share a geographical territory and a culture. As these definitions indicate, culture and society are dependent concepts. One cannot exist without the other.

Within societies there are often smaller groups that are similar in many ways to the larger society and yet are distinguishable from it. These groups are called subcultures. A subculture may be defined as a pattern of norms and values that are distinguishable in significant ways from the larger culture and yet maintain an overall similarity to the larger culture.

NORMS AND VALUES

The definition of subculture given above introduces another word, *norms*, into the sociologist's vocabulary. Since culture consists of learned and shared attitudes, values, and behaviors, one would expect the members of a society to behave in similar ways. A member of a society learns how to behave in a given situation. Not only does the member behave in that manner, he or she also expects other members of that society to behave in that way. These prescribed and expected patterns of behavior are called norms.

Not all norms are of equal salience in a society. Therefore sociologists distinguish between levels of norms. Folkways are the least salient or lowest level of norms and refer to the norms dealing with politeness, etiquette, styles of dress, and other customary behavior. Mores are the more salient norms—those considered essential to the maintenance of the society. Mores are related to a society's values and concepts of right and wrong. Laws, a third level of norms, are social mechanisms that enforce those mores considered most critical to the survival and maintenance of a society.

Norms organized around functions that are most salient to a society are called *social institutions.* In studying modern societies sociologists have discovered there are five basic functions around which norms may be clustered. These basic functions are called social institutions. The five basic social institutions are the family, economics, the government or political leadership, education, and religion. Each of these social institutions will be dealt with in later chapters.

In defining both culture and mores, the term *values* was used. Values are cultural goals and standards that are the bases for evaluating persons, behaviors, objects, and ideas.

LEARNING AND LANGUAGE

The definition of culture developed in this chapter used the concept of learning. This concept is important to the understanding of culture and humankind as culture-bearing creatures. Behavioral scientists have discovered that all animal behavior may be classified as one of three types: reflexive, instinctive, or learned. A reflex is an automatic muscle reaction to a stimulus, for example, blinking when an object approaches the eye. While a reflex is a simple behavior, an instinct is a complex pattern of behavior that is inherited and genetically controlled.[1] Morgan and King state three conditions that must be fulfilled for a behavior to qualify as instinctive:

1. It must be generally characteristic of a species.
2. It must appear full-blown at the first appropriate opportunity without any previous training or practice.
3. It must continue for some time in the absence of the conditions evoking it; that is to say, it may be triggered by a stimulus, but not controlled by the stimulus (1966:40).

The third classification of behavior is that which is learned. Learned behavior is acquired by processes such as instruction,

---

[1]Although American behavioral scientists generally use the term *instinct* to refer to behavior, some European scientists, particularly those of the psychoanalytic school, use instinct to refer to drives and needs. I am using instinct in the American sense to refer to behavior.

observation, practice, trial and error, and guidance. The importance of this discussion is that humans appear to have few, if any, instinctive behaviors (Holland, 1978:62; Morgan and King, 1966:41). If humans have few, if any, instincts, then all human behavior is learned except for simple reflexive behaviors. Since all complex human behavior is learned, the importance and pervasiveness of culture becomes apparent. The process of learning one's culture is called *socialization,* which will be more fully discussed in chapter 4.

One of the most important behaviors a person learns, and one that makes possible most other learning, is language. By way of definition, *language* is the verbal[2] communication of ideas, concepts, feelings, and facts by the systematic use of word symbols. Language is essential to the communication of much of culture.

Language has an even greater effect on culture. Those persons who share a culture also share a language. Anthropologists Edward Sapir and Benjamin Whorf studied the languages of various cultures and discovered that different languages treat reality in different ways. They developed a theory, the Sapir-Whorf hypothesis, that basically states that a language gives the members of a culture eyeglasses through which they see the world and that each culture is using a different set of eyeglasses. The study of the effect of language on society is called sociolinguistics.

CULTURAL RELATIVITY

William Graham Sumner, in his classic work *Folkways,* defined ethnocentrism as the "view of things in which one's own group is the center of everything, and all others are scaled and rated with reference to it" (1906:13). Basically ethnocentrism is the practice of making one's own culture and its norms and values the standard by which all other cultures are judged.

Sumner went on to define cultural relativism[3] in the following way: "Everything in the mores of a time and place must be regarded as justified with regard to that time and place" (1906:65). In other words the concept of cultural relativity is the position that

---

[2]Written language and sign language are based on spoken language. Spoken (verbal) language is the basis for all other forms of language.

[3]The terms *cultural relativism* and *cultural relativity* are used interchangeably in this chapter.

ideas, actions, and objects should be evaluated by the norms and values of the culture in which they are found rather than by another culture's norms and values. Also the norms and values of each culture should be evaluated in the light of the culture to which they belong. As Sumner says, "'Good' morés are those which are well adapted to the situation. 'Bad' morés are those which are not so adapted" (1906:65).

The concept of cultural relativity implies that "any cultural trait is socially 'good' if it operates harmoniously within its cultural setting to attain the goals which the people are seeking" (Horton and Hunt, 1976:59). While most sociologists hold to the position of cultural relativity, at least as a methodological approach, there has been some criticism of the position.

One of the criticisms of cultural relativity is that it has little value in resolving cross-cultural conflict. It is said that if two cultures are in competition or conflict, to use the term *good* to describe the actions of both does nothing to resolve the conflict. In fact, in any conflict the sociologist must sit back and see which participant wins over, or dominates, the rival. In other words, pushed to its extreme, cultural relativity would seem to advocate that might makes right, or that the doctrine of the survival of the fittest is moral.

A second criticism of cultural relativity is that the concept itself is said to be ethnocentric. The concept is a Western idea and reflects a Western bias. A thing is good if it is functional or efficient. Functionalism and efficiency are Western values. Related to this Western concept is the problem of who determines if something is operating "harmoniously within its cultural setting to attain the goals the people are seeking." The whole process can quickly become quite subjective with a Western bias.

Another criticism is that, as some have argued, cultural relativity is actually self-contradictory. Cultural relativity implies that all values are cultural and therefore relative. Yet "cultural relativism itself posits a fundamental value: respect for cultural differences" (Broom and Selznick, 1977:73). Cultural relativists state that all cultures are equally good and should be respected equally. Cultural relativists have in fact made an a priori judgment of all cultures based on a value from their own culture: equality.

Finally, it may be argued that cultural relativity leads to ethical

51

relativity. As Broom and Selznick point out, "It is sometimes said that cultural relativism precludes the belief that some values are good for all humanity" (1977:73). Horton and Hunt state, "Sociologists are sometimes accused of undermining morality with their concept of cultural relativism" (1976:59). To use an extreme example in order to demonstrate the moral dilemma of cultural relativity, let us suppose a sociologist studied the Nazi extermination of Jews during World War II and found that this policy operated "harmoniously within its cultural setting to attain the goals which the people are seeking"; then, according to the definition of cultural relativity, it would have to be called good. Yet few, if any, sociologists would want to call the Holocaust good. Cultural relativity seems to leave us without a basis for human morality.

BIBLICAL AUTHORITY

Although cultural relativity seems to leave us without a universal morality, Christians claim a universal moral standard in the Word of God, the Bible. As the National Association of Evangelicals states it, "We believe the Bible to be the inspired, the only infallible, authoritative Word of God" (NAE, no date, back cover of pamphlet). The article on Scripture in the doctrinal statement of the college where I teach develops this doctrine of the authority of Scripture more fully:

> The Old and New Testaments, inerrant as originally given, were verbally inspired by God and are a complete revelation of His will for the salvation of men. They constitute the divine and only rule of Christian faith and practice (Saint Paul Bible College Catalog, 1978-1980:8).

God created humans as spiritual, biological, psychological, and sociological beings. Humans have developed cultures to meet the needs arising from their nature. While cultures vary, humankind is one and is responsible to God. God has revealed Himself to humankind through creation, through the spoken word (prophets and apostles), through the written Word (Scriptures), and preeminently through the incarnate Word, Jesus Christ. The written Word is the testimony to the spoken word and the living Word. Richard Quebedeaux points out that evangelicals

> accept Scripture as *both* history and revelation. They view the redemptive historical events recorded therein as the mighty acts of God, culminating in the life, death and resurrection of Jesus Christ. But for

them, the Bible also embodies the divinely given Word of God as spoken by the prophets, and which interpret Christ's earthly kingdom of God (1974:74).

The Scriptures are both divine and human and are, as Quebedeaux says, "at the same time the words of God *and* the words of man recorded in a specific historical [cultural] time and context" (1974:75). God, by inspiration, worked through the human authors as products of their cultural situations. As George Ladd puts it, "The result is not a mere product of history or religious insight: it is a normative, authoritative, divinely initiated and superintended account of who God has revealed himself to be and what He has done for man's salvation" (1966:216). The importance of the doctrine of inspiration is to impute authority to the biblical principles and teachings.

In speaking of the inspiration and authority of the Bible, we must remember that the Bible derives its authority from God; it is the Word of God. As Throckmorton says:

> we must remember that the Christian's final and absolute authority is God as He is revealed in Jesus Christ. No statement regarding the authority of scripture can be allowed in any way to contradict this. The authority of the Bible must be related to the authority of God in Christ (1959:207).

BIBLICAL AUTHORITY AND CULTURAL RELATIVITY

Several criticisms were earlier leveled against the concept of cultural relativity. It also appears to be diametrically opposed to the concept of biblical authority. One might ask, Is there any place for a concept such as cultural relativity in a Christian world view? Several evangelical social scientists believe there is.

Both Eugene Nida (1954) and Charles Kraft (1979) see ethnocentrism and cultural relativity as two ends of a continuum. They claim that if we go to the ethnocentric end of the continuum, we absolutize human institutions; and if we go to the cultural relativity end of the continuum, we relativize God and the Bible. Nida therefore posits a position, which Kraft adopts, of "relative relativism" and Nida describes it as follows:

> In contrast with the absolute relativity of some contemporary social scientists, the Biblical position may be described as a "relative relativism," for the Bible clearly recognizes that different cultures have different standards and that these differences are recognized by God as

having different values. The relativism of the Bible is relative to three principal factors: (1) the endowment and opportunities of people, (2) the extent of revelation, and (3) the cultural patterns of the society in question (1954:50).

In further explaining the three principal factors of his "relative relativism," Nida turns to the Scriptures for illustrations. He points out that the Bible teaches that rewards and judgment are relative to a people's endowment and opportunities. He cites the parable of the talents in Matthew 25:14–30, as well as this statement from Luke 12:48: "From everyone who has been given much, much will be demanded."

Nida says the Bible teaches that people are responsible to God relative to the extent of revelation they have received. To support this point he cites Jesus' upgrading of the Old Testament positions on retribution for evil and divorce in Matthew 5, as well as Luke 12:47–48, which says, "That servant who knows his master's will and does not get ready or does not do what his master wants will be beaten with many blows. But the one who does not know and does things deserving punishment will be beaten with few blows."

Nida also sees the Bible as relative to different cultures. To support this point he cites 1 Corinthians 9:20–21:

> To the Jews I became like a Jew, to win the Jews. To those under the law I became like one under the law (though I myself am not under the law), so as to win those under the law. To those not having the law I became like one not having the law (though I am not free from God's law but am under Christ's law), so as to win those not having the law.

In concluding his discussion of "relative relativism," Nida defends his position by saying that it

> is not a matter of inconsistency, but a recognition of the different cultural factors which influence standards and actions. While the Koran attempts to fix for all time the behavior of Muslims, the Bible clearly establishes the principle of relative relativism, which permits growth, adaptation, and freedom, under the Lordship of Jesus Christ. The Bible presents realistically the facts of culture and the plan of God. . . . The Christian position is not one of static conformance to dead rules, but of dynamic obedience to a living God (1954:52).

Marvin Mayers (1974) has also attempted to integrate biblical authority and cultural relativity. He sees ethnocentrism and cultural relativity as antithetical ideas. Mayers has developed a paradigm that involves two sets of opposing concepts. The first set includes cultural absolutism (ethnocentrism) and cultural relativism. The second set of concepts includes biblical relativism (that the teachings of Scripture are relative) and biblical absolutism, or biblical authority (that the teachings of Scripture are authoritative). Mayers' paradigm involves pairing either concept from one set with either concept from the other set, giving the possibility of four combinations as listed: (1) Biblical relativism and cultural absolutism; (2) Biblical relativism and cultural relativism; (3) Biblical absolutism and cultural absolutism; (4) Biblical absolutism and cultural relativism.

Mayers sees each of these four combinations resulting in four distinct positions that are shown in the diagram:

		BIBLICAL	
		RELATIVISM	ABSOLUTISM
CULTURAL	ABSOLUTISM	Situation Ethics	Tradition-alist
	RELATIVISM	Antinomian	Mutual Respect

Mayers labels persons who hold to a position of biblical relativism and cultural absolutism as situation ethicists. In this position, when Scripture and culture clash, culture is absolute and Scripture is relative; and therefore Scripture yields to culture. The major proponent of this position is Joseph Fletcher, who writes:

> The situationalist enters into every decision-making situation fully armed with the ethical maxims of his community and its heritage, and he treats them with respect as illuminators of his problems. Just the same, he is prepared in any situation to compromise them or set them aside in the situation if love seems better served by doing so (1966:26).
>
> The situational factors are so primary that we may even say, "Circumstances alter rules and principles" (1966:29).[4]

---

[4]Fletcher would no doubt argue that he is not abandoning Scripture but that he is appealing to love, the highest principle in Scripture. However, his position absolutizes the situation, for he allows the situation to determine what serves love; he relativizes the Bible by going against its teachings if that serves love in a situation. The issue is, Which best informs us on what best serves the principle of love, culture itself or culture in obedience to Scripture? Fletcher has opted for culture itself.

Mayers goes on to label the person who holds to the position of biblical relativism and cultural relativism as an antinomian. The antinomian is bound neither by the Scriptures nor by culture. The antinomian acts without principle. This person will equally violate scriptural principles and cultural mores when it furthers his or her ends.[5]

The third combination is biblical absolutism and cultural absolutism, and Mayers sees a person holding this position as a traditionalist. This person applies the Scriptures to a situation in his or her own culture. The person absolutizes the solution in a form compatible with his or her own culture and makes this absolutized form the standard for evaluating all other cultural forms. For example, an American traditionalist would take his or her subcultural form of worship and make it the standard by which all other subcultural forms of worship would be evaluated. The traditionalist would argue: I follow the Bible and this is how I do it; therefore, deviation from how I do it is deviation from the Bible. The traditionalist easily becomes a legalist. The tendency of a traditionalist, once he or she has absolutized a cultural form, is to give that form precedence over the Word of God.

The fourth combination, that of biblical absolutism and cultural relativity, according to Mayers, leads to a position of mutual respect. Mutual respect allows each person to follow the Scriptures in a manner that is compatible with the individual's culture. Mayers argues that there can only be mutual respect of cultures with biblical absolutism. He writes:

> The approach of biblical absolutism and cultural relativism affirms that there is a supernatural intrusion. This involves act as well as precept. Even as Christ, through the incarnation, became flesh and dwelt among us, so precept or truth becomes expressed in culture. However, even as the Word made flesh lost none of his divineness, so precept loses no truth by its expression via human sociocultural forms. It is always full and complete as truth. So long as sociocultural expression is approached crossculturally it can be recognized as truth as well. The moment truth is wed to one cultural expression there is high potential

---

[5]While it is certainly true that a person holding this position could be an antinomian, Mayers, in my opinion, overlooks other options. A person holding this position could also be a situationalist. Also, a person could disregard the Scriptures, hold to cultural relativity, and still maintain a highly moral and ethical lifestyle by his or her culture's standards.

for "falsehood" in any other culture. More seriously, since any given culture is in the process of change, there is an even higher potential for falsehood within the culture that locks truth into one expression (1974:233).

After having examined two different models for integrating the concepts of biblical authority and cultural relativity, we see that these two concepts appear more compatible than one might have believed at first. This writer finds Mayers' model more satisfying than that of Nida and Kraft since Mayers is willing to integrate the full concept of cultural relativity.

Building on Mayers' model, one can argue that the position of biblical authority and cultural relativity not only can integrate the concepts, but that only a person who holds to biblical authority can truly practice cultural relativity. The position of biblical authority and cultural relativity is able to answer each of the criticisms of cultural relativity raised earlier in this chapter.

One of the criticisms of cultural relativity is that it has little value in resolving cross-cultural conflict. That is because the actions of persons from each culture in the conflict, according to cultural relativity, are to be evaluated in the light of their own culture. Therefore, there is no common ground for evaluation and resolution. However, with the position of biblical authority and cultural relativity, there is the common ground of the Bible. The Bible as God's Word rises above both cultures, that is, its teachings are supracultural. Thus it becomes the basis for evaluating the actions of each culture as well as the basis for resolving the conflict.

Another criticism of cultural relativity is that it is, in fact, ethnocentric. Since no person is culture-free, the values of the person's culture will always influence the determination of what is good or harmonious in a culture. However, the position of biblical authority and cultural relativity makes possible—at least in theory—the potential for a nonbiased cultural relativity (an ideal that probably never will be fully attained). This is so because the basis for what is good does not come from the values of any culture but rather from the supracultural principles found in the Word of God.

The third criticism of cultural relativity is that it is self-contradictory. Cultural relativity begins with the assumption that all cultures are equally good, equality itself being a cultural value.

In contrast, the position of biblical authority and cultural relativity would see all cultures as (1) adequate for meeting the needs of its members,[6] (2) manifesting human sinfulness, and (3) potential vehicles for God's interaction with humanity (Kraft, 1979:52). The values for this position are drawn from the Scriptures rather than from any specific culture.

The fourth criticism is that cultural relativity leads to ethical relativity. The only basis that cultural relativity has by itself for making moral evaluations is functionalism. However, the position of biblical authority and cultural relativity has a supracultural standard, the Word of God, by which moral judgments may be made in all cultures. The position of biblical authority and cultural relativity calls for biblical principles to be applied directly in each culture. If the principles come by way of a second culture, the model has been violated and the result is ethnocentrism.

The cultural norms for naming children in the United States and among the Kwakiutl Indians of British Columbia illustrate the point. In the United States given, or first, names are considered to be in the public domain. Anyone may name a child Robert, Mary, Frank, or Sue regardless of whether any other person has that name. Among the Kwakiutl Indians, names are considered private property, and no one may give to a child the name of a living person. As people die, their names may be given, or willed to others. In looking at the act of naming a child after a person still living, we may inquire how one determines if that action is right or wrong. The following questions, adapted from Mayers (1974: 233), can serve as a guide in the process of evaluation:

1. What is the cultural norm? (this is the expression of cultural relativity)
2. Is the norm in keeping with biblical principles? (this is the expression of biblical authority)
3. Is the action in keeping with the norm? (this defines the situation)
4. Does the action violate either the norm or biblical principles? (this is the integration of biblical authority and cultural relativity)

Let us see how these four questions help us as we think about the action of naming a child after a living person in each of the two cultures.

---

[6]God has created humans with basic needs that must be met. A culture that did not meet these basic needs would cease to exist.

1. What is the cultural norm? Names in the United States are in the public domain and may be freely used. Among the Kwakiutl Indians names are private property and one may not use another's name.

2. Is the norm in keeping with biblical principles? The Scriptures teach respect for the property of others (Exod. 20:15, 17; Mark 10:19; Rom. 2:21; Eph. 4:28) but do not prescribe what things are or are not to be considered private property. This is left up to each culture. Neither the United States norm nor the Kwakiutl Indian norm violates biblical principles.[7]

3. Is the action in keeping with the norm? In the United States, naming a child after a living person would be in keeping with the cultural norm. Among the Kwakiutl Indians it would violate the norm.

4. Does the action violate biblical principles? In the United States, naming a child after a living person would not violate biblical principles, but among the Kwakiutl Indians it would.

This illustration demonstrates that an action may be right in one culture and wrong in another. It is important to note that it was not the culture that determined the rightness or wrongness of the action; rather, it was the biblical principles. Each culture defined the situation (cultural relativity), but it was on the basis of the biblical principles (biblical authority) that the action was evaluated.

HERMENEUTICS

Two applications of this integration of biblical authority and cultural relativity will be examined. The first application is to be the area of hermeneutics, or interpretation of the Scriptures.

Evangelicals generally take the Bible literally. As Lindsell shows,

> All that is meant by saying one takes the Bible literally is that one believes what it purports to say. This means that figures of speech are regarded as figures of speech. No evangelical takes figures of speech literally. . . . The Scriptures use phenomenological language, as we all do (1976:37–38).

---

[7]Not all cultural norms will be in keeping with biblical principles. Even as humans are sinful, so are their cultures. For example, the norms for divorce in the United States seem to be at odds with the biblical concept of marriage. When cultural norms violate biblical principles, the Christian is responsible to the biblical principles.

Evangelical hermeneutics is aware of the importance of understanding a passage in the light of its cultural context (Berkhof, 1950:113–32; Johnson, 1976:128–61; Mickelsen, 1963:159–77; Ramm, 1956:136). However, this principle is often either ignored or applied selectively. For example, when Paul talks of greeting the brothers and sisters with a holy kiss (Rom. 16:16), or of women having their heads covered during a worship service (1 Cor. 11:2–16), many evangelicals recognize these as cultural forms. The items of most importance are the principles that lay behind the cultural forms, namely, greeting the brothers and sisters warmly and dressing moderately and appropriately for worship services. As George Ladd points out, "The essential principles embodied in the ancient historical [cultural] situation have permanent validity, even though the particular historical [cultural form] . . . has passed away with the ancient world" (1966:173). However, frequently when this principle of interpretation is discussed in evangelical circles, a question that typically arises is: What parts of the Bible do we take culturally and what parts do we take literally?

The mistake in the above question is the assumption that understanding a passage culturally and understanding a passage literally are opposing principles of interpretation. However, the position of biblical authority and cultural relativity leads to a hermeneutic that understands all of Scripture culturally and all of Scripture literally. The correct question is: What did this passage literally mean in its cultural context? If we are to be consistent in the interpretation of Scripture, it is important that "the principles we apply more or less automatically in cases where the biblical culture is considerably different from our own, we should be applying all the time, even in apparently clear cases" (Johnson, 1976:135).

It is important to remember that all cultures are relative, and this includes the cultures in which the Scriptures were given. Just as we must be careful not to absolutize a cultural form in our own culture and make that the standard for other cultures, even so we must be careful not to absolutize the cultural forms found in the Scriptures and make them the standard for other cultures. As Johnson puts it, "the Word of God is expressed by the cultural forms, but the cultural specifics are not the message" (1976:134). We must look behind the cultural form recorded in Scripture to the divine, supracultural principle that will find its expression in a form compatible with the receiving culture. When Jesus washed the disciples' feet (John 13:1–11), He practiced a cultural form. The principle being taught in this passage is not that we should wash each other's feet but that we should humbly serve each other. In our culture that might involve holding the door for others, or being willing to get the coffee, or taking out the garbage.

One might ask, How does this principle of interpretation apply to a passage that states a principle rather than gives a cultural example, as for instance Ephesians 5:23, "For the husband is the head of the wife"? Again, we must begin by attempting to determine what the passage meant to those to whom it was first written. We must guard against assuming that statements of principle in the Scriptures are not cultural. In the instance cited above, what is meant by the word *head?* We will immediately recognize that the word was used figuratively. Paul was obviously not referring to the physical organ that has hair on the top and eyes, nose, and a mouth in front. If the word *head* is used figuratively, what does it mean? In our culture the word *head* in this context would be understood figuratively to mean boss or leader. However, in first-century Greek culture it had more the idea of "that which *nourishes* the rest of the body and draws it to its goal" (Johnson, 1976:136). It can be seen how these two different figurative uses of the head lead to different understandings of the passage. In fact, an understanding of the cultural setting of the Pauline epistles is essential to an understanding of Paul's teachings regarding husband-wife relationships in particular, and the role of women in society and the church in general. There is a simplistic school of interpretation that attempts to apply the words of Paul directly to our cultural situation today without considering their cultural context; this method usually results in a subordination of women. However, when Paul's teachings are understood in the light of the cultural situations he was addressing, the result is usually an elevating of the status of women (Gundry, 1977; Scanzoni and Hardesty, 1974; Williams, 1977). As Johnson explains,

> Recognizing, then that the Word of God comes to us in the New Testament in the specific cultural/historical language of the first century, we need a bicultural approach to scripture. In this approach, the interpreter attempts to see the immediate historical context of the wri-

ter. . . . While he searches for the author's full context, he [the interpreter] constantly keeps in mind the possibility that he is reading into the text his own culture and making the biblical statements agree with his own notions and traditions (1976:134).

At this point one might ask, If the interpretation of a passage depends so heavily on an adequate knowledge of the cultural context of the passage, how can the average person read and understand the Scriptures correctly? Johnson gives a very adequate answer to this question:

In the first place, we do find in some circles a somewhat naive view of Bible interpretation. It is readily assumed that if the Bible is read in a good, modern translation and the sense seems to be quite plain, then this is all that is needed. While certainly some measure of the Bible's message and meaning can be gained from repeated readings in a good translation, the fact remains that the Bible is still an ancient book and its expressions, images, and literary genre require an awareness of the ancient world for the most fruitful understanding. Interpreting the Bible correctly demands hard work (1976:42).

There are some basic tools that can greatly assist the untrained person in understanding the Scriptures in the light of the cultural context. First, a good introduction to the Old Testament (e.g., Jensen, 1978; Young, 1958) and to the New Testament (e.g., Gromacki, 1974; Harrison, 1964; Tenney, 1961) will give the Bible student some insights into the historical/cultural context of the various books of the Bible. Next, a Bible dictionary (e.g., Davis, 1972; Tenney, 1963) can help us understand specific traits found in the cultures of Scripture. Finally, commentaries on specific passages should be consulted.

CONTEXTUALIZATION

The second application of the integration of biblical authority and cultural relativity will be to cross-cultural ministry. When a person has been raised in one culture as a Christian and enters another culture to bring the gospel, the person brings more than just the gospel. The person is bringing his or her cultural understanding of the gospel and cultural manifestation of it. In other words the gospel has been contextualized in the culture of the Christian. Buswell defines *contextualization* as

theology done from inside a system, rendering the supracultural Christian absolutes not only in the linguistic idiom but also within the particular forms that "system" takes within the system: concepts of priority, sequence, time, space, elements of order, customs of validation and assertion, styles of emphasis and expression (1978:90).

As we introduce the gospel in another culture, we must attempt to lay aside our own cultural understanding and manifestation of the gospel and allow understandings and manifestations of the gospel to develop in the light of the host culture, that is, to become contextualized.

At this point we might ask, Is there not only one gospel and is it not the same for all cultures? This question has been dealt with by the contributors to the *Willowbank Report:*

> it is important to identify what is at the heart of the gospel. We recognize as central the themes of God as Creator, the universality of sin, Jesus Christ as Son of God, Lord of all, and Saviour through his atoning death and risen life, the necessity of conversion, the coming of the Holy Spirit and his transforming power, the fellowship and mission of the Christian church, and the hope of Christ's return.
>
> While these are basic elements of the gospel, it is necessary to add that no theological statement is culture-free. Therefore, all theological formulations must be judged by the Bible itself, which stands above them all. Their value must be judged by their faithfulness to it as well as by the relevance with which they apply its message to their own culture (1978:12–13).

In order to be effective in ministering cross-culturally, we must be cultural relativists as well as advocates of biblical authority. It is important to realize that the members of any culture are going to emphasize some facets of the gospel while the members of another culture will tend to emphasize other facets of Scripture. As the *Willowbank Report* continues:

> The Bible proclaims the gospel story in many forms. The gospel is like a multi-faceted diamond, with different aspects that appeal to different people in different cultures. It has depths we have not fathomed. It defies every attempt to reduce it to a neat formulation (1978:12).

For example, in developing a theology of conversion, our Western culture with its emphasis on individualism has tended to emphasize the individual nature of the conversion experience, drawing on Scripture that supports that position (e.g., Acts 8:26–40). However, those who are from a culture where group and communal decision making are emphasized will tend to emphasize the corporate nature of conversion, drawing on Scripture that reports communal conversions (e.g., Acts 10:44–48; 16:33; 1 Cor. 1:16). Once again we quote from the *Willowbank Report:*

> Conversion should not be conceived as being invariably and only an individual experience, although that has been the pattern of western expectation for many years. On the contrary, the covenant theme of the Old Testament and the household baptisms of the New should lead us to desire, work for, and expect both family and group conversions. . . . Theologically, we recognize the biblical emphasis on the solidarity of each *ethnos*, i.e., nation or people. Sociologically, we recognize that each society is composed of a variety of subgroups, subcultures, or homogeneous units. It is evident that people receive the gospel most readily when it is presented to them in a manner which is appropriate—and not alien—to their culture, and when they can respond to it with and among their own people. . . . We recognize the validity of the corporate dimension of conversion as part of the total process, as well as the necessity for each member of the group ultimately to share in it personally (1978:22).

CONCLUSION

In this chapter we have attempted to integrate the concepts of biblical authority and cultural relativity. We pointed out that the Word of God is supracultural, that is, it stands above culture. However, although the Word of God is supracultural, it is given to us within a specific cultural setting. Therefore a working knowledge of culture and its role in human society is important to both interpreting the Bible in the light of its cultures and applying the principles in our own culture as well as cross-culturally. From the discussion in this chapter, the importance of understanding the nature and dynamics of culture should become apparent. In studying culture, we must keep in mind that culture is relative, whereas the Word of God is authoritative.

DISCUSSION QUESTIONS

1. What are some basic folkways, mores, and laws in your culture? How do they relate to the value system of your culture?
2. This chapter points out that humans have few, if any, instinctive behaviors. Can you think of any? Do they satisfy the three criteria of Morgan and King for behavior to be instinctive?

3. Can you cite examples of biblical absolutism and cultural absolutism from your experiences in Christian organizations?
4. How much does a person need to know about the cultures in Scripture to be able to interpret Scripture?
5. Can the gospel and Christianity exist apart from culture, or will the gospel always take a cultural form?

SUGGESTED READING

Stephen A. Grunlan and Marvin K. Mayers, *Cultural Anthropology: A Christian Perspective* (Grand Rapids: Zondervan, 1979). A basic introduction to cultural anthropology that provides a background for understanding the nature and dynamics of culture.

Alan Johnson, "History and Culture in New Testament Interpretation" in *Interpreting the Word of God,* S. J. Schultz and M. A. Inch (eds.) (Chicago: Moody Press, 1976). An excellent discussion of the importance of interpreting Scripture in the light of its cultural context. Discusses issues and gives examples.

Marvin K. Mayers, *Christianity Confronts Culture* (Grand Rapids: Zondervan, 1974). An excellent approach to cross-cultural communication of the gospel. Deals with the issue of biblical authority and cultural relativity and applies it to contemporary situations.

Eugene A. Nida, *Customs and Cultures* (Pasadena, Calif.: William Carey, 1954). An application of cultural anthropology to missions. An early attempt to deal with the issue of biblical authority and cultural relativity.

The Willowbank Report—Gospel and Culture (Lausanne Committee for World Evangelization, Wheaton, 1978). A report of the consultation on the gospel and culture held at Willowbank, Bermuda, in January, 1978. A good discussion of contextualization and cross-cultural ministry.

4

ROBERT McCLUSKEY
St. Paul Bible College,
Minnesota

SOCIALIZATION

Although the topic of personality and socialization is impossible to cover comprehensively in a short essay, some overview of the field must be given to provide a proper perspective. There are many theories, but most theorists admit that their knowledge is incomplete and their concepts are in flux.

Personality may be defined as the characteristics and tendencies that typify an individual's behavior. These behavioral traits are peculiar to the particular person. Expressions of thought, self-concept, attitudes, and intellect are included. In short, personality is that particular combination of elements that makes each person unique.

Socialization is the "process whereby an individual learns the skills, roles, rules, and values of a society and develops a social (self) identity. Socialization is a life-long process that usually involves learning in different but related subgroups (family, peer group, occupation)" (Lowry and Rankin, 1977:160).

Socialization therefore may be seen as the process by which innate behavior patterns are modified to produce personality. The final product may be more or less a result of innate or learned functions, but since more control may be exercised over the socialization factors of personality, social scientists choose to devote more study to them.

One commonly accepted categorization divides theories of personality and socialization into (1) ethological theories, (2) psychoanalytic theories, (3) social-learning theories, and (4) cognitive-developmental theories (Bee, 1978). Most students of the subject agree that no one of these theories completely explains all observed phenomena, and it is also true that each theory does explain some particular phenomena better than the others. For those reasons many students of personality and socialization prefer to maintain an eclectic approach to the subject, that is, they borrow from each theory those concepts that enable them to construct a comprehensive model. However, because everyone brings in some degree of bias, it would be difficult in practice to find either the pure theorist or the pure eclectic. We will briefly discuss the theoretical categories referred to above.

ETHOLOGICAL THEORY

"From the ethological point of view, the human infant is not a completely naive being, but possesses a legacy of potential behavior patterns which at one time assured the survival of the organism even without the aid of social learning or customs" (Hess, 1970:31–32). John Bowlby (1969) made what is perhaps the most complete statement of an ethological theory related specifically to personality development. The emphasis is on innate, instinctive patterns of behavior in the infant. The child provokes attention and care through crying and squirming and then prolongs it through smiling, cuddling, and instinctive behavior. The major theoretical debate surrounding ethology concerns the degree to which more complex behavior, such as aggression, is instinctive or reflexive.

It is in connection with these behavioral patterns that the old concept of instinct as an internal force determined by the genes and independent of environmental (learning) stimulation has largely been abandoned. Contemporary ethologists now accept some version of the view that heredity determines a preprogrammed physiological system that reacts to a broad range of environmental stimulation; in other words, the environment interacts with genetic potential to produce the organization of each response system. In humans, the environment, perhaps because of its greater diversity relative to lower animals, has a greater impact on genetic potential and thus plays a more active role in determining action patterns (Meyer and Dusek, 1979:57).

Both the strengths and weaknesses of ethological theories stem from the same circumstance, that is, an incomplete approach. It *does* explain perhaps better than any other viewpoint, the earliest manifestations of personality and interpersonal relationships in infants. On the other hand, little attention is given to the individuality of infants or the potential for the production of long-term individual differences by the environment. This might be expected, given the origin of the theoretical perspective in studies of animal behavior and its distinct evolutionary bias. In short, ethological theory emphasizes more than any of the others the effects of heredity on personality and socialization.

PSYCHOANALYTIC THEORY

Psychoanalytic theories are predominantly associated with the work of Sigmund Freud. Like the ethologists, Freud emphasized the instinctive bases of behavior (Bee, 1978:305). It should be pointed out, however, that Freud's use of the term *instinct* is not precisely the same as that of the ethologists. Whereas ethologists understand instinct to encompass specific innate behavior patterns, Freud's use connotes only that certain drives and needs are innately present.

Especially important for psychoanalysts are those instincts associated with sexual gratification. Attachment to others and the perception of self are manifestations of the child's sexual instincts. Freud understood the child to pass through several distinct psychosexual stages, with shifts from one stage to another being caused by changes in sensitivity in various areas of the body. Five stages may be summarized as follows:

1. *The oral stage: From birth to one year.* Because the infant first experiences the world through the mouth, it provides the first region of pleasure. Thus the individual who first provides pleasure through the mouth will be the one with whom first attachments are formed.

2. *The anal stage: Ages one to three.* Because postnatal physical development proceeds from the head downward, the infant be-

comes more aware of lower trunk functions as he or she grows older. As a result, the child becomes more aware of bowel movements as both a source of pleasure and a reliever of discomfort. In addition, toilet training focuses the attention of parents on the elimination processes as well. The net result is to shift the center of attention from the oral to the anal zone.

3. *The phallic stage: Ages three to five.* As the genital area becomes fully developed, the child is capable of pleasurable feelings from this zone. Masturbation commonly begins. It is at this stage that a most important event takes place—the "Oedipal conflict." In boys there develops an intuitive awareness of the mother as a sex object (Rappoport, 1972:74). Consequently, a boy must view his father as a sexual rival who will castrate him if the rivalry is not eliminated. The conflict is resolved through the boy's repression of his sexual attraction to the mother and "identification" with the father. Thus the boy adopts an appropriate sex role.

Although the identification process for girls is not as clear in psychoanalytic literature, it is more important to understand that the phallic stage is essential to the development of the identification that produces morality, sex roles, and attachment, all of which are essential factors in socialization.

4. *The latency stage: Ages five to twelve.* This is a "resting stage," during which cognitive activity (beginning school, for example) apparently absorbs the energy of the child.

5. *The genital stage: Ages twelve to eighteen and older.* If the Oedipal conflict has been satisfactorily resolved, the hormonally induced sexual energies of puberty will produce sexual attachments to persons of the opposite sex. Confused identification, however, affects personality through an inability to cope with sex-biased relationships, as well as many other potential problems.

Although Freudian theory, as related above, has fallen somewhat into the background of psychological respect, it is well to remember the important place it holds historically in the development of the social sciences. Few contemporary theorists espouse the emphasis placed on sexual phenomena as primary determinants of interpersonal and social relationships; but we must appreciate Freud for focusing our attention on the importance of maturation (stages of development) and the interaction between children and care-givers. While his dynamics are subject to serious question, his description of the development of personality has been invaluable.

An alternative theory, that of Erik H. Erickson, falls within the psychoanalytic framework and is very much in the contemporary mainstream. Erickson gave attention to the development of the rational part of Freud's personality framework, the ego. At any given stage a healthy or unhealthy quality can be developed. The early stages parallel the psychosexual stages of Freud. The eight-stage theory of Erickson can be summarized as follows:

1. *Basic trust versus mistrust.* This stage occurs during the oral stage, between birth and age one. During this stage the infant develops a sense as to whether the world is predictable and whether he or she can produce consistent results through behavior. Obviously, the care-giver is crucial in this process. Consistent responses to the child's behavior can produce trust, while erratic or harsh responses produce mistrust. Clearly, the basic trust or mistrust that the child carries out of this stage will profoundly affect the outcome of the following stages.

2. *Autonomy versus shame and doubt.* This stage corresponds to the anal period, the second and third years of life. The greater mobility of the child produces an increased range of choices, with corresponding possibilities of success or failure. If the child experiences success at independence, autonomy will result. If repeated failures, ridicule, and punishment result from the newly found freedom, shame and doubt will occur. Again, parents are vital to the insurance of maximum potential for success and the rewarding of achievement. Erickson sees toilet training as being a particularly critical occurrence.

3. *Initiative versus guilt.* Paralleling Freud's phallic period, this stage occurs around ages four and five. The child is now becoming aware that he or she not only is mobile and able to exercise influences over the environment, but that influence may be planned, initiated, and organized toward goals. More important, the child recognizes that he or she is accountable for these actions—that they may be right or wrong. This brings about a fear in the child that this newly found initiative may be judged criti-

cally. Further, the process of identification internalizes the values of the parents in the child. In order for the child to emerge from this stage with initiative and without guilt, the parents must insure that the child is given clear-cut values and that initiative is directed into acceptable behavior.

4. *Industry versus inferiority.* This stage occurs during the latency period, ages six to twelve. New cognitive and physical challenges, particularly related to school, require the child to win approval through productivity. Failure to develop the skills required to produce will result in feelings of inferiority.

5. *Identity versus role confusion.* Associated with puberty, Freud's genital stage, the adolescent is here confronted with the requirement of developing, according to Erickson, a "sexual identity" and an "occupational identity." These require integration of the self with the world and have long-range significance. Without a firm personality emerging from previous stages, and appropriate guidance and support, the profusion of roles visible to the child can be confusing.

6. *Intimacy versus isolation.* This stage, ages nineteen to twenty-five, stems from the need to merge one's identity with another. There is no implication, however, that the individual is willing to *sub*merge his or her identity into another. Hence, an inability to merge, because of a weak ego produced by inadequate resolution of previous stages, will drive the person into isolation.

7. *Generativity versus stagnation.* During the period of mid-twenties to about forty, the emphasis on the pleasure of the sexual experience itself shifts to the pleasures of conceiving and rearing children. According to Erickson, the ability to focus attention on children is an outgrowth of the successful resolution of earlier stages. If this is not achieved, a sense of stagnation or purposelessness may be the result.

8. *Ego integrity versus despair.* As the individual ages and approaches death, he or she must have a secure sense of value (which Erickson called "ego integrity") or despair will result.

The strengths of Erickson's theory are not only in its very comprehensive descriptive base but, even more, in its relationship to cognitive as well as sexual development. He recognized that how people think plays a large part in personality and social development, as well as in how they feel. An additional strength is the consideration of adult socialization, which is a sparsely covered field of significant concern to sociologists.

SOCIAL-LEARNING THEORY

A basic premise of all social-learning theories is that the ways in which people interact with others are *learned*. A strict version of such a theory would contend not only that the infant comes into the world *tabula rasa* (as a blank tablet), but that the contingencies of the child's behavior in social intercourse determine the patterns that define personality. All types of learning might be involved—classical conditioning, operant conditioning, observation, and discovery. For example, what is termed attachment—the special relationship that an infant seems to have with the mother—is viewed as stemming merely from the mother's repeated reinforcement of the child for expression of his or her needs. Eventually, because the child associates the mother with pleasure and comfort, the mother herself becomes a good object as well.

There are at least two reasons for the popularity of social-learning theories during the past several years. Their popularity has been due partly to their success in providing explanations of a wide range of behavioral phenomena; this popularity also has been partly due to their empirical research techniques, that are able to satisfy the preoccupation of contemporary science with technical precision. Since social-learning theories tend to emphasize the external, behavioral components of personality to the exclusion of concern with cognitive and affective components, they are able to claim that their evidence is "measurable," "replicable," and "unambiguous."

Unfortunately, theorists who are enamored of such empiricism often view the consideration of internal processes as meaningless because such processes are not subject to observation or precise measurement. Thus they tend to overlook causation and concentrate on description, and so their social psychology is expressed in correlations instead of concepts. According to Bee,

> Most theorists in this tradition, including Bandura, Sears, Bijou, Baer, and many others, have not been very interested in changes with age in the *type* or quality of dependency, or aggression, or peer behavior. The primary concern has been to account for the differences in

quantity—individual differences in the strength or vigor of the behavior (1978:315).

However, social-learning theorists have been very much on the scene of late, and their research has done much to provide useful techniques for the establishment of effective socialization and intervention in deviant socialization. An excellent example is the classic work of Albert Bandura (1973) on aggression and role modeling, particularly the effects of television on aggression. Because Bandura rather conclusively demonstrated a connection between violence in children and the amount of violence they observed, concentrated efforts have arisen to minimize the amount of violence viewed by children in the media. It is probably fair to say that as a consequence of these types of influences, we are currently more under the influence of social-learning theorists than of any other group.[1]

COGNITIVE-DEVELOPMENTAL THEORY

Finally, there are those who recognize that people do think (as well as behave), and that they think in different ways at the various stages of their lives. These *cognitive-developmental* theorists are beginning to strongly supplement and influence the dominant position of the pure social-learning theorists. In many ways cognitive-developmental theories encompass all of the above perspectives, but they tend to emphasize the cognitive, or thinking, aspect. Maccoby and Masters state, "Any behavior of a child is a function of the level of cognitive development he has achieved" (1970:91). Charles Horton Cooley was an early proponent of the notion that what people think profoundly affects what they do. Using the analogy of a looking-glass, Cooley explained that we develop ideas about ourselves by imagining what others think about us. "For Cooley, the *looking-glass self* has three main elements: the way we imagine we appear to others; the way we imagine others to judge that appearance; and the way we feel about those judgments" (Light and Keller, 1978:113). George Herbert Mead (1934), Cooley's contemporary, expanded this concept by positing that infants, through their interaction with others,

---

[1]Exchange theory in sociology draws heavily on this theoretical perspective.

acquire a vocabulary of "significant symbols," or conventionalized gestures, that others understand. This process shapes thoughts and behavior patterns that cause children to think of themselves as others do. As children play and mature they work out relationships with specific, important people (themselves, parents, siblings) whom Mead calls "significant others." In time these relationships generalize and children develop a concept of what is expected of them; they see their capabilities as social creatures and where they fit in a larger society—the "generalized other." The emphasis of these views is on the role of thinking in the process of socialization and personality development. There is a cognitive assessment of the expectations and norms of the context, and appropriate behavior follows.

In the area of the development of thinking, Jean Piaget is probably the most influential contemporary voice for the cognitive-developmental view. His detailed observations and experiments, which led to his theory of increasing cognitive skills as stemming from progressive decentration, are classic, and are required fare for students of human development all over the world.

Piaget's stages of cognitive development have been summarized as follows:

1. *Sensory motor intelligence (0 to 18 months).* During this stage the child at first does not distinguish between itself and its environment. The child is egocentric, and reacts to objects based on their physical characteristics rather than their symbolic meaning.
2. *Preoperational intelligence (18 months to 7 years).* During this stage the child acquires language, is still egocentric, and deals with objects based on their symbolic meaning.
3. *Concretely operational intelligence (7 years to 11 years).* During this stage the child begins to become less egocentric and begins to see things from the other person's perspective; it develops more complex patterns of thought but still based on concrete objects.
4. *Formally operational intelligence (11 years and upward).* At this stage the individual begins to adopt adult thought processes including abstract reasoning (Grunlan and Mayers, 1979:77–78).

The work of relating models such as Piaget's to personality acquisition and socialization has, in qualitative terms, just begun. A notable attempt is that of Lawrence Kohlberg in the area of "moral development" (Scharf, 1978). Kohlberg's recent appearance as a developmental theoretician of substantial repute bespeaks the current enthusiasm toward comprehensive and rational models of personality development.

Kohlberg contends that children adopt a set of internalized rules for determining whether a particular act is right or wrong. These rules are essentially a function of the cognitive development of the child, or the extent of progress from the absolute egocentrism of the infant. During the process of maturing the child is more and more able to take the perspective of others. The most widely accepted Kohlberg model, and the one that still appears in many textbooks, describes six stages of development through which an individual might pass. The stages range from the Obedience or Reward Orientation, in which the physical consequences of an act determine its goodness or badness, to the Universal Ethical Principle Orientation, where what is right is a question of the individual conscience and judgments are based on fundamental and universal principles:

KOHLBERG'S STAGES OF MORAL DEVELOPMENT

A. PRECONVENTIONAL STAGES

Stage 1: Obedience or Reward Orientation—Behavior is motivated by avoidance of punishment.

Stage 2: Instrumental Exchange or Marketplace Orientation—Behavior is motivated by the desire for reward or benefit.

B. CONVENTIONAL STAGES

Stage 3: Conformist Orientation—Behavior is motivated by anticipation of approval or disapproval of others.

Stage 4: "Law and Order" Orientation—Behavior is motivated by the anticipation of dishonor and guilt over harming others.

C. POSTCONVENTIONAL STAGES

Stage 5: Social Contract or Legalistic Orientation—Behavior is based on a concern for maintaining the respect of others as well as self-respect.

Stage 6: Universal Ethical Principle Orientation—Behavior is based on concern for one's own ethical principles and self-condemnation for violating them.

Kohlberg's attempt to formalize the notion of moral thinking has undergone substantial modification and criticism (see below and Muson, 1979:48); nevertheless, the widespread acceptance of his model and the proliferation of practical human interventions that it has spawned give evidence both to the trend and to the promise of cognitive-developmental theorization. No doubt the increasing integration of social-learning and cognitive-developmental theorization will produce more rational and comprehensive applications to the processes of personality development and socialization.

THE ASSUMPTIONS OF SOCIALIZATION

The following discussion is in no way intended to exhaust the subject of assumptions. Its purpose is to point out some ways in which the study of personality and socialization is most vulnerable to false or incomplete assumptions. More complete discussions of Christian perspectives on the assumptions of science may be found in the suggested readings.

A perfunctory review of introductory sociology textbooks reveals that the *nature/nurture,* or *heredity/environment,* argument is at the heart of a substantial number of issues in the field. Briefly defined, the issue to be decided is as follows: Which is most influential in determining the direction of personality development and socialization, the effects of heredity or the effects of environment? For example, is a person more aggressive than others because he was "born that way," or because he was "raised that way"? Each theoretical perspective will emphasize these determinants of personality to a different degree. The cognitive-developmental theorists will focus on maturational components that in turn direct attention to the genetically determined unfolding of species characteristics. On the other hand, the social-learning theorists will tend to look at the rewards and punishments that shape what they view as mere reflexes into complex behavior.

The danger in the nature/nurture issue for Christians, however, is not in what the various theories say, but in what by implication they leave out. If Christians allow themselves to become caught up in the nature/nurture conflict, they are apt to forget to ask the most important question of all: What part of human behavior is not controlled by either heredity or environment; specifically, how much of one's personality is determined by his/her own will, or by submitting to God's will?

The latter question will be quite foreign to most nontheistic sociologists. In our modern culture with its scientific orientation, many people assume that *all* human behavior is motivated and modified by heredity or environment. All behavior is said to be determined by empirically measurable causes. The following question is often posed: Is it not the case that all the accumulating evidence from the biological and behavioral sciences points more and more to the conclusion that a human being's belief in freedom of choice and freedom of action is nothing more than a comforting illusion? If the answer to this question is yes, there arise far-reaching implications for Christian beliefs. For example, if humans have no freedom of choice, how can they be held responsible for their acceptance or rejection of the claims of Christ? Or again, if they have no freedom of action, in what sense can they be held morally culpable for behavior that breaks God's laws (Jeeves, 1976:112)? Scripture, however, demands choices from Christians and non-Christians alike. For example, men are invited to come to Christ (Matt. 11:28) and to receive Him (John 1:12). The Bible further says that those who refuse to believe in Him are held accountable for their refusal (John 3:17–18; 5:22–25). Such admonitions run strongly counter to the assumptions of determinists, who must ultimately contend that no individual is truly free to choose and thus is not accountable for who he is or what he does. Another objection to the notion of choice stems from what David G. Myers calls "divine determination" (1978:216). This concept is an even more critical determinist problem to Christians, because it has its roots in a well-established segment of orthodox Christianity, the so-called Calvinist perspective. Without digressing into a theological discussion or debate, the issue revolves around such concepts as predestination and the sovereignty of God. Since arguments on all sides of these questions have continued unabated for years, no attempt will be made to reconcile them here; but another perspective of the problem may be useful: "As Augustine reasoned, either God cannot abolish evil or he will not; if he cannot, he is not all-powerful; if he will not, he is not all-good. John Stuart Mill saw this as an 'absolute contradiction at the center of Christian faith.' It is a mystery with which all Christians live" (Myers, 1978:216).

Fortunately, it will not be necessary to resolve the theological dilemma in order to provide a theistic perspective to some pressing social issues. This is true because most antitheistic social philosophy tends to arise not from false assumptions about the causes of attitudes and behavior, but because of conclusions reached about *accountability* for those attitudes and behaviors. As to this question, no perceptive orthodox Christian should be confused.

> The only sensible perspective on our own present situation for us to take is to assume responsibility for our actions, even though an omniscient mind looking in from the outside may foreknow our choices. Our experience joins the Scriptures in simultaneously affirming the reality of responsibility, from the human perspective, and of divine omnipotence, from God's perspective. The future is in God's hands, and yet responsibility for the future is ours. In other words, "Work as if all depended on you, pray as if all depended on God." Paul senses this paradox when he writes, "I . . . : yet not I, but the grace of God which was with me." Both divine sovereignty and human responsibility must be asserted (Myers, 1978:222).

A social problem arises from extending the assumption that our personalities and behavior are determined by forces over which we have no control and for which we are not accountable. In brief the problem is that all values soon become relative to the interests of the immediate group, or disappear altogether. This problem with values can be seen by asking a typical question that arises: If a person murders because of the influence of television models, or because of abuse at home, or because chemicals have broken down inhibitions, can the person be called bad and be punished?

The nontheistic social scientist will object that the implications of this question completely ignore environment as a defense against judgment. Are, for example, individuals from certain cultural subgroups more evil than others because they are arrested more, or abuse children more, or have higher divorce rates? The Christian can only respond that in terms of accountability the answer is yes. The lost person is condemned by personal sin, and the saved person suffers loss by failure to deserve rewards (1 Cor. 3:13–15). It is not necessary however to ignore the issue of causation in order to understand the clear teaching of the first three chapters of Romans that humans are evil because they choose to be evil. The fact that humans are accountable in no way diminishes the predictability of their behavior.

We are beginning to see in our society the logical extension of determinism. B. F. Skinner (1971), for example, has completely surrendered his vast behaviorist domain to it. He has acknowledged without reservation that everyone is controlled, and his most constructive suggestion is that the controls be placed in the hands of those who control the best. Even more serious is the view, recently expressed by a child psychology teacher, that although children might be told that a certain behavior was *wrong*, it would be better to say that it was *unhealthy*. In this view criminals should not be *punished* for their crimes; they should be *rehabilitated*, or at worst *quarantined*.

Christians who fail to discern the fallacy of determinism often use God's intellectual provision to buy into an assumption that will ultimately be the disillusionment and demise of any science that embraces it. Karl Menninger, in his well-known book *Whatever Became of Sin?* (1973), acknowledges that the disappearance of right and wrong from our society may herald the end of civilization itself.

It is beyond question that heredity and environment play important parts in determining the day-to-day relationships of people with one another. The social sciences *are* sciences because behavior is statistically predictable. The day-to-day functioning of society requires that the background and experience of individuals make predictable what they are going to do. But consider the case of an experienced and violent criminal who is the son of experienced and violent criminals. Could such a person, frustrated and subject to normal fight or flight reactions, when slapped in the face, choose to turn the other cheek? Of course he could; and he must if his will and God's will have become one. Skinner says that only the most expert of human controllers can make such a criminal into a social creature, but the Christian will quickly reveal the fallacy of this human determinism if he asks, Who controls the controllers, and who controls the controllers of the controllers, and—? In view of the conclusion that individuals are accountable for their behavior, and to some degree are controlled by heredity and environment, the subject of socialization becomes very important to Christians. Does socialization predetermine behavior? Or does it merely predispose? And to what degree?

An answer that might resolve the issue could go something like this: Socialization (nature/nurture) determines all behavior in which no individual will is involved. Because this would include most behavior, socialization predisposes almost all behavior; that is, we do the vast majority of things without conscious thought. This is even true of some quite complex activities, such as driving a car. Occasionally, circumstances will cause us to become aware of behavior that is usually habitual. At that point we may choose among alternatives as to how it will be done. Further, even a conscious behavior that is chosen from among other options will contain some elements that are carried out from habit. For example, you may choose a particular route by which to walk home, but you are unlikely to think about the tempo of walking, or how your arms will be swung. These however are really major components of walking home and to some degree determine what we call personality.

Thus humans may be seen as homeostatic creatures with a conscious override. Such a concept will allow for both the highly predictable nature of behavior and the apparent ability of individuals to occasionally act contrary to their normal pattern. It will also explain why the so-called higher order behaviors seem to be less predictable; they presumably would involve more conscious intellectual thought and, consequently, more exercise of the will.

All individuals are accountable to conform to God's will (Rom. 3), but only the Christian has the power to do so. Because of the predominant role of basic needs in early socialization, all persons tend to respond strongly to their fleshly desires. This is the source of the war that Paul found in his members (Rom. 7:21–23). But through the power of the Holy Spirit, Christians are able to win this war (8:12–14).

Equipping Christians to be strengthened with power in their inner beings (Eph. 3:16) and to be made new in the attitude (spirit) of their minds (4:23) are important functions of the family and the church. Because of the Fall every individual must be resocialized after the new birth if he or she is to have the mind and will of Christ. Resocialization for Christians is necessary for two reasons. First, they need a new set of habits—unconscious behaviors.

When appropriate Christian habits have been formed, such habits can be said to be products of a new will, even though they may not involve an exercise of the will itself. In terms of the earlier discussion, the resocialized Christian will be predetermined by his new habits to a different set of unconscious behaviors. These presumably will largely be correct, or good, habits.

Second, and perhaps more important, areas of *concern* to the individual will be different after the new birth. Behaviors that were previously matters of habit will become matters of choice, and vice versa. The Bible tells us that certain Christians are qualified to participate in the more complex and difficult aspects of the faith because they "have their senses trained to discern good and evil" (Heb. 5:14 NASB). This is resocialization. A major concern of Christian leaders today is the inability of many Christians to do what is right because they don't have the ability to *discern* what is right. No degree of will can be exercised when there is no conscious awareness that choices are being made.

Closely related to the fallacy of determinism is that of *relativism*, which in sociology often takes the form of an adaptation of values to reflect current cultural norms. The biblical pattern is, of course, the opposite—cultural norms are to be conformed to absolute values (see chap. 3 for a discussion of this issue).

An example of such relativism is the statement of Kohlbergian theorists (see above) that different behavior might be moral in different circumstances. In fact, although Kohlberg's theory purports to be about moral thinking, he contends that the individual's level of moral development is determined not by what he does, but by how he decides what he is going to do. Suppose, for example, the case of two people who are given the opportunity to lie with the result that one lies and the other tells the truth. If they both reach their conclusions by similar thought processes, it could be concluded, according to Kohlberg, that both are in identical stages of moral development. Apparently there is little, if any, consideration given to the possibility that certain actions might always be wrong.

Another example of relativism is the willingness of sociologists to alter the meanings of terms to absorb the pejorative impact of changes in norms. Until recently, for instance, few reputable commentators would have applied the term *nuclear family* to any unit less than a married couple. We are now beginning to see the term *family* applied quite broadly so that it includes such units as a man and a woman who are not married and households with children in which the parents are divorced or have never married. The danger in this rapid change in meanings is that traditional moral values will become attached to all concepts encompassed within the broadened definition. Thus single-parent families will be seen as being good in the same sense as the traditional nuclear family. In many cases it is probably the intent of such changes to produce this effect.

There is a potential two-level problem with this practice. First, the value implications may not be true. There appears to be little question that the traditional nuclear family produces better socialization circumstances than, for example, single-parent families. The formation of multiple attachments is augmented by the presence of both parents in the home; the presence of models of both sexes contributes an appropriate self-image for the child, and so forth.[2]

Another potential problem, perhaps more important for the Christian, is that models permissible under expanded definitions may not be permissible in God's design. Continual bombardment with unbiblical models, however, will ultimately produce diminishing discernment.

Unfortunately, because we live at such close quarters with the secular world and with its unbiblical philosophy, it is very easy for us to fall into the habit of accepting secular terms and definitions while adapting biblical truth to fit. The area of social science is no exception and may be, in fact, one of the most susceptible to the tendency.

THE AGENTS OF SOCIALIZATION

Having examined in general two of the assumptions underlying views about personality development and socialization, it is time

---

[2]This discussion does not imply that the presence of two parents in the home is a guarantee that a child will be "good." Two "good" parents should produce "better" children than two parents who are less effective in their parental roles. It is also possible that one "good" parent will raise a "better" child than two inferior parents. However, proper socialization is facilitated by the presence of both parents.

to consider the two factors that play the predominant roles in personality development and socialization.

1. *Parents*. Until recently most theorists would have agreed that the first and most important point of contact that people have with society is their parents. It has now become fashionable, however, among sociology textbook writers and teachers to point out that the nuclear family is less important than previously thought. Frequently cited evidence concerns the experience of the Israeli kibbutz, in which the role of the biological parents is minimized and the community assumes much of the responsibility for the rearing of the children. Advocates of such child-rearing programs point out that there appears to be little negative effect on the socialization of kibbutz children and that they are better socialized in some ways than children reared in nuclear families (Light and Keller, 1978:373–74). However, wherever there appears to be a contradiction between a biblical model and scientific evidence, the Christian must assume that the biblical model is correct and that the conclusions from the research need to be reexamined.

This case illustrates the danger of accepting the conclusions of the secular theorists. The interpretation of socialization research done in kibbutzim is no doubt valid in the secular context. However, there is no consideration of the effects of communal parenting on *spiritual* development. How, for example, can a kibbutz child develop an understanding of one God, the Father, who is personal and loving and yet alone requires accountability for sin? It seems clear to me that this is a primary role of the father within the family. As the young child thinks in only concrete terms, the father provides the concrete model from which the child will ultimately conceive of the spiritual God. It would appear that the child reared in a multiple-parenting situation will have a no more complete understanding of ultimate authority than that of the community and the state. This is not accidental on the part of the government of Israel (Vander Zanden, 1979:136), nor is it accidental that the trend in the United States is in the same direction.

It is important for the Christian sociology student to understand that social acceptability does not guarantee the best answer to a social need. If a trend lacks biblical support, it will also lack the support of adequate research, that is, research that accounts for spiritual as well as physical and intellectual well-being.

One author notes:

> Slightly more than half of American children under eighteen years of age (and 62 percent under the age of six) who are living in homes with a female head also has a family income that falls below the poverty level. Single parents find that the responsibilities for family living fall on one adult rather than two and often call for a good deal of juggling of time and energy. Their circumstances are frequently made more difficult by the fact that schools and workplaces have inflexible hours, and these hours do not coincide (Vander Zanden, 1979:432).

Is this lifestyle, so commonplace and widely accepted in our society, according to God's perfect will? Christians must learn to apply the test of their faith to all processes of life, including socialization: (1) Is it according to biblical doctrine or pattern? (2) Will investigation bear out the soundness of the hypothesis or action physically, intellectually, and spiritually? (3) Does it seem right? It sometimes appears that the processes of socialization advocated by secular society are tested backwards, incompletely, and without authority. Secularists begin with how it seems to the flesh. They may seek to determine through investigation whether it is sound, but only physically and intellectually so; and they will never consider the spiritual implications. This results in the feeling of incompleteness that many people have today. To be socialized in such a manner is like sailing on the ocean in a vessel with no power and no rudder; people know they are in the water, but they don't know where they are or where they are going.

Another area in which Christians are cautioned to closely examine the assumptions of contemporary secular sociology with regard to parenting is in the acquisition of sex roles. First, it must be acknowledged that there *is* a sex-stereotyping problem in our culture. Evangelical Christians are not immune to this problem and may be infected worse than non-Christians. The problem is not, however, in the assessment of differentiated sex roles for men and women, but in the *valuation* of sex roles for men and women.

Many studies have shown that the treatment of boys and girls is different right from birth (Weitzman, 1975). Books, electronic media, and display advertising reinforce stereotyped sex roles. The expectations and modeling of parents and others lead children into male or female roles. Conversely, less stereotyped environments lead to less stereotyped behavior. In short, evidence for the high influence of social factors in the production of sex roles from the earliest hours is conclusive.

Students of sex-role acquisition often use research findings indicating the strong influence of environmental factors to imply that males in Western culture are provided with some arbitrary and unfair advantages in life that can and should be eliminated. There are several problems with this inference.

First, differences in the sexes are not arbitrary. As this writer understands biblical propositions, God intentionally created males and females differently and made them just as He wanted them. Second, God is unfair to no one, by name or gender. Each individual is unique and infinitely valuable. Gender cannot detract from that value. God has designed a unique role for each individual, and gender is a parameter of that role. In other words, as God has selected each of us for His special purpose, He has equipped us according to His sovereign will. If one must see his or her God-ordained circumstances as delimiting (as has been done since the Garden of Eden), then one must at least recognize that maleness or femaleness is no more delimiting than shortness or tallness, blondness or brunetteness, or left-handedness or right-handedness.

It follows, then, that men and women cannot be exactly alike; but it also follows that all are equally valuable in the roles God has chosen and given. To say that "to love" is better than "to obey" is to deem God unfair, and those who seek to escape their roles are as wrong as those who seek to demean them.[3]

2. *School.* After parents, the second most potent agent of socialization is the school. Although chapter 12 of this book deals especially with education, it will be useful here to briefly allude to some of the factors of schooling that directly affect socialization.

The acquisition of identity, self-worth, and sex roles occur primarily in early stages of socialization under the auspices of parents; in contrast, the acquisition of values is a much more continuing process. As cognitive-developmental theorists teach,

---

[3]It needs to be pointed out that all evangelicals will not be in agreement on what the Scriptures teach on male-female roles, and husband-wife relationships. Some evangelicals may understand the Bible differently than others on this issue.

children reason differently as they mature and, in general, their capacity for social adjustment through the adoption of more numerous and sophisticated perspectives is enhanced as they grow older. For example, in the Piagetian model, the attainment of the formal operations stage is an absolute prerequisite for the attainment of Kohlberg's higher levels of moral reasoning. It is thus clear that the school has *great* potential for intervention in this aspect of socialization. This area is usually referred to as *values acquisition* or *values clarification*. In this regard the Christian needs several cautions.

First, it should be understood that American public education was historically oriented toward basic Christian values. The concept of the school as a promoter of pluralistic secular values had its real beginning only recently, with the influence of John Dewey. Our country was founded with an appeal to "the Supreme Judge of the World for the rectitude of our intentions" and "with a firm reliance on the protection of divine Providence" (Declaration of Independence). A quick look at early textbooks and the predominantly religious training of early teachers will reveal beyond reasonable doubt the firmly theistic values of early American education. Furthermore, publicity given to the bibliocentric religious leanings of Americans today convincingly demonstrates that we still are a theistic nation. Finally, it is now commonly acknowledged that the values of a teacher, faculty, school board, or community are as inextricably a part of their existence as their dialects or their ethnic mix.

It is absurd, therefore, for schools to attempt or claim to be value-free or value-neutral. The extent of this absurdity has been conspicuously revealed by findings in both the philosophical realm (Rushdoony, 1976) and the legal realm (*Torcaso v. Watkins,* 376 U.S. 488). These findings show that attempts to eliminate theism in the classroom have resulted in the establishment of secular humanism, which is itself a religion.

The Christian sociology student is thus cautioned against indiscriminate references to secular or humanistic values in education. The rapid proliferation of sectarian schools, especially evangelical Christian ones, is impressive testimony that the consumers of education expect the schools to impart values that not only satisfy the body and the mind, but the spirit as well. The opposition of government to the growth of these schools is adequate testimony as to where the interests of the state lie.

An example of the attempt to inculcate pluralistic, value-free principles into the socialization process in schools is the widespread introduction of the moral development principles of Lawrence Kohlberg (see above). Kohlberg recognizes that people use different reasoning processes as they mature, which is a scientific and valuable observation. However, he develops his educational philosophy and techniques from the perspective that when the school has intervened to advance the mode of moral reasoning, the behavioral outcomes are secondary and of no concern to educators. Further, the variety of Kohlbergian intervention theory that appears in most textbooks claims to raise the moral reasoning of the most mature individuals to a level at which they can transcend outside authority. That is, the individual who has learned to view every perspective before making a moral judgment will make decisions that may be contrary to any single point of law, authority, or expertise; yet, according to Kohlberg, the person's decisions will be right because they correspond to universal principles. Again, it is interesting that Kohlberg does not claim that two individuals at his highest stage and in the same situation will make the same decision. In fact, he is not now sure that anyone reaches this stage, apparently because it can be successfully demonstrated that every decision one makes is ultimately predicated upon some authority.

The question is, Whose authority? It is here that the Christian student has much to teach the non-Christian teacher. Kohlberg contends, but without adequate emperical support, that as a person becomes more mature the person is less dependent on authority. This persistence of human nature to verify its intellectual desires is not science, but pride. A truth of Scripture is that we are all under authority, though we may choose whom to serve. Admittedly, Satan is willing to disguise his mastery in the lovely cloaks of humanism, relativism and naturalism until the title deed to his slave is sorrowfully turned over by God. God, however, has freely revealed what science can never discover—that to be truly mature is to become as a little child, accepting the benevolent lordship of Christ and the riches of peace, joy, and love that service to self can never bring.

DISCUSSION QUESTIONS

1. Which of the theoretical approaches discussed do you think is most compatible with a biblical understanding of human nature? Why?
2. What effect does the nature/nurture issue have on the concept of human responsibility?
3. To what extent do you believe that humans have free will or free choice? To what extent are humans responsible for their behavior?
4. What is your response to the author's concept of the church being a center for resocialization after a person has accepted Christ?
5. What are the implications for Christians of the effect of socialization on personality development?

SUGGESTED READING

Kenneth O. Gangel, "Toward a Biblical Theology of Marriage and Family," *Journal of Psychology and Theology* (1977, 1, 55–69; 2, 150–162; 3, 247–259; 4, 318–351). An excellent four-part series outlining in some detail the roles and responsibilities of Christians within the family, the roles of the family as a social structure, relationships within the family structure, and issues and problems relating to parenting. The influences of culture are considered.

Paul D. Meier, *Christian Child-Rearing and Personality Development* (Grand Rapids: Baker, 1977). Meier, a physician and psychiatrist who teaches at Dallas Theological Seminary, here provides a longitudinal presentation of principles related to personality and socialization. It is not a technical book, but offers a practical approach to the application of biblical and scientific principles.

David G. Myers, *The Human Puzzle* (New York: Harper and Row, 1978). The subtitle of this book, "Psychological Research and Christian Belief," summarizes its theme. It is an excellent commentary on the assumptions of research and their biblical implications. No Christian student of the social sciences should proceed without reading this book.

Rousas J. Rushdoony, *Intellectual Schizophrenia* (Phillipsburg, N.J.: Presbyterian and Reformed, 1976). An examination of the philosophical implications of secularized education, with a Christian perspective. This book will cause you to think. Although not primarily a volume about socialization, chapter 1 is entitled "The School and the Whole

Person," giving evidence of Rushdoony's understanding that schooling plays a large part in forming the personality.

Peter Scharf (ed.), *Readings in Moral Education* (Minneapolis, Minn.: Winston, 1978). Although the Christian student is cautioned to view this book with discernment, it offers a good example of the progress being made in the application of cognitive-developmental socialization theory. Actual interventions for the purpose of changing attitudes and behavior are described.

5

RUSSELL HEDDENDORF
Geneva College,
Pennsylvania

STATUS AND ROLE

Much of what we know as modern sociology is barely forty years old. Many of the crucial concepts and principals used today were largely unformed, if not unknown, before then. Sociologists seek the most succinct way to phrase a principle or concept. And when successful, their results became bench marks in the development of the field.

It is generally recognized that American anthropologist Ralph Linton provided the first and most useful explanation of *status* and *role* in his classic text *The Study of Man* (1936). The fact that sociology is indebted to an anthropologist for this breakthrough only emphasizes the importance of the concept of culture in sociology and the common roots nurturing these two disciplines.

THE MEANINGS OF STATUS AND ROLE

Linton's definitions of the concepts were so precise and yet so simple that one could hardly do better than quote him: "A status, as distinct from the individual who may occupy it, is simply a collection of rights and duties" (1936:113). "A role represents the dynamic aspect of a status . . . (when a person) puts the rights and duties which constitute the status into effect, he is performing a role" (1936:114). Consequently a status is inseparable from a role, and one cannot exist without the other.

In another sense "a status, in the abstract, is a position in a particular pattern" (Linton, 1936:113). This meaning of the concept refers to the fact that a person in his or her status has a place in society. Stated in another way, one is socially located. But since each person has a number of positions in society, he or she also has a number of statuses and, of course, corresponding roles at the same time.

Social positions such as student, salesman, parent, soldier, and girl friend are typical examples of statuses. Once having acquired a status, an individual learns a whole series of norms that apply to him or her in that status. One sociologist properly refers to these norms as "agreements" that define and condition relations among persons in those statuses (Babbie, 1977:109). These agreements function as a social glue to help individuals conform to the expectations of society as well as to the expectations of others with whom they interact.

A status, then, requires that a person make a contribution to society and to others by conforming to their expectations. In return, the status provides the individual with an awareness of his uniqueness as this is expressed in his differences from others. It assists in the formation of a self-identity by rewarding him with approval. This occurs for students, for example, when they fulfill the college's norms and gain a clear and rewarding awareness of themselves as students. In this way they are motivated to conform to the norms, and their behavior is rewarding for themselves and others.

Statuses and roles do not just link people with their society; they also locate them within a total fabric of interacting persons, all of whom share some common purpose. People's responsibilities in society are best understood in terms of this vast network of interacting beings who are responsible to them as well. In addition, these interacting persons help individuals to understand how others depend on them and how they may relate to others. In short, people learn to become complete humans and social beings in their statuses and roles (Cooley, 1949:287–89).

The kind of relationships found among members of a baseball

91

team is typical of these network arrangements. No position has meaning unless its relationship to other positions is understood. The catcher has no purpose on the team without the pitcher and vice versa. Each expects the other to perform some action and, in turn, behaves accordingly. If the catcher is successful in calling for pitches, the pitcher gains greater self-esteem as well. Together, the pair helps shape the success of the team and its awareness of its potential.

The smooth functioning of the team, then, depends on the maximum adjustment of the players to their statuses and roles. The team's morale is influenced by the success or failure of this adjustment. As new expectations develop, the team gains a unique identity that separates it from other teams. In other words the team's success or failure influences the player's attitudes toward opposing teams as well as toward their own. The result is the formation of a common purpose not shared by other teams.

But if team members are to perform well, they need some expertise or special competence in a status. Members of a Little League team usually can play at several positions, but such versatility is not common for major league players who have learned that they are most effective at particular positions. The question arises, How is the decision made to move into one position or another? Stated another way, we might ask, Why does one person become located in one position while another is in a different position?

ASCRIBED AND ACHIEVED STATUSES

Linton's original distinction between ascribed and achieved statuses is now well accepted. An *ascribed status* is assigned to persons without regard for innate differences or abilities, and the required tasks could be performed by most anyone. Housekeeping chores, wood cutting, and farming are typically unspecialized jobs assumed by persons in ascribed statuses. *Achieved statuses,* however, require specialized qualities because of the more technical kinds of tasks involved. Practicing medicine, designing bridges, and singing in an operatic role are activities that require the abilities of persons in achieved statuses. While *ascribed statuses* are usually assigned to persons at birth, *achieved statuses* are left open to be filled through competition and individual effort. Rites of passage, signifying a new set of expectations and role interactions, further mark the movement from one type of status to another.

In those societies with little need of technical skills, ascribed statuses are especially numerous and provide for the ordinary requirements of daily living. In modern societies, however, this pattern is reversed. The importance of achieved statuses and roles is vastly increased and, by comparison, ascribed statuses lose importance. Even though they may provide for some of society's most fundamental needs, the unspecialized nature of ascribed statuses weakens some of their attractiveness.

The most basic ascribed statuses assigned at birth are age, sex, and race. The biological qualities of these statuses define the minimal responsibilities expected by society. Only a woman, for example, can bear children and perform the biological functions of a mother. Although any woman is capable of reproduction, being a good mother is difficult and is rewarded by recognition as Mother of the Year. Similarly, citizenship responsibilities are limited to adults. It is necessary to remember, however, that not all adults make good citizens and some women are very poor mothers. In short, even ascribed statuses demand some conformity to social expectations, and social problems may occur if this guideline is not observed.

To illustrate, there is the homosexual who chooses, for one reason or another, not to abide by the norms for his or her sex. There is also the gifted black artist who, because of inherited skin color, is expected by bigots to limit himself to an unskilled trade. Similarly, a woman may forego graduate school at marriage to assume the responsibilities of a housewife. In other words there is always some strain between the expectations assigned by society to a status and the interpretation a person brings to it.

A low social position may be accepted as a mere "accident of birth." Whether justifiable or not, the ascribed status is to be accepted as interpreted by society (Davis, 1948:112–13). Another way of seeing the problem is to suggest that a status may be differently interpreted by the person (Davis, 1948:113–15). Because of high motivation or special gifts, achievement may be stressed instead of ascription. In spite of these differing interpretations, the major point is this: while ascribed statuses provide the security of known cultural expectations, achieved statuses should stimulate individual effort while locating the right persons in appropriate social positions.

Unfortunately, the process of status ascription and achievement rarely works in such an ideal fashion. Few people regularly conform to the expectations inherent in statuses and roles. In other words deviance may be just as "normal" as conformity (Durkheim, 1962:10–13). Spouses are as likely to hate each other as to love and parents may abuse children as well as cuddle them. The sociologist can neither completely predict nor understand why such deviances occur. Still, there are certain principles that help to explain why these problems may exist.

STATUS AND ROLE PROBLEMS

Change in status expectations. Statuses cannot be expected to remain static in a modern society. Changes in prestige of statuses require new behavior and norms that, in turn, influence the statuses. At one time women were denied rights currently permitted to them. Similarly, blacks have gained increased status in matters of race. And when achieved statuses, such as that of teacher, gain increased prestige, there will also be a comparable increase in power and influence. These trends suggest that the changing norms of society produce new standards for statuses.

Changing statuses also stimulate new expectations in the individual. The experiences of a senior student differ from those of a freshman and channel interests away from the school instead of toward it. Similarly, the mutual expectations of a newly married couple for each other will not necessarily be the same after ten years of marriage. Unless behavior adjusts to these changing expectations, some deviance is inevitable. In short, an individual's changing patterns of status expectations produce deviance as well as conformity to new norms (Johnson, 1960:21–28).

This fact leads to the crucial point that deviance may be constructive as well as destructive. To illustrate, the unwillingness of a black woman to sit in the segregated section of a bus did much to stimulate the civil rights movement of the sixties. This simple act questioned traditional definitions of the status of blacks and produced a legitimate strain among whites and blacks. Questioning society's expectations in this way requires adjustment in the status system to the emerging and, hopefully, more suitable norms.

Status and role imbalance. A status system is well adjusted when there is an equality between the status rewards expected by a person and his role performance. Imbalance occurs when the person receives too much reward for his role performance or less reward than his status deserves. The problem, of course, centers on how society and the individual define these rewards and performances.

The movie star, for example, receives a high degree of status rewards. Many would claim these are unwarranted when measured against the real contributions that person could make to society. Any justification of these rewards rests on the value the actor has for the movie industry itself. In economic terms his value may far exceed his contribution to moral standards. To understand the relationship of statuses and roles, then, it is necessary to consider the values implicit in them.

Conversely, a person may be given a low status for an important role contribution made to society. Black slaves in the South provided the essential labor for the maintenance of an entire society, but were treated with scorn and segregation in return. This imbalance was also justified in economic terms although, by any other measure, its illegitimacy would be apparent. One hundred years later the civil rights movement sought to adjust this long-standing imbalance of status and roles with, of course, only partial success.

The fact that society seeks to adjust the status system, regardless of the time span involved, suggests the importance of this system. Ideally the individual should be in the right status and properly motivated to perform it well. When this occurs his behavior is mutually rewarding for society, others, and himself. Furthermore, he learns that all other forms of behavior are inappropriate for him, and principles of morality are clarified and renewed. The status of husband, for example, sets a man off from an unmarried male. The husband is aware that sexual relations are legitimate only with his wife, and the unmarried male is governed by a completely different set of moral expectations. To confuse these statuses, or worse, to ignore them altogether, leads to the moral chaos characteristic of modern society.

Status as an end. The question of moral behavior emphasizes an important point: statuses are always linked with proper role performance. Parents are expected to refrain from abusing children and students are required to take tests. Persons unwilling to accept the role requirements should not seek a status for its rewards alone. The result can only be disregard for others and destruction of the social ties among persons.

Nevertheless, some statuses are too often sought only as ends for self-gratification. The salesman is usually seen as someone motivated by a personal profit motive and without regard for the customer's needs. Other statuses may change from stressing role performance to an emphasis on status as an end for self-gratification. Historically, the teacher stressed service to the community with little consideration of personal gain. The current emphasis in the profession reverses this pattern and encourages working for greater personal benefits and financial rewards. In other words when statuses are sought as ends in themselves, self is stressed instead of society.

It is characteristic of modern society that people lose awareness of larger responsibilities and are concerned only about immediate needs and circumstances. This fundamental lack of responsibility to others too often produces a distortion of social relationships and the meaning of the status itself. The father who prods an unwilling son to join a Little League team is a case in point. The father uses the son to live his own childhood again and mistakenly believes this to be good parenting. In fact, it is nothing more than a form of manipulation.

The point is that manipulation of others is often resorted to when status alone is emphasized. The other's status and, indeed, his person as well may be seen only as a means to maximize one's own status (Moberg, 1970). A reversal of this pattern is needed, along with a realization that another's status is at least as important as one's own. Once recognized, this idea of the Golden Rule is seen as one of the great principles for social relationships (MacIver, 1970). Going one step further, one sociologist has emphasized the necessity of the biblical principle of altruistic love— sacrificing oneself for the good of the other (Sorokin, 1950).

Before equality in human relationships is possible, there must be an awareness of one's position in relationship to others. Instead of focusing on oneself alone, an individual needs to develop an appreciation of others and the importance they have in themselves and in society. A teacher must see the value and potential of his or her students if the teacher is to gain a positive evaluation of himself or herself, and parents must value their children in order to relate to them. In short, a status is not to be an end for self-gratification but a means for relating to others.

Role as an end. One important way by which people relate to each other is by means of paired role responsibilities: minister and parishioner, landlord and tenant, doctor and patient, and so on (Bierstedt, 1963:253). These are status relationships that occur primarily because of the interrelationship of the behavioral aspects of the status positions both persons hold and not because of who they are. The emphasis is on doing the right thing in order to maintain the relationship. Thus the role must be stressed if the status is to be maintained.

Each status relationship carries its own value system. The widely accepted taboo on nudity, for example, must be abandoned by a patient in a doctor's office. An unwillingness on the patient's part to shed clothing will prevent a normal and necessary doctor-patient relationship. Note, however, that the taboo is still in effect for the doctor in his office and for the patient meeting the doctor on the street.

When roles are stressed in this way, the person loses importance. Indeed, confidentiality is absolutely necessary in doctor-patient and minister-parishioner relationships. But such confidentiality only illustrates the loss of human qualities of patients and parishioners who now are identified as "cases" instead of as persons.

While all status relationships have this dehumanizing tendency built into the roles, some are more demanding in this regard. The bureaucrat-client relationship is a case in point. The client is treated as a case by the bureaucrat in order to determine the rules and regulations that might apply to him or her. Once these are determined, the bureaucrat then proceeds to solve the client's problem. Usually the bureaucrat has an interest in only one area of an individual's life. At no point is it necessary for the bureaucrat to consider the client's total needs as a person.

The extreme effect of living a role is that persons may become what their role expects them to be. The bureaucrat, for example, may develop a personality that is no longer limited to meetings with clients (Merton, 1952:361–71). Many bureaucrats treat all persons as clients and show no flexibility in meeting the demands of other statuses. Consequently they exhibit little awareness of how to treat others as human beings who have a wide variety of needs and desires.

Role conflict and role strain. This problem of adjusting one's role behavior to fit the needs of a situation produces other difficulties as well. Little harm is done when a primary-grade child refers to a teacher as his or her mother. There is a different problem, however, when an employer perceives his secretary as a wife and speaks to her in endearing terms.

Another type of problem occurs when a person has difficulty calling out a necessary response. Faced with two role responsibilities in a situation, the person must first make a decision on priority. This condition is known as role conflict and occurs when a person must respond to two incompatible situations at the same time. There is the man, for example, who promises his wife that he will promptly return from work so she can have the car. Later, as a result of an urgent and unexpected meeting, he finds it necessary to work longer than expected. Clearly, he could have avoided some problems if he had been able to make some priorities and communicated them to the persons involved.

The problem of role conflict, then, occurs when role responsibilities are considered to be of equal importance. As long as this condition exists, the individual is faced with the dilemma of determining priorities. But when one role is so dominant that it is seen as the end for which all others are the means, the problem is largely solved. Role conflict, then, causes few problems when persons are guided by ultimate and determining values.

But this seldom happens. It is more likely that people will only respond to the immediate demands of a situation. Usually this occurs in a *role set*, a term that refers to all the social positions related to a role. The role set of a teacher, for example, includes students, administrators, peers, janitors, and parents. Role strain occurs when the members of a role set make conflicting demands on the teacher; for example, a parent might request a conference at the same hour a faculty meeting is scheduled. Again, some priorities are needed. But unless the person is a Christian and has absolute and ultimate values, he or she is more likely to resolve the problem on the basis of immediate, personal interests; and the person is apt to experience role conflict.

Some roles, on the other hand, require conflict and inconsistent forms of conduct (Broom and Selznick, 1977:37). The professor's role, for example, calls for impartial evaluation of the student's work. But the professor is also expected to stress the human qualities of the student and to develop academic potential. Flexibility is needed as both professor and student call out the proper response to meet the demands of the situation.

Of course, such flexibility is often lacking. Errors in judgment and response produce strained relations when expectations are not met. The student, for example, may expect a positive and supportive letter of reference. The professor, however, recognizes personal responsibility to the potential employer and supplies an objective and less favorable recommendation. The result is conformity to the employer's expectations and deviation from the student's.

Because of role conflict and role strain, complete conformity to role requirements is never possible. The web of social relations and mutual responsibility is so complex that some deviance is inevitable. Thus failure to fill role obligations adequately is not necessarily the individual's fault. True, the individual is responsible for personal behavior and is expected to fulfill any commitments he or she brings to a role, but society also shares some of the responsibility for failures in role performance.

STATUS AND ROLE REQUIREMENTS

If status and role problems are to be minimized, attention must be given to certain requirements for status relationships. How these requirements are interpreted and whether they solve status and role problems depend on how society and individuals handle them.

Status definition. Before the role associated with a status may be performed well, a person must have a clear definition of the status and its role requirements. It is not enough to say that spouses should love, honor, and respect, or that fathers should refrain from provoking their children. These expectations are necessary but also vague and incapable of evaluation by others.

The corporate world attempts to solve the problem with job descriptions, that is, lengthy statements of an employee's expected behavior for which the person is to be held accountable. Even this provision is often inadequate and open to interpretation. Furthermore, in most areas of our society, job descriptions seem improper, if not absurd. How do we define a good husband? What can a parent reasonably expect from a child today? And if all the roles of the virtuous woman in Proverbs 31 became the model for a contemporary wife, many women would reconsider the prospects of marriage.

The problem becomes more complex when we realize that status definitions are often not constant but are dependent on social situations and their interpretation. In general, students understand their role requirements: they are to attend class, study course material, and take tests. But the expectations of teachers differ so greatly that diversity rather than similarity is the model for the definition of what a student is or does. And when it is realized that a teacher's expectations often vary from one course to the next, it is a hopeless task to define a student's role clearly for all classes.

Status definition then often depends on the social situation in which the role is performed. Rather than stressing some status definition, as vague as it might be, the person is more inclined to accept cues from his or her immediate social context. To illustrate, a student understands the need to study for a test. However, when faced with peer pressure to take a break and spend the rest of the evening at a pizza shop, the student is more likely to redefine his or her role accordingly. Status definition then may be controlled by the person in that status rather than by society through some set of values.

Accountability, as suggested earlier, is explicit in the attempt to define a status with a job description. But few statuses today even imply accountability. Even the trend to no-fault divorces suggests that a spouse is not accountable for personal behavior. And if responsibility cannot be assigned, role requirements lose meaning and at best are vague and ill defined. In short, few people today define their statuses in terms of requirements, and many fail to take them seriously. They prefer to receive instead of give.

Status rewards. It is more likely that statuses will be viewed in terms of rewards rather than requirements. On the one hand this attitude is desirable, for status rewards can encourage proper role behavior. On the other hand not all rewards are beneficial. A mother may seek the immediate reward of so-called smother love with its selfish absorption of her child's personality. A far greater reward however may come only after patient sacrifice and the child's independent expression of appreciation for her understanding love.

This willingness to postpone rewards is referred to as the principle of deferred gratification (Bredemeier and Stephenson, 1962:108). Medical students need to follow this principle as they postpone the benefits of their status until the completion of their education. The gambler however follows the principle of immediate gratification in the pursuit of a good income without exerting extensive effort. Some labor unions have turned to strikes rather than increased productivity in their attempts to gain immediate gratification.

This last point illustrates the important fact that inappropriate means are sometimes used to gain certain kinds of status rewards. Some status rewards, for example, are legitimate only when deferred. If immediate gratification is sought, the rewards may become illegitimate. A good example of this fact is marriage, which offers the reward of legitimate sexual relations to the partners. But couples sometimes seek the pleasures of sexual relations without the benefit of marriage. Rather than deferring their gratification until marriage, they seek it immediately in premarital sexual relations. The result is a violation of the biblical rules governing the sexual union. It is a physical experience that is less than satisfying, for God intended it to have spiritual overtones and to occur within marriage.

The point, of course, is that status rewards have a proper meaning only when there is a clearly defined status and role relationship. In marriage this occurs when certain legal procedures are followed. Even if the role requirements are not clearly stated, the marriage partners and their friends know they are married and have certain obligations, as vague as they may be, binding them. But once the couple moves into society, their marriage may be unknown to strangers. Their anonymity as husband or wife requires some symbolic way of communicating this status to others.

Status symbols. A status symbol simply makes possible the perception of one's status by others. It does not necessarily imply some particular high quality or rank. An army private's status symbol is a chevron and a captain's is a set of bars worn on the shoulders. Rank in this case is explicit because the army requires a hierarchical arrangement of soldiers to provide for military discipline. Upon noting the captain's bars, the private defers with a salute that is returned by the captain. In this case a complete set of responses is controlled by the symbols, although our society does not generally insist on such a precise response to status symbols (Bensman and Rosenberg, 1963:193–96).

A wedding band, for example, identifies the married person in a crowd. Although it does not establish any inherent ranking or necessary behavior, the ring does facilitate determining relationships between the sexes. A certain awareness and etiquette clarify the expectations men and women have toward each other. A husband who removes a wedding band, however, becomes anonymous once again and the women he meets may see him as a possible suitor. In short, he misrepresents his status and manipulates the expectations of those he meets with the symbol, or role sign as it is sometimes called (Smelser, 1973:532–33).

The point here is clear: because a status symbol only represents something, it must be handled with sincerity and integrity. If not, the owner gives the impression of actually having what the symbol represents. A Jaguar sports car bought with a $1,000 down payment, even though the owner has a $15,000 annual income, is a status symbol of this sort. The owner implies by his action that he in fact has the wealth suggested by the auto. Thus status symbols such as wedding bands may be removed or added. They may also be used to enhance a status beyond that which is actually possessed. In each case the perception of a person by others is influenced by the image he or she wishes to convey.

It is quite possible then that a great difference will exist between who a person is and who he appears to be. In fact, society is always ready to aid in creating these illusions. Whenever we are encouraged to go into debt to buy an expensive car or home, we learn to live beyond our means. For some, the gap between their potential and their goals is insignificant and easily bridged. For others, it is great and produces failure or, at best, frustration. A shocking example of this point was made in a news account some years ago of a high school student who was not accepted into the local university attended by many of his friends. Somehow the young man was able to misrepresent himself as a student, attend classes, and take tests without official registration. For four years he deceived his family and friends, fully aware that he would be unmasked at commencement. When that day came, his inability to face reality caused him to commit suicide.

Status performance. The most basic requirement for holding any status is that a person have the requisites to perform the role requirements. Too often motivation exceeds ability, as is the case with some high school students. Whether lacking the ability, the money, or the necessary grades, a student may not qualify—at least by the university's standards—to be a student. Indeed, whenever we either ignore or do not understand our inability to fill certain role requirements, social problems may occur.

Motherhood is a case in point. Because a woman is biologically capable of bearing children, it might be automatically assumed that she is also capable of being a good mother. But the number of abused children suggests otherwise. Motherhood involves exceedingly delicate as well as demanding requirements that cannot be met automatically by every woman. Indeed, motherhood may require a necessary mental discipline and flexibility beyond the natural capacity of some women. If so, motherhood cannot be taken for granted; instead, it must be reserved for the "gifted," or, as is more likely, taught to those lacking the necessary qualities.

This illustration returns us to the point made earlier that one should not choose a status simply for the rewards offered. Too many social problems may occur when reward is the only basis for choosing a social status. Divorce, alcoholism, drug addiction, and crime may all be related in some way to a person's inability to fulfill role requirements simply because of a lack of some personal quality. But as long as society stresses rewards rather than requirements, problems are likely to continue.

Poor status performance, then, is not necessarily the fault of the person alone. Society may encourage persons to achieve statuses in which they will not perform well. It also may use improper means to measure a person's performance. Is there any reason to assume, for example, that an Ivy League student will perform better in an elite graduate school than a student from a land-grant institution? If the person is not above the use of illusions or reliance on status symbols to gain or maintain a status, can we expect anything more from social institutions? Indeed, society may so distort the meaning of statuses and roles that we find it difficult to perform in them at all

CHRISTIAN IMPLICATIONS

The fact that we are both not "of the world" and yet "in the world" is a most profound Christian as well as sociological truth (John 15:19; 17:11 KJV). Because we are socially located in our statuses, we are "in the world"; but in our Christian lives we are not to be "of the world." This tension is usually not clearly perceived by the Christian and may not be understood even when recognized. And yet Scripture as well as sociology provides clear principles for dealing with these problems. Having developed the sociological principles, the scriptural principles may be briefly outlined.

The first principle is that God does indeed intend that people be socially located. Even though made in the image of God, humans are to be "in the world" and not try to escape it and its responsibilities. Citizens are to pay taxes (Matt. 17:24–27) and be subject to rulers (Titus 3:1). Husbands are to love, wives are to respect, and children are to obey (Eph. 5:22–6:1). These are all social statuses requiring shared expectations if the ordered society God considers beneficial for His children is to exist.

Second, statuses and roles do more than order society; they also afford the person an opportunity for understanding his or her uniqueness as a human being. When Christ told the disciples He would make them "fishers of men" (Matt. 4:19), He did more than merely describe their uniqueness in terms of a common status. He assured them that they would fulfill His purpose for them only if they understood what it meant to be fishermen. An extraordinary example of this principle is the case of Ruth and Boaz. Because of their faithfulness in fulfilling the expectations of their ascribed kin statuses, the line of inheritance was continued and resulted in the birth of Christ (Ruth 4:17–21; Matt. 1:1–16). Thus faithfulness to one's role requirements may fulfill God's purposes as well as provide for the benefits of others and oneself.[1]

---

[1]It needs to be noted that some societal role requirements may go against the teachings of Scripture. The Christian's first responsibility is to be obedient to the Word of God.

Third, God provides spiritual gifts to people for the fulfilling of role requirements or "for the common good" (1 Cor. 12:7). In fact, certain persons are intended by God to fill certain statuses "so that the body of Christ may be built up" (Eph. 4:11–12). Human uniqueness then should be the basis for an achieved status as well as the result of it. Even marriage, Jesus claims, should be only for those without the special gift for celibacy (Matt. 19:11; cf. 1 Cor. 7:37–38).

A fourth principle is that the Christian's status expectations should agree with his or her God-given abilities. That is why the Christian is told, "Do not think of yourself more highly than you ought" (Rom. 12:3). Christians should not take their gifts for granted and seek statuses for which they are unprepared. Nor should they be like Moses and deny the capabilities that God has given them (Exod. 4:10–12).

Fifth, the expectations that Christians have of themselves should be consistent with the image they convey to others. Rather than use symbols to give false impressions of their status, they are to be realistic about their importance. Jesus advised guests not to take the most important seats at a banquet. Instead, He suggested they take the humblest seats so that the host could then assign them more important seats (Luke 14:8–10).

Sixth, status definitions should not be based on social situations. Peter, for example, does not accept the extraordinary deference of Cornelius as a basis for gaining higher status (Acts 10:25–26). Nor does he accept the common notion that social encounters should be based on differences among persons (Acts 10:28). When Jesus met the Samaritan woman, He did not decide to accept or reject her on the basis of her status in the town. Instead, He defined her status in terms of her deepest needs (John 4:7–26).

This leads to another important principle: people should not act more importantly than their status or role. The Jews were insensitive to this principle largely because they stressed status instead of godly behavior. It was the Good Samaritan, Jesus taught, who treated the wounded man as a "neighbor" (Luke 10:29–37). Christ, of course, illustrated the principle many times with His miracles. His willingness to heal the man on the Sabbath illustrates this point (Matt. 12:9–14). The man's need was most important to

Him, not the fact that He was clearly visible in the temple at the time. Jesus' concern was with helping the man, not with protecting His status.

Jesus' actions point to another principle: Christians should seek deferred rather than immediate gratification. Indeed, the whole gospel directs us to eternal and not current rewards. This is illustrated with the parable about the marriage feast and the reminder that the host will be rewarded at the Resurrection (Luke 14:12–14). Jesus, of course, takes the principle one step further and illustrates with His atoning death the necessity of immediate punishment rather than gratification. This principle is further illustrated by His teaching that Christians should store their treasure in heaven rather than on earth (Matt. 6:19–21).

A related principle is that we are to choose a status for its responsibilities rather than its rewards. Certainly, Jesus never suggested to the disciples that their present rewards would match their efforts (Matt. 10:5–10). Indeed, Noah's faithfulness responded only to God's commands without consideration of reward (Gen. 6:22; 7:5). The New Testament also records the faithfulness of the patriarchs to the requirements given them by God: "They did not receive the things promised" (Heb. 11:13).

Finally, status symbols should be used with care when relating to others. Christ's denouncement of the teachers of the law always stressed this need (Mark 12:38–40). Their apparent objective was not only to increase their own status, but to lower the status of others as well (Mark 7:3–5). Paul, on the other hand, spoke of the fact that he had been trained in the law under Gamaliel as he witnessed to others of God's claim on their lives (Acts 22:3–16). Raised a Pharisee, Paul used the symbol of his status to glorify God and not himself.

CONCLUSION

It is helpful to view statuses and roles as a vast network of potential relationships among persons. This invisible weblike structure links people by means of mutual opportunities and responsibilities. All of us are located at some point in this network with considerable latitude to move from one set of relationships to another.

It is necessary for us as Christians to see this system as a means by which God allows us to be faithful to Him through the decisions we make. We can either abide by His commandments and manifest the gifts granted to us, or else we can be disobedient and conform to the distorted expectations offered by society. How we view our statuses and roles provides a real test for our Christian maturity.

But the problem is not only the individual's. The sinfulness of society has weakened and, indeed, even broken much of the web. Consequently some persons lack equal opportunities to move from one status relationship to another. The social corruption of society can be measured by conflicts existing among social groups that act as barriers to the assumption of new status opportunities and role responsibilities. In this way society is fragmented and stratified into social classes that form the basis for many of our social problems today. Armed with a knowledge of sociology and the authoritative principles of the Word of God, Christians are in a unique position to minister to our society and its ills.

DISCUSSION QUESTIONS

1. What are some of your ascribed statuses? Achieved statuses?
2. Does one's status as a Christian lead to any role strain or conflict in our society? Why? Why not?
3. Is it possible for people to become prisoners of their statuses and roles; that is, can role expectations govern their behavior completely? What should a Christian's attitude be toward role expectations?
4. Should a Christian put greater emphasis on status rewards or role requirements? Why? Why not?
5. Should Christians ignore status in dealing with people? Why? Why not? How should they treat status differences?

SUGGESTED READING

Peter L. Berger, *The Noise of Solemn Assemblies* (Garden City, N.Y.: Doubleday, 1961). One of Berger's earliest works in which he argues for the necessity of personal conversion. Although a statement in the sociology of religion, it deals effectively with the problem of commitment and role responsibility.

Harry Blamires, *The Christian Mind* (Ann Arbor, Mich.: Servant Books, 1978). This essential book on the topic asks, "How should a Christian think?" and argues that if the Christian thinks in a consistently Christian fashion, the believer's behavior will be in agreement with Christian standards and be different from the world's standards.

Charles Martin, *How Human Can You Get?* (Downers Grove, Ill.: Inter-Varsity, 1973). Starting with a consideration of the nature of man, this British author discusses various roles and relationships in which man must participate. He concludes with a statement on the Christian's calling.

Udo Middleman, *prō-ĕxĭst-ĕnce* (Downers Grove, Ill.: Inter-Varsity, 1974). Considering "the place of man in the circle of reality," the author concentrates on the values of work and property in a consideration of how the Christian is to live.

Calvin Redekop, *The Free Church and Seductive Culture* (Scottdale, Pa.: Herald, 1970). Although primarily a discussion of the Free church tradition and organization, there are several excellent chapters on the problems of human relationships and how the Christian is to relate to others through his statuses.

6

DAWN McNEAL WARD
Trinity College,
Illinois

SOCIAL STRATIFICATION: SOCIAL CLASS AND SOCIAL MOBILITY

> Modern man cannot endure economic equality because he has no faith in self-transcendent, otherworldly immortality symbols: visible physical worth is the only thing he has to give him eternal life (Becker, 1975:86).

An understanding of social stratification is crucial for an overall understanding of any society and the individuals in that society. *Social stratification* refers to the social class system that reflects the degree and the structure of inequality in a society. Whether we are talking about the family, religion, education, socialization, or politics, social class is an important concept to consider. A group's or an individual's position in the class system is related to family life, sexual practices, where they live, their health and chances of reaching old age, how often they attend church, their style of worship, their happiness, and even their conception of God. This chapter will first consider the nature of the social class system in American society. Then it will focus on social mobility—the movement of individuals and groups within the class system. Next it will focus on an analysis of the American class system in relationship to some contemporary social issues. Finally, it will conclude by offering some challenges to Christians in dealing individually and collectively with the issues of social class and social mobility.

Sociologists with differing theoretical perspectives will approach the study of social stratification in different ways. Throughout the first half of this chapter, we will consider three sociological perspectives on social stratification. These will correspond to those perspectives described in chapter 1 of this text. We will refer to them as the functionalist approach, conflict approach, and interpretive approach (symbolic interactionism in chap. 1).[1]

SOCIAL CLASS

Sociologists are not all agreed regarding the nature, number, and relationship of social classes in American society. However, there are some points on which most sociologists agree. First, in modern societies there are scarce resources (resources with limited supply relative to demand) that must be distributed in some fashion. Second, these scarce resources can be divided into three major categories, which were first distinguished clearly by Max Weber, a nineteenth-century German social scientist. Their distribution makes social stratification multidimensional and thus very complex. Simply put, we can say that the three scarce resources in society are *privilege* (wealth or property), *power* (political or social influence), and *prestige* (honor or respect). Third, these scarce resources are distributed in a routine manner. The procedures for distributing them are standardized at any given point in time. Fourth, these resources are distributed unequally—some get more than others. Fifth, these resources are distributed unequally primarily to groups rather than to autonomous individuals. These groups can be described in various ways. For example, they may be seen as social classes, as occupational groups, or as groups described in terms of sex, age, race, or geographical location.

Functionalist approach. A *social class* may be viewed as a "stratum of people of similar position in the social status con-

---

[1]These approaches correspond to the paradigms in sociology developed by Howard Boughey in his introductory text *The Insights of Sociology* (1978). He refers to these paradigms as functionalism, activism, and naturalism. I will rely on several of his insights in analyzing social stratification.

tinuum" (Horton and Hunt, 1980:313). In this view social class is seen largely as a way of life or a subculture. Members of a class regard one another as equals and share certain attitudes, values, and behaviors. There is no way to specify an exact number of social classes. The number of social classes is not fixed, and the boundaries between social classes are not definite. Class differences are real, however, and are related to differences in income or wealth, occupation, and education. Consequently, for research purposes, functionalists tend to assign people to social classes based on their income, occupation, and education.

In a classic statement of the functionalist theory of social stratification, Davis and Moore (1945) argue that stratification is not only inevitable but is necessary (or positively functional) for society. The essence of their argument is that substantial rewards (privilege, power, prestige) must be built into certain important positions in society. These rewards will motivate talented people to undergo the sacrifices involved in training for, and performing, those important roles. In summary, the functionalists argue that social classes are subcultures with differing amounts of privilege, power, and prestige related to the importance of the positions held by people in those classes.

Conflict approach. The conflict approach is critical of the class structure of American society. Classes are not viewed primarily as subcultures, but as conflict or special-interest groups. Because the conflict theorists tend to focus on the economic institution as the most foundational in society, they define social class primarily in economic terms. However, a class is not defined in terms of the amount of income of its members. A class is a group of people who share a common relationship to the means of production in a given society, for example, land or factories (Boughey, 1978). In some conflict theories, the capitalist world is seen as moving toward a two-class system in which one class (the bourgeoisie) owns and controls the means of production, while the other class (the proletariat) simply works for the bourgeoisie. This condition is seen as undesirable because the workers as well as the owners become alienated from the work, themselves, and each other. Furthermore the workers are seen as being exploited and oppressed in many overt and subtle ways by the owners.

Functionalist and conflict theorists sometimes disagree because they are speaking about different issues and asking different questions. For example, functionalists ask, How can talented people be motivated to fill important positions in society? The conflict theorists counter by asking, Why are some talented peoples such as blacks and women excluded from privileged positions in society? The functionalist argument for social stratification was not intended to answer the latter question. But some functionalists have dealt with this issue. For example, Talcott Parsons (Johnson, 1975) suggests that as society "adaptively upgrades" itself, it will "progressively include" groups that have previously been excluded from important positions in society. This is quite an optimistic view of social and economic development in modern society. The conflict theorists do not share this optimism.

The conflict theorists offer several other criticisms of the functionalist argument. First, it does not take into account the extent to which those in positions of power, for example, medical doctors and political leaders, try to protect and increase the rewards inherent in their positions. These rewards tend to become disproportionate in terms of the actual sacrifices involved in the positions. Also, the functionalists assume that certain positions are functionally more important than others. This point is controversial. However, it is clear that it is in the interests of the powerful that their positions be thought of as important and demanding. In fact, several powerful groups in American society, including medical doctors and political leaders, have threatened the public with poor performance if they are not adequately rewarded. This is, in part, the medical doctors' argument against socialized medicine. Finally, the functionalist argument is based on a utilitarian view of human nature and fails to consider other sources for human motivation. The issue of motivation will be considered further in the last section of this chapter.

One goal of the conflict theorists is to minimize the inequalities of our social-class system. This generally involves some kind of redistribution of the wealth, either through economic reform or revolution. Their initial goal is to develop "class consciousness" (Boughey, 1978). Class consciousness is a recognition of one's true class interests. It involves the breakdown of people's individualistic orientations and of their antagonism toward others with problems similar to their own. In essence, the oppressed class must join together and work for a common goal—a more just and less alienating society. In order to do this, racial, sexual, ethnic, and age barriers that have been exploited by the well-organized, powerful groups in society must be broken down. In summary, the conflict theorists see social classes as more real than the functionalists. Social classes are seen as actual groups of people who are, or should become, united to work toward common interests.

Interpretive approach. Interpretive sociologists are primarily concerned with people's perceptions of social class rather than with a measurement of, or precise definition of, social class. Because of the ethic of equality, Americans tend not to want to admit that they have clear notions of social classes. They generally perceive the class structure as involving four social classes—upper, upper middle, middle, and the lower classes (Storer, 1980). When asked, the vast majority of Americans describe themselves as members of the middle or working classes.

People are also involved in what the interpretive sociologists call "doing social hierarchy" (Boughey, 1978:140). This involves creating social hierarchies in social interaction. In many social encounters there is a tendency to create inequality—to assign one person a subordinate (submissive) role and another the superordinate (dominant) role. This defines who has the most prestige and power in the situation. Social interaction can become a "contest for dignity" (Boughey, 1978:140). This contest takes place between such categories as teachers and students, physicians and patients, waiters and customers, and husbands and wives. A consistent loser in the contest is apt to store up deep resentments over a period of time. In summary, the interpretive approach views social classes from the subjective perspectives of the actors involved in the situation.

SOCIAL MOBILITY

The American dream takes for granted the possibility of individual access to upward mobility in the social class system. Millions of immigrants have come to America with the hope of upward mobility. We are currently witnessing a widespread fear of collective downward mobility among the American people because of various economic conditions and world politics. Sociologists are concerned with understanding various systems of mobility and various means for achieving mobility. They agree that *social mobility* is the movement of individuals or groups upward or downward in the social class structure. They also agree that the two major ideal types[2] of social class systems are: (1) an *open-class system* where class position is based on achievement, for example, hard work and education, and where mobility is frequent; and (2) a *closed-class system* (caste system) where class position is based on ascription, for example, heredity, sex, and race, and where movement is infrequent. Sociologists disagree about the degree of openness in the American class system.

Functionalist approach. Horton and Hunt suggest that two factors determine the opportunities for mobility in American society, namely, (1) "changes in the occupational structure and (2) the individual's response to occupational opportunity" (1980:339). Regarding changes in the occupational structure, Horton and Hunt are optimistic regarding upward social mobility in the future. Technological changes will continue to decrease the demand for unskilled labor and increase the demand for trained personnel. The individual's response to occupational opportunities will determine who will move up as the occupational structure changes. The two keys will be (1) acquiring valuable skills through education and (2) having attitudes adapted for upward mobility, particularly the ability to defer gratification.

In a controversial book, *The Unheavenly City Revisited,* Edward C. Banfield (1974) suggests that the lower, middle, and upper classes have different time horizons that influence their responses to opportunities for upward social mobility. The lower class is radically present oriented; they are unable to plan for the future, are preoccupied with immediate gratification, and feel powerless over their own destiny. The middle class is more future oriented; they plan for the future of their immediate family, defer gratification, and feel a mixture of anxiety and power regarding their future. The upper class is even more future oriented; they are

---

[2]Ideal types are logical extremes that do not describe any actual situation accurately. Actual social class systems are analyzed to see how they compare to each ideal type. The term "ideal" does not refer to the goodness of these systems but rather to their abstract nature.

concerned for the future of their descendants, the community, and mankind. They have a sense of power regarding the future. Although this analysis is somewhat speculative, it suggests that the orientation of the lower class around the present prohibits them from taking advantage of chances for upward mobility.

Conflict approach. Conflict theorists attempt to show how certain groups are systematically limited in their opportunities for upward mobility by discrimination and structural features of American society. At the same time they attempt to demonstrate that certain groups have little chance of downward mobility due to hereditary advantage. They view racism and sexism as ideologies that prevent the mobility of blacks and women. They also maintain that it is in the interests of the upper classes to emphasize consumption through the mass media and to instill fears of downward mobility in the middle classes in order to maintain the current class structure.

It is extremely difficult to demonstrate conclusively the degree of upward and downward mobility among various social classes in American society. The best evidence available at the present time suggests that the American class system is open at some points and relatively closed at others. For example, there appears to be quite high intergenerational mobility in the middle occupational categories, that is, the skilled trades, but limited mobility at the extremes of the class structure (Mueller, 1980).[3] Other evidence suggests that when blacks and whites use the traditional paths to success, for example, the educational, the payoff is generally greater for whites than for blacks (Marrett, 1980). It appears that there remain significant structural barriers to upward and downward mobility in American society.

Interpretive Approach. Interpretive sociologists are interested in analyzing the symbols people use to display their upward mobility. Concepts such as *conspicuous consumption* are used to explain consumption patterns of upwardly mobile groups. By displaying their financial abilities through engaging in certain types of class

---

[3]Social mobility is generally measured intergenerationally. The social class positions of two or more generations of kin, for example, father and son, are compared to see if upward or downward mobility has occurred. Sociologists have traditionally shown little interest in mobility among women.

behavior, people hope to validate their class position. This type of behavior characterizes people who are not yet secure in the class into which they would like to move. Some common symbols of class mobility in our society have been new homes, college educations for the children, having leisure time to travel, and participation in sports, for example, jogging and tennis. The mass media and mass production have standardized many middle-class symbols so that truly status-conscious people must continue to search for new symbols to adequately display their individual mobility.

A SYSTEMATIC ANALYSIS
OF THE AMERICAN CLASS SYSTEM

In his chapter on "The Assault on Class" in *Facing Up to Modernity* (1977), Peter Berger presents one possible way of responding to the current class system and the various attacks on it. Although not agreeing with all of Berger's conclusions, I believe his analysis of the current situation is valid and his response authentic within his Christian perspective. A summary of his views is presented as a springboard for further discussion of a Christian response to the issues of social class mobility.

The American class system involves three fundamental class premises that are currently under attack. The first premise is that "parents are entitled to hand on to their children the benefits of their class position" (Berger, 1977:45). Many parents have achieved upward mobility themselves and want to hand on the benefits of this to their children—they do not want their children to struggle as much as they did. Thus the hereditary or ascribed aspect of the American class system is that children benefit from their parents' class position. This class premise is being threatened by proposals to integrate the public schools racially and consequently in terms of social class. The reason some have resisted integration is that they want their children to continue to associate with children of comparable class position and thus avoid many of the social and cultural realities of lower-class life —physical violence, drugs, and poor educational attitudes. Consequently, when faced with school integration, particularly through busing, many middle-class parents have moved or developed private schools to maintain their class benefits. There may of course be racial as well as class factors operating in these situations.

The second premise of the American class system is that the physical and social quality of one's neighborhood and home should be a benefit of one's class position and a reward for social mobility (Berger, 1977). The trend has been for the upwardly mobile to move into the best available housing in basically homogeneous neighborhoods. Zoning laws and racial discrimination have helped to keep these neighborhoods from containing lower-class people. Government programs recently have challenged this premise by attempting to build low-income housing in middle-class neighborhoods. This has been resisted and perceived as an assault on the basic class system.

The third premise of the American class system is that individual competition and achievement determine an individual's relationship to the occupational system and his or her opportunities for upward mobility (Berger, 1977). This has been challenged by recent programs for affirmative action in education and occupations, particularly those programs based on *quota systems*. In these systems, group identity as well as individual merit are taken into account in the recruitment process. Racial and sexual groups that have been discriminated against in the past are given a competitive advantage in these programs. Using group identity as a basis for recruitment is viewed as a threat to the individualistic premises of the class system.

Berger both criticizes and defends the American class system. He believes this system is a viable social reality that should be defended but not idolized. He says in essence that the American class system is based on the premise of achieved rather than ascribed status. This premise has often been violated but still serves as a strong motivating force in society. He suggests that we should maintain the current class system while attempting to correct the injustices within it, particularly the racial injustices. He recommends that the role of the government should be to encourage economic growth, thus opening up the opportunity structure, rather than challenging the class system itself.

How should Christians respond to the class system in American society? This response should take place at two levels. First, Christians should respond as individuals in the class system; and second, they should respond as participants in the church, which is also part of the class structure. Before we look at some possible

Christian responses, we first need to examine the social class situation in the church.

THE CHURCH AND SOCIAL CLASS IN AMERICAN SOCIETY

Americans are segregated by social class.[4] This situation is reflected in the church as well. According to H. Richard Niebuhr in *The Social Sources of Denominationalism* (1929), social class has been at least as responsible as theology for the development and growth of new denominations. In particular, the Methodist and Baptist denominations developed from lower class roots. Members of a particular denomination may experience upward mobility over a period of time. When this occurs the whole style of the denomination quite frequently changes (Horton and Hunt, 1980). Formerly in the lower class, the so-called shouting Methodists have become middle class Methodists with dignified worship services. Some of the lower and working class fundamentalists of the early twentieth century have become the more sophisticated middle class evangelicals of the 1970s and 1980s. Meanwhile many Christians remain in the lower class in terms of their economic positions.

How should Christians respond to class segregation and inequality in society and in the church? Christians differ in their answers to this question. Some Christians join with activists in suggesting that there are evil structural barriers to justice for the lower classes in our society and throughout the world. They actively work for change at the individual, political, and economic levels. Magazines such as *The Other Side* and *Sojourners* reflect this approach. Other Christians would agree with Berger that they should defend the American class system and its individualism and work for greater justice within it. There are also large numbers of Christians who have never seriously considered the nature of, or the problems in, the American class system. The following section will examine the relationship of the Christian lifestyle to the issues of social class and social mobility. The section will focus on applied rather than theoretical integration, and it will examine the

---

[4]Although social class segregation is related to racial segregation, the two forms of segregation and the prejudices related to them are not identical. In this chapter we directly consider only class segregation in order not to confuse the two issues.

implications of sociological thought for Christian thought and life rather than attempt to develop an alternative sociological perspective.

THE CHRISTIAN, SOCIAL CLASS, AND SOCIAL MOBILITY

Increasing one's access to privilege, power, and prestige (that is, upward social mobility) is a highly stressed goal in American society. A belief in the American dream has been a defining feature of our society for hundreds of years. Our educational system, the mass media, the political institution, the economy, and even our churches emphasize the virtue of upward mobility. The middle class family and good neighbors are viewed as defenses against the downward mobility of middle-class children. The lower classes also share the goal of upward mobility. However, this emphasis on the value and virtue of upward mobility is not universally shared in our society. Studies of social stratification in various communities have resulted in the concept of the "unranked status group" (Karp et al., 1976:180–81). These groups contain persons who have rejected the values, symbols, and norms of the social system and have developed values, symbols, and norms of their own. Tramps, intellectuals, artists, and revolutionaries may form such groups. A key characteristic of these groups is that they are not dependent on nongroup members for their sense of social solidarity and identity. As a result of their autonomy, they are in a position to challenge and question the existing social order. Because they reject the social class definitions based on privilege, power, and prestige, they are free to challenge the existing class and mobility systems.

The concept of unranked status groups is useful in developing a Christian response to the American class system. This usefulness is three pronged. First, Christians should not be dependent on society's emphasis on privilege, power, and prestige in developing self-identity and socioeconomic goals. Second, Christians should be free to question many of the assumptions regarding class and mobility in American society. We have no ultimate allegiance to any class system, although we may prefer some over others. Third, Christians should consider the group nature of their social class identities in view of the extreme social class segregation in American churches. It may be that much of what Christians

119

describe as *unity in Christ* is primarily a unity of class-based sub-cultural similarities.

One practice to which unranked status groups would not fall prey is what psychologists Ludwig and Myers have described as "poortalk," that is, "affluent people talking as if they're poor" (1980:10). Poortalk pervades casual conversation and media presentations in American society. It is part of a vicious cycle involving reference groups, adaptation, and relative deprivation. The cycle goes like this. Society encourages us to strive for upward mobility. We choose a social class reference group that represents our social class values and goals. This group is slightly higher than our own social class, and so we feel deprived relative to them. When we achieve the goals of our reference group, we are satisfied for a while; but then we adapt. We move on to a slightly higher reference group and on and on we go. We will feel perpetually deprived even though we are affluent relative to many other groups in our society and the world. Any economic trends in society that suggest a decline in the standard of living are likely to stimulate poortalk. This analysis of poortalk shows how crucial our choice of a reference group is in shaping our class and mobility orientations. Also, it shows how relative the feeling of deprivation is, and it suggests that much middle class poortalk reflects and perpetuates insensitivity to true poverty and deprivation.

Privilege, power, and prestige—how should a Christian relate to the scarceness of these resources? Jesus had a great deal to say about one's personal economic lifestyle. He never explicitly developed a model for a class system, but spoke in ways that challenged the contemporary system. As John Alexander (1978) has pointed out in an article in *The Other Side,* Jesus chose to attack the system at its nerve and to focus on motives and values. He used this approach rather than openly attacking the particular system of His day in which were the evils of injustice and inequality. In developing a Christian response to privilege, power, and prestige, we will consider some New Testament teachings.

Privilege. Even though the Scriptures never condemn being rich in and of itself, they speak sharply and clearly regarding a person's attitudes and actions with regard to wealth. Jesus speaks to the heart of the matter in the parable of the rich fool, saying, "Be on your guard against all kinds of greed; a man's life does not consist in the abundance of his possessions" (Luke 12:15). This means that from God's viewpoint our identity and worth as persons are not determined by the amount of wealth or privilege we possess. There is more to life than gathering possessions. True, we need certain things—food, shelter, and so on—simply to survive. God is keenly aware of these needs, but our highest goal in life is not to acquire more and more wealth for our present use and as a guarantee for our future care. The rich fool was hoarding and storing up for the future. He was on the right track in the sense that he was making preparations. His error was in storing up the wrong things for the wrong future. Jesus commands us to store up "treasures in heaven," not "treasures on earth" (Matt. 6:19–20). Here Jesus is suggesting a radical alternative to society's reward system. In His system rewards are incorruptible—there is no anxiety over downward mobility. Taxes, inflation, and thieves cannot touch these rewards. Also, these rewards are not in short supply. Jesus is proposing a radical alternative for the Christian in terms of social class identity. The rewards to be gained are not to be confused with the rewards of material possessions. However, the rewards promised by Jesus may be a result of the way we share our present material possessions (Matt. 10:42). An appreciation of the "treasures in heaven" requires a radical orientation concerning the future that reaches beyond that of the upper class of Banfield, mentioned earlier. Jesus calls His followers to a life of faith that involves giving priority to spiritual realities, whether we are contemplating the present or the future.

It is tempting to suggest that the Christian is simply to develop a proper attitude toward riches. But attitude and action are closely related. This idea was expressed in the parable of the rich fool when Jesus said, "Where your treasure is, there will your heart be also" (Luke 12:34 RSV). As we build up privilege on earth, our hearts, minds, values, and time will be dedicated to caring for that privilege. Defending our class position may dictate where we live, and with whom we associate, as Berger has suggested. To be concerned with material wealth is dangerous because, as Jesus said, "No servant can serve two masters. . . . You cannot serve both God and Money. . . . You [Pharisees] are the ones who justify yourselves in the eyes of men, but God knows your hearts" (Luke 16:13–15). Paul concurs regarding the danger of seeking riches

(1 Tim. 6:9–10). People are hardheaded on this point in part because their culture suggests that material concern is normal and desirable. Jesus was aware of this tendency, and so He went on to tell the parable of the rich man and Lazarus that is recorded in Luke 16:19–31.

The Scriptures are also clear regarding the means and the results of upward mobility. Certain means of gaining material wealth are condemned, specifically those that involve the exploitation of others, particularly the poor (James 5:1–6). Obtaining wealth while others remain in need puts one in a position of responsibility (Luke 12:48; 16:19–31; 19:12–27). Paul suggests that earning more than one needs is good *because* it allows us to share with the needy (Eph. 4:28).

Power. Ideas regarding power and prestige are closely related in Jesus' teachings. To be powerful in God's kingdom is to be a servant (Mark 10:35–45). Jesus' concept of power as service is in direct contrast to society's concept of power as authority and influence. Paul also discusses why God chooses to reveal His power among those who are weak according to social standards (1 Cor. 1–4). The Christian need not live in fear of those with political and military power. Jesus revealed His own power when he refused to compete according to the rules of the powerful in their contest for dignity (Matt. 27:11–14). He reassures His followers of His power in the most intimidating circumstances (Matt. 10:26–33).

Prestige. As with riches, Jesus gets to the heart of the matter with regard to prestige, suggesting in Luke 22:24–27 that being great in God's kingdom involves being a servant. Here again we have a radical alternative to the values of our society where we display our prestige by having others serve us. In addition, James 2:1–13 teaches that we should not show varying degrees of respect to others based on their social class positions. Two reasons prohibiting such partiality are given. First, the poor are chosen to be the rich in faith—they will inherit the kingdom and deserve the respect of their status as heirs. Second, the rich are the oppressors and blasphemers in society. It makes no sense to give the rich of this world more respect than the rich in faith. It is perhaps difficult to apply a passage such as James 2:1–13 to partiality among Christians today because of our homogeneous and class-segregated local churches. Perhaps this passage needs to be contextualized to relate it to partiality in denominations and in the church as a whole.

The Scriptures do not inform us regarding the precise levels of privilege, power, and prestige that are optimum for us as individuals, families, and social groups. There are no legalistic standards that can be used to comfort or judge ourselves or others. God has called us away from considerations of quantity and from viewing our class standing relative to the less-advantaged peoples of our society and the world. The Scriptures do not exhort us to suppress the desire of the poor and oppressed for justice and equality based on spiritualized notions of privilege, power, and prestige. That would be a dangerous misapplication of these ideas.

The Scriptures do teach us to live by an alternative system of values. Sociologists interpret social class and social mobility in terms of the values and goals prevalent in society. The Christian should be aware of another social reality that transcends but yet can transform society. In this reality, privilege, power, and prestige as defined by society offer no immortality, power, or ultimate significance.

The churches are to stand as models of the values of the kingdom of God. In India the church is struggling to overcome the grip of a caste system that relies almost exclusively on ascribed status. Samual and Sugden write, "In India the victory of Christ proclaims liberation from the grip of caste, the curse of *karma*, the lust for power, and social inequality; men can become sons of God and brothers in Christ. The church is demonstrating that all are one in Christ Jesus" (1979:18). American Christians might find it easy to criticize a caste system, especially in the church, because it is rooted in Hinduism. We may not feel so comfortable when called on to challenge and reconsider our participation in the American class system. If Christians can collectively orient themselves to the alternative reward system that Jesus promises, we can stand as "unranked status groups" that can model Christ's love and challenge the premises and the injustices of the American class system.

DISCUSSION QUESTIONS

1. Which of the three theoretical approaches discussed—functionalist, conflict, or interpretive—do you think best explains social class? Why?

2. Do you think one of the above approaches is more compatible than the others with a Christian perspective? Why? Why not?
3. What social class are you in? How have you determined this?
4. Do you believe "parents are entitled to hand on to their children the benefits of their class position"? Why? Why not?
5. What should the Christian's attitude be toward upward social mobility? Why?

SUGGESTED READING

Ronald J. Sider, *Rich Christians in an Age of Hunger* (Downers Grove, Ill.: Inter-Varsity, 1977). A biblical study of world hunger focusing on biblical ideas regarding the poor economic relationships in the church, attitudes toward property, structural evil, simple lifestyles, and changes.

Ronald J. Sider (ed.), *Living More Simply* (Downers Grove, Ill.: Inter-Varsity, 1980). A series of papers on various aspects of simple living presented at the U.S. Consultation on Simple Lifestyle held April 25–29, 1979, in Ventnor, N.J.

Peter Berger, *Facing Up to Modernity* (New York: Basic Books, 1977). The chapter entitled "The Assault on Class" is a good representation of defending the ideals of the American class system in spite of its failings.

The Other Side (Philadelphia: Jubilee). A monthly magazine about Christian discipleship and justice that often has articles dealing with social class and mobility.

═7

DON GRAY
Eastern College,
Pennsylvania

DEVIANCE AND SOCIAL CONTROL

No other issue seems to elicit the concern of the American public so strongly and consistently as crime. It is almost impossible to glance at the front page of a newspaper or watch the local news on TV without being confronted with the sordid facts concerning a series of rapes in the subway, payoffs to government officials, a shooting allegedly connected to organized crime, or a "drug bust" by federal narcotics agents. Given this constant exposure, it is no wonder that crime is a major social problem in the mind of the American public (Cole, 1979:6–9).

Sociologists are concerned about crime as part of a broader category of human behavior they call *deviance*. This term is typically defined as any activity that violates social rules. Crime and delinquency are acts by adults and juveniles, respectively, that violate social rules presently incorporated into legislative statutes.[1] Thus while deviance involves such serious and nonserious crimes as

---

[1]Strictly speaking, there may be some illegal acts whose deviance is questionable because the laws prohibiting these acts no longer receive significant social support. Sunday "blue laws" would seem to fall in this category.

murder, shoplifting, tax evasion, and overparking, it also includes some things that, although legal, significant elements in society tend to disapprove of, avoid, feel uncomfortable around, or stigmatize. Thus deviance also includes mental illness and breeches of social etiquette; and, in our secular age, even taking one's religious faith too seriously might be considered deviant by some people. Sociologists who study deviance are interested in investigating why some acts are considered deviant while others are not, why some people violate social rules, and how society attempts to control those it defines as deviant.

Some of these questions also intrigue many laypersons. However, there tends to be much public dissatisfaction with the way sociologists approach the study of deviance. At least two major conflicts are evident.

First, in their study of deviance sociologists find that there are vast differences of perception concerning what is deviant and concerning the degree of seriousness with which people regard any particular form of deviance. Some people interpreted Watergate as a major threat to our democratic institutions, while others saw it as merely the effort of one political party to discover the secrets of its rival. Some think marijuana smoking is a serious threat to one's health and morals, while others see it as a key to wisdom and happiness. Some think environmental pollution should be eliminated at all costs, while others see it as a risk we must accept in order to maintain a high material standard of living.

Sociologists account for these differences by emphasizing the *relative* nature of deviance. For them, deviance, like beauty, is in the eye of the beholder. This does not mean that sociologists are immoral or amoral. It only means that for the purpose of understanding deviance they attempt to avoid moral judgments that can distort their efforts to analyze empirical data objectively. As citizens they may be as involved as the next person in seeking either to control deviants or to restrain those who condemn them. The public however tends to distrust any approach to deviance that is not committed to moral absolutes. The dominant sociological approach to drug use, for example, tends to offend both the narcotics agent and the drug devotee because this approach does not affirm the moral stance of either party. This does not mean that the results of sociological investigation cannot be valuable to both parties in providing an understanding of the interaction in which they are engaged. At the end of this chapter it will be argued that the sociology of deviance provides a body of knowledge that can enhance the ministry of the church.

Second, most sociologists are concerned with explaining deviance as well as describing it. These explanations often take a form in which individual deviant activity is the dependent variable, and some variable located in the social environment is the independent variable or causal agent. Hypotheses specifying these relationships tend to be phrased in such a way that they can be taken to imply environmental or social determinism. This raises the whole spectrum of issues surrounding the classical problem of freedom and determinism. Although this problem arises in relation to all sociological research involving human action, it is especially crucial in the area of deviance because of the assumption of moral responsibility that underlies the imposition of social sanctions. Many sociological theories of deviance are taken by laypersons (and some sociologists as well) to imply that deviants should not be held accountable for their actions. Their reason is that these actions are seen as the result of environmental forces over which deviants have no control rather than as the result of their own independent choices.

Some sociologists are philosophical determinists while others are not. In practice sociologists do not require that their hypotheses explain every relevent empirical case, but only a statistically significant proportion of cases. If it were otherwise, there would hardly be any empirically supported theories in the social sciences. This suggests that in the social sciences the statement "X causes Y" is best interpreted to mean "X influences Y" or "X facilitates Y." These latter statements need not be inconsistent with a philosophical perspective that views humans as free moral agents. One need only grant that their choices tend to be influenced in specific directions by certain social conditions. Without such influences it might be difficult for social life to exhibit an adequate level of orderliness and predictability.

One purpose of this introduction is to persuade the reader not to jump prematurely to the conclusion that a Christian world view is incompatible with the judicious use of deviance theory and research. There is a growing interest among evangelical Christians in the issue of social justice. This interest reflects a recognition that God is concerned about whether social relationships are conducted according to His righteous standards. Although evangelicals have accepted the principle of living by biblical standards, they often have been captive to the secular culture when it comes to putting the principle into practice. One result has been a strong tendency to be passive toward a criminal justice system that is relatively severe in its punishment of street crime but highly tolerant of various forms of economic exploitation. This writer would contend that while sociological insights concerning deviance cannot in themselves provide us with a blueprint for a just social order, they can motivate us to reexamine the biblical tradition and can provide us with insights that will help us apply that tradition more effectively in a modern industrial society.

SOME COMMON FORMS OF DEVIANCE

Perhaps the reader has already noticed that the definition of deviance as a violation of group rules applies to a wide variety of behavior in a pluralistic society such as our own. Here only a few important forms can be discussed briefly. These forms are considered important because there exists a relatively high level of consensus as to their deviant character and because they illustrate some crucial theoretical insights to be discussed later.

Murder. There has been an increasing concern with violence in American society, especially as reflected in efforts to restore capital punishment in a number of states.[2] Statistics on homicide tell an interesting story that has definite implications for efforts at social control. In proportion to their numbers, murderers are more likely to be male, relatively young, poor, and occupationally unskilled. Homicide is much more likely to occur in the evening and early morning hours, especially on weekends and during holiday periods such as Christmas and the Fourth of July. Homicides often

---

[2]The Supreme Court decision on capital punishment in 1972 did not forbid its use constitutionally, but only invalidated existing laws allowing for the death penalty because of obvious biases in the way courts had used their discretion to apply the law. More recently, the court has struck down mandatory death penalty codes but has allowed to stand guided-discretion statutes that set forth specific conditions under which the death penalty may be applied (Robin, 1980:312–18).

occur in homes and involve family members. The majority of homicides do not involve strangers, but persons who know each other, and they often seem to result from trivial motives. Homicide rates tend to be highest in those social groups where manliness is defined in terms of a willingness to resort to violence as a response to insult and argument.

Wolfgang and Ferracuti (1967) concluded that these data point to the existence of a "subculture of violence" that tends to be most prominent in those segments of American society that are relatively deprived, both materially and culturally. Perhaps because of the difficulty deprived persons have in obtaining the services of social institutions in order to resolve their grievances, they tend to resort to more direct and (for them) immediately effective techniques, one of which is violence. Also, deprived males in America have few resources other than their masculinity with which to build a favorable self-image. Thus most murders seem to be the result of a relatively unplanned response to a symbolic threat to someone's personhood. For this reason I doubt that the widespread use of capital punishment would be an effective deterrent to the dominant form of homicide in America. We might have more success in the long run by attacking the two main sources of the subculture of violence. The two problem areas seem to lie in the general cultural identification of masculinity with violence and in the lack of responsiveness on the part of our social institutions to the plight of the poor.

Professional crime. The professional criminal can be distinguished from the amateur by the degree of skill used and the strength of commitment to crime as an occupation or way of life (Gibbons, 1977:273). The professional is usually a specialist who concentrates his efforts on one type of crime such as shoplifting, check forgery, counterfeiting, pickpocketing, con games, or robbery. While some professionals necessarily use violence, the vast majority rely on their ability to outmaneuver and to manipulate the victim. These skills and others, together with a view of the world in which "everyone has a racket," are learned from other professionals during a period of apprenticeship.

Perhaps the most colorful of professional thieves is the con man, who swindles victims out of their money by presenting them with a bogus get-rich-quick scheme that usually involves behavior of highly questionable legitimacy. The victim, or "mark," is enticed to invest money in the scheme and then is led to believe that the scheme failed. Meanwhile the con men make off with the victim's money. One elaborate con game, known as the "wire," involves convincing a mark that one has inside advance information regarding the outcome of horse races. The mark is even led to believe that a bet or two has been won in order to be convinced to invest his or her savings in a subsequent race. The mark is then advised that he or she misunderstood the betting instructions and incorrectly placed the bet. The gambling club where the bet is placed is an elaborate fake that the con men set up themselves (Sutherland, 1937:57–60).

Professional thieves tend to enjoy long and profitable careers, and efforts to bring them to justice are usually unsuccessful. Due to embarrassment on the part of the victims, their crimes are often not reported; and even if there is a report, such thieves usually leave little at the scene of the crime that would allow them to be traced. If detected, they are often able to "fix" their cases either by bribing their victims or by working through a corrupt lawyer to bribe some official in the justice system. Professional thieves experience little motivation to cease from their activities as long as they are able to operate profitably. The reality of the collusion of official agents of justice and the willingness of ordinary citizens to be involved in their schemes continually reinforces their belief that honest men are few and that the only difference between themselves and the typical citizen is that their racket happens to be illegal. There may be more merit in their contention than many people are willing to admit.

However, some social scientists believe that most professional criminals are different from conventional persons in at least one fundamental sense. Professional criminals are committed to a world view that makes crime and criminal lifestyles seem meaningful, even preferable to conventional ways of living (Schmalleger, 1979). This world view is reinforced by a criminal subculture with which the professional identifies and from which he receives support in his efforts to exploit the conventional world. Professional criminals are thus unlikely to give up their criminal activities until their criminal world view is effectively challenged. For the individual this means undergoing an identity crisis in which the criminal world view is rejected for a new conventionally oriented outlook. This drastic switch in basic commitments can be likened to a conversion experience.

Occupational crime. Sutherland (1949) coined the term "white collar crime" to refer to crimes committed by respectable persons during the practice of legitimate occupations. Akers identifies two major types of white-collar, or occupational, crime:

1. Crimes against the public committed by agents of corporations, governmental officials, businessmen, or professional practitioners. Examples of such crimes are tax fraud, environmental pollution and false advertising as well as obstruction of justice and other types of "Watergate" crimes.

2. Crimes committed within a corporation or governmental agency by some members of the organization against other members. Included here are embezzlement, inventory theft, discrimination in promotional practices, and various forms of political extortion. The ultimate cost to the public of these crimes is many times more than the annual loss due to all street crimes combined (burglary, auto theft, robbery, and the like) (1977:224–25).[3]

Most occupational crimes probably remain undetected. One famous case that came to light in the early 1960s, now known as the Great Electrical Conspiracy, involved around thirty electrical companies, large and small, in a conspiracy to fix prices on bids for government contracts for electrical equipment (Geis, 1967). Company executives, who officially espoused a free enterprise ideology, seemed to have little inward difficulty in justifying an elaborate pattern of secret agreements to fix prices. They showed little evidence of guilt concerning their hypocritical stance. These executives had learned on their way up the corporate ladder that those who did not cooperate in this illegal venture would simply not be promoted. They also had learned to rationalize their actions by viewing them as illegal, but not unethical (Smith 1962:359).

Embezzlers also make use of various rationalizations to justify

---

[3]Estimates of the cost of various crimes are continually becoming outdated due to inflation and economic expansion. The President's Commission (1967:42-43) once estimated annual loses due to tax fraud alone at $25 to $40 billion!

taking money from their employers. As they see it, they are merely "borrowing," or perhaps taking what is really theirs, since they are not being paid a decent wage. These rationalizations are not invented anew by embezzlers, but are adaptations or justifications that are common to the larger culture in which they participate (Cressey, 1953:137). The Watergate conspirators also used commonly accepted rationalizations to justify their crimes. However, they also relied on the more insidious justification that moral considerations were irrelevant and that the only important consideration was a pragmatic one, namely, would it work? Similarly, this amoral stance was not invented for Watergate. It is an orientation that appears to be all too common (perhaps even dominant) in the upper echelons of our political and corporate structures. It has also begun to permeate the lower echelons of the social structure where most people live out their daily lives.

Sexual deviance. Perhaps the most controversial forms of behavior in America today are those related to the expression of human sexuality. Our sexual mores are becoming increasingly tolerant of a wide range of sexual practices. Among other things this has resulted in a greater willingness on the part of sexual minorities to come out into the open and organize for the purpose of seeking social legitimacy and respectability. Homosexuals in particular have been partially successful in achieving legal change and in reducing discriminatory hiring practices.[4]

Evangelical Christians have been in the forefront of opposition to efforts to liberalize public restrictions on homosexuals. These efforts raise the question of how and when it is appropriate to impose a biblical standard on the secular world. Paul was so concerned about the maintenance of biblical standards within the Christian community that he instructed the Corinthians not to associate with those who flouted those standards while claiming to be Christians. However, this sanction is not intended for nonbelievers, whose judgment is to be left to God (1 Cor. 5:9–13). Some evangelicals have reversed Paul's emphasis by supporting stringent legal restrictions on sexual deviates while at the same

---

[4]Twelve states in the 1970s legalized homosexuality among consenting adults. Also, a number of large corporations have made it a policy not to discriminate against homosexuals in hiring (Thio, 1978:214).

time being generally lax with regard to discipline within their own community. As a result the responsibility to enforce Christian standards of sexual conduct has effectively been placed in the hands of secular authorities, a situation that Paul cautions the Corinthians to avoid (1 Cor. 6:1–11).

One outcome of depending on secular authorities to enforce biblical standards has been a distortion of those standards. This is especially evident in the case of prostitution; in some states the law applies only to the prostitute, not to her customers. Paul seems to put at least as much responsibility on the customer (1 Cor. 6:15–16). Even where the law applies to both parties, it is rarely enforced on the customer (Glaser, 1978:355–56). This discriminatory pattern of enforcement probably reinforces the belief held by some prostitutes that they are morally superior to the conventional world and more honest in their sexual relationships.

This discussion should not be construed as an argument in favor of eliminating all societal controls on sexual deviance. However, it would behoove evangelicals to reexamine their position on how best to control such deviance. Minimally, it would seem only just to seek controls that do not discriminate against one particular party to a deviant transaction. Beyond this, it would also be prudent for evangelicals to recognize that the New Testament calls on Christians to witness by the quality of their lives, but not to impose that quality indiscriminately on an unevangelized society. Evangelicals might also pray for the humility to recognize and correct their own lack of consistency in living by biblical standards.

Drug use. Sociologists use the term *victimless crime* to refer to crimes such as prostitution and illegal drug use that involve an exchange among willing participants. By contrast, other crimes involve at least one party who is coerced, deceived, or otherwise victimized. Victimless crimes present certain difficulties for law enforcement agents. Parties to these crimes seldom, if ever, report the crime or willingly act as witnesses. Thus enforcement depends on such tactics as using undercover agents and paid informants and raiding private premises, all of which may result in the violation of constitutional rights. Drug laws also tend to produce certain broader problems of social control. In particular, laws governing addictive drugs like heroin can encourage addicts to turn either to theft or to the recruitment of new customers to whom they can sell drugs in order to support their expensive habits.

Some sociologists have argued that these problems could be largely avoided if our drug laws were less punitive. Yet most social policy makers have been reluctant to accept this recommendation. This reluctance seems to be due in part to the apparent lack of success of conventional efforts to treat addiction and to the belief that illegal drugs have adverse and irreversible physiological effects on their users.[5] Available evidence suggests that the fears of policy makers concerning the effects of illegal drugs on their users are somewhat exaggerated. Most addicts are eventually able to achieve abstinence, though relapse rates are higher among those who are less educated and occupationally unstable (DeFleur, Ball and Snarr, 1969). The latter may be due in part to the fact that in some disadvantaged neighborhoods being a successful addict is considered challenging and exciting compared to other available options (Preble and Casey, 1969). Moreover, while the sustained and heavy use of some illegal drugs such as LSD may have irreversible physiological effects, it is still highly debatable that the effects of moderate doses of marijuana are as harmful as the typical pattern of tobacco use.[6]

Again, this challenge to the conventional wisdom is neither an endorsement for drug use (I hesitate to use aspirin) nor a proposal for complete decriminalization. It is an argument for a more intelligent social policy on drugs that does not defeat its own purposes through overly punitive and alarmist reactions. Empirical evidence in the late sixties and early seventies did show a relationship between marijuana use and the rejection of conventional values (Suchman, 1968). A more enlightened policy might profitably begin with a careful review of legal drug use, including medical use. In a society as permissive as our own toward the use of legal drugs to produce and control various feelings, it can hardly

---

[5]Some officials may be alarmed by what they perceive to be the beginnings of a drug epidemic. Recent polls show that slightly over half of America's young adults have tried marijuana (Akers, 1977:104). It is widely believed (though without adequate justification) that the use of marijuana leads to the use of hard drugs such as heroin.

[6]Some new research seems to indicate that the long-term effects of marijuana may be more serious and negative than anticipated earlier.

be expected that the illegal use of drugs will not be a problem.

Organized crime. The counterproductive aspect of some of our past policies on drugs is well illustrated by their relationship to the rise of organized crime in this century. Crime syndicates dealing in services such as gambling, prostitution, loan sharking, drugs, and various black market items have been in existence since the early beginning of American society. These syndicates became especially powerful when the profits from illicit liquor swelled their coffers during Prohibition.

These profits were used to extend syndicate influence in ways more corrosive to a democratic society. One way is racketeering, a simple form of which is protection. Here, businesses are sold bogus services under the thinly veiled threat that harm may come if these "purchases" are not made. Organized crime has also infiltrated labor union leadership, from which it has been able to extort both union members and employers through excessive dues and bargains to avoid labor troubles (Akers, 1977:150–51).

Even more profitable for organized crime is the control of legitimate business. A businessman with poor credit who turns to a loan shark may soon find that the local syndicate is his business partner. Legitimate business can be a source for the investment of illegal profits, a front for tax evasion, or a base of operations for a number of fraudulent schemes. Included in the latter is bankruptcy fraud, in which a business controlled by the syndicate buys goods on credit and immediately resells them. The receipts from resale are pocketed, and the firm is placed in bankruptcy without paying the suppliers (Thio, 1978:348).

The most insidious activity of organized crime is its efforts to corrupt public officials. Lower-level agents of enforcement are rather easily corrupted by way of payoffs to overlook the delivery of illicit goods and services, especially when one party to the crime is typically a "respectable" citizen, as in the case of gambling and prostitution. Higher-level officials can be corrupted by both bribes and the assistance that crime syndicates offer in election campaigns.[7] Those who cannot be bought can sometimes be duped.

---

[7]Often this includes using "repeaters" who vote many times under the names of persons who have died or left the precinct but are registered as voters. For a description of these activities, see Whyte (1955:235–40).

Crime syndicates have been known to support the efforts of religious groups to keep a county "dry," thereby keeping the demand high for bootleg liquor.

Organized crime has commonly been portrayed as a monolithic force that has invaded American society from the outside. Supporters of this view tend to rely on a description of the Mafia as a nationwide alliance controlled by twenty-four families of Italian descent (Cressey, 1969). The best evidence, however, suggests that most syndicated crime operations are locally based and historically have involved a variety of ethnic groups (Albini, 1971). This implies that organized crime is largely an internal phenomenon that has developed in response to American social structure and values. Further evidence for this view is seen in the similarities between the tactics of organized crime and those of American business in the early stages of its development (Bell, 1959:148). Some of these tactics, such as bribery and the selective use of violence, have not disappeared from our corporate structures even today.

These unpopular conclusions concerning the roots of organized crime would seem to call for a reassessment of our social control policies. One crucial question to be asked is, do present efforts to control the provision of illicit services merely increase the profits of crime syndicates and broaden the scope of corruption among law enforcement agents? This question implies that evangelicals might find it profitable to reconsider their views on how certain moral problems can best be dealt with in a secular society. Certainly, when organized crime supports the efforts of Christian groups to keep liquor illegal, it is time for evangelicals to ask themselves what it means to be "wise as serpents" (Matt. 10:16 KJV) in our generation.

SOCIOLOGICAL EXPLANATIONS OF DEVIANCE

Social scientists do not merely strive to gather facts about deviance, but to develop theories that explain those facts. These explanations often suggest that there is a relationship between the way a society is organized and the forms of deviance that are prominent within that society. This section will summarize several major theories of deviance and compare selected insights from these theories with the biblical perspective on human society.

Anomie theory. Robert Merton (1938) challenged the conventional wisdom of his day when he contended that rather than discouraging deviance, a society often inadvertently encourages deviance; moreover, he added that this is done through attempts to instill that society's highest values. Merton examined two main features of a society—the cultural goals that are internalized in its members through socialization, and the opportunities the society provides its members to achieve those goals. Much deviance results from a disjunction, or "strain," between goals and means.

Merton argued that American society places a heavy emphasis on success (symbolized by wealth) as a goal to be sought by *all* Americans. However, not all Americans are given similar opportunities to achieve success in socially approved ways. The result of this disjunction is a social condition called "anomie," or lawlessness, in which deviance rates are high because many persons turn to deviant means in order to compete more successfully. Moreover, those coming from working- and lower-class backgrounds do not have the same chance to succeed as those from middle- and upper-class origins. As a result it is to be expected that lower-class persons will be more likely to turn to certain forms of deviance as an alternative means of achieving the goal of success. Thus an attractive but uneducated young woman from a poverty-stricken family may be tempted to turn to prostitution in order to achieve the American dream of material success.

Although various forms of the anomie theory have been much criticized, this perspective on deviance still has many adherents.[8] The reason is due in part to its emphasis on the social roots of deviance, a way of thinking that is alien to that of many evangelicals, who explain deviance primarily in terms of individual characteristics. However, Scripture does not limit itself to an individualistic frame of reference. In warning His disciples not to give this world's possessions high priority, Jesus recognized that society's values emphasize material acquisitions and that this emphasis has a variety of destructive outcomes (Matt. 6:31–34). Therefore one cannot serve such values and serve God as well (Matt. 6:24).

---

[8]Many have attempted to extend or modify Merton's perspective, especially with regard to explaining juvenile delinquency (Cohen, 1955; Cloward and Ohlin, 1966). For a variety of criticisms of the anomie theory, see Clinard (1964).

Jesus did not limit His admonitions about striving for success to material values. He also warned about seeking the chief seats at public gatherings (Luke 11:43; 14:7–11; 20:46), and this would seem to imply that there is danger in any social system that establishes systematic status distinctions and encourages competition for the higher positions. Rather than urging His disciples to strive for success (however it may be defined), which ultimately results in the domineering exercise of power, Jesus urged His disciples to strive for servanthood. This is one way in which the church is to be salt and light in a barren, dark world.

One gets the clear impression that some of our churches are too caught up in the American success syndrome to take Jesus' words about success seriously. How else can their competitive efforts to build huge edifices and thus establish a successful ministry be interpreted? Merton's theory elucidates one of the less obvious features of a society in which success rather than service to God and others becomes the chief aim of people.

Cultural transmission theory. One of the major criticisms of anomie theory is its tendency to identify deviant behavior with the lower status segments of society. This results in the neglect of those forms of deviance, for example, occupational crimes, that are typical of middle- and upper-class segments. Cultural transmission theories focus on the general principles by which social definitions conducive to deviance are learned in all segments of society. The dean of cultural transmission theorists is Edwin H. Sutherland (1947). Sutherland began to develop his theory in the 1930s when it was popular to view deviance as the outcome of biological or psychological abnormality. He rejected both of these orientations for a social-learning approach that has become known as "differential association."

Sutherland's perspective became formalized in nine statements in 1947. The first three statements propose that criminal behavior is learned primarily within the context of intimate personal relationships. The fourth and fifth statements suggest that this learning involves both techniques and general attitudinal orientations. Statements six and seven, the core of the theory, not only state that deviance results when social definitions favorable to crime are prevalent, but also suggest some crucial dimensions for the evaluation of the relative influence of various definitions.

Specifically, the influence of a particular definition is thought to be proportional to the frequency, duration, intensity, and temporal priority of those personal associations in which it is encountered. Finally, the last two statements of Sutherland's theory reiterate his view that deviance is not the result of either abnormal learning experiences or abnormal needs and values.

Though at first glance the differential association theory may appear to be an elaboration of the obvious, it contains a number of implications that are not so obvious. One of these is that attitudes favorable to deviance can be learned in association with otherwise conventional persons. This is common in the case of occupational crime, where values such as the importance of showing a profit are learned from work associates and applied to rationalize price fixing, environmental pollution, and other types of corporate crime. It is also common in the case of so-called "folk crimes," such as cheating on one's income tax. Here, beliefs such as corruption and waste in government become the primary justifications. Even a crime such as murder often seems to be related to a widely accepted "subculture of violence" that places a high evaluation on defending honor, preserving autonomy, and maintaining a reputation.

The differential association theory has been criticized for being vague about what constitutes a definition conducive to deviance. Without some guidelines, it is possible to argue that just about any attitude or belief, given the proper conditions, is conducive to deviant conduct. In any event it does appear that a broad spectrum of attitudes and values has the potential to support many forms of deviance. Perhaps this is one reason why Jesus set forth a rigorous standard of righteousness that encompassed not only deeds but also words and attitudes (Matt. 5:17–37). If Sutherland's theory has any merit, eventually even one's innermost thoughts influence not only one's own actions but those of others as well.

Social control theory. Social control theories differ from the previous theories discussed in that they do not assume that any special motivations or rationalizations are necessary for deviant activity. Most deviance, in this view, is the result of common everyday motives that the deviant shares with conventional members of society. The difference between the deviant and the non-deviant lies in the degree of control that society is able to exert over each. When social controls are weak, persons will tend to pursue those courses of action that offer a maximum return for a minimum of effort. Such a strategy usually involves deviance since it is much easier, for example, to steal a valued object than it is to earn it.

Travis Hirschi (1969), who formulated one of the more comprehensive control theories, believes the key to controlling human behavior lies in the social bond between the individual and society. Hirschi conceives of this bond as having four major elements—attachment, commitment, involvement, and belief. Attachment refers to the kind of intimate relationship we have with others that makes us become sensitive to their feelings and expectations. To the degree that we are attached to others, we seek to avoid doing things that will hurt them or otherwise cause them to think less of us. Commitment, more or less, is a rational process in which an individual decides that the potential gains to be derived from deviance are not worth the risk of losing the rewards of conventional living. The degree of commitment, then, depends on one's assessment of such factors as the relative rewards of conventionality and deviance, the losses that might result from being caught at deviance, and the probability that participation in deviance will result in detection. Involvement merely refers to the extent to which a person's time is tied up in conventional activities, thereby reducing the time available for deviance. Beliefs that bond the individual to society include the conviction that social rules are morally valid and should be obeyed and the feeling that various authority figures deserve respect.

These elements tend to be positively related; and thus persons having strong attachments to others will also be highly committed to conformity, believe strongly in the validity of social rules, and so forth. Yet most control theorists would also perceive these elements to be somewhat interchangeable; hence if one or more elements of the social bond are weak, other elements may still bind the individual strongly to society.

There is much empirical support for the control theory.[9] This is interesting in view of the consistency between the implications of

---

[9] Hirschi (1969) and Nye (1958) test their control theories in a fairly comprehensive manner. Hirschi finds strong support for both the social control and cultural transmission theories of delinquency.

the theory and biblical insights concerning human relationships. Perhaps the most crucial of these relationships involves parents and their children. The control theory suggests that the normal attachment to parents can be a basis for the development of strong conventional commitments on the part of youth. However, this depends on how parents exercise their authority. To fail to discipline a child is to remove the parental bond as a vital force in social control. On the other hand, to exercise discipline arbitrarily and without affection can erode the bond of attachment. Wise parents use discipline with discretion in order to guide their children into conventional commitments (Briar and Piliavin, 1965). This seems to be what the Scriptures advocate when they equate discipline with love (Prov. 13:24) and urge parents to guide their children in a manner that does not elicit resentment (Eph. 6:4).

Labeling theory. Labeling theorists have been critical of other approaches to the study of deviance for not giving enough recognition to the relativity of deviance. In their efforts to stress this principle, labeling theorists have tended to focus their observations on how a social group defines and reacts to deviance rather than on the deviant himself (Becker, 1963:10). This approach, though not unique to labeling theorists, has been carried further by them than by representatives of the other major deviance theories described above. The result has been some very important insights, two of which will be touched on here.

First, persons are labeled deviant by others, not merely because of what they have done, but also on the basis of their social position in the group. More specifically, this *social disadvantage thesis* predicts that the poor, minorities, and others who lack social power are most susceptible to labeling. This thesis also implies that persons who exhibit certain undesirable social characteristics —for example, being a dropout or coming from a broken home— are more likely to be discriminated against in the labeling process. Some labeling theorists go so far as to contend that social disadvantage is more important than deviant behavior *per se* when it comes to determining who experiences the societal reaction.[10]

---

[10]Many sociologists contend that this position overstates the case. Empirical evidence suggests that the perceived seriousness of the offense has a stronger influence on labeling overall than the social characteristics of the offender (Gove, 1975:170, 194, 295).

A second thesis closely related to social disadvantage is that of *deviance amplification*. This is the view that the societal reaction to deviance often serves to perpetuate deviance rather than to extinguish or control it. This idea is implicit in the belief, more or less popular, that prisons are really schools for crime. Labeling theorists suggest that societal reactions sometimes create a vicious circle in which a person once labeled as deviant is isolated from conventional society. As a result he is virtually forced to affiliate with other deviants and make a living by deviant means. A prime example would be the ex-convict, who finds that conventional members of society are very hesitant to hire or otherwise to associate with him.

Labeling theorists have provided much impetus for recent efforts to divert youthful offenders from the formal sanctions of the criminal justice system in order to avoid some of the negative outcomes of labeling (Schur, 1973:154–55). However, the labeling theory has been criticized for exaggerating the negative effects of labeling and ignoring its deterrent effects, especially for the young or novice offender (Thorsell and Klemke, 1972). Perhaps the greatest contribution of the labeling theory has been to make us aware of the importance of how society reacts to the individual deviant. While it would be detrimental to ignore certain types of behavior, it is also detrimental to react in a way that cuts a person off from any hope of eventual reintegration into society and isolates that person from conventional affiliations and influence. Love and wisdom go hand in hand in Jesus' words concerning forgiveness (Matt. 18:21–35) and in the emphasis elsewhere in the New Testament on the restoration rather than the rejection of the deviant (Gal. 6:1). American society would profit greatly from a reexamination of its correctional system from the standpoint of such principles.

Critical theory. Recently there has emerged a new perspective on deviance that transforms the labeling emphasis on social disadvantage into a Marxian-style critique of modern industrial society. Critical theory views the creation and application of social rules, not merely as being biased against powerless persons, but also as reflecting the interests of a ruling capitalistic elite. In particular, this theory predicts that laws will be rendered ineffective when they threaten corporate profits but will be strictly enforced when they serve corporate interests and the political structures that serve those interests. This means, for example, that there will be few convictions for violations related to pollution, unsafe working conditions and monopolistic business practices but severe and certain punishment for protest activities that interfere with the construction of nuclear facilities or the production of military weapons. Justice systems in capitalist societies are viewed as servants of dominant economic interests rather than as neutral arbiters of justice (Quinney, 1979:78–80).

Capitalist societies are also charged with inciting high rates of deviance in at least four ways. First, the ethos of capitalism encourages persons to act in competitive, selfish, and acquisitive ways (Bonger, 1916). One can expect that in a capitalist society the activities of the salesman and the business executive will become almost indistinguishable from those of the professional thief and the organized crime boss.

Second, the various classes of society tend to reinforce and encourage each other's deviance. The powerful encourage the powerless by the hypocritical way in which the former condemn street crime while at the same time engaging in such occupational and political crimes as, for example, Watergate. The powerful also act so as to heighten the degree of inequality in society, thereby provoking the powerless to use deviance as a means of individually redressing the imbalance. On the other hand, the deviance of the powerless deflects the attention of social control efforts from the less visible deviance of the powerful and gives the powerful a sense of moral superiority because their deviance is less likely to be socially condemned (Thio, 1978:84–89).

Third, criminal justice systems in capitalist societies are ineffective when it comes to controlling street crime as long as that crime is largely a matter of the poor exploiting the poor. This is so because it is in the interest of ruling elites to establish a public image of deviance as being the result of the moral defects of the poor. Attention is thereby deflected from the defects of the social system—especially unjust economic relations—that are seen as the real causes of crime (Reiman, 1979:117–18). Because criminal justice systems in class societies support these unjust relationships, they are themselves unjust.

Finally, advanced capitalist economies develop a reserve labor pool of unemployed persons in order to increase competition for scarce jobs and thereby control wages. These marginal workers tend to be involved in various forms of deviance. They steal in order to obtain what the elite-controlled media tell us everyone needs. They may turn to violence as a response to powerlessness and frustration. They may experience stress and anxiety that results in alcoholism, mental illness, or even physical illness (Balkan, Berger and Schmidt, 1980:53–54). Eventually, the degradation involved in a capitalist economy seriously weakens the commitment of the most exploited classes to the class system itself. This can bring on revolutionary activity that threatens the very foundation of class rule.

The critical theory has been questioned for what appears to be an overemphasis on the degree to which criminal justice represents the interests of ruling elites. If elites have complete control over the legal system, why are there laws against such activities as pollution and price fixing in the first place? Moreover, is not even the present level of enforcement of these laws contrary to elite interests (Clinard and Meier, 1979:87)? However, the biggest controversy raised by the critical theory concerns its ideological stance. Some sociologists would contend that sociological theory should not mix objective analysis with value judgments concerning the social institutions under investigation. The critical theory violates this principle by calling for fundamental changes in a social order that it has already determined is unjust and oppressive. Sociological analysis is a tool for making people conscious of this oppression and for determining the most effective way to bring about the disintegration of capitalist society and the emergence of a new socialist order. Many critical theorists are not satisfied with existing attempts to establish socialist societies, especially in the USSR and China.

Because it is a pioneering attempt to unite a sociological perspective with an explicit ideology oriented to social action, the critical theory provides a model for those who wish to engage in similar efforts, even though they may have serious reservations concerning both its value commitments and its scientific claims. Christians who wish to integrate a sociological perspective into their own world view might profit from a close examination of the critical theory. They might be surprised to find that the indictment of modern society advanced by critical theorists is not as alien to a biblical point of view as the Marxian origins of the former would lead one to believe.[11]

THE SOCIOLOGY OF DEVIANCE
AND THE MINISTRY OF THE CHURCH

There has been a strong tendency in evangelical circles (not entirely unwarranted) to view the perspectives of sociology with suspicion. This chapter has summarized several theories of deviance, an area where evangelicals are especially likely to take issue with sociological interpretations. A case in point is the dominant tendency among deviance theorists to view deviance in extremely relative terms. This may appear at first glance to be irreconcilable with the Christian perspective, which emphasizes moral absolutes. However, when it is recognized that sociological perspectives emphasize a nonjudgmental, analytical orientation for the purpose of achieving understanding, at least some of the conflict disappears. The church may then incorporate the valid insights of sociology into its own normative framework in order to enhance its ministry. Since these insights often challenge popular conceptions of deviance, they can be useful in identifying areas where the conventional wisdom of the church has become conformed to the world (Rom. 12:2) and in motivating evangelicals to reassess their attitudes toward social issues in the light of a more biblical perspective.

One implication arising from this analysis concerns attitudes toward various forms of deviance in American society. We who are evangelicals have tended to assent to the dominant societal trend that takes a strong stand against the deviance of the powerless—those who commit various street crimes—but is relatively unconcerned about the deviance of the powerful—those who pollute the environment and fix prices. By so doing we have distorted a biblical sense of priorities concerning sin and its impact on society (Prov. 29:4). If I am correct in this assessment, then a thorough review of what the Scripture has to say about deviance is in order. It is unlikely that such a review will diminish our

---

[11]Sometimes we can learn the most from those we disagree with the most.

concern over robbery, mugging, burglary and the like. Rather, I suspect that it will heighten our concern about the more subtle forms of economic exploitation and oppression, especially those forms that most affect the poor (Sider, 1977:87–112). While sociological insights themselves do not inform us concerning biblical priorities, they can help us to understand the degree to which our own attitudes toward deviance are influenced by our cultural traditions rather than by biblical standards.

The sociology of deviance also sensitizes evangelicals to the problems of relying too heavily on formal legal controls to deal with deviance problems in a secular society. A candid assessment of the scope of these problems should cause evangelicals to think carefully before promoting state intervention as the primary means of social control. Hopefully, such an assessment will help evangelicals to recognize that there are limitations to even the most effective social legislation. It should also serve to remind us that social involvement *per se* cannot be a substitute for our mission to proclaim the gospel by word and deed.

Sociological insights concerning deviance can also assist the church in ministering more effectively to the deviant and potentially deviant segments of the community. An understanding of the social forces that promote forms of deviance can help the church to structure its own communal life so as to offer more comprehensive support to those who struggle with these temptations.[12]

---

[12]One note of caution should be added. The evangelical church is becoming increasingly aware of its responsibility to minister to those people who have been caught up in deviant behavior and lifestyles but who are reaching out for help and love. Thus there is a genuine need in the church for ministries to the homosexuals, single parents, and youth with criminal records. But the very existence of these ministries has a subtle effect of reducing the negative connotation of such behavior. There is a fine line between no longer being shocked at certain deviant behavior and accepting it as a necessary evil—between overlooking the sinful past of a repentant believer and condoning similar behavior among Christians. A case in point is the prevailing attitude by some evangelicals toward divorce. Some have moved from shock to accepting it as normal in society to condoning it among Christians.

To prevent such subtle slippage, the Christian must be continuously alert to his Teacher, the Holy Spirit, and must have his senses sharpened so as to be able to discern deviance that is in violation of God's propositional standard (Heb. 5:14).

In this connection a crucial but neglected area of ministry is that of making laypersons entering various occupations aware of the pressures toward deviance they can expect to encounter and providing them with the resources to resist these temptations.[13] The church must also make its members aware of the fact that in today's world there are those career criminals who espouse a world view from which, according to some deviance theorists, they must be converted if they are ever to adopt conventional lifestyles. Sociological knowledge of the content of various deviant world views can help the church to develop a more effective evangelistic ministry to specific deviant populations. Furthermore, as the church begins to understand the relationship between deviance and the dominant cultural trends in American society, it can develop ways to counteract the corrosive effects of these trends. Moreover, a knowledge of how society rejects the deviant can help the church to communicate more clearly the offer of God's acceptance in Christ. There is much in the labeling perspective that suggests how hope for the future can be translated into a present reality.

Finally, sociological knowledge can help us to address the problems of social and economic injustice by making us more aware of the specific shape of these problems in our own day. If there is a connection between poverty and crime, as some theories of deviance imply, positive contributions to the former problem may also be an effective way to deal with the latter. One way the church might begin to address economic issues is by making a more direct application of biblical standards to the conduct of economic life. Studies of occupational crime can assist this effort by making us aware of informal ideologies and practices that are predominant in the business world. The critical theory is fundamental in considering problems of social injustice because it links these problems to the basic characteristics of the American social system, especially to its economic structures, and calls the church to reexamine its relationship to the modern secular order (see chap. 10). Have we not lent support to unjust and exploitive social

---

[13]If the attitudes that promote such crimes as embezzlement and political corruption are as pervasive as past research suggests, then this ministry may eventuate in a thoroughgoing critique of the American value system.

structures that God has promised to overthrow (Isa. 10:1–3)?

The reluctance of the church to face this question would seem to be due to more than its tendency to identify with conservative social and political viewpoints. To be faithful to a biblical view of social justice may require radical criticism, not only of our criminal justice system, but also of other major institutions in American society that influence criminal justice practice. It may also require dissent from the materialistic value orientation that governs the functioning of these institutions. Such a critical emphasis would not be well received by the powers of this age and would probably eventuate in a loss of much of the tolerance the church has enjoyed in Western secular society. Christians who identify with this critical stance may even find themselves classified among the deviant elements of society. Although this will tarnish our image in the eyes of conventional society, it cannot help but enhance our opportunities to minister to deviants.

DISCUSSION QUESTIONS

1. Is deviance always bad or wrong? Why? Why not?
2. What is your reaction to the statement in this chapter on the usefulness of capital punishment? Why? What evidence do you have for your position?
3. Do you believe morality can be legislated? Should Christians attempt to impose their values and standards on society? Why? Why not? If we were to eliminate all laws that legislate morality, what would be left?
4. What should be the function of laws and the legal system? Why?
5. What is your reaction to the author's critique of the American justice system? Why?

SUGGESTED READING

Ronald L. Akers, *Deviant Behavior: A Social Learning Approach* (2nd ed.) (Belmont, CA: Wadsworth, 1977). An upper level text written from a cultural transmission perspective. Evaluates major theories of deviance and examines a wide variety of deviant activities.

Joseph L. Albini, *The American Mafia: Genesis of a Legend* (New York: Appleton-Century-Crofts, 1971). Considers major issues related to the nature and development of organized crime in America. Takes a historical perspective that is highly critical of efforts to identify organized crime with any particular ethnic group.

Travis Hirschi, *Causes of Delinquency* (Berkeley: University of California Press, 1969). Probably the most comprehensive presentation and empirical evaluation of the social control theory. Contrasts the basic tenets of several major deviance perspectives.

Edwin M. Schur, *Radical Nonintervention: Rethinking the Delinquency Problem* (Englewood Cliffs, N.J.: Prentice-Hall, 1973). A critical review of various approaches to the treatment of delinquency. Examines theoretical assumptions underlying these approaches and contrasts them with those of the labeling theory. Also draws out the correctional implications of labeling.

Jeffrey H. Reiman, *The Rich Get Richer and the Poor Get Prison: Ideology, Class and Criminal Justice* (New York: Wiley, 1979). A radical critique of the American criminal justice system. Claims that the system is designed to fail and that this failure serves elite interests.

Edwin H. Sutherland, *The Professional Thief* (Chicago: University of Chicago Press, 1937). A colorful account of the activities of professional thieves, as told by an experienced member of the profession. Written from a cultural transmission perspective.

8

WINSTON A. JOHNSON
Houghton College,
New York

GROUPS

What kinds of families develop a family scapegoat or "blacksheep," and what functions does he or she serve for the family?

What can the television camera teach you about the "games people play" in groups?

How do friendship groups affect a person's development?

What was the role of small groups in Mao's Chinese revolution?

How do therapy groups develop, and how do they change people?

What group process turned the People's Temple into tragedy?

What are the best bargaining strategies to use in negotiations?

What made the Knicks one of the greatest teams of all time?

How do groups use their leaders, and how can leaders be more effective?

Why do musicians prefer to play in quartets rather than in trios?

How do group processes affect jury decisions?[1]

Questions such as these suggest that groups, especially small ones, are important objects of investigation for everyone. The purpose of this chapter is to introduce the reader to the subject of

---

[1]These questions are from a brochure outlining research activities at the Center for the Study of Human Groups, State University of New York at Buffalo.

how and why groups function as they do. Most texts that introduce students to the sociology of groups do not go beyond the importance of the family as the main agent of socialization. Beyond initial socialization, the group—especially the small, face-to-face group—is not seen as particularly important. In this chapter the student will be introduced to the field of small groups, concentrating on the important and continuing role these groups play in the lives of individuals. This chapter will present research activity that suggests the importance of knowledge about these groups in order to provide information about small groups in general and how they can operate in the life and work of the church in particular.

In order to understand what happens in groups, it is necessary to know what is meant by *human interaction*. Shaw (1976) has concluded that small group communication is virtually the same as interaction. Thibaut and Kelley similarly suggest that interaction means individuals emit behavior in each other's presence, create products for each other, and communicate with each other (1959:10).

THE SMALL GROUP DEFINED

What is it that distinguishes a collection of individuals from a group? Research indicates that there must be some *interaction* of the members before a collection of individuals can be considered a group. Groups also come to develop a set of *norms*. These norms serve to set boundaries that determine how interpersonal communication is to be maintained. As time passes groups determine *roles* for their members. Roles are assigned positions within the group that involve certain expected behaviors. Groups develop sets of interpersonal likes and dislikes that affect how members deal with each other.

Another important dimension of the group is *personality*, which is that aspect of individual behavior that tends to be consistent over time and across groups. As has been mentioned the group is a setting in which the personality comes into close relationship with culture. An individual's behavior in the group is an attempt to make sense out of the unique configuration of personalities that come together in groups. Frequently, *culture*—that is, the customs of the community or society at large—is something the group begins to rally around as a model for their own structures. Various personalities deal with culture in different ways and the result can be conflict. The life of the group involves dealing with these conflicts. In the course of negotiations the group develops a culture of its own, taking both personalities and the culture at large into account.

Most of the research on groups has dealt with groups of five to thirty members. In life people are primarily involved in groups of this size. However, many of the generalizations about small groups may be carried into a larger context with the appropriate modifications. Many definitions of a small group have been attempted. Robert Bales' definition in *Interaction Process Analysis* is a classic and is quite useful:

> A small group is defined as any number of persons engaged in interaction with each other in a single face-to-face meeting or a series of meetings, in which each member receives some impression or perception of each other member distinct enough so that he can, either at the time, or in later questioning, give some reaction to each of the others as an individual person even though it be only to recall that the other person was present (1950:36).

However, a more comprehensive definition of a group has been given by Tubbs: "A group is a collection of individuals who influence one another, derive some satisfaction from maintaining membership in the group, interact for some purpose, assume some specialized roles, are dependent on one another, and communicate face-to-face" (1978:8).

This definition is particularly useful as we consider the church. Elton Trueblood (1967) has noted that there are two areas of concern to the Christian and the church in its development of fellowship—the church itself and the "field," or world. Trueblood's insight provides some approximation of the church's sociological function. This "base" is where members "derive some satisfaction from maintaining membership, where they 'interact for some purpose' and 'assume specialized roles'" (1967:86). Whatever *koinonia,* or close fellowship, may mean spiritually, this definition helps us understand it sociologically. More specifically, it helps us understand that true *koinonia* exists in the small face-to-face group. To quote Trueblood, "A base is not a true Christian base unless it is a center of affection, in which the members accept the principle of unlimited liability for one another" (1967:86).

THEORETICAL PERSPECTIVES ON GROUPS

Within the sociology of small groups, three main schools may be distinguished. One is the *sociometry* school that grew out of the tradition of Jacob L. Moreno. As a medical student in Austria, Moreno used to spend his lunch hour watching children play. He would tell the children stories and have them act out the tales. From this came his idea for "spontaneity theater," which he established in Vienna. During the Depression of the 1930s he came to New York City and made a living with a company of young actors acting out news stories of the day. This led directly to psychodrama and its use with veterans in World War II. Eventually this technique took the form of role playing in which actors portrayed various social situations in an attempt to understand the feeling of various individuals in the real world. This has been useful in exploring race relations and other social problems. Moreno focused largely on emotional relations in group situations. Eventually Moreno developed the sociometric test in which individuals were asked who they would like to have as fellow participants in a group. The purpose was to allow individuals to participate in groups with individuals to whom they were attracted. This test was used extensively in the American school system and the army.

Today, thirty years after Moreno initiated his ideas, proponents of sensitivity training use role playing and the acting out of social relationships as ways of allowing individuals to cope with the role expectations of society.

Kurt Lewin, the founder of the second school, came to the United States from Germany. With him he brought a new direction to the study of groups. Along with Lippitt, White, Cartwright, and Zander he conducted research on the effect authoritarian and democratic leaders have on groups. His focus was on the *life space* of the actor in a social situation. Life space refers to the set facts, both social and physical, that compose an individual's surroundings. Lewin believed that social behavior was subject to scientific laws and that these laws were discoverable through a knowledge of both psychological and social forces. Lewin's main concern was the impact of the group on the individual. (Lewin is also credited with making the term *group* acceptable to psychologists.)

The most influential figure for sociologists studying groups is

153

Robert F. Bales. In a volume entitled *Working Papers in the Theory of Action* (1953), Talcott Parsons, Robert F. Bales, and Edward A. Shils presented a sociological theory of group interaction that focused on group problem solving. This third school is concerned with the operation of the social system which was of special concern to Bales and which is discussed later in this chapter. The social system is the set of interacting elements that characterize any one group. Bales signaled a significant switch in research to focus on the individual's impact on the group and also on the social situation of the group. He is also responsible for the development of the *self-analytic group* as a tool for learning how groups function. A self-analytic group meets for the sole purpose of understanding its own process. This will be discussed in more detail later in the chapter. Bales' work has influenced a number of prominent social researchers including Theodore Mills, Dexter Dunphy, Philip Slater, Richard Mann, Graham Gibbard, and John Hartman. In the 1960s Bales brought to the attention of sociologists the importance of understanding personality as a variable in the group setting.

A useful way of studying a group is to recognize it as an array of interdependent forces, each of which can be interpreted and analyzed within the perspective of other forces. The group is regarded as a *social system* in which events are a result of complex, multiple-caused interrelation. This approach will guide the discussions in the sections that follow in this chapter.

Tubbs (1978) has provided us with a useful model for observing and understanding small group interaction. He suggests there are three important variables: (1) *relevant background factors,* that is, the input into the group in the form of characteristics of individuals composing the group; (2) *internal influences* that vary with the nature and function of the group (much of group life consists in working toward a satisfactory combination of these influences); (3) *the general outcomes of the group at any point,* also referred to as the group's consequences. These variables are easy to discern in groups that have specific goals to guide them. Each of the three variables in the model has a means of being fed back into the system to enable the group to develop and change.

The social system framework readily permits complex interpersonal processes to be divided into five levels: behavior, emotions, norms, group goals, and group values (Parsons, Bales, and Shils,

1951:3–29, 53–79 or Mills, 1967:58). Mills has defined each of the levels as follows:

1. Behavior: How persons behave overtly in the presence of others.
2. Emotions: The drives persons experience, and the feelings they have toward one another about what happens.
3. Norms: Ideas about how a person should act, should feel and should express their feelings.
4. Goals: Ideas about what is most desirable for groups as units.
5. Values: Ideas about what is most desirable for groups to do and to become (1967:58).

It is evident that each of the levels defined above has its expression in individual personality and behavior. However, Mills believes that these levels can be seen as groups interact. Recognizing that the group is a social system, one is aware that there is a complex interrelation of these levels and that events within these levels have multiple causes.

Within the social system that is the interacting group, Mills notes that there are subsystems concerned with each of these levels:

1. Behavior: The sub-system is the interaction system—the organization of overt action among persons over time.
2. Emotion: The sub-system is group emotion—the set of emotional responses to events as they occur.
3. Norms: The sub-system is the normative system—the organized set of ideas of what should be done and felt. It regulates behavior and applies sanctions when appropriate.
4. Goals: The sub-system is the technical system—that which decides what the group should accomplish and plans the procedures for such accomplishment.
5. Values: The sub-system is the executive system—that which interprets what the group is, what is desirable for it to become and how to become that (1967:58–59).

All of these levels are empirically related. An event that takes place on one level has impact on the other levels of interaction.

One of the principal virtues of the systems approach is its ability to account for change and growth within the social system. As such, it presents a dynamic rather than static model of social interaction. A weakness of this model is the value bias it carries. The model assumes that infinite movement of the social system toward growth and change is a positive value.

All of the features suggested in Tubb's three variables and Mills' definitions of the five levels of group process have been and continue to be objects of investigation for the small group researcher.

PRIMARY AND SECONDARY GROUPS

In early sociological studies the individual remained in dramatic opposition to the total society. Groupings in between were overlooked, for example, small groups and families. The importance of intermediary groups came into much clearer focus in the work of Charles Horton Cooley (1909).

Cooley was interested in the role that values play in group life. Specifically, he was concerned with how society's values were passed on from one generation to the next. In the course of his research he recognized the importance of primary groups such as families and peer groups in the socialization process:

> By primary groups I mean those characterized by intimate face-to-face association and cooperation. They are primary in several senses, but chiefly in that they are fundamental in forming the social nature and ideas of the individual. The result of intimate association, psychologically is a certain fusion of individualities in a common whole, so that one's very self . . . is the common life and purpose of the group. Perhaps the simplest way of describing this wholeness is by saying that it is a we; it involves the sort of sympathy and mutual identification for which the "we" is the natural expression (1909).

Primary groups are primary in that they give the individual his earliest and most complete experience of social unity. As Cooley suggests, the relationships in primary groups do not change to the same extent as more "elaborate relations." In fact, the stability of primary relationships "form a comparatively permanent source" out of which more complex and less personal relationships evolve. Of particular importance is Cooley's observation that the relationships in primary groups are not isolated from the larger society, but are strongly influenced by it. Similarly we note that the personality of the individual comes to be directly involved in the primary group. This is through the intimate association that we suggested earlier as a characteristic of the primary group. Thus in Cooley's seminal work called *Social Organization* (1909), the group comes into focus as the interface between the individual and the society.

Secondary groups are larger and more impersonal than primary groups. Cooley did not make specific reference to these types of groups, but sociologists have found the distinction useful.

The idea of the primary groups brings with it images of positive, close relationships that we associate with families and peer groups. Secondary groups suggest the "cold impersonality and formality of large-scale modern bureaucracies and urban communities" (Nixon, 1978:15). Neither of these forms may be said to exist in their pure form. Each carries with it aspects that are both primary and secondary.

How does one enter primary groups? The best-known group is the family. For the most part individuals remain a part of their family of origin for their entire lives. The impact of this primary group is great indeed. Most people grow up and select mates and begin families of their own. Of interest to the sociologist is how location in society influences those choices. For example, it is known that one-half of the people in America marry someone who lives within a mile of them (Clark, 1952:17–22). Primary group location, both geographically and socially, determines such a choice.

Similarly the people one chooses as friends are socially associated. They become part of the primary groups formed outside the family. People are most likely to have a close friendship with those with whom they associate frequently. This was demonstrated in a study done at the Massachusetts Institute of Technology (Festinger et al., 1950). The study involved married graduate students in a housing development. They were assigned apartments at random so that interests were no more or less likely to be the same in the same building. The study showed that families were more likely to be friendly with those in the same building. What is more surprising about this study is the importance of space in the development of relationships. The study showed that the closer another's door was, the more likely they would be friends.

Research has also shown that values influence the development of friendship (Lazarsfeld and Merton, 1954:18–66). People tend to become friendly with others whose values are similar. Individuals generally select friends who agree with this perspective in matters of importance. These findings have important implications for the church. This is one explanation for denominationalism.

157

THE STRUCTURE OF GROUP INTERACTION

One of the most interesting aspects of observing groups is seeing how they organized their interaction. Using the definition of the social system presented earlier, Bales developed a scoring scheme that focuses on two sets of problems that groups must solve in order to survive. The first set involves *instrumental* problems that refer to the group's difficulties in meeting its specified goals. The second set involves *socioemotional* problems—those that directly affect the group's ability to become a cohesive working unit. Many times both of these sets or problems are related to the interpersonal conflicts that occur whenever people get together. The socioeconomic also includes mobilizing the group for action and matching individual needs with the needs of the group.

Bales was also concerned with how roles developed in groups. This came out of his work on the family done with Talcott Parsons in 1955 *(Family, Socialization and Interaction Process)*. This is a classic study in primary groups because of its presentation of basic role allocation in the family. In that work the authors identified the role of the *instrumental* husband and the *socioemotional* wife. Unfortunately, the effect of the work was to reinforce stereotypical roles for the husband and wife since the authors did not articulate the best way to get things done in the family.

More observations led Bales to the conclusion that with most groups there emerge individuals who lead the group in the completion of its task. There also emerge those who become expressive or socioemotional leaders. However, the groups may also develop role specialists, including the joker, rescuer, scapegoat, hero, and others. The scapegoat, for example, is the object of much aggressive hostility from other group members.

Small groups in the church. In his preface to *The German Mass*, Martin Luther suggested that one way in which the church might be formed was through *ecclesilae in ecclesia*, little churches within a church consisting of groups of lay people meeting for prayer and instruction in homes. Although Luther himself never followed up on this suggestion, the Swiss reformer Martin Bucer later in the sixteenth century did use small groups in Strassbourg. The Puritans in England used a similar technique. Johann Arndt made use of the *collegia pietatis*. His influence, coupled with that of Dutch Puritanism, led to the *collegia* being included in the works of

Philipp Spencer, most notably his work suggesting the structures for reform entitled *Pia Desideria.*

Lovelace, in *The Dynamics of Spiritual Life,* views the band system of reformer Count Zinzendorf as "the most deliberate and successful use of the small group principle in history. . . . This microcommunity of Herrnhut, . . . was analogous to the Mennonite open communities in many ways but [was] informed by an urgent sense of mission to send the gospel to the world and to bring renewal to every Christian denomination" (1979:166). Their system involved subdividing the community into group meetings for sharing, mutual correction, confession, and prayer. The meetings characteristically used lay leaders.

Much of the fervor involved in the use of small groups in church history centered in the quest for the intimate community of the true body of Christ. Concern was focused on the need for believers to be involved in face-to-face communication developing commitment, cohesion, and continuity in time. Many of the reformers saw these types of groups as the key to renewal within the church. The trend continued into the work of John Wesley through the mid-1700s. His class meetings were designed to nurture converts and press for the reform of the Anglican church. In contemporary Methodism these groups are missing. Lovelace suggests that this may point to some of the weakness within the denomination today:

> It is startling that a strategy as obvious and effective as small groups could be discovered and widely used in history and then apparently lost until its modern rediscovery in popular religious movements . . . the loss can only be explained by the resistance . . . to the entrance into light which these groups demand when they are correctly handled, and by the hostility and obscuring tactics of the powers of darkness (1979:167).

Elsewhere, Lovelace suggests ways in which the local congregation may be renewed through changing some of its structures. The local congregation needs to form and strengthen small groups within the church, the most basic of which is the family. As mentioned early in this chapter, the family is the small group with which most of us are familiar. Understanding its dynamics and the functions or roles of its members can help build the church up as well as the family unit itself. The family is an important interface or link between us as individuals and the society at large. In it primary values are taught and reinforced. The right use of this basic and "naturally occurring" group can strengthen both the individual and the groups to which a person belongs.

For those who are not directly attached to a family unit, small groups are also important. The formation of pastoral support groups for Bible study and prayer and mutual caretaking should be a vital part of any church's program. Such groups are widespread in American churches today. Lovelace maintains that "without such mechanisms for the interchange of grace and the movement of known truth into action, the weekly pattern of Sunday church attendance can become a stagnant routine consisting of passive intake of truth which is never turned into prayer and work for the kingdom" (1979:226).

One of the least discussed uses of small groups in the local congregation is for understanding how people work together. Our churches, whether large or small, use many committees. These committees are important to the church's operation. Most persons know how personality comes into these situations but are ignorant of how groups with specific tasks function. It is in part the aim of this chapter to introduce the recurring aspects of groups. Models of how roles emerge in groups have been suggested, and levels of interaction have been discussed. All these things should make church members more aware of the dynamics of the groups in which they participate. This awareness does not mean things are always going to go smoothly when they participate in groups, but it does mean that church members will be better able to cope with different situations that arise. Secondly, awareness should be used cautiously. It can sensitize church members so that they become ineffective in their groups. A little knowledge is sometimes a dangerous thing. The unwise use of the knowledge of group processes can cause unnecessary conflicts that defeat the purpose of the group. Certainly, church members should be conscious of the fact that a church committee is not the best place to work on interpersonal problems. There are other mechanisms available within the local congregation for the solution of such difficulties, be they groups or individuals.

Awareness of what is happening in groups also has the advantage of at times increasing a person's capability for changing the group process. An understanding of what is going on in a situation can enable a person to make necessary adjustments to ensure successful solutions to problems. Not only is this true for individuals, but groups also have capacities to understand themselves. As the group uses the mechanisms above and becomes more aware of itself and how it is functioning, it can alter its capacity for change.

Through a sensitive and realistic understanding of people as they come together in groups, the church can increase its capacity for diversity in support groups and ministry. However, it is good to be aware that increased knowledge and understanding also contribute to the development of structures that have greater rigidity and less flexibility. Such groups are headed toward closure or self-destruction. The tragedy of the Jim Jones cult in Jonestown, Guyana, is an example of such a group. A greater understanding of the world and knowledge of the impossibility of escape from it led to greater isolation and more rigid structures within the Jonestown community. The results of this downward spiral are well known; namely, the suicide-murder of virtually all its nine hundred plus members.

Group structure and the church. "A small group of eight to twelve people meeting together informally in homes is the most effective structure for the communication of the gospel in the modern secular-urban society" (Snyder, 1979:139). With this statement Howard Snyder begins his chapter on small groups in his book on the need for change in church structures. Believing he has built a sufficient case for this conclusion, he proceeds to suggest that given the structure of the small group, the possibilities for the church are limitless and highly consistent with a biblical view of the church. Unfortunately, Snyder considers the small group best because it takes us back to the primary relationships found in Acts and away from the secondary relationships discussed earlier. Rather than focusing on the primary quality of the Christian community as described throughout the Pauline epistles, Snyder points back to a time when Christians were so scattered that they could do little else but meet in small groups. The small group should not become a technology of the church because it is a reaction to impersonal relationships. Rather, it is the structure to be employed because it characterizes the relationships that make the body of Christ what it is; namely, a community in which

Christian Perspectives on Sociology

believers support and serve each other and the world in an intimate manner.

The behavioral sciences attach great significance to the importance of the small group. It is an important tool in business and
industry for training workers and managers. Group counseling
and therapy groups are commonplace. And the church has become
suspicious of some of the publicized excesses of the small groups
movement. Nonetheless, it is the conviction of this writer that
although renewal within the church begins with the individual,
the group life of the church must be utilized to bring about
growth, support, and service in the Christian life. The important
matter here is not the small group as a structure but the quality of
relationships it manifests. Lawrence Richards, author of *A New
Face for the Church,* describes it this way:

> To learn to trust, and to become trustworthy—to learn to love, and to
> become loving—we must become deeply involved in the lives of
> others, to whom we commit ourselves in Christ. To develop this kind of
> relationship we need others to share themselves with us. All of this
> demands time. More than this, it requires a face-to-face relationship. A
> relationship we can have only with a few others at a time. And thus a
> church is forced to move into a small group structure (1970:153).

In addition to the need of people to know one another intimately
within the church, there are other reasons for the usefulness of the
small group. One of the most important is the type of spiritual
growth sought within the church. Other small groups are designed to change ideas or beliefs. The small group within the
church is designed to transform attitudes, values, and even personality (Richards, 1970:155). Involvement in all groups is an-
chored in social relationships. Christians need a new set of
relationships if they are to accomplish a new work within. The
small group is the key. "If one wishes to change attitudes and
subsequent behavior of a group, discussion and decision where all
members participate as directly as possible tend to be more effective than enlightenment or persuasion by the lecture method"
(Hare, 1976:287).

Perhaps the most succinct presentation outlining the value of
the small group for the church is found in Gulley's book *Discussion, Conference, and Group Process.* He suggests four values of the
small group:

1. There is clearly stronger commitment to a decision when those affected participated in its formulation.
2. In most situations, groups apparently produce higher quality decisions than do an equal number of equally able individuals working separately.
3. Group discussion participants gain increased understanding of other persons and learn to get along better with others.
4. Members learn about collective responsibility and irresponsibility, group action and inaction, and similar matters (1968:366–69).

The aim of the small group *in* the church is to function *as* the church. Notice that the group is not to be a microcosm of the institutional church. It is the church in its purest and most intimate sense. This concept has been illustrated by Richards (1970:154) in the following diagram:

Aspects of the Small Group as the Church

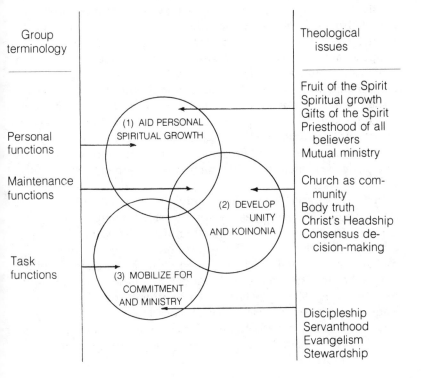

163

Each of the three circles presents a function of the small group within the context of the church. As members become more aware of one another, they increase in their abilities to meet each other's needs. Through the exercise of various roles as evidenced by various gifts, members begin to grow and changes take place within both the group and the individual. But the small group referred to here moves beyond sharing concerns and thus fosters personal and spiritual growth. Group members come to identify themselves as a collectivity distinct from other collectivities. They develop a sense of belonging and unity. The collectivity becomes a discernible group, evidencing *koinonia*, or deep-rooted fellowship. Unfortunately, groups can become ingrown and close themselves off from the world outside. The kind of group that can function usefully within the church must also be able to reach out from the group and awaken others and draw them into similar groups.

This model is especially helpful in terms of the earlier discussions in this chapter. A glimpse may be caught of how both personality and the world outside the group (culture) come to manifest themselves in the life of the group. Individuals meet to support each other and in the process come to identify with each other as a group. They come to see themselves as having a similar relationship in terms of the world outside the group, and they work to make that relationship a reality. Note that there is a developmental sequence involved. These phases in the life of the group come out of various functions that must be met to insure survival and growth of the group. Personal growth leads to common identity, which leads to accomplishment of the group task and mobilization for ministry.

In his most recent book, *Community of the King*, Howard Snyder (1979) speaks of the necessity for the small group to minister. Church structure is such that small groups exist within the larger community of the church. These small groups provide for growth, nurture, and evangelism in the larger church structure. In other words the small group is called as much to missions as to community (Snyder, 1979:155). There is a legitimate role for a central leader for the larger community unity, allowing for diversity of interests and approaches to both the concepts of community and mission. At the same time the universal call to discipleship serves as a common bond.

Snyder suggests two qualifications for the structural significance of the small groups in the church:

1. All Christians should be involved in some sort of small group that allows members to take responsibility for each other;
2. The Church needs to recognize "patterns of obedience" which respect diversity of calling, but admit the universal nature of discipleship (1979:155–57).

In order for any of this to be accomplished, it must be recognized that groups within the church are subject to the dynamics discussed earlier in this chapter. The only way to create more effective groups is to confess the weaknesses in the ones that exist. Then the church can begin to structurally reconstitute the groups by using the knowledge of human interaction and the biblically based model suggested above. Where there are no such groups, Christians must commit themselves to their necessity in the realization that such groups are reflections of the quality of life the church community claims to possess.

If small groups are as important as suggested, then the church should be prepared to make a substantial commitment to their development. There are those in the church who regard such notions as another passing fad. However, Scripture seems to reinforce their importance within the context of the larger church, which is so often regarded as *the* most important structure and is epitomized by the Sunday gathering. With goals in mind, the Christian should be prepared to critically examine the traits exhibited by church groups and make corrections. Knowledge and enthusiasm are the two key components in making such changes.

DISCUSSION QUESTIONS

1. What are some groups of which you are a member? Which are primary and which are secondary?
2. Is the church you are attending a primary or secondary group? On what basis did you decide?
3. Should a church be a primary group?
4. How much training should pastors have in group dynamics? Why?
5. What is your reaction to the statement in this chapter that Christian growth and service are best accomplished in group life? Why?

SUGGESTED READING

Darwin Cartwright, *Group Dynamics: Research and Theory* (Evanston, Ill.: Row and Peterson, 1962). Good introduction and review of small groups.

Robert S. Cathcart, *Small Group Communication* (Dubuque, Iowa.: Brown, 1971). Introduction to the dimensions of interpersonal communication in groups.

Dexter Dunphy, *The Primary Group* (New York: Appleton-Century-Crofts, 1972). A classic—deals with the various components of a variety of types of small groups.

Alexander P. Hare, *Handbook of Small Group Research* (New York: Free Press of Glencoe, 1976). The most thorough review of the literature in small groups.

Richard Lovelace, *The Dynamics of Spiritual Life* (Downers Grove, Ill.: Inter-Varsity, 1979). Although not exclusively devoted to the small group, this book conveys the role and impact the small group could and should have in church renewal.

T. M. Mills, *The Sociology of Small Groups* (Englewood Cliffs, N.J.: Prentice-Hall, 1967). Excellent introduction to the area from the classic social system perspective.

Howard A. Snyder, *Community of the King* (Downers Grove, Ill.: Inter-Varsity, 1979).

_____ *The Problem of Wineskins* (Downers Grove, Ill.: Inter-Varsity, 1976). Both of these books are excellent sources for considering the role small groups can and should play in today's churches.

Trueblood, Elton, *The Incidiary Fellowship* (New York: Harper and Row, 1967). Good theological understanding of the relationships that should characterize the church, and meet human needs.

9

DONALD L. CONRAD
Bethel College,
Indiana

MARRIAGE AND THE FAMILY

A radiant, blushing bride accompanies her proud father down the aisle to meet a nervous groom. He will then recite after the minister, "I take thee, to be my lawful wedded wife—"

An awed, but beaming, young father and an exhausted, but triumphant, new mother rejoice together in the delivery room as the doctor holds up a crying infant. The miracle of new life—their baby!

Dad and Mom, sons and daughters, all seated around the Thanksgiving dinner, the Christmas tree, or the vacation campsite. Memories. Fun times. *Family* times.

The familiar scenes described above have almost universal parallels, for all cultures have marriage rites, new babies, and family interaction. Yet how differently would many people in some cultures describe *their* wedding, *their* first birth, and what *their* family does together. As Arnold Green notes, "We need to view others to know how universal some *functions* are, and how unique some *forms* are" (1972:272).

SOCIAL INSTITUTIONS AND THE FAMILY

The complex set of beliefs and practices that a society institutes

167

and maintains to meet a basic human need is called a *social institution*. David Dressler says

> a social institution is an enduring organization of procedures, rules, and policies that enables people in a society to satisfy one or more long-range essential needs. Institutions make up the relatively permanent framework within which culture and social structure operate. . . . To provide continuity and predictability in social relations, there must be routine and legitimate ways to handle the recurring problems of living (1976:287).

The major social institutions treated in most sociology texts are family, economic, political, education, and religion. To these basic five, various authors have added the following: law and recreation (Green, 1972), business, transportation, war, journalism, television, baseball, medicine, entertainment, and drama (Bierstedt, 1970), and science, law, charity, sport, and the military (McGee, 1980). Other items could be added such as institutionalized racism, sexism, and internal colonialism against poor whites and ethnic minorities.

Talcott Parsons (1951) approached the study of society from a functionalist perspective, arguing that every society needs to solve four basic system problems through its cultural arrangements in order to survive. These are (1) *adaptive*—within its environment, to produce and distribute enough food and goods to meet subsistence needs; (2) *goal-attainment*—decision-making mechanisms to determine the group purposes and appropriate means, and to maintain societal order; (3) *integrative*—to tie together the various institutions and individuals into a functioning and meaningful whole; and (4) *pattern-maintenance*—to pass on the knowledge, values, and skills to new members and motivate them to assume roles essential to the group.

The family is basic to the maintenance of all the rest of culture. The family is distinct from economic institutions that focus on the adaptive needs and from politics that deals with goal setting and attainment; yet the family is a vital unit in both the economic system and the political process. Religion binds together a culture and gives a sacred integrative quality to its essential features, and education helps transmit the cultural patterns; but it is the nuclear family and kinship group that produces, nurtures, and socializes the next generation in its economic, political, and religious values.

The form and function of the family must be adaptable to the survival needs and other values of the culture. Each culture must adapt to its own habitat and live off the resources available there. Among the Northwest Coast Indians in British Columbia, this meant catching salmon and seal; hunters on the Great Plains went after the buffalo; tribes living in the California forests cooked acorns; and in much of Africa people dig manioc roots. The pygmies of the Ituri Forest gather bananas, women in the Australian "outback" spend hours searching for grubworms to roast, while American women spend time looking for the best bargains in the delicatessens and modern supermarkets. Residence rules, sex roles, property rights, authority patterns, and family structures are all deeply intertwined with what the society does to survive in their natural habitat. In fact, Whiting and Child (1953) concluded, in an extensive cross-cultural study of family forms, that child-rearing practices, concepts of God, and means of social control were each correlated with the type of economic subsistence.

In primitive societies family and kin carry out nearly all the basic societal functions, or at least are deeply integrated into them. In almost all technologically modernized, urbanized, industrialized societies, much of the work involving formal education, politics, religion, social control, security, care of the ill and aged, and economic production is done outside the home by specialized institutional processes and structures. Still the family is often involved to some extent with each of these areas and continues to fulfill in significant ways several essential personal and societal functions.

THE FUNCTIONS OF THE FAMILY

Some today question the need for any social rules governing sexual, marital, or parental behavior. Scoffing at the necessity for "a piece of paper," they cohabit, mate, and reproduce with little regard for the accumulated wisdom of human cultures or the teachings of God's Word. But no culture is disinterested. All known cultures have developed systematic norms to provide a secure environment for children and to make some adults responsible for their care and training. Dressler says that institutionalized family norms are "universally used to regulate the mating behavior of adults and to provide for the rearing of chil-

169

dren (1976:291)." In fact, probably every culture defines what marriage and a family are, *who* may mate with whom, *when, how,* and *where* people are to marry and even *why*.

Queen and Habenstein, in their much-quoted historical and cross-cultural study of the family, conclude that there is an amazing variety of practices, rules, and sentiments in the domestic institutions of different peoples; but through all the varied forms of family life, the following patterns stand out rather clearly: (1) a mother-child bond in the early years; (2) the dominance and prevalence of monogamous marriages; (3) rules regulating sex relations; and (4) the identification of the family with several basic functions (1974:10—11). Authorities are pretty much in agreement that the family serves five major purposes in almost all societies: continuation of the species, sexual control, nurtural care, cultural transmission, and status ascription.

Bierstedt points out that these purposes also meet *individual* needs. If we were not rewarded by also having our own personal needs met, probably few of us would be willing to conform our behavior just to meet societal needs. A condensation of Bierstedt's treatment of the interplay of individual and societal purposes may make this much clearer.

1. Society needs a regular system for *replacing the members* lost through mortality and mobility. Disease, war, catastrophe, migrations and normal mortality demand that constant replacements be provided. On a personal basis, we received life only through the sexual union of the living and, in turn, create new life to continue our identity, our kin group, our beliefs and property.

2. Societies have all found it necessary to place some *control on the expression of sexual urges*. Without constraints, many women would be either pressed into sexual union or denied it at the whim of the stronger males; babies would be born without responsible parents, etc. Marriage provides for the individual maximum opportunity in a stable relationship for a lifelong erotic relationship. It minimizes temptation and conflict and maximizes opportunity for growth in intimacy and understanding.

3. Society needs to insure the biological preservation and *protection of its new members*. As individuals we need someone to give us nurturance, security and love until that age when we are mature and self-sufficient. In the human species, this is nearly one-third of our lifetime.

4. Society must guard the *transmission of its culture,* to provide members who are motivated to work, who identify with their nation,

ethnic group, social class, and other cultural continuities, and who respect the goals, values, beliefs and authority which are essential to the group's survival. We need to learn the rules, roles and relationships; the morals, manners and methods of the social milieu within which we live. This includes not only the norms with its reward and sanctions system, but also the flexibility in those norms, and its patterns of evasion and deviance. Our sub-cultural groups, and especially our family, provide the microcosm which reinforces, filters and modifies cultural values.

5. *Status ascription* is essential for an orderly maintenance of the patterns and regularities of the culture. New members must be given an efficient place of entry and opportunity in the role-allocating system. On a personal level, we need a name, a social network to give us legitimacy and support, and a beginning point of identity in terms of race, nation, class and other cultural regularities. Our family of orientation gives us a home, kindred, our initial church, social class, political party, geographic placement and social identity (1970: 394–403).

To bring up an infant into a well-adjusted, role-fulfilling human being requires a stable unit that protects and nurtures and that provides basic socialization into the values, language, and behavioral norms of the culture. The family is the most pervasive social group in the world. For this reason Charles Cooley, one of the founders of the symbolic interactionist perspective in sociology, called the family the most basic *primary group.* He defined a *primary* relationship as the form of interaction between persons that is characterized by intimate, face-to-face association and cooperation.[1] The newborn infant first meets the culture through the family that plays a primary role in the development of the child into a functioning adult. Cooley believed a most important aspect of these relationships was in the fact they produce a blending of

---

[1] In order to be an intimate and primary group, it does not need to be continually face to face, however. W. I. Thomas and Florian Znaniecki, in their classic study (*The Polish Peasant in America,* 1918. Richard Badges, Boston) of letters sent from European peasant families to relatives who had immigrated to this country shows that family bonds can be enduring and influential, though separated by many miles. Most college students who check their mail boxes every day hoping for news, money, or counsel from home know that family ties can bridge the miles. Many also have experienced, as Znaniecki found, that eventually distance, time, and new associations can begin to weaken the old ties. "Absence makes the heart grow fonder . . . of the ones who are nearby."

individuals into a sense of mutual identity that causes one to feel a part of the beliefs, values, and purposes of society. In his view the major primary groups are the family, the playground of children, and the adults of the neighborhood (Lowry and Rankin, 1977:53).

One of the strongest evidences of the basic importance of the family in preserving culture is the extent to which it is attacked by those who seek to radically remake society. For example, in the USSR and mainland China, when authoritarian political systems sought to radically change those countries, the Bolsheviks and Maoists saw the power and conservative influences of the family as counterrevolutionary. Concerted efforts were made to remove child-rearing functions from the parents, to reduce parental authority or filial piety, and to minimize any religious and legal prohibitions against premarital and extramarital liasons, abortion, and divorce. The consequences, though temporarily useful to the revolution, soon became threatening to the social order itself, and in less than twenty years it became necessary to reinforce family values again (Lowry and Rankin, 1977:418). It is instructive to note that much of the rhetoric and reasoning of the radical branches of the women's liberation movement draws upon the writings of Marx and Engel (Spencer, 1976:353).

THE FORMS OF THE FAMILY

To make it possible to organize the comparative study of the family in hundreds of diverse cultures, sociologists and anthropologists have developed a specialized terminology involving scores of terms. Based largely on Latin and Greek roots, they describe marriages (-gamous), inheritance lines (-lineal), authority (-archal), residence (-local) and naming (-nymic). To these endings are attached prefixes such as mono-, poly-, patri-, avuncu- (uncle), neo-, and ambi-. For example, the dominant family pattern in the United States is monogamous,[2] nuclear, neolocal, patrinymic, bilateral, patriarchal, matricentric, and moving toward egalitarian. Further amplification of these terms and others is found in nearly all sociology and cultural anthropology texts dealing with the family.

---

[2]However, as many have noted, our pattern of "serial monogamy" through legal divorce and remarriages is a form of sanctioned polygamy.

The binding and blinding power of our own culture causes us to assume that our way of life is normal. Not surprisingly, many native peoples around the world call themselves *the people,* inferring that the center of the universe lies in their hometown, and outsiders are somehow *nonpeople.* It is often startling to students in a college course in marriage and the family to find how unusual many of our beliefs and customs seem to people of other cultures.

In Murdock's (*Social Structure,* N.Y., Macmillan, 1949) study of a sampling of 234 cultures, only 18 percent require monogamy, and just over 30 percent use our bilateral system of kinship structure; few have traditionally had our neolocal pattern of residence after marriage, only 15 percent are matrilineal, and many do not take the name of the father's family as we do. In some cases the biological father has little to do with the rearing of his own children, and the wealth he accumulates goes to his nieces and nephews, or belongs to the tribe and village of his wife. Few cultures have had our system of dating and mate selection. Being "in love" has little to do with getting married, and being "unhappy" has little to do with divorce, though some have higher divorce rates than we do.

The discovery that one's own culture is often out of step with much of the rest of the world makes several responses possible. The first, and most likely, is to assume that one's own ways are correct, normal, and best, whereas the ways of others are incorrect, deviant, and inferior. A second response is to take a relativist position and say that whatever people have come to view as right for them is right. A third possible approach would be to uncritically borrow from others whatever looked appealing or try to remove from another culture whatever seemed different. This would deny the cultural relatedness of cultural institutions.

As Grunlan notes in chapter 3, cultural relativism must be balanced with biblical authority. Not all practices can be judged cross-culturally, but all must be examined in the light of biblical principles. David Lyon speaks clearly to this issue when he says:

> Built into [the] Christian sociology, however, will be the assumption that men in society are sinful, and that conflicts, deviance, even certain social institutions, may exist as a result of sin. They are less than ideal; in terms of the creation order, they are abnormal. What "is" is not necessarily what "ought" to be (1976:66).

Grunlan and Mayers (1979:164–68) note that cultural diversity is possible within biblical guidelines, but that some cultural patterns fall outside the biblical principles and therefore are in violation of the Word of God in that respect, even though they are probably acceptable on other points. The Christian standards for marriage and family values in our own culture cannot be determined by taking a Gallup poll, doing a Kinsey study, or comparing them with Murdock's sample. Even though a Christian learned that only one-third of the cultures prohibit premarital or extramarital sex, or that Kinsey, Reiss, or Gallup had discovered that most people in this culture thought "permissiveness with affection" was acceptable, the knowledge of what others do could never make an immoral act normative for one's own life. For the evangelical Bible believer, the essential question is, What does God's Word say about this? Because the believer accepts or receives the Bible as inspired and authoritative, it is believed that what it teaches should be applied to one's culture and to every area of one's own personal life.

THE FORMATION OF THE FAMILY

The family institution, according to Perrucci, et al., is a "structure that is supported by norms and involves the marriage of a man and woman for the purposes of sexual cohabitation, affection, companionship and the bearing of children" (1977:274). Green adds, "Elaborate or simple, the marriage rite has the same essential purpose . . . the seeking and affirmation of public approval . . . and always and everywhere is followed by joyful celebration" (1972:272).

The marriage ceremony has three major purposes, according to Kelley (1979:281–83). First, it is a *rite of passage* that marks the change from single to married status, moving the couple from dependence on parents to support from the broader community. Second, it legally establishes a new family unit with all the economic and social aspects that centuries have built into the meaning of that new contractual relationship. Third, this new status and new economic position of the couple is publicly witnessed to in an interpersonal commitment that expresses love, kindness, caring, and responsibility by promising "I will," "I promise," "I do."

Not all cultures repeat vows of endearment in a ritual as we do.

Dressler (1976:290–91) tells of the Cuna Indians found on islands along the coast of Panama. The parents arrange the marriage. When the day comes, the marriage maker and helpers pick up the groom and carry him to the prospective bride's house calling "husband, husband." They place the bride and groom in a single hammock. By custom he jumps out and runs away. They recapture him, and if he refuses to go back, there is no marriage. If he consents, they return him; and he runs away four times. On the fifth he stays, and they lie awake together all night. Neither sleep nor intimacy is allowed. The next morning he goes with her father to the Panamanian mainland to help him fetch wood. This act publicly seals the marriage and symbolizes parental blessing. That night sexual union consummates the marriage.

Among some African cultures, the different aspects of marriage and the stages of involvement of the two familial groups is formalized by bride wealth gifts in three segments. The first, in *connubium*, secures the right to exclusive sex; the second, in *exorium*, obtains the right to her labor; and finally, rights in *genetricium*, pertain to her offspring. Only when a child is born and the last cattle exchanged is a person fully married. In our culture the complex nature of marriage can be seen in terms of our philosophy as to what all is involved in marriage from the personal, familial, social, and spiritual aspects. Physical union is a very intimate act, involving much more than the pleasurable interaction of two sets of organs. For both sexes, but especially for the woman, the first act of intercourse etches something indelibly in the consciousness. On a fundamental level, physical mating *is* marriage, and most women and many men have reserved that ultimate act of physical consummation for the legal marriage partner. Yet mere sincerity and sex are still not marriage in this culture or others.

On a gradient of degrees, marriage can be seen as moving along a continuum from promiscuous union to full Christian marriage. *Promiscuity* is known in all cultures, but is not recognized in any culture as the marriage norm. *Pair bonding*, though found often in nature until the young are viable, among humans would be an "affair" without ritual and permanence. *Cohabitation* would move on to the level of mutual consent and public knowledge, but also lacks social legitimacy. *Common-law marriage* involves a stable union without ritual or legality; although in some countries it is ultimately given legal standing, it is still considered inappropriate and deviant, and it often lacks responsible commitment. Advocates of alternatives to the traditional family often suggest some form of these three. *Legal* marriage adds the dimensions of contract and community recognition through some social ritual. *Sacred marriage* requires the approval of the prevailing religious representatives who may also symbolically represent the cultural continuities and mores and provide linkage with the clan and ancestors. Full *Christian marriage* moves one step further, for it includes the previous essentials, but also involves following biblical teaching on seeking God's will in mate selection, having a Christian ceremony and assuming sacred responsibilities.

It is apparent that there is a progression in the above analysis from a very personal view of marriage—mating with whomever one pleases—on to mutual consent, to family and clan approval, to broader social legitimation and involvement, and finally to divine approval.[3] This speaks to the questions often raised by youth. When is a person really married? What constitutes marriage? Can two people enter into a legitimate and Christian marriage by just sincerely giving themselves to each other? If you have sexual union, does that make you married in God's sight? Can you be legally married, but still not be legitimately married? Is it the family, the state, the church, society, or the couple themselves that determines what marriage is and when it is valid? In my own view a couple are not fully married in the degree that God has planned unless their marriage includes consent, commitment, contract, social confirmation, church sanction, consummation, and Christ's approval. This sevenfold cord of love is not easily broken (Eccl. 4:12), for it commits self, mate, family, friends, society, the church, and God Himself to this enduring and important human tie.

---

[3]One useful way to view this interrelationship between the personal, civil, and social aspects of marriage is to picture it as a triad: the couple, God (and the church), and society (Small, 1959). Throughout history there has been some tension between individual autonomy, secular control, and ecclesiastical control. Among the Quakers there is still a form of self-marriage. On the other hand, in two states only a minister can legally perform marriages. In the rest of the states either a minister or a civil official can do so. About 75 percent of all marriages are performed by clergy.

A Christian approach would be first to seek God's approval; then, that of the intended mate; next that of the minister, family, and friends; and finally to make it legal and public by certificate, ceremony, and celebration. God's blessing should come first and last in a Christian approach to marriage. "Be ye well assured, that unless ye are joined together as God's Word allows, ye are in no wise married" (old ceremony).

THE FINALITY OF MARRIAGE

As has been indicated throughout this chapter, marriage is not just a personal matter between two individuals. The purposes served are broad in their societal impact and eternal in their consequences. Every culture considers divorce disruptive and unfortunate. Some make it very difficult to obtain, but others are more permissive. Some cultures have a higher divorce rate than does the United States; in others, divorce is very rare. In all cultures there is a recognition that some circumstances make continued marriage or parenting nearly impossible; so provision is made for divorce or for removing children from an intolerable situation. Like marriage, such a rite of passage is hedged about by ritual and rules that underscore essential cultural values even at the time of their strain. Divorce, perhaps even more than death, is a threat to the shared meanings that undergird our existence. It may be likened to suicide, which shocks and challenges the community even more than a natural death. Like suicide, the "death" of a marriage not only reminds us of our human frailty, which every death does, but it also infers a personal repudiation of the intentional allegiance that we are to have to life and to larger social responsibilities.

The tendency to define marriage only in personal "me-ism" terms may be one factor explaining the considerable increase in divorce. Some see marriage as primarily a search for personal happiness and fulfillment rather than as an assumption of responsibilities that are both temporal and eternal. Holding such a view, a person who is unhappy, uncomfortable, or unfulfilled may feel justified in severing his or her relationship and trying again to find a more compatible and congenial companion. While God did not create marriage to make people miserable, nor did He intend the family to be a wretched institution, on the other hand, it is clear from the response Jesus gave to the Pharisees that divorce was not in God's original purpose and that the trivial reasons men used in His day to justify it violated God's command (Matt. 19:3–4; Mark 10:1–12; Luke 16:18; Deut. 24:1–4).[4]

FURTHER CHRISTIAN PERSPECTIVES AND ISSUES

Some sociology books start explaining the basis and beginning of the family in terms of biological differences in males and females that made man the "protector" of the pregnant or nursing female and of her dependent offspring. Others claim that marriage evolved from herd behavior to polygyn, which gave exclusive sexual rights to the strongest males, up to socially enforced monogamy, which secures a mate for nearly everyone.

The Bible starts on a different basis. Though all creation bears the mark, image, and life of God, only of humankind was it said that they were made "male and female" in the image of God and that He had breathed into them "the breath of life" (Gen. 1:27; 2:7). As creation neared completion, God asked the first of the humankind to observe, categorize, and name all the other created beings. None was deemed suitable for the companionship and mating of the first man; he was lonely, unfulfilled, and childless. God said of all the rest that He had done, "Behold, it is very good" (Gen. 1:31), but of Adam He said "It is not good that the man should be alone" (2:18). God did not form a new creation from the earth, but fashioned a parted-self, a "womb-man" from near Adam's heart to be of the same essence "bone of my bones and flesh of my flesh" (Gen. 2:21–23) and as suitable as to Adam's nature, needs, and destiny, as he was to hers. God gave them into the naked clasp of each other in order that they could "become one flesh" (Gen. 2:24).

Marriage in this account starts with God, not man. Its primary purpose was companionship and spiritual communion, not sexual opportunity or producing babies or legitimizing them. Yet sex and reproduction are explicitly stated to be in the plan and purpose of God from the beginning. A careful study of Genesis 1–3 outlines

---

[4]In Jesus' day there were both strict and liberal views concerning divorce among the rabbis. Some taught that divorce was permissible if one's mate "didn't please them," or if they "found someone they liked better." Jesus' evaluation of our current, lenient, no-fault, upon-demand divorce practices would undoubtedly be just as negative.

the major purposes of marriage and the family for both male and female: (1) to convey the image of God (1:26–27); (2) to control the earth and its creatures (1:26, 28); (3) to commune with God and each other (2:20–24; 3:8–9); (4) to cohabit and consummate in sexual union (2:24–25); and (5) to fill the earth by being fruitful and multiplying (1:28). The major purposes of marriage are much higher and broader than to justify sexual union or legitimize parentage. God didn't wait to perform the first wedding until after Eve became pregnant. Rather, He first instituted a stable and permanent relationship of companionship, homemaking, and partnership in worship and service into which children would come only after the parents had come to a deep knowledge of each other (Gen. 4:1). Those who advocate union without spiritual communion, sexual recreation without permanent responsibility, or affection without legal affiliation are not on biblical grounds. Nor is it scriptural to say, as some Victorians did, that the only reason for marriage or sexual union is for procreation. The Pauline view that even marriage needs to be subordinate to discipleship was distorted by some church fathers into being considered a burdensome concession to our lower natures. That is not what God said in Genesis 1 and 2; Proverbs 5:18; Ecclesiastes 9:9; or Hebrews 13:4; it is not the message of the "Book of Loves" (Song of Solomon), and is the opposite of what is implied when Jesus used the happy occasion of a wedding reception as the opportunity to perform His first public miracle and to begin His public ministry (John 2:1–11). God is for marriage, He is for loving companionship, He is for sex, and He is for having children. In His plan they all go together but in proper order.

Children Need a Home and Two Parents

It is almost universally recognized that marriage gives a legitimate status to babies at birth and fixes the responsibility for their care. Every child deserves the "birthright" of having a name, both a father and mother, and being nurtured in a caring and secure home. But not all are so fortunate.

The number of illegitimate births recorded in this country in 1938 was only 145,000 out of a total of 2,500,000 births. Twenty years later the figure had only risen to 200,000 out of 4,255,000 births. But in the next fifteen years, it had more than doubled to

179

407,000 out of a total of only 3,141,000 births.[5] Coupled with the greater accessibility and utilization of contraceptives and abortion, this clearly indicates that premarital sexual activity is extensive and that "permissiveness with (or without) affection" is widespread. Illegitimate union will produce illegitimate babies. Even married couples, who are experienced with contraceptives and are trying to space children, have a rather high failure rate. Nearly half of all babies born are unplanned, though not necessarily unwanted. In 1975, some 800,000 babies were conceived by girls fifteen to nineteen years old. Of these, 200,000 were unmarried at the time of giving birth, 200,000 married after conception, and more than 200,000 received an abortion. In that age bracket it appears that nearly three-fourths of the pregnancies were not intended and many were not wanted. But once a baby is born, 87 percent of the unwed mothers now keep the child, who is raised with the help of the mother's family and various assistance programs.

Increasing numbers of youth—especially college students—are living together illegally, committing fornication, and taking very lightly the offense against both human and divine standards. Richard Hettlinger commented on this growing pattern as follows:

> First, I would ask whether the act of intercourse, with all its unique quality and intimacy, can be rightly or meaningfully experienced apart from the permanent commitment of marriage. Does not love, in any profound sense, remain unfulfilled until the couple are actually responsible for each other? And if so, can the act which expresses and seals the unity of love be justified in advance of that moment? Should the man who has not yet taken the decisive step of committing his future to a girl ask of her this risk to her future? . . . After the wedding they are legally, socially and personally committed beyond recall, no longer independent centers of action but "one flesh." . . . a trial marriage is a contradiction in terms, because the essence of marriage is that (at least in intention) it is not a trial at all, but a permanent bond. And if the full meaning of sex is to be discovered in personal relationships, the ultimate intimacy of intercourse should be reserved until the ultimate commitment to another person, which is represented by marriage (Kelley, 1979:229–30).

---

[5]The trend toward fewer illegitimate births among nonwhites reversed again during the sixties, so that more of the illegitimates born in 1973 were among nonwhites. Even allowing for this, a greater number of births by white mothers were also illegitimate.

As the youth culture becomes increasingly open and permissive in sexual attitudes and behavior, it places serious peer pressure on Christian youth to forsake the time-honored biblical standards of chastity and purity (cf. 1 Tim. 5:22; 1 Cor. 6:18; Gal. 5:19; Eph. 5:1–17). Most teens are now involved in premarital sex, and more than half of teen brides are pregnant when they marry, including many youths in our churches. Most evangelical churches have opposed abortion, sex education at school, and the availability of contraceptives to unmarried youth. It is apparent that Christian homes and the church must give greater attention to assisting our youth to form moral guidelines to bring their sex lives under the lordship of Christ.

Abusive Parents

A second issue, centering solidly in the family, has to do with child abuse, battering, and maltreatment. A major function of the family is the physical and emotional nurturing of the children; another is to provide a network of intimacy and caring within a primary group; yet another is to provide a role model for the growing child as to what good parenting means. Unfortunately, perhaps as many as one million children each year are physically damaged and emotionally scarred by their own parents and siblings (Fontana, 1973).

Christian families brought up to believe that to spare the rod is to spoil the child (cf. Prov. 13:24), or that a child's perverse and stubborn will must be broken (cf. 23:13–14), often feel justified in disciplining their child in ways their neighbors may perceive to be beating and battering. Legislation to insure humane treatment of children and to protect the rights of the child have been strenuously opposed by some fundamental and evangelical groups who interpret it to be a move to take the rearing of children away from the parents and make it the responsibility of the state. Furthermore, it is argued, if the state or legal agencies can tell you how to discipline your child, who is to say that they will not someday take children away from their parents because they teach them faith in God rather than atheism, as has occurred in Russia and China?

Although concern for the integrity of the family, and the rights and responsibility to rear their children and discipline them, is legitimate and well rooted in both Scripture and history, evangelicals must be on guard against justifying maltreatment as being "the will of God." Bible-believing church people dare not be the biggest obstacle to protecting children from abuse. Well-informed opposition to the efforts by some liberals to weaken the family should be accompanied by well-informed support and leadership for agencies that minister to parents who abuse and sexually molest their children and for prosecuting those who maim, kill, and traumatize their own offspring.

Considerable public and professional attention is also being given today to sexual abuse in the family. Current estimates are that perhaps twice as many youth are sexually abused as are physically abused. The number may exceed two million children. Children are frequently conditioned while very young to believe this is appropriate family affection. Guilt comes when they learn the opposite from their peers, and they must live with the fear of discovery, of rejection, or of creating family problems.

Various theories have been offered to explain the almost universal incest taboo against coitus between those in the same household, close blood relatives, and certain clan members. Freud called it a "reaction-formation" against a repressed and unconscious desire; Westermarck believed a person would not be sexually attracted to someone he or she grew up with. Malinowski was convinced that it would create family conflict and kindred confusion to try to be both a wife and daughter, mother and sister, and niece and sister-in-law. Furthermore, exogamous marriages reduce conflict and cement ties between villages and tribal groups that might otherwise get caught up in blood feuds or other controversies.

In any event, we know that Leviticus 18 carefully outlined the specific degrees of relationship that were forbidden in sexual relationships among the Israelites. Ember and Ember (1973:168) portray a page from a recent Anglican Prayer Book in which thirty specific categories of kin, close by blood and marriage, are expressly forbidden as mates: grandparents (three), uncles (six), fathers (three), brothers (three), sons (three), grandsons (six), and nephews (six). Today we would add to this list all the blood cousins of the first degree and, in some states and faiths, also the second cousins and great-uncles and great-aunts.

God underscores these marriage rules by stressing five times "I am the LORD" or "I am the LORD your God" and God adds, "Ye shall therefore keep my statutes. . . . None of you shall approach to any that is near of kin to him, to uncover their nakedness" (to know sexually) (Lev. 18:2, 4–6, 30 κJV). To the specific list of seventeen kindred that God taboos, He added the neighbor's wife, other men, and animals. God calls sexual violations among the kin "wickedness" (v. 17 κJV), homosexuality is an "abomination" (v. 22), and bestiality He calls "confusion" (v. 23). All of these were prevalent patterns among the nations surrounding God's people, and the existence of these wicked and perverted patterns of family life and religious worship explains why God in judgment forced the native inhabitants out of their land and gave their land to the Israelites (vv. 24–30). If the Israelites did any of these, the penalties were immediate and severe (Lev. 20:10–23).

Though almost every culture has explicit incest rules, and sometimes very serious sanctions, violation of the rules is known in all cultures too. If familiarity breeds contempt, or if this taboo is instinctive, it hardly seems we would need the rule, or that there would be so much violation. In a typical community of a thousand families in the United States today, probably fifty or more will have this problem; and it will cut across all classes and professions. Most of the persons reading this paragraph will know at least one such case. Only God knows the long-term genetic, moral, and spiritual consequences of violating the rules He so solemnly gave, but teachers, counselors, pastors, and those working in juvenile runaway shelters can all testify to how damaging psychologically and socially it is to a young girl who is sexually used and abused by her father.[6] Confrontation may be necessary, as Paul recommends in 1 Corinthians 5, but usually little is to be gained by putting either of them in court or in jail. In many cases psychological and spiritual counseling has corrected the situation and brought healing to deep scars. The church should be in the forefront in ministering to these homes, expecially since research shows that often such abuse is found in closely knit, religious and respectable families where the father is dominant and authoritarian.

---

[6]Although there are few studies and little data, sexual liasons between mother and son and brother and sister also occur frequently. The guilt and sexual anxiety produced is thought to be a major factor in adult homosexuality in males and in prostitution and lesbianism in females.

"A WOMAN'S PLACE IS IN THE HOME"

Even a cursory scanning of sociology texts, books on marriage and the family, and literature of changing sex roles in contemporary society will show that Christian teachings are frequently cited as a major factor in the father's dominance in the home, traditional and inferior roles for women, and the Victorian sexual ethics and double standard.

One can't deny some of the quotes or attitudes expressed by Origen, or some other second- or third-century church father, or of some medieval monks, but it is a "bad rap" on the Christian church to suggest that statements by a few individuals quoted out of context represent *the* Christian view, or biblical teaching. Even today some assume great authority and claim to teach "a Bible view" of the chain of command, the submission of women, and their spiritual safety under the husband's "umbrella"; but many reputable Bible scholars would have trouble with the hermeneutics involved in using only a few passages to build such a dogmatic system.

No consideration of the changing roles of women can escape certain realities of both demography and our economy. Women are living several years longer; but even more important, they are confining child bearing and child rearing to a much shorter portion of their married life. Large families are no longer needed to supply adequate workers for the home-based farm work and household productivity. Most children now live to maturity. Thus most women have only two or three children, and these are born within ten years of marriage. The children usually have all entered school by the time mother is thirty, and have left home by the time she is forty or fifty years old, leaving her at least twenty years of relatively free time to either focus on her grandchildren, community and church service, or gainful employment. Many women have found it difficult to reenter the job market after a twenty-year dropout, for they are rusty in skills they once did well, or their job has become obsolete. Moreover, they discover that challenging jobs are difficult to get and pay scales are usually discriminatory.

If a woman enters the work force and stays in it through all but a few months of her child-rearing years, she needs to be a "Super Mom" in order to keep up with the combined expectations of dual roles. She may neglect one or the other somewhat and feel guilt over what she failed to accomplish. Men, too, may find it difficult to maintain career advancement, an adequate parenting role, and to share in other household and familial roles.

Double-digit inflation may make it almost necessary to have two incomes in order to maintain the affluent standards to which many people have become accustomed. An important issue that Christians need to face is whether or not a less affluent lifestyle would be more in keeping with maintaining the high priority that the Bible puts on parenting on the part of both the father and mother.

It also needs to be stated that the church would undoubtedly have a greater ministry if it would assist parents in their parenting tasks rather than condemning the bulk of mothers who now work full time outside the home.

CONCLUSION

Controversy swirls about the family as an institution. Can permanent, exclusive monogamous unions survive the fracturing forces of the postindustrial society that Toffler so dramatically described in his best-selling book, *Future Shock* (1970)? Is it too much to expect one's partner to provide so much emotional satisfaction, especially since women may not feel adequately rewarded for the roles they must play? Is it fair to bring children into such a messed-up, overpopulated world? If children are not intended, why marry?

But, as one text concludes, the conventional family is not about to disappear. "No institution that has evolved and survived as long and as universally as the family will disintegrate because of critics, innovators or experimenters. The basic social institutions are usually very resilient" (Ritzer et al., 1979:408). Margaret Mead underscored several times that although one function or another can perhaps be better performed by other agencies, no institution can do so many of them so well as the family. Mead herself found out how resilient family norms are when she proposed the "two-step" form of marriage in which couples live together for a time in a "trial marriage" type of betrothal and then solemnize it into full marriage before any children are conceived. Though some couples had been following this pattern, and Mead was a respected public figure, the outcry her proposal raised led her to conclude that traditional mores concerning marriage are still very deeply held in this country.

Changes have occurred, however. Scanzoni (1975) notes that today there is less control of mate selection by the extended family, family authority is more equalitarian, commitments carry less of the "forever" quality, and greater emphasis has been placed on the search for personal happiness. In spite of discriminatory wage scales, women have greater economic opportunity and better legal protection in contracts, inheritance, and divorce proceedings. All of these may have contributed to the higher divorce rates, though in themselves some may be desirable changes.

A Garden of Eden there was and a heaven there will be, but God wants us to live out our faith in the now of today. In our yearning to get away from the problems, struggles, and pressures of the present, there is a tendency to put a halo over a nostalgic past that never was or to dream of a utopian future that exists only in storybooks. Historians and sociologists often yearn for the past that might have been, or they anticipate a day in the future that could hopefully come. The danger lies in comparing the present with conditions in the past or future that exist only in the imagination. Many changes have occurred, and they are not all good. Other changes are occurring today that cause some to question whether the family will survive in the future, and if so, in what form. But to panic because the current scene doesn't match a fictional past or future is not good scholarship, good politics, or a good Christian witness.

The calling of the church and of the Christian is not to keep the family from changing, but to endeavor to maintain the essence of that union, set forth in Scripture, between Christ and the church. According to the Bible, men and women were not created for the sake of the family, but the family was instituted for the good of humankind. God's plan and purpose in marriage has been marred by selfishness and sin, but a primary setting for Christ's redemptive work in the world is in the caring and sharing relationships that we call marriage and the family.

DISCUSSION QUESTIONS

1. Do you think the nuclear family is necessary for the maintenance of society? Why? Why not?
2. What do you believe constitutes a Christian marriage? Do you agree or disagree with the teaching in this chapter? Why?

3. Do you believe there are biblical grounds for divorce? If so, explain the grounds.
4. Should an unwed mother keep and raise her child? Why? Why not? What are the rights and duties of the father?
5. What do you believe are the biblical roles for husbands and wives? Why?

SUGGESTED READING

Harold T. Christensen (ed.), *Handbook of Marriage and the Family* (Chicago: Rand McNally, 1964). A comprehensive review of the literature on the family by recognized authorities in each specialized area.

Peter DeJong, and Donald R. Wilson, *Husband and Wife: The Sexes in Scripture and Society* (Grand Rapids: Zondervan, 1979). This book should be in everyone's library and be read. And reread! It gives a careful exegesis of scriptural teaching about masculine and feminine roles, and it challenges many traditional sexist views about what the Bible teaches.

V. A. Demant, *Christian Sex Ethics* (New York: Harper and Row, 1963). A professor at Oxford and Anglican canon of Christ's Church speaks sensitively to the many issues raised by the sexual revolution of the sixties. He speaks of chastity, eroticism, gender differences, meaning of marriage, cohabiting, and many other current issues from historical, ethical, and biblical standpoints.

Maureen Green, *Fathering: A New Look at the Creative Art of Being a Father* (New York: McGraw-Hill, 1976). A secular writer examines an area that most books almost totally ignore—the importance of fathering in the family constellation, especially in those homes where divorce or separation has occurred. Everyone who is, or wants to be, a father should read it, but especially mothers should read it—and also divorce court lawyers and judges.

Dwight Harvey Small, *Design for Christian Marriage* (Westwood, N.J.: Revell, 1959). An older book that has had very wide usefulness in colleges, churches, and homes. Rich in scriptural interpretation, allusions to literature, and utilization of social science, it succeeds in integrating them in an interesting and helpful way. This book should be in every person's library. Chapter 4 on "Sex as Symbol and Sacrament" is an especially good correction to distorted views about sex found both in the church and secular society.

Tim Timmons, *Maximum Marriage* (Old Tappan, N.J.: Power Book, 1976). A practical self-help book written by a minister-counselor who conducts Christian family life seminars. Humorous and helpful, it seriously examines Scripture to show the biblical plan for marriage, parenting, and headship.

10

STEPHEN A. GRUNLAN
St. Paul Bible College,
Minnesota

ECONOMICS

All humans share the same basic needs for the maintenance of life. These needs include food, shelter, protection, and health. Since all human societies share these needs, each society must develop social patterns and organizations to exploit its environment to meet these needs. The economic institution is made up of the standard and routine behaviors and social organizations in a society used for the production, distribution, and consumption of goods and services. Like other basic social institutions, the economic institution is integrated into the whole social fabric of the society. It is influenced by many noneconomic factors such as societal values, traditions and customs (Babbie, 1977:249–50; Gordon and Harvey, 1978:84; Perrucci et al., 1977:160).

Social scientists categorize economics by five basic subsistence technologies. From least to most advanced these are (1) hunting and gathering, (2) animal husbandry, (3) horticulture, (4) agriculture, and (5) industrialism (Otterbein, 1977:40–42). The more advanced technologies will often incorporate elements of less advanced technologies. For example, industrialized societies usually utilize agriculture and animal husbandry.

188

Hunting and gathering, which includes fishing, is a technology that exploits its environment without controlling or changing it. Native game in the area is hunted, but there is no attempt to control the game or to introduce new species. The vegatation, including fruits, that grows naturally in the environment is gathered, but there is no attempt to cultivate the vegetation or to introduce new varieties.

Animal husbandry involves the breeding and raising of animals. Animals are domesticated and maintained to provide food, skins, and transportation. This level of technology allows humans to have the animals at hand as opposed to having to go out and hunt for them.

Horticulture is a farming technology that involves raising crops with the use of hand tools such as digging sticks or hoes. This technology involves clearing a field of grass, brush, and trees. The ground is then broken up with a digging stick or hoe. Crops usually consist of grains such as corn, wheat, and millet, or roots such as manioc, yams, and potatoes. The field is weeded as the crops grow, and when the crops are mature they are harvested. These fields usually decline in fertility in two or three years. They are then allowed to return to their natural vegetation and new fields are cleared. In societies where these first three subsistence technologies are practiced, the whole population is generally involved in food production.

Agriculture is a farming technology that utilizes the plow and either draft animals or tractors. Agriculture also involves more intense cultivation. Farmers use fertilizers—either animal refuse or chemicals—and rotate crops. With intensive cultivation, the same fields can be used permanently and plantings yield larger harvests per acre. Agriculture is usually such an efficient means of producing food that a significant part of the population is freed from food production to engage in manufacturing and trade. Agriculture makes possible the transition to industrialism. The freeing of a major segment of the population from food production leads to five major social changes related to the emergence of industrialism: (1) increased occupational specialization, instead of each family providing all of its needs, it specializes and overproduces in a few areas; (2) a market for the exchange of goods and the development of a barter economy; (3) the emergence of political leadership and a governmental structure; (4) a management of labor and allocation of resources; and (5) different rewards for different tasks, leading to a status system and stratification.

While the above five factors figured in the development of industrialism, three additional factors were responsible for the continued growth of industrialism. The first of these was the development of money. By using tokens of fixed value, economies could advance from barter economies to cash economies. With the development of a cash economy, wage labor was possible. With the advent of wage labor, further industrialization was possible. Instead of one person making the whole shoe so as to have something to barter or trade, several shoemakers could work for one industrialist, one making heels, one making soles, one making bodies, and another assembling the shoes. The owner of the business could sell the shoes for cash and pay wages that the workers could use to purchase their necessities.

The second factor responsible for the growth of industrialism was the development of the alphabet. When people became able to read and write, further industrial development was possible. Messages did not have to be carried personally but could be written and delivered by another. This facilitated increased trade and enabled governments to operate more efficiently. The development of writing and reading also led to the development of postal services.

Even with the development of money and the alphabet, the growth of industrialism would still have been limited if it had not been for the third factor, mechanical technology. As mechanical technology advanced, more efficient farming implements were developed, allowing each farmer to produce more food and freeing more workers from the land. The latter migrated to the cities and entered the wage labor market. As mechanical technology increased, the need for wage laborers increased. New factories began to open and the need for skilled artisans such as blacksmiths decreased, while the need for laborers increased.

However, the real growth in industrialism took place during the industrial revolution. Although not all historians agree on the cut-off dates for the industrial revolution, 1760 to 1918 would be accepted by most. With the invention and development of steam for industrial use, factories began to spring up in urban areas

Economics

where there was a ready supply of laborers (Hawley, 1971:63–86).

Anthropologists do much of their research among hunters and gatherers, pastoralists (those who practice animal husbandry), and horticulturalists, whereas sociologists are primarily concerned with examining contemporary industrialized societies.[1] Some of the areas that sociologists are interested in include the division of labor, specialization, unionization, labor-management relations, economic systems, and manifest and latent functions of organizations and associations.

In the field of economics, another area of concern is poverty. Poverty is a major social problem in America. According to the 1970 U.S. census figures, more than 25 million Americans live in poverty. More than half of these people are children and old people. About 30 percent are black, 9 percent are Latins, and some 60 percent are white. Many people living below the poverty level are employed either full time or part time. More than three-fifths of families living in poverty are headed by men. Only about one-third of those living in poverty receive any welfare benefits (Horton and Leslie, 1974:337).

EFFECTS OF POVERTY

Although poverty has many harmful effects on people, one of the worst is malnutrition. As was pointed out earlier, economics is concerned with meeting human needs that are related to the maintenance of life. One of the most basic needs is nutrition. The poor are often undernourished because they cannot afford an adequate diet. For example, in 1979, the average welfare payment for a family of four in Philadelphia was $360 a month. The federal government estimated a family of four needed $516 a month, about $6000 a year; for minimal survival (*The Other Side*, 12/1979: 99:36). Therefore the poor tend to eat food that is high in starch and carbohydrates and low in protein.

Both psychological and medical researchers use animals in research projects that have implications for humans. One of the more frequently used animals in this research is the rat. The ad-

---

[1]It should be noted that anthropology is becoming more involved in studying industrialized societies. For example, urban anthropology is a growing field of study.

vantages of using rats for research related to humans are that rats have a diet and a metabolic process similar to that of humans (note that they scavenge human refuse). Another advantage is that rats reproduce themselves every few months. This means that several generations of rats can be studied in a few years.

In a recent issue of *Psychology Today*, Margot Slade (1979) reported on a research project carried out with a colony of rats at the London School of Hygiene and Tropical Medicine and Boston University Medical School. Researchers from these schools and Massachusetts Institute of Technology kept the colony of about three hundred rats alive on a diet of 8 percent protein as compared with the normal rat diet of 25 percent protein.

The researchers used a standard maze device for testing the rats' ability to learn. First, they tested a group of rats fed a normal diet to discover how long it took normal rats to learn the maze. Next, a group of rats that had been undernourished for one generation and a group of rats undernourished for two generations were tested. The undernourished rats took significantly longer to learn the maze.

That undernourished rats on low protein diets should perform less well than rats on a normal diet in a learning test is not surprising. It is the next two parts of this study that have far-reaching implications. The researchers then took a group of rats from the undernourished colony and fed them normal diets for two generations. After one generation the rats looked healthy; but after two generations on a normal diet, the rats had still not recovered normal learning skills.

In the last part of the study, the researchers took a group of rats from the undernourished colony and fed them a normal diet for three generations. During the four to twelve days before a rat's eyes open, the researchers took pups from their nests and put them in another part of the cage. Normal pups are able to find their way back to the nest in three minutes or less. Even after three generations of normal diets, these offspring of undernourished rats took significantly longer to find their nests.

Although this may be all very interesting, how does this rat research relate to people? Scientists have already demonstrated that a protein-deficient diet negatively affects the learning ability of humans. The researchers went on to declare that the results of these studies are directly applicable to humans. They state, "The implication of these findings is quite clear; giving food to people who have starved for generations simply isn't enough" (Slade, 1979). The implications of this research are staggering. How many generations will be limited to a less-than-normal life because of the undernourishment taking place today?

Another effect of poverty is seen in the area of health. Almost half the mothers who had their children in public hospitals (city, county, or state) received no prenatal care. The infant mortality rate for children born to poor women is almost double the national rate. Approximately 50 percent of children in families living below the poverty level are incompletely immunized against smallpox and measles; over 60 percent of these children have never been treated by a dentist. The chance of a poor person dying under age thirty-five is four times the national average (Geiger, 1971:242). Research indicates that the poor are almost three times as prone to psychiatric illness as the rest of society (Harrington, 1969:130).

Another area in which people are affected by poverty is education. The poor are often educationally deprived. For example, the state of Illinois has set per capita spending limits for all school districts. The objective of this law was to insure that wealthier suburban school districts did not spend more money per pupil than the poorer inner-city school districts. Yet many high-school graduates from the inner-city schools were functionally illiterate, while many of the suburban high-school graduates were going on to college. How could that be if the same amount of money was being spent per pupil? In the inner-city schools a larger proportion of money had to be spent on building maintenance because these schools were generally older, while suburban schools were newer. In the inner city more money was spent to repair the effects of vandalism; moreover, money had to be spent on security guards and truant officers. In the suburban schools the corresponding money was paid to special-education teachers. In the inner-city mothers worked; in the suburbs mothers donated time as volunteer aides to teachers.

It is easy to see how these effects of poverty are cyclical. Malnutrition affects health. Health and malnutrition affect education. Education affects occupation, which affects income, which affects

Christian Perspectives on Sociology

the level of poverty. The side effects of this recycled poverty include crime, violence, apathy, and all the other social problems associated with being poor.

POVERTY AND SCRIPTURE

What should be the Christian response to poverty? Christians look to the Bible for direction and instruction concerning the issues of life. The Word of God is not silent on the issue of poverty, but rather addresses the issue head-on.

The Old Testament teaches that food should be provided for the poor (Exod. 23:11; Lev. 19:9–10). In fact part of the tithe was to be used for this purpose (Deut. 14:28–29). The Old Testament also teaches that those who help the poor will be blessed (Ps. 41:1, KJV; Prov. 14:21; 22:9). Another Old Testament teaching equates one's treatment of the poor with one's treatment of God; the one who oppresses the poor is reproaching God, while the one who is generous to the poor honors God (Prov. 14:31). Also, being kind to the poor is lending to God (Prov. 19:17). Caring for the poor is seen as an evidence of righteous living (Ezek. 18:5–9). Also, true fasting and true worship are equated with care for the poor (Isa. 58:5–11; Jer. 7:2–7; Amos 5:21–24).

The Old Testament goes on to teach that if people shut their ears to the cries of the poor, God will shut His ears when those people call on Him (Prov. 21:13). The Scriptures also teach that the righteous are concerned for the rights of the poor, but that the wicked lack such concern (Prov. 29:7).

The prophet Jeremiah condemned God's people for being fat and well fed but lacking in concern for the poor (5:28). He went on to command the people of God to practice justice and help those being oppressed (22:3) and pronounced a woe on kings who do not pay for labor (22:13–17). Oppression of aliens, orphans, and widows is also condemned by Ezekiel (22:7) and is equated with the sin of adultery by Malachi (3:5).

Jesus picked up the theme of our treatment of the poor being equated to our treatment of God when He taught that if we feed the hungry, clothe the needy, visit the sick, and minister to the imprisoned, we are doing it to Him (Matt. 25:31–46).

Jesus also addressed the believer's responsibility to the poor. He told the rich young man that to be complete, he needed to sell his possessions and give to the poor (Matt. 19:21). Jesus also taught that when we give a party, we should not invite the kind of people who can return the favor, but the poor who cannot (Luke 14: 12–14).

Paul was also concerned for the poor (Gal. 2:10) and took up special offerings for them (Rom. 15:25–26; 1 Cor. 16:1–3). James teaches that true faith is evidenced by our treatment of the poor (James 2:14–20). John teaches that Christian love results in helping the poor and needy (1 John 3:17–18).

There are two passages of Scripture dealing with the poor that are often misunderstood. The first is Matthew 26:11: "The poor you will always have with you, but you will not always have me." The context concerns the story of the woman who anointed Jesus with expensive perfume (Matt. 26:6–13). The disciples thought the perfume should have been sold and the money given to the poor, but Jesus responded, "The poor you will always have with you." Some have understood Jesus to mean that there will always be poor people; so Christians should not worry about them but concentrate on spiritual ministries. However, the Lord actually was saying that the woman had performed an act of worship and that there were many opportunities to help the poor—and by implication that they should do so. Jesus alluded to the phrase "there will always be poor people" in Deuteronomy 15:11. The whole verse reads, "There will always be poor people in the land. Therefore I command you to be openhanded toward your brothers and toward the poor and needy in your land."

The second misunderstood passage is 2 Thessalonians 3:10: "For even when we were with you, we gave you this rule: 'If a man will not work, he shall not eat.'" Actually this verse does not even refer to the poor, although some try to apply it to them. In its context (2 Thess. 3:6–12), this rule governing working and eating refers to busybodies in the church community and not the poor.[2] The evidence from the Word of God is clear: the Christian is to have a concern for the poor and to reach out and help the poor.

---

[2]It should be noted that although this verse is not addressing the poor, it does reaffirm the Scripture's emphasis on the dignity of work (cf. Gen. 2:15; Prov. 10:4; 12:11; Eccl. 3:13; Eph. 4:28). The Scripture does not condone laziness or the poverty resulting from it.

POVERTY AND SOCIAL STRUCTURE

Any Christian who takes the teachings of the Bible seriously will be concerned for the poor and will want to help alleviate poverty. What should be our approach? For the most part, evangelicals have practiced an individual-orientated approach. They have reached out to help individuals or groups through charity and relief ministries such as deacons' funds and rescue missions. Often the individual-orientated approach has been followed because many have tended to see poverty as an individual or personal problem. Individuals are poor and needy either because of personal shortcomings or some misfortunes.

However, some evangelicals are beginning to see poverty less in terms of personal shortcomings and misfortunes and more in terms of social structure and social injustice (e.g., Olson, 1974:54–59; Sider, 1977:131–70). They would see the individual-orientated approach as treating the symptoms rather than the cause They believe much of the poverty in society results from the social system. They would argue that if we want to truly alleviate poverty, we must work to change the system that is causing so much of the poverty.[3]

Many social scientists see much of the poverty in a society as a by-product of the social system. One of these social scientists, Oscar Lewis, developed the concept of "the culture of poverty." He says:

> I have tried to understand poverty and its associated traits as a culture . . . with its own structure and rationale, as a way of life passed down from generation to generation along family lines. . . . The culture of poverty, however, is not only an adaptation to a set of objective conditions of the larger society. Once it comes into existence, it tends to perpetuate itself from generation to generation because of its effect on the children. By the time slum children are age six or seven they [have] usually absorbed the basic values and attitudes of their subculture and are not psychologically geared to take full advantage of the changing opportunities that may occur in their lifetime (1968:4–6).

Lewis sees six conditions as necessary for the culture of poverty to exist. They are:

---

[3]In saying this these evangelicals do not deny that some individuals are poor because of laziness, preference, or other personal causes. The poor can also be sinful.

1. A cash economy, wage labor, and production for profit.
2. A persistently high rate of unemployment and underemployment for unskilled labor.
3. Low wages (for unskilled labor).
4. The failure to provide social, political, and economic organization, either on a voluntary basis, or by government imposition, for the low income population.
5. The existence of a bilateral kinship system rather than a unilateral one.[4]
6. The existence in the dominant class of a set of values that stresses the accumulation of wealth and poverty, the possibility of upward mobility, and thrift, and explains low income status as the result of personal inadequacy or inferiority (1968:4–5).

Oscar Lewis means that poverty tends to recycle itself. The social structure creates a set of circumstances that forces some people to live in a state of poverty. These people make adjustments in their world view, lifestyle, and psychological outlook; in short, their culture is to cope with poverty. This culture of poverty is then passed on to their children.

People who live in the culture of poverty are aware of the culture of the majority. They know what the middle class values are; they will talk about them and claim they are living by them, but in reality they do not. It is important to distinguish between what they say and what they do. This is not an indictment of those who live in the culture of poverty, but a fact that must be recognized before one can begin to have an effective ministry among the poor. It is also important to note that these are not racial characteristics, but apply equally to whites, blacks, Latinos, or any other group that lives in the culture of poverty.

It is also very important to distinguish between being poor and living in the culture of poverty. While going to college I paid seventy-five dollars a month for a third-floor attic where my wife

---

[4]Bilateral kinship refers to a person being equally related to his or her mother's and father's families. In a unilateral kinship system, descent is figured either through the mother's or the father's clan, but not both. In societies with a unilateral kinship system, a person is a member of his mother's or father's clan, depending on how the kinship is figured. The clan cares for the individual and provides social organization and keeps a culture of poverty from developing. The United States has a bilateral kinship system (except for some Indian tribes). For a further discussion of kinship systems, see Grunlan and Mayers (1979:171–88).

washed out diapers in the bathtub because there was not even enough money for the laundromat. Our family was poor but not in the culture of poverty. Instead of being trapped in poverty, we were making a temporary sacrifice in order to get ahead. The culture of poverty is not measured in dollars and cents but is rather a psychological frame of mind. It sees no escape from its condition.

All six social conditions necessary for the culture of poverty discussed by Oscar Lewis exist in the United States. Herbert Gans (1975:218–24) suggests that these conditions are allowed to exist because they are functional. He argues that poverty and the poor perform several functions in American society. One of these functions is to supply a pool of workers to perform society's "dirty work," the dirty, dangerous, menial, and temporary work the nonpoor do not want to do. Gans points out that society has two ways of getting its dirty work done. One is to pay such high wages that workers are attracted to the work, and the other is to force people to do it who have no other options. In American society poverty provides a pool of cheap labor for dirty work.

A second function of poverty, according to Gans, is to subsidize the nonpoor. For example, the low wages paid farm and migrant workers provide less expensive food for society. Inexpensive domestic help subsidizes the lifestyle of the upper class. The poor provide guinea pigs for training doctors and medical research.

A third function of poverty suggested by Gans is to provide jobs for the army of professionals who serve the poor. What would happen to all these workers if they won the war on poverty? Many people in America have a vested interest in the continuation of poverty.

A fourth function of poverty, according to Gans, is that the poor consume goods and services no longer wanted by the nonpoor, thus prolonging their use. The poor purchase day-old bread, secondhand clothes, and deteriorating cars and buildings. They also provide clients for physicians, lawyers, and other professionals who are too poorly trained or too incompetent to attract more affluent clients.

Gans offers as a fifth function of poverty the fact that the poor provide negative role models. They can exemplify personal failure and prove that the values of the dominant class are superior.

A sixth function of poverty, according to Gans, is that the poor help guarantee the status of the nonpoor. In every hierarchal system someone has to be at the bottom, but in America the poor provide a basis for status comparison.

Another function of poverty seen by Gans is that the poor provide a cushion to absorb the costs of change and growth in the American economy. Gans also sees the poor facilitating the American political process. The Republicans rarely get support from the poor and so ignore them. The Democrats are all but guaranteed the votes of the poor who vote; so they pay lip service to the poor and then develop policies to benefit the working class in order that they do not lose those votes to the Republicans.[5]

It has been seen that social structure can hold people in a condition of poverty and that the larger society often benefits from this system. How did this system come about? Did someone plan it that way? The social structure that led to these conditions was unplanned. It developed from long-standing social patterns.

Sociologists generally divide economic systems into four categories: capitalism, socialism, communism, and mixed economy. Capitalism is an economic system in which the means of production and distribution (capital) are privately owned. Profits from production and distribution go to the owners. Socialism is an economic system in which most of the means of production and distribution are owned by the state. Some private property is permitted. Wages are based on contribution, and the profits from production and distribution are used to benefit society. Communism is an economic system in which the state owns all property. The means of production and distribution are utilized for the benefit of the people. All share in the production and all share in the benefits, or in Marx's famous dictum, "From each according to his abilities, to each according to his needs" (Babbie, 1977:253). Mixed economy is a system that mixes capitalism and socialism.

The American economic system is primarily capitalistic, although it has aspects of mixed economy. How did American capitalism come about? In 1776 Adam Smith published *An Inquiry into the Nature and Causes of the Wealth of Nations.* In this work he

---

[5]Although we may not agree with every aspect of Gans's critique, we need to honestly consider what he is saying. See chapter 6 in his book for a discussion of Berger's defense of the system.

saw that the key to economic well-being was self-interest and competition. In competitive free enterprise systems, Smith argued, every producer will provide the best product or service at the lowest possible cost because that will bring in customers and is in the producers' self-interest. Basically, Smith sought to harness human selfishness (self-interest). He pointed out that people will not serve the best interests of society out of generosity but they will do so to make a profit. What happened to Smith's idea?

Bill Tabb (1979:44–49) points out that in 1776, when Smith was presenting his ideas, four-fifths of the people in the free labor force were in business for themselves as farmers, blacksmiths, shop owners, and professionals. The free enterprise system Smith envisioned involved individual businesses. Today four-fifths of the work force is employed by someone else. Employers became larger and larger while workers became more and more specialized. Organizations became so large that individuals lost influence over them. Today one percent of American corporations produce two-thirds of all goods produced in America (Tabb, 1979:45).

The above discussion has been a rather severe critique of the American economic institution. It is easy for Americans to become defensive and to avoid an honest examination of their social system. I personally believe that the American free enterprise system has tremendous potential as an economic system. That potential is evidenced in America's industrial production and the high standard of living of most of the citizens. However, I recognize as a Christian that sin has affected all humans and, through them, their social institutions. Therefore, although capitalism may be an effective economic philosophy, the way it manifests itself will invariably be affected by human sinfulness (this is also true for socialism or any other system). The American economic system has been affected by human sinfulness, and in many cases this has gone beyond individual sinfulness and has become institutionalized. True patriotism does not consist of overlooking the country's wrongs, but of working to correct those wrongs in order to build a better country. Although everyone will not agree on what might be the most helpful approach in correcting some of these problems, the problems need to be recognized, and Christians need to work for change as their consciences dictate. As a first step toward change, some criteria for evaluating social systems are presented below.

CHRISTIANS AND THE ECONOMIC INSTITUTION

Sociologists generally agree that poverty is more the result of the economic and social system than personal shortcomings or misfortunes. If this is true, and sociological research seems to indicate that it is, then what is our reponsibility as Christians? First, it seems that we need to evaluate our present economic systems. Philip Wogaman (1977:51–53) suggests five criteria that Christians should apply in evaluating economic systems. The first criterion is the meeting of the material well-being of all the members of the society. Until a person's basic physical needs are met, it is not possible for him or her to reach human fulfillment. God created humans as material beings as well as spiritual beings and provided for both kinds of needs.

The second criterion is concerned with the basic unity of humankind as opposed to alienating people from each other. The measure of success of the economic system should be in terms of the human values rather than monetary output.

The third criterion involves human freedom and opportunity. The economic system should be one that frees people rather than enslaves them. The system should allow for individual creativity and expression.

The fourth criterion is the consideration of human equality. All people are equal before God, and all are created in His image. While all have sinned and the image is marred in all, God has provided a way of redemption, available to all, through Jesus Christ. An economic system should both espouse and support the essential equality of all humans.

The fifth criterion is that the economic system must take seriously the universality of human sinfulness. The system should realistically take into account human selfishness and greed. It needs to guard against the sinful human tendency to exploit others and the environment for personal gain.

Beyond evaluating economic and social systems, Christians need to be involved in seeking to correct those aspects of the social system that tend to produce and recycle poverty. The Christian needs to work for social justice. The Scriptures speak out against unjust social systems (cf. Isa. 5:8–11; 10:1–4; Amos 5:11; 6:4–24) and command the people of God to work for justice (cf. Ps. 82:3–4; Jer. 22:3; Amos 5:12–14).

SUMMARY

In this chapter we have looked at the economic system as a social institution, with particular emphasis on the problem of poverty. An attempt was made to show that poverty should be understood from the level of social structure as well as the individual level. The teachings of the Word of God on poverty and the Christian's response were examined. And, finally, a call for Christian involvement was presented.

Neither solutions nor specific actions have been advocated in this chapter. The basic purpose has been to raise the issue of structural causes of poverty and to make the reader aware of some of these causes and their consequences. It is hoped that the reader will both think and pray through these issues. Christians are not called to remain faithful to any particular economic, political, or social system. They are called to remain faithful to the Word of God.

Evangelicals are often fond of saying that the way to change society is to change people's hearts. If that is true, then those whose hearts are already changed should be working to change society. If a system is unjust, then converting all the people in that system to Christianity may make them all honest and fair, but it won't make the system more just. Only when the Christians in a system work to change that system will it become more just. A concern for social justice should not detract from the Christian's task of evangelizing the world, but should be part of it.

DISCUSSION QUESTIONS

1. Do you believe that most poor people could improve their position if they really wanted to? Why?
2. Look up the Scripture passages cited in this chapter. Do you think they have been properly interpreted? Why?
3. How many of Oscar Lewis's six social conditions necessary for poverty do you see in American society?
4. What aspects of the American economic institution do you believe tend to recycle poverty? Why?

5. What can Christians do about those aspects mentioned in question 4?

SUGGESTED READING

R. J. Sider, *Rich Christians in an Age of Hunger: A Biblical Study* (Downers Grove, Ill.: Inter-Varsity, 1977). A good study of the teachings of Scripture on poverty and hunger. It contains an extended discussion of structural evil. The closing chapters have some interesting and, at times, controversial suggestions for a Christian response to poverty. This book takes a global view of the problem.

J. Philip Wogaman, *The Great Economic Debate: An Ethical Analysis* (Philadelphia: Westminster, 1977). This work studies the ethical basis for evaluating economic systems. He then examines various economic systems in the light of the criteria established. He calls for all Christians to influence economic life for human good.

Neil J. Smelser (ed.), *Readings on Economic Sociology* (Englewood Cliffs, N.J.: Prentice-Hall, 1965). A collection of essays examining sociological perspectives on economics. The essays look at the interplay of economics and social structure. They also examine the processes of production, distribution, and consumption.

M. Harrington, *The Other America: Poverty in the United States* (New York: Penguin, 1969). A vivid look at poverty in America. Although this work is over ten years old, most of the conditions discussed still exist today.

John White, *The Golden Cow* (Downers Grove, Ill.: Inter-Varsity, 1979). An examination of the lifestyle and materialism of evangelicals. While this work is weak on solutions, it is an excellent critique.

11

STEPHEN G. COBB
Northwestern College,
Iowa

POLITICS

Politics, organizations, power, government, and law are inseparable and deeply interrelated. Politics is a term often used, misused, and abused, but seldom clearly defined. This confusion creates all kinds of difficulties when discussing it.

POLITICS DEFINED

This discussion must begin with a working definition of politics. *Politics* is a process that deals with the distribution of material goods—for example, food, shelter, clothing, and physical resources—and nonmaterial goods—for example, a sense of security, belongingness, and honor. This definition assumes that human beings have basic material and nonmaterial needs to be satisfied by the distribution of goods. Key issues, then, involve who decides how needs are defined, who assigns their priorities, and who decides how goods are distributed. What are the sources that determine the criteria that define the meaning of equitable or just distribution? Who are in positions of power and how did they gain access to the control and direction of political processes?

Robert Ellis and Marcia Lipetz define politics as "the institution concerned with the *organization of power, maintenance of social order,* and *regulation of relations* with other societies . . . a set of rules about certain kinds of behavior" (1979:379) (emphasis is mine).

Kenneth Dolbeare and Murray Edelman, in their text *American Politics: Policies, Power, and Change,* define politics as follows: "Politics is a *process* (a) in which *power is employed to gain rewards,* and (b) through which the *interests* of broad segments of the population are *affected*" (1971:10) (emphasis is mine).

Integrating these definitions, we can see that the process of distributing material and nonmaterial goods, the effectiveness of that process, and the degree that material and nonmaterial needs are satisfied relate directly to "maintenance of social order," "rewards," and "interests." In addition, to lessen conflict in the search for ways to satisfy needs in the midst of a goods scarcity, politics is necessarily involved with the regulation of behavior and the organization of collective action to satisfy such needs.

POLITICS AND POWER

The preceding definitions imply the vital role of power. Definitions, rules, laws, and policies related to goods distribution are useful only when those governing, or in control, have the necessary power to implement and enforce their decisions. *Power,* simply put, is the capacity to get what we want or, as the German sociologist Max Weber puts it, power exists when the will of one person or a group can be exercised so as to determine the behavior of others (1947:152).

Weber also made an important and useful distinction between *power* and *authority.* Power infers the capacity to control others, perhaps even causing them to behave in ways other than what they would prefer. This means that power is coercive and relies on effective sanctions such as rewards and punishments that can in fact be mobilized by those in control.

Power is enhanced and/or qualitatively altered, said Weber, if it is accompanied by authority. This means that those governing must be recognized as having the legitimate right to govern. This recognized legitimacy via the internalization of its rationale helps induce a sense of "oughtness" to obey (1958:181–95). Coercion by itself, without such authority, lacks long-range effectiveness when it comes to having power to maintain social control. The many recent examples of this truism include events in Nicaragua, Iran, Cuba, Afghanistan, El Salvador, and elsewhere.

Weber describes three kinds of authority, or "legitimate rule": (1) *Tradition,* which is based on the *traditional* beliefs of a society, such as with tribal or clan chiefs, kings and queens, and others who inherit their positions; (2) *charisma,* which is based on personal qualities valued in a particular culture and which was possessed by such people as John F. Kennedy, Winston Churchill, Adolph Hitler, and Charles de Gaulle (and certainly Jesus Christ has charisma); and (3) *legal-rational,* which derives authority from the position, and not the person, as, for example, in the case of members of Congress or police officers (Rose, Glazer, and Glazer, 1977:163–64).

Weber then points out that having political power necessitates having a legitimizing base. To be considered authorities, those in power must be recognized as having the *right* to command and must induce an *obligation* to be obeyed. Such a relationship would be exemplary of legitimate power or control. There are, of course, those who have power—the capacity to get what they want—but who do not have a legitimate base. Their power however is much more tenuous. Again, it would seem that recent events in El Salvador, Nicaragua, Iran, Afghanistan, and Cuba are bearing witness to these premises.

Our discussion thus far leads to another distinction, that between politics and power manifested at both the individual and the collective levels. Power manifested at the collective level is *government.* This term is reserved for those situations in which power and authority are exercised at the level of some group of society. It therefore is proper to refer to the government of a family, of a trade union, or of the United States. Although specific individuals may make and enforce decisions on all members of the group, the power is exercised on behalf of the group as a whole and is usually legitimized by reference to some notion about the welfare of the group as a whole (Rose, 1976:320). As shall be discussed later, legitimacies by reference to the welfare of the group as a whole may be rhetoric only, with the operative goal being the protection of a particular group's vested interests.

The state then is one particular form of government. "It is the government found among people who occupy a given geographic territory . . . having a monopoly of the legitimate use of physical force within a given territory" (Rose, 1976:320).

Therefore if a state is to carry on political activities effectively and according to the definitions of the term *politics* discussed above, it must have a *legitimizing* base and effective sanctions.

Politics, then, requires organization; and organized government, specifically the state, is institutionalized politics. Organizations, simply put, are tools in the hands of their creators and are created for collective goals.

> An organization is a collectivity with a relatively identifiable boundary, a normative order, ranks of authority, communications systems, and membership-coordinating systems; this collectivity exists on a relatively continuous basis in an environment and engages in activities that are usually related to a goal or a set of goals (Hall, 1977:22–23).

What soon occurs is the proliferation of competing organizations, each lobbying and jockeying to gain access to power via access to the political process and political organizations. Their goal is to affect the carrying out of political activities in ways most favorable to their vested interests, and they develop intricate ideologies—world views—to rationalize and justify their behavior. The church, big business, organized labor, and others are involved in this organizational jockeying for access to political power. This phenomenon, which appears to be universal, is convincingly discussed in Robert Michels' book *Political Parties: A Sociological Study of the Oligarchical Tendencies of Modern Democracy* (1960), in which he develops his "iron law of oligarchy."

Within this system of competing interest groups, all groups do not have equal access to political power. C. Wright Mills assures us in his classic work *The Power Elite* that equal influence of interest groups is certainly not the case in the United States.

> The top of American society is increasingly unified, and often seems willfully coordinated: at the top there has emerged an elite of power. The middle levels are a drifting set of stalemated, balancing forces; the middle does not link the bottom with the top. The bottom of this society is politically fragmented . . . increasingly powerless (1956:28–29).

Rose, Glazer, and Glazer in their introductory sociology next describe Mills's "power elite" well:

As partial evidence Mills and the elite theorists argue that it is people from similar backgrounds and of similar political and economic interests who are in control of the major organizations of American society. Not only do the corporation executives, generals, and high government officials frequently come from the same class background, attend the same parties, and belong to the same clubs, but they also tend to move from a position in one elite to a comparable position in another. High-ranking military men retire to become executives in defense-related corporations. Corporation presidents in turn become cabinet officers as heads of regulatory agencies. They may change jobs, but they continue to serve the interests and maintain the perspectives of the groups from which they came. . . . Mills quoted Charles Wilson, the president of General Motors who became secretary of defense in the Eisenhower administration: "What's good for General Motors is good for the country." This, claimed Mills, shows how the people who make the critical decisions in this country actually believe that the interests of the government are identical with those of major corporations (1977:168).

The power elite, then, is composed of the "military-industrial establishment"; that is, a dominant few from military, industrial, and political groups. These select few make major decisions by informal consensus, being united by social interaction at country clubs, resorts, and business gatherings. G. William Domhoff, in *The Higher Circles: The Governing Class in America* (1971), makes a case similar to that of Mills. Ellis and Lipetz summarize Mills's and Domhoff's view of the power elite:

> Their power derives from several sources. They own or control much of the corporate economy; they finance both political parties in order to minimize issues and slow down change; and they use media to divert the public with entertainment and maintain the appearances of democracy. Instead of seeking total domination, they exert great influence on crucial areas. For example, they have encouraged heavy defense spending and the protection of big business. In such a view, elections make little difference (Ellis and Lipetz, 1979:375).

Other sociologists, such as Arnold Rose, doubt that power is quite as unified as Mills and Domhoff assert, but rather emphasize that political power is divided among many groups with diverse interests, including political parties, government bureaucracies, corporations, and labor unions. To reach a consensus on major issues, these interest groups bargain behind the scenes, create alliances, lobby, wage propaganda programs, apply political and economic pressures, and strike compromises. Power shifts from one group and alliance to another (Ellis and Lipetz, 1979:376).

However, the difference between Mills, Domhoff, and Rose is a matter of degree and emphasis. They all assert that the people in general have little real political power compared to those in the various "higher circles."

This matter of competing interest groups seeking access to political power raises an important issue often referred to as state interventionism or imperialism. In contemporary societies it is increasingly difficult for a given state, for example, to be self-sufficient as it tries to use its own various material and nonmaterial goods to satisfy needs. There is therefore a growing expansiveness in world capitalism and world communism, to mention the two most prominent examples. The tendency to reach out causes states to intervene in the affairs of others for such things as resources, goods, and security. Of course, this expansiveness and intervention are based on particular definitions of the situation, especially defined ideologies. Therefore part of the problem, as well as the solution, lies in defining and redefining operative political ideologies.

There is also internal *intrastate* interventionism as well as *interstate* interventionism. For example, political power, influence, and intervention in the United States have reached into many areas of our social life:

> The mingling of politics and economics is so extensive that some sociologists expect the loss of their separate identities. Already all governments combined employ one in six persons. A defense budget of $118.5 billion in 1977 represented about 5.5% of the GNP. And the federal government uses its taxing, spending, hiring, and regulatory powers to maintain prosperity and employment. Politics continues to make inroads into education . . . the federal government uses higher education for research and expects public schools to promote racial equality. Policies regarding admission, texts, buildings, and teachers are increasingly regulated by state and federal law. Family life is more influenced by political decisions with time. Child abuse is more scrutinized; building codes make housing more safe; and welfare aids poor families. The institution of politics has lapped over into religion. The government long ago replaced the church as the source of learning and charity. Beyond that, political beliefs, rituals, and leaders are becoming quasi-religious. Robert N. Bellah labels it the American civil religion. Patriotic discourses often are in terms of us as "the chosen people" and ours as "the promised land." As in religion, heretical beliefs such as Marxism are met with hostility more than with reason. Political rituals performed at national cemeteries or on national holidays sometimes

command a sacred atmosphere. And the unifying figures of the nation have been great presidents, some of whom have the aura of sainthood. Although this civil religion lost some of its sacredness due to the Vietnam War and Watergate, Bellah expects (perhaps it would be better to say "hopes for") new prophets and its resurgence (Ellis and Lipetz, 1979:379–80).

BIBLICAL PERSPECTIVE

What is suggested, then, is the development of an approach to sociology, and the sociology of politics specifically, that has a *radically*[1] Christian orientation—that has its reference point for research and analysis grounded in normative Christianity.

Such an approach to sociology would obviously be value-laden and idealistic. However, lest Christian sociologists feel somewhat guilty or less than scientific in developing such a sociology, it should be emphasized that many humanistic sociologists have laid the groundwork.

For example, Christian sociologists can be assisted greatly by the critical approach to social problems promoted by Kenneth J. Neubeck in his excellent textbook *Social Problems: A Critical Approach.*

Neubeck's analysis of how a sociologist approaches the study of social problems in general is pertinent to the study of politics specifically. In identifying social problems Neubeck asserts that a sociologist's own values must inevitably become involved. For example, it would be impossible to identify something as a social problem without making explicit reference to an assumed ideal societal state, that is, to a vision of the ways in which society should operate (Neubeck, 1979:12–13).

Neubeck suggests a vision, or ideal, against which his text defines social problems and measures the status quo. Neubeck's vision possesses the following characteristics:

1. Differences in personal wealth and income should be minimal, so that the life chances of all Americans are relatively equal and so that all share more equitably in the goods and services being produced.
2. Members of American society should be able to actively participate in or directly influence those political and economic decisions that affect them.

---

[1]By radically is meant a position that is totally Christian. Such a position will always be radical in a world where sin pervades.

3. Each individual should have ready and continuing access to the education and training needed to develop his or her interests and capabilities to the fullest extent.
4. There must be no personal and institutionalized discrimination against individuals on the basis of group membership (e.g., race, ethnicity, and sex).
5. None of America's resources should be devoted to military aggression and violence against other peoples of the world. Instead, our nation and others must move toward disarmament and the peaceful settlement of differences.
6. Resources must be devoted to the preservation and conservation of the natural environment, and technological decisions must take into account the well-being of future generations.
7. Work must be freely available to all. It should be organized cooperatively, with special attention to providing meaning, dignity, and satisfaction.
8. Members of American society should be at peace with themselves and with one another. The vicarious rewards associated with such activities as crime, violence, and drug abuse should have no attraction, and the anxieties that provoke mental troubles and suicide should be absent (1979:13).

Christian sociologists could benefit from considering Neubeck's ideal reference point, but they could further enhance it by articulating the contributions that normative Christianity might make to that ideal societal state.

The meaning of normative Christianity and its implications for defining an ideal societal state and, specifically, the role of politics are discussed in detail later in this chapter. Let it suffice at this point to say that the source of normative Christianity is God, who has revealed Himself in creation and in the Bible. In the Word of God are found such truths as those concerning the historical Christ, the ministry of the Holy Spirit, and what God has to say about the nature of the universe, humanity, the human predicament, and the solution to that predicament. The Christian sociologist, then, in *defining the situation* in sociological analysis, is aware of operative, causative, and facilitating factors of which the secular sociologist lacks knowledge. The Christian sociologist knows, for example, of humanity's being made in God's image and of humanity's misuse of freedom. He knows also of human sinfulness and of the sinfulness of human institutions. He knows of God's offer of forgiveness and regeneration to repentant sinners made possible by the atoning sacrifice of the person of Jesus Christ, God incarnate. He understands the necessity of never giving up on God's creation because it is His. He accepts the sovereignty of God and His lordship. Although Christian truth is real and operative, the Christian sociologist must still endeavor to discover the position of the subject being dealt with in terms of how the subject views, or defines the situation.

Thomas and Znaniecki provide a helpful reminder at this point. Within the quotation bracketed comments and italics have been introduced for emphasis:

> We must put ourselves in the position of the subject who tries to find his way in this world, and we must remember, first of all, that the environment by which he is influenced and to which he adapts himself, is *his* world, not the objective world of science [or that provided by Christian normative subjectivity]—is nature and society as *he* sees them, *not* as the scientist sees them [and not as the normatively subjective Christian sociologist sees them]. The individual subject reacts *only* [this is too strong—it is a large factor, but not the only one; i.e., the innateness of "God within," etc., are factors] to his experience, and his experience is not everything that an absolutely objective observer [or normatively subjective Christian observer] might find in the portion of the world within the individual's reach, but only what the individual himself finds. . . . If men define situations as real, they are real in their consequences (1927:68).

This quotation expresses the heart of Thomas's well-known "principle of the definition of the situation."

Now, as the bracketed notes indicate, the Christian sociologist would have to consider the impact of the innateness of God within on the definition of the situation. However, the thrust of Thomas's point is crucial for the *objective* Christian sociologist with a normatively Christian approach to bear in mind. Certainly the Christian sociologist would assert that certain operative causation/facilitation factors are contributing to the defining of the situation for the subject, and they are operative regardless of the subject's awareness of these factors. These factors are part of the subject's experience whether he or she is aware of them or not.

On the other hand, it is still important to realize that there are subjects who are not aware of, or conscious of, such operative factors and who then manifest consequences based on the "as ifness" of their definition of the situation.

Several points have been raised that are of crucial importance to

Politics

Christian sociologists as well as to Christians concerned about sociological and political issues. These are issues that revealed Christianity (the created order, Scripture, the person of Christ, and the Holy Spirit) addresses in varying degrees of specificity and intensity. Does the Christian perspective (recognizing there is great diversity of understanding and interpretation within Christendom), for example, address the following questions with particular definitions, directions, criteria, guidelines, judgment, affirmation, or condemnation?

How, and by whom, are material and nonmaterial needs to be defined and given priority? How, and by whom, are material and nonmaterial goods to be distributed and/or allocated? What are the criteria that determine equitable, fair, and just distribution? What are the criteria that determine the setting of priorities for needs and goods so that it is known which are more and which are less essential? What are the criteria for determining responsible versus wasteful stewardship of resources and goods? What are the criteria determining the responsible and moral use of power and the relationship of means to ends?

Are there biblical guidelines concerning the how and degree to which the masses as opposed to a select elite ought to participate in the political process? Are biblical guidelines available for the relationship that exists when a few are trustees for many (or, stated another way, when many are submissive to a few)? Are there guidelines, on the one hand, concerning the balance between law, order, and homogeneity to preserve stability, and, on the other hand, concerning permissiveness and heterogeneity to preserve individual integrity? Are there guidelines as to the functionality or dysfunctionality of conflict in the political process?

Can Christians be good politicians on the one hand and true to their faith on the other? Are there just wars? Should there be capital punishment if one considers biblical ethics and mandates? Are there "Christian" ways of using force or sanctions in general?

What are the appropriate activities of a Christian public office holder in a heterogeneous society consisting of many non-Christians and what is his commitment to the separation of church and state? Does the Christian understanding of the nature of the universe and of humanity, and man's predicament and the solution to it, have anything to say about carrying on political activities? Do Christians find themselves under certain mandates that those with a secular understanding do not recognize? (The items listed for Suggested Reading at the end of this chapter pursue these questions in detail.)

Rather than offering what would have to be simplistic answers to the above questions in this brief chapter, I would remind the reader that it is more important to also ask and pursue these questions. Asking the right questions is the key to meaningful answers. Hopefully, the reader will delve further into the sources of normative Christianity for specific direction.

In seeking to answer the above questions, we need to keep in mind the following biblical mandates: "Be fruitful and increase in number; fill the earth and subdue it. Rule over . . . every living creature" (Gen. 1:28); "God . . . gave us the ministry of reconciliation" (2 Cor. 5:18); God not only gave us the responsibility to recognize different gifts (1 Cor. 12:27–31) but also gave us the command to be good stewards of what we possess (Matt. 25:14–30). The "greatest commandment" is "Love the Lord your God with all your heart and with all your soul and with all your mind"; the "second" is "Love your neighbor as yourself" (Matt. 22:37–39). These biblical mandates, the ideal societal state suggested by Neubeck, and the vision that normative Christianity provides, all suggest deep political involvement. These criteria certainly suggest that material and nonmaterial needs must be given priority according to God's vision. God loves all people and treats all impartially, and these attitudes should be reflected in the use and distribution of life-chance opportunities. These criteria further suggest that political power ought not to be manifested to protect the interests of the few but rather those of the masses. God expects the church to be involved in these processes, and He appreciates diversity and different gifts and does not demand coerced homogeneity and dead leveling. Conflict is not necessarily bad but ought to be responsible and humane.

There have been Christians, particularly over the past two centuries, who have struggled with the kinds of questions cited above. These people have come from diverse backgrounds, have spoken from diverse perspectives, and have preferred diverse labels. There have been those who concluded that Christ and the early church were socialistic and that therefore politically sensitized Christians ought to have socialist alignments. Indeed, many carried the banner of Christian socialism. Others have developed a so-called "liberation theology," a "theology of hope," and have challenged Christians to see social change through effective political action. Still others have taken a "naturalistic providential" view of things, asserting that God was in control, that His will was naturally evolving toward fulfillment, that His "hidden hand" guided this development, and that the status quo therefore represented a stage in His plan. And some, for all practical purposes, dropped a sacred canopy over the status quo and assumed that "what is" represents God's will, otherwise the "is" would be "isn't"!

Space does not allow a thorough or even superficial treatment of all these voices. Therefore what follows is an example of one particular group of voices that endeavors to define and implement Christian politics. This group, though varying in emphases and methodologies, has often been designated as Christian socialists. This does not imply that politically concerned Christians or Christian sociologists must be socialists, or that all of those voices so categorized appreciate the label. However, a discussion of Christian socialism will help clarify some of the efforts and difficulties in attempting to define and implement Christian politics.

CHRISTIAN SOCIALISM

It is interesting to note that in the late 1800s and early 1900s, many Christian socialists in the United States were great promoters of value-laden sociology in universities and seminaries. They saw sociology as an obvious way for persons seriously interested in the betterment of society to develop perspectives and tools for an intelligent critique and reform of social injustices.

For example, Ralph Ely, a professor of economics first at Johns Hopkins University and later at the University of Wisconsin, encouraged the application of sociological studies to industrial problems. Christianity, for Ely, was summed up in what he saw in the two commandments cited by Jesus to love God and to love people. The first command gave us theology, while the second "when elaborated becomes social science or sociology" (Dombrowski, 1966:52). Ely suggested that theological students should spend half of their time studying sociology and that seminaries should become the intellectual centers for this discipline.

W. D. P. Bliss emerged as a key figure in the Society of Christian Socialists and a contemporary of Ely. In espousing that *all* of society had to be redeemed for the potentialities of life to be free and develop, Bliss said, "Long enough has the church tried to build the temple of God by polishing each stone without caring how the stones were laid together. . . . Society *moulds* individuals as truly as individuals mould society. To forget this has been the cardinal mistake of the church. . . . Sociology must be wedded to theology" (Dombrowski, 1966:103).

It is clear that when many Christian socialists urged the wedding of sociology and theology, they were promoting value-laden sociology and searching for revealed Christian criteria and assumptions that would direct their participation in sociology and politics.

These American voices were, however, preceded and influenced by many English voices. The early English Christian socialists such as Frederick Denison Maurice and Charles Kingsley advocated the establishment of cooperative workshops based on Christian principles. Their concerns grew out of the conflicts between Christian ideals and the manifestations and effects of competitive, capitalistic business and the problems associated with the industrial revolution.

An influence upon Kingsley and Maurice, and of import to sociologists concerned about politics and social justice, was Claude Henri de Rouvroy Saint-Simon (1760–1825), a French social philosopher, who as a young man served in the American Revolution as a volunteer with the colonists. He was concerned about the social injustices accompanying industrialization and called for the reorganization of society by scientists and industrialists on the basis of the "new Christianity." This new Christianity would entail a scientific division of labor resulting in automatic and spontaneous social harmony (or so he idealistically thought). In 1825 he wrote a book called *The New Christianity* in which he asserted that any hope for the development of true brotherhood must accompany scientific organization.

For all sociologists, it is significant to know that August Comte, the "father of sociology," was for a time a pupil of Saint-Simon in his salon for scientists. Compte's credo was "to know in order to predict and to predict in order to control." And his interest was in developing a science of humankind to help in moving toward the creation of "the good society." (Coser and Rosenberg, 1976). Saint-Simon's influence on Comte is obvious. Saint-Simonians promoted ideas of socialism, a federation of the nations of Europe, the abolition of individual inheritance rights, public control of means of production, and gradual emancipation of women (*The New Columbia Encyclopedia*, 1975:2402).

Christian socialism saw a revival in England at the end of the nineteenth century, and it appears that the primary motivations were twofold and interdependent. On the one hand, there were the problems of a rapidly industrializing society, with the accompanying problems of the Guilded Age, social injustices, inequitable distribution of resources and goods, and class stratification. These difficulties were accompanied by a materialistic, consumptive, secularized popular culture. On the other hand, there was the problem of the alienation of the masses from an organized religion that seemed to lose its relevancy, did not address the needs of the masses effectively, and did not have the sensate appeal of the new popular value structure. Therefore Christian socialists at the end of the nineteenth century were addressing the needs of an industrialized society and a faltering church.

Christian socialism at the end of the nineteenth century was a part of the general socialist and reform revival that included the social gospel, discoveries of science, biblical criticism, and comparative religion studies. However, it was certainly possible that Christians, like others, could become socialists for a variety of reasons. There were Christians who just happened to be socialists, and there were socialists who just happened to be Christians. However, others were peculiarly *Christian socialists*, that is, they were socialists *because* they were Christians. These people tried to develop uniquely Christian grounds for their socialist convictions. Peter Jones wrote a book in which he reviews the spokespersons from the various organizations involved. Jones believes that Christian socialists active during the end of the nineteenth century usually stood for one or more of these theological arguments, or variations of them:

1. From patristics: that many of the church fathers were socialists and communists.

2. From the New Testament and the ethics of the Sermon on the Mount: that Jesus Christ was a socialist.
3. From the sacraments and the Book of Common Prayer: that the modern church in its worship, symbol, and ritual exhibits a socialist faith.
4. From the doctrine of Divine Immanence: that God's presence everywhere in nature and in man, destroys the artificial distinction between the "sacred" and the "secular" worlds, sanctifies the material life, and supports the socialist call for a Kingdom of God on earth (1968:86–87).

At this point a major problem should be cited that runs through Christian socialism and involves Christians in politics in general. This is the common problem of translating a general, theoretical, and/or theological critique or analysis of societal conditions into realistic, implementable political programs and policies. Unfortunately, in former times, as now, it was much easier to critique and theorize than to develop and implement a political program that was pragmatically useful.

For example, Christian socialists in the United States made basically the same critiques as have been discussed above, but then often seemed afraid of the possible radical consequences of their call for justice. They therefore tended to espouse "gradualism" and "reformation," as opposed to "revolution," so that their call for change often amounted to little more than a plea for some vague "organic unity of the race" or piecemeal reform (Dombrowski, 1966:26).

Christian socialists appeared to have the same rather naïve understanding of individual, corporate, and organizational nature that still plagues us today and that tends to lead to promoting voluntary regulation as the way to solve our political problems. Such thought assumed that *good* will sort of evolve naturally as a stage in ongoing social evolution, with the help of logical, moral persuasion and humanity's natural capacity to respond to what is good. Such thought, it would appear, rests on a rather naive ahistoric and unbiblical understanding of humanity's sinfulness and the nature of corporations and organizations to seek the maximization of profits and self-interests.

Christian socialists tended, as politically involved Christians do today, to underestimate the resistance of selfish vested-interest groups. Therefore Dombrowski's observation is as relevant to our present conditions as it was when referring to the past century. "When the good-will ethic was translated into a practical strategy, it took the form of upholding law and order and opposing all forms of rebellion and revolt. The end result was that social Christianity was delivered into the hands of the ruling class as one more instrument for keeping the proletarian group quiescent" (Dombrowski, 1966:26).

Politically concerned Christians are readily "co-opted," to use a good sociological term. Early Christian socialists suffered from a disease similar to that of many contemporary optimistic, idealistic, and naïve Christian reformers. They underestimated the power and resistance of entrenched vested-interest groups, especially in the corporate realm, that knew it was to their advantage to leave things as they were. Entrenched vested-interest groups do not readily respond to moral, humanitarian persuasion if it threatens to undermine their advantaged positions.

What follows is an example of a politically concerned Christian who manifested these two basic tendencies: on the one hand, to be caught up in the difficulty of developing and implementing a political program that was realistic and pragmatically useful; on the other hand, to believe in the methodology of logical moral persuasion in a rather naïve manner. William Carwardine was a Methodist minister who espoused a form of Christian socialism during the Pullman strike of 1894. He referred to his position as "applied Christianity, the gospel of mutual recognition, of cooperation, of the 'brotherhood of humanity'" (Carwardine, 1894:123). Carwardine encouraged government regulation unlike George Pullman, president of the Pullman Company. In his stand Carwardine also was unlike many corporate executives today who urge the government to stay out of regulation and depend on voluntary controls and who promote governmental laissez-faire (hands off) policies and competition. Here is a contemporary substantive and normative issue: What is the extent of competition today, and is competition Christian? Carwardine was realistic enough to realize the necessity to play the game of power politics, that is, to organize and get important and powerful people on his side.

Because of the negative connotations of Marxian socialism for many people, Carwardine constantly separated himself from that approach. He recommended what he called the "socialism of the Sermon on the Mount," which encouraged the "love of neighbor as one's self." The problem here, of course, is the problem cited throughout our discussion of Christian socialism and Christian politics in general; that is, the problem of translating such general, idealistic phrases as the "socialism of the Sermon on the Mount" into actual political programs and policies concerning resource distribution.

It is one thing to say Jesus Christ was a great political economist, who espoused various social, moral, and economic teachings; it is another thing to define just what this means in the realm of resource distribution programs and policies. Certainly, the Christian community today still lacks consensus on this issue.

CHRISTIANS AND POLITICS: CONTEMPORARY IMPLICATIONS

There are still Christians seeking political involvement in the tradition of Maurice, Kingsley, Carwardine, and others. At the Christian-Marxist dialogue conference at Rosemont College in Philadelphia during May 26–28, 1978, expressions of Christian socialism were heard. One can read *Religious Socialism*, a quarterly newsletter of the Religion and Socialism Committee of the Democratic Socialist Organizing Committee and find that elements of Christian socialism are still alive today. There are still assertions that American democracy is a facade for the rule of the oppressing class; there are assertions that we need "democratic centralism" and affirmations that long before Marx the Hebrew prophets had provided sharp class analyses that Jesus Christ and the early church fathers further developed. Still other Christians, whose ideas are expressed in the periodical *Sojourners*, advocate political critique and involvement but do not identify with Christian socialism as such.

There is considerable diversity among Christians who seek political relevancy and activism and who appeal to a variety of rationales, criteria, and values. Yet they do have something in common—their assumptions and hypotheses at the start, and their proposals at the end, are value laden. After all, can anyone who would desire to move from point A to point B do anything other than make value judgments as to why we should move from point A to point B and then theorize as to the correct way to make the move?

Politically concerned and involved Christians have stressed the necessity for anyone to be value-directed who would get active in sociology and apply its principles to problems of resource, goods production, and distribution. Such persons also illustrate the problems involved in the process: the selection of norms and criteria for value judgments; the translation of idealism into programs; not letting what "we would like things to be" stand in the way of "seeing what is"; and, finally, moving from critique to programs and policies that are in fact capable of implementation.

It is absolutely necessary that Christians in general, and Christian sociologists in particular, become involved in the development of *radically Christian sociology*. By the emphasized phrase I mean that it is not enough to say Christian sociology is simply Christians doing sociology as anyone else would; instead, Christians must seek the implications for sociology of the biblical understanding of the nature of the universe and humanity, the human predicament, and the solution to that predicament. Christians must also engage in the struggle to discover just what this means in terms of political theorizing, critique, and action. To fail to integrate our faith, theory, and political involvement is to join those who for too long have dined sumptuously at intellectual feasts that feature accumulated knowledge served under glass!

A *radically Christian sociology*, then, would be rooted in constant reference to revealed Christianity, the created order, Scripture, the person of Christ, and the Holy Spirit. It must address itself to a uniquely Christian understanding of the nature of the universe and humanity, to a diagnosis of the human condition, and to a prescription for reconciling that condition. The *radically Christian sociologist* must be convinced that he or she operates from a normativity, a reference point of the highest truthfulness and certainty that is based on the revelation of God himself as Creator and Lord.

It would appear that at a minimum a Christian sociologist would refer to the following operative assumptions and then seek to discover and define their implications for the doing of politics.

God exists. "In the beginning God created the heavens and the earth" (Gen. 1:1).

221

All that is reflects God's design or permission. "In the beginning was the Word, and the Word was with God, and the Word was God. He was with God in the beginning. Through him all things were made; without him nothing was made that has been made" (John 1:1–3).

God is good and His creation is good. After the various acts of creation are these words: "And God saw that it was good" (Gen. 1:10, 12, 18, 21, 25, 31).

God is sovereign. "Our God is in heaven; he does whatever pleases him" (Ps. 115:3).

God is transcendent and immanent. "Since what may be known about God is plain to them, because God has made it plain to them. For since the creation of the world God's invisible qualities—his eternal power and divine nature—have been clearly seen, being understood from what has been made, so that men are without excuse." (Rom. 1:19–20).

Humanity is made in God's image and is therefore good; the human social order is therefore good. "Then God said, 'Let us make man in our image, in our likeness, and let them rule. . . .' So God created man in his own image. . . . God . . . said to them, 'Be fruitful and increase in number; fill the earth and subdue it. Rule . . .' God saw all that he had made, and it was very good" (Gen. 1:26–31).

Humanity has the capacity to choose and abuse; humanity has the capacity to love, express freedom, and be self-aware. "'For God knows that when you eat of it your eyes will be opened, and you will be like God, knowing good and evil.' When the woman saw that the fruit of the tree was good for food and pleasing to the eye, and also desirable for gaining wisdom, she took some and ate it. She also gave some to her husband, . . . and he ate it" (Gen. 3:5–6).

Abuse of freedom and choice via the criteria revealed in creation, the prophets, the law, the Scriptures, the Holy Spirit, and God incarnate in Jesus Christ further compounds humanity's state of sin. "For if the message spoken by angels was binding, and every violation and disobedience received its just punishment, how shall we escape if we ignore such a great salvation?" (Heb. 2:2–3).

Since humanity is sinful, human interaction and institutions—the total social order—is affected by sin and out of harmony with God. "As it is written: 'There is no one righteous, not even one'" (Rom.

3:10); "They are darkened in their understanding and separated from the life of God because of the ignorance that is in them due to the hardening of their hearts" (Eph. 4:18).

There is hope of renewal for humanity and the social order due to God's love; this is possible through repentance, conversion, and faith in Jesus the Christ, the Messiah, the Atoner, God incarnate. "Repent, then, and turn to God, so that your sins may be wiped out, that times of refreshing may come from the Lord, and that he may send the Christ, who has been appointed for you—Jesus" (Acts 3:19–20).

Christ makes atonement (at oneness with God) possible for individuals and the social order through His life, teachings, atoning death, and resurrection. "Therefore, if anyone is in Christ, he is a new creation; the old has gone, the new has come!" (2 Cor. 5:17).

Redeemed humanity can manifest redemption in the social order and is obligated to do so, reconciling brokenness in individuals and their structures. "All this is from God, who reconciled us to himself through Christ and gave us the ministry of reconciliation. . . . We are therefore Christ's ambassadors, as though God were making his appeal through us" (2 Cor. 5:18–20).

Though individuals and social structures are sinful, they are capable of redemption and being brought toward perfection. Christians are to be in the process of becoming more like their heavenly Father, and God's future kingdom on earth is the divine ideal for the social order. "Be perfect, therefore, as your heavenly Father is perfect" (Matt. 5:48) (Cobb, 1979:17–26).

It appears rather obvious that these fundamental Christian assumptions have many implications for anyone involved in sociology in terms of theorizing, conceptualizing, defining, describing, analyzing, hypothesizing, attributing causation, suggesting correction, manifesting empathy and yet judgment, and other activities. The Christian sociologist and the Christian lay person alike, in seeking political relevance—whether developing political policy, critique, implementation, or counsel—must do so within a framework of "givens" derived from revealed Christianity. A politically involved Christian, appealing to such criteria, will inevitably be prophetic, a function painfully needed. Of the priestly and prophetic functions, there has been an overabundance of the priestly, and a dearth of the prophetic!

DISCUSSION QUESTIONS

1. This chapter points out that the "power elite" come from the same backgrounds, intermingle freely, and interchange positions. Do you believe this is good or bad? Why?
2. Do you agree or disagree with those sociologists who say the ordinary American citizen has very little power? Why?
3. How would you evaluate Neubeck's eight ideals for American society? Naive? Socialism? Biblical? Why? (If you prefer another descriptive term, which one?)
4. Do you believe Christianity and socialism can be joined? Why?
5. Should Christians be willing to live within the rules of any political order that allows them freedom to worship? Should they strive to "redeem" the political order? Why?

SUGGESTED READING

Robert G. Clouse, Robert D. Linder, and Richard V. Pierard (eds.), *Protest and Politics: Christianity and Contemporary Affairs* (Greenwood, S.C.: Attic, 1968). A series of essays dealing with such topics as, "How can a Christian be in politics?" "Communism, realism, and Christianity," "Christianity in public schools," and "Responsibility of the Christian voter." Good reading.

G. William Domhoff, *The Higher Circles: The Governing Class in America* (New York: paper, Vintage Books, 1971). This book clearly explains and extends the Mills thesis concerning the power and influence of power elites related to the naive belief in government by and for the people in general.

Robert D. Linder (ed.), *God and Caesar: Case Studies in the Relationship Between Christianity and the State* (Terre Haute, Ind.: Indiana State University, Department of History. Conference on Faith and History, 1971). Several good case studies in the relationship between Christianity and the state.

C. Wright Mills, *The Power Elite* (New York: Oxford University Press, 1956). The classic and still very contemporary statement of the power and influence of the powerful few to the detriment of the larger whole, still expressed by Domhoff and others.

Michael Parenti, *Power and the Powerless* (New York: St. Martin's Press, 1978). A good treatment of the meaning, use, and abuse of power; the decline of pluralism and the organization of wealth; the legitimatizing of class dominance and its influence in the rule of institutions; democracy as a ritual.

Leslie Stevenson, *Seven Theories on Human Nature* (New York: Oxford University Press, 1974). A short but thought-provoking book that summarizes, compares, and contrasts seven perspectives on, on the one hand, understanding the nature of the universe and humanity, and, on the other hand, the human predicament and its solution. The Christian perspective is included and stimulates further development of the political implications of such a perspective.

Robert E. Webber, *The Secular Saint* (Grand Rapids: Zondervan, 1979). An interesting treatment of Christian social responsibility from an evangelical perspective. Webber discusses and critiques three models found in evangelical circles.

12

MARILYN J. WELDIN
St. Paul Bible College,
Minnesota

CHARLES E. WELDIN
St. Paul Public Schools,
Minnesota

EDUCATION

"Each generation of teachers, pupils, and adult laymen should feel a responsibility to improve schooling for the current generation . . . and establish models for generations to come" (Doll, 1974:3). Every society is the product of past generations of education and serves as a catalyst for the future.

The institution of education involves both formal and informal learning settings. The formal programs range from preschool to higher education, including all age groups. They are diverse in nature and purpose within each society and from one culture to another. Yet all societies are a part of a world of unprecedented complexity and changes that affect the institution of education. The family, church, school, economics, and government of industrial societies influence each other. Preliterate societies tend to be less influenced than industrial societies, which require interdependence for survival.

Contemporary events or situations may become factors that educators cannot ignore. This has been true, for example, of the problem of the American hostages in Iran, the Arab-Israeli conflict in the Middle East, the upheavals in the developing countries of

Africa and South America, environmental concern in industrial nations, and world-wide problems such as racism, hunger, and disease. Some of the most important educational changes in this century have occurred since the Russian launching of Sputnik I in 1957.

FUNCTIONS OF EDUCATION

The institution of education must be society centered and person centered. The functions of education serve to transmit the existing culture, develop new knowledge, and to equip each individual to function within the society. Education is interrelated to economics and government, but is more closely related to the family and religion.

Functions serving society. The continuance and stability of any society depend to a large degree on the persistent performance of activities by members in that society. However simple or complex, any society must have a means of communication through language. In a developed society, language is both spoken and written and differentiates in syntax, vocabulary, and pronunciation.

Each society must have a division of labor based on ability, training, and expertise. Status-role assignment depends to a large extent on birth, intelligence, and education. Likewise, social stratification will reflect the values ascribed to these factors within each society.

In preliterate societies, division of labor is based primarily on sex and age. Technology is primitive and job-related skills are learned through imitation. Education is informal. Children learn through observation, storytelling, and prescribed customs and ceremonies. The educational process is an integral part of daily life through normal patterns of behavior, and the cultural transmission occurs without conscious effort. In primitive societies a person can have an understanding of most of the knowledge, traditions, and arts of that society. In a modern society the volume of information is too massive for one person to master.

From the earliest recorded history of man through the present, preindustrial societies have existed where education is noncompulsory. In some societies that have a written language, only select members are taught to read and write. Children from wealthy families and a few highly gifted children are permitted to attend formal schools. In Bible days literacy for the masses of Greeks, Romans, and Jews was unheard of. During the Middle Ages in Europe, formal schools were founded and operated by the Roman Catholic church for sons of the elite families who wished to enter such professions as the priesthood, teaching, or law. About 85 percent of the population were serfs receiving no formal education; so the transmission of the culture occurred in the same way as in preliterate societies.

Until World War I university education in Europe was reserved for those of the privileged classes. The goal was to develop aristocrats. In the primarily agricultural society, manual labor by the masses was seen as more essential than literacy.

Even today in some preindustrial societies, education is noncompulsory. Dressler points out that in Nepal, 85 percent of its population are illiterate (1976:342).

When societies become industrialized, technology becomes more sophisticated and there is increased complexity in the division of labor. Uneducated persons are in less demand while educated members with specialized skills are needed for the survival of the industrialized society.

Change is related to new knowledge. Most societies rely heavily on institutions of higher learning such as colleges and universities to develop and transmit new knowledge. Researchers are awarded grants to permit a wide variety of studies ranging from human behavior to new energy sources and ways to improve efficiency. The use of the scientific method insures a systematic way to investigate a problem and gather information with maximum objectivity and consistency.

In addition to the functions of transmission of culture and the acquisition of new knowledge, education in a modern society will help to preserve the status quo, delay the entry of young members into the labor market, and procure persons into occupational positions.

Functions serving the individual. Among the functions affecting an individual through formal educational programs, four benefits are the most important.

Providing custodial care is the first benefit to be noted. The average child in the United States spends about one thousand hours a year in school. Some services that were once performed by the home are now being provided by the school. For example, for a nominal charge or fee, many children receive a hot lunch at noon and some schools even provide breakfast. Sex education, once discussed only in the home, is now a normal part of the curriculum of most public schools. The priorities and wealth of the school system determines the amount and kind of physical and psychological care a child receives. Most schools provide medical screening and tests for vision and hearing. Dental and speech therapists, nurses, and psychologists are a part of the regular staff.

The federal Public Law 94-142, passed 29 November 1975, assures that all handicapped children between ages three and eighteen will have available to them a free appropriate public education. Leeper, Skipper, and Witherspoon stress that a tremendous responsibility is placed on the care centers and schools to aid parents through providing care and teaching, for children are the hope of the future (1979:11).

A second benefit received by individuals in school is that each person is helped to *gain knowledge, skills, and understandings* that build a foundation for making the numerous choices throughout life. The basic three Rs are expected to be learned along with a wide variety of subjects and skills. Education is the primary means by which persons gain knowledge and skills that will influence their place in society and their social mobility. The continual evaluative process in terms of performances in various areas of school life aids the student in gaining insight into himself or herself. The record of these evaluations often serves to aid or hinder the person in the larger society.

A third area of benefit in education is that it *channels students into occupations* that will influence their social positions during the rest of their lives. Interests, values, abilities, efforts, and opportunities all influence the person's choices. Since American schools tend to focus on middle class values and styles of life, children from foreign countries or from low-income families tend to be at some disadvantage. Most school systems provide special programs to accommodate these children. Through the guidance of a professional staff, the student can discover his or her own strengths and weaknesses. Interests and talents are more closely defined. The problem of selecting an occupation from the thousands of possibilities could be overwhelming. Yet schools can help the individual to become aware of those possibilities that match the individual's interests and capabilities.

A fourth benefit is that schools tend to *promote a youth subculture*. Children are socialized through the peer group as well as through educators. Teen-agers try to behave like other teen-agers. This becomes apparent through observing their styles of dress, speech, and activities. During adulthood the tendency is for subcultures, styles of life, and occupations to be factors that promote variant norms and values; and the latter tend to distinguish a group of people from others in the culture.

THE ORGANIZATION OF EDUCATION

Education in an industrial society is big business. In most countries of the world, schools are run by one central agency, usually the church or the government. In the United States the public schools are under the control of the state boards of education, and these boards give local districts the major responsibility for decision making. Teachers are certified by the state and must meet the standards required by law. The school administrators work under the guidance of the local school board. "Ninety-five percent of the school boards in the United States are elected, usually in a nonpartisan special election" (Rich, 1974:200). The functions of the school board include selecting the superintendent, establishing educational policy, developing the school budget, determining salary schedules, and allocating funds for buildings and equipment (Rich, 1974).

The main source for funding education is through local property taxes, but there has been an increase in the contributions given by state and federal governments. Both federal and state support has been given in the form of indirect assistance that provides for such things as buildings, supplies, equipment, food, and special programs. It is recognized that the influence of the federal government is great, and federal laws pertaining to schools, such as laws against sex or racial discrimination, are often enforced through the threat to withhold funds.

The organizational structure of American education is multiphasic and can be viewed from many perspectives. Three aspects will be considered.

Age level. Public schools maintain an educational program for all children from first through high school, and in most states kindergarten through high school. Increased support has been given to preschool. Day-care programs are offered and in some states there is college and vocational training available to students, either free or partially subsidized. Adult educational programs of many kinds encourage continuing formal opportunities for learning throughout life.

The values of education in America are deeply embedded in our culture. Americans believe that education is a good thing for all citizens. So strong is this value that laws require all children to attend school at least to age sixteen. Americans are practical minded and want education to do specific and observable things for the individual. Competition is emphasized; yet democracy and equality of opportunity are important themes throughout American education.

Curriculum structure. It is misleading to discuss similarity in public schools without pointing out diversity. Local control creates considerable diversity in the quality of programs. All schools provide instruction in the basic skills of reading, writing, and mathematics. There is great diversity in curriculum content and instructional methods. Curriculum content reflects the influence of class, racial, and ethnic considerations.

The launching of Sputnik I stirred the nation to cite presumed deficiencies in the schools at all levels. The federal government responded with larger-scale efforts to stimulate improved teaching in specifically designated areas. Because the government assumed that deficiencies were in such areas as science, mathematics, and foreign languages, it poured vast resources into curriculum development and academic in-service education for those subjects.

During the 1960s the nation's social problems led to civil rights movements and the formation of pressure groups for certain racial/ethnic minorities. Often public schools became the designated social institution for correcting social ills. Educators tended to approach curriculum development in a patchwork, piecemeal fashion as a reaction to events rather than an action toward positive, purposeful change. Inlow points out that the curriculum of the public schools has developed cumulatively through time;

however, for the most part, the development has occurred as products of convenience and expediency rather than through a prior plan that included the process for effective curricular design (1973:40). Dressel confirmed that institutions of higher education have generally muddled through crises with minor modification or stopgap procedures rather than by researching according to basic assumptions and principles (1963:39).

In the 1970s Silberman maintained that there was a "crisis in the classroom"; his prime denunciation of the "grim, repressive, joyless places most schools are now" was documented by vivid examples of incidents he observed in diverse schools (1970:122). As a reason for this, Silberman cited mindlessness—"a failure to think seriously or deeply about the purposes or consequences of education" (1970:73). He argued that schools can be humane and still educate, can be child centered as well as subject centered, and can stress esthetic and moral education without weakening the three Rs.

Following the negative and critical appraisals of the schools during the 1960s and 1970s, educators attempted to conceptualize and develop alternatives. LaBell (Goodlad, 1975:30) placed the various approaches into three categories according to their primary objectives: (1) relevance, or educational responsiveness to human needs and problems; (2) efficiency, or fiscal responsibility; and (3) equality, or equal opportunity to gain access to societal resources and to participate in societal decision making.

Fantini stressed that education on all levels should provide alternatives for all students. His alternatives were placed on a continuum of seven major divisions from freedom to prescriptive. It is possible to analyze the curriculum design of both public and private schools through Fantini's model:

1. Free: Learner-directed and controlled. Learner has complete freedom to orchestrate his own education. Teacher is one resource.
2. Free-Open: Opening of school to the community and its resources. Noncompetitive environment. No student failures. Curriculum is viewed as social system rather than as course of studies. Learner-centered.
3. Open: Learner has considerable freedom to choose from a wide range of content areas considered relevant by teacher, parent and student. Resource centers in major skill areas made available to learner. Teacher is supportive guide.

4. Open-Modified: Teacher-student planning. Teacher centered.
5. Modified: Prescribed content is made more flexible through individualization of instruction; school is ungraded; students learn same thing but at different rates. Using team teaching, teachers plan a differentiated approach to the same content. Teacher and programmed course of study are the major sources of student learning.
6. Modified-Standard: Competitive environments. School is the major instructional setting. Subject matter-centered.
7. Standard: Learner adheres to institution requirements uniformly prescribed what is to be taught—how, when, where, and with whom. Teacher is instructor-evaluator. Student passes or fails according to normative standards (1973:447–48).

Sponsorship. Private schools are controlled through a local church board or another designated committee and are usually subject to denominational or sponsoring group requirements. Funding for the operation of private schools comes through tuition, gifts, grants, and fund-raising campaigns. Little or none of the support is provided through state or federal taxation. Parents who send their children to private schools find themselves paying double, since they pay both taxes and tuition.

HISTORICAL REVIEW

Education had an integral part in the life of God's chosen people, the Hebrews. Mason says, "Through the temple rites on the great feast days, the synagogue with its reading and interpreting of the Scriptures, faithful instruction in the home, and emphasis upon teachers and teaching, the faith of Israel was preserved" (Hakes, 1964:25). Children received education by their parents' instruction through symbolism and religious rites. Hebrew values and norms were passed on to each generation. The rabbi, the Jewish teacher, was given a high status position. The synagogues were schools of instruction as well as worship.

Jesus is referred to as teaching thirty-one times in the Gospels and He referred to Himself as a Teacher five times. As the master Teacher, He used such basic methods of teaching as lecture, discussion, questioning, object lessons, storytelling, and drama. The basic methods of teaching used by Christ were practiced throughout the centuries and continued to be evident during the early Colonial Period in America; educators still use these methods today.

233

The strong religious beliefs of the pioneers encouraged a child to learn to read so that the Bible could be read and understood. In 1642 the General Court of Massachusetts enacted a law that "encouraged" citizens to provide for their children's education; then in 1647 another law "required" towns to provide for the education of youth.

Throughout the colonies a wide variety of elementary schools sprang up, but all had some religious curriculum. The first secondary school was established at Boston in 1635; and in 1636, Harvard, the first college, was founded for the purpose of preparing ministers.

The aims and objectives of American public education have gradually changed over the years. The schools have moved from a religious orientation to a secular emphasis. Prayer in public schools is now forbidden. The numerous problems in the public school system have caused many parents to seek private education.

The modern Bible college movement grew out of the need for trained lay and semiprofessional workers to supplement the regular ministry. In 1881 A. B. Simpson founded the first Bible college, which was named Nyack Missionary College. Five years later (1886), D. L. Moody founded the Moody Bible Institute. These two schools became the pattern for many other similar schools. The two-year courses of the 1920s and 1930s were expanded to three-year programs, and later to four-year degree programs (Witmer, 1964:379–91).

Today a typical Bible college, like a Christian liberal arts college, contains three subject areas—biblical, general, and professional. At the beginning the Bible college movement lacked in commonly accepted standards and professional association. Ten of the schools were recognized by state boards of education and other accrediting agencies. As schools steadily moved in the direction of collegiate institutions by lengthening their programs and offering more general education, the need for an accrediting agency became apparent. In 1947 the Accrediting Association of Bible Institutes and Bible Colleges was organized, and in 1957 the name was changed to Accrediting Association of Bible Colleges (AABC) (*AABC Manual*, 1957:7).

GROWTH OF EVANGELICAL CHRISTIAN SCHOOLS[1]

Private evangelical Christian elementary and secondary schools constitute the fastest-growing segment in American education. While some authors accuse "Christian" schools of being segregation academies, recent research indicates that the motivation behind this new growth of schools is more complex than escaping racially integrated public schools. It is most difficult to judge the motives of parents who move their children from public schools to private schools. It is possible that sometimes racism may be the reason for the change.

A basic difference in philosophy that relates to the nature of the human species brings sharp differences between the evangelical Christian school and the public school educator, not only in what should be taught, but in how content should be assimilated. John Dewey, the father of American secular education, held that the child is inherently good. Christian evangelicals hold to the Scriptures, which teach that man is by nature lost and sinful. Romans 3:23 says, "For all have sinned and fall short of the glory of God." Man is totally depraved and is therefore in need of salvation. This conversion takes place when the individual places his or her faith in the substitutionary death and resurrection of Jesus Christ. The experience of salvation moves one from the lost, unsaved group into the family of God. Strict discipline, Bible reading, prayer, and a return to the "basics" characterize the Christian Protestant schools. (Those clientele of the Christian Protestant schools decry the secular humanism, lack of discipline, and inferior quality of teaching of the three Rs in public education.)

No matter what the subject, the Christian teacher must know the Scriptures and, under the direction of the Holy Spirit, skillfully

---

[1]Several terms are used in current research to describe these schools. Some terms used are fundamentalist schools, Christian schools, Protestant evangelical schools, Protestant fundamentalist schools, and private schools. Frequently, writers use the terms synonymously; however, at times clear distinctions are made between some fundamentalist schools and other schools that are referred to as Christian. There is great diversity among these schools. Therefore, for purposes of this research, the term Christian Protestant schools will be used as a general term that applies to all private Protestant schools, unless otherwise quoted by various authors.

apply them to achieve an intellectually honest integration. Thus all parts of the formal curriculum in the Christian school have their first point of reference in the Word of God, draw their materials from the Bible wherever possible, and return to the Bible with their accumulation of facts for interpretation and practical application as illustrated in the diagram by Byrne (1961:67).

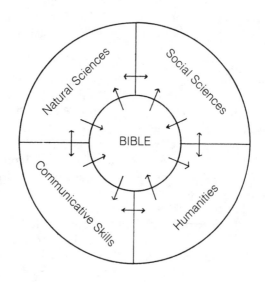

John Dewey's teaching that human nature is basically good and that the child will naturally seek the highest level is seen as in direct opposition to the teachings of Scripture.

A difference in values causes the focus of the public school and the Christian Protestant school to be visibly *different*. State and federal control of the Christian Protestant schools is rejected by teachers and administrators in those schools. Legislation that prescribes mainstreaming and nonsexist practices and policies do not apply to the private schools. Court cases have successfully challenged the right of the state to regulate Christian schools in Ohio, Vermont, Kentucky, and North Carolina. Fundamentalist groups resist any attempts of the state or federal government to impose any regulations (Nordin and Turner, 1979:394). The issue has not been finally resolved, and so there will be further court tests to determine whether or not the state and/or federal government should be excluded from some kind of control in the Christian Protestant schools.

Paradoxically, the Christian school movement is exploding at a time when other segments of private education are recording a decline (Kienel, 1974:14). Most Christian Protestant schools refuse to make public their enrollment figures. Exact figures are difficult to obtain because these schools belong to one of four major organizations: the National Association of Christian Schools, the American Association of Christian Schools, the Association of Christian Schools International, and Christian Schools International.

Evangelical Bible-believing Christians are establishing Christian schools, preschool through high school, at the rate of two new schools a day in the United States. On 28 October 1976, Tim LaHaye predicted before a convention audience of 3,178 Christian school educators in California that by 1990, if present trends continue, 51 percent of the students in America will be educated in Christian schools (Kienel, 1978:1).

A study of Christian Protestant schools in Wisconsin and Kentucky indicated that parents and administrators insisted that they were not opposed to integrated education. It was found that more than 90 percent of the students enrolled in such schools in these two states were white and fewer than 2 percent were black. No black teachers were employed by fundamentalist schools in either state (Phi Delta Kappan, February 1980:392).

EDUCATIONAL ISSUES

Both public and private schools are affected by social issues that lead to educational concerns. Three issues will be discussed that have caused Christians to wrestle with the implications.

Mainstreaming. The Education for All Handicapped Children Act of 1975, also known as Public Law 94-142, requires the state and local governments to provide:

1. identification programs that find and evaluate all handicapped children in each area;
2. a special education designed to fit each child's needs, while the child maintains normal school activities as much as possible;
3. related services including transportation, diagnosis and treatment needed to help each child get an education.

Public Law 94-142 affects students who require special education and related services due to physical or sensory handicaps and/or intellectual or emotional problems. Physical or sensory handicaps include speech handicaps, hearing impairments, visual handicaps, and physical disabilities. Intellectual or emotional problems include mental retardation, learning handicaps, emotional disturbances, and multiple handicaps.

School systems must adapt to meet the needs of their handicapped students. Training must be provided for teachers and other personnel who deal with students. Regular teachers will learn how to teach children with special needs. Special education teachers must be trained to meet the new demand. Academic and vocational courses of study must be adapted for handicapped students. The level of achievement, age, and handicapping condition of the student is to be considered in the learning process. School buildings must be opened to all handicapped students. This includes ramps, low drinking fountains, bathrooms to accommodate wheelchairs, low telephone seats, and elevators.

Related services that public schools must now provide are defined in six categories: (1) diagnostic medical services; (2) transportation; (3) speech pathology and audiology; (4) psychological services; (5) therapy; and (6) recreation.

The role of parents in educational planning for their handicapped children has been greatly changed. The school no longer makes an educational plan and tells parents and students what that plan is to be. Parents have the right to be consulted before the school makes a decision about their child. Parents have access to all records that pertain to their child's education evaluation and placement. They have the right to object to the school's decision about their child and may demand a hearing. Parents should be involved in the design of the individual educational plan (IEP) for their child.

St. Paul Public Schools, St. Paul, Minnesota, is a forerunner in setting a model for the implementation of the process of facilitating the intent of Public Law 94-142. The model designed by St. Paul is nationally recognized.

Since Christian Protestant schools are exempt from government control, mainstreaming does not have to be addressed. Most Christian Protestant schools do not offer specialized programs and can reject children with special handicaps. Christian Protestant schools need to address the following needs: (1) How can special educational needs, such as the mentally handicapped, be met? (2) What provision should be made for the physically handicapped? (3) What should a parent do when he or she cannot in good conscience send the child to public school because of a conflict in philosophy when his or her child's needs are not being met in a private school? (4) What is the Christian private school's obligation in meeting the individual needs of students?

SEXISM—TITLE IX

Title IX of the Education Amendments of 1972 says, "No person . . . shall, on the basis of sex, be excluded from participation in, be denied the benefits of, or be subjected to discrimination under any education program or activity receiving federal financial assistance."

Three terms need to be clarified in order to deal with the problem.

Sexism. This term refers to the degree to which an individual's beliefs or behaviors are prejudiced on the basis of sex. When an institution such as a school is sexist, it reflects prejudice on the basis of sex in its policies, in its practices, and in the way it is structured.

Sex-role stereotype. This term assumes that the male half of our population has in common one set of abilities, interests, and roles; and the female half of our population has in common another set of abilities, interests, values, and roles. Sex-role stereotyping reflects oversimplified attitudes about males and females. It completely ignores individual differences. For example, the belief that all or most boys are good in math and science is a sex-role stereotype. The belief that all or most girls are quiet and passive is another sex-role stereotype.

Sex discrimination. This is the denial of opportunity, privilege, role, or reward on the basis of sex. When a school practices sex discrimination, it excludes persons or treats them differently on the basis of sex. Discrimination may affect either males or females. A school policy that allows only girls to take home economics is one example of sex discrimination; one that gives boys first choice of athletic activities is another.

Sexism in the schools can be identified by examining the following components found in the schools: books; ways teachers teach; ways counselors counsel; sex segregation; vocational education; physical education and athletics; extracurricular activities; and staffing patterns.

The issue of sexism in the church is one of many major concerns. While there is agreement among evangelicals regarding the inspiration and authority of the Bible, vast differences are evident in the interpretation and application of God's Word. What is a biblical absolute and what is a cultural factor? When the Scripture speaks of slaves and masters, does that mean that every society must have slavery? When the Bible speaks of a male-dominant and male-centered society, is it saying Christians must always live in a society similar to that of Jesus' day? Fraser put it this way: "God does not insist that His people live in male-dominated, polygamous, sheep-herding families. Nor does He insist that they gather in male-led sanctuaries that exclude Gentiles and women from its central worship and teaching" (Hestenes and Curley, 1979:140).

The exegesis of such biblical passages as 1 Corinthians 11:1–15; 14:33–36; and 1 Timothy 2:9–15 often is done in such a way as to limit women in the use of spiritual gifts. Some groups believe that the roles of males and females are as God ordained. Others see culture as ascribing the roles, with biological factors the only major difference.

In many churches and church-related schools, people are strapped into a limited space of ministry and growth because they were born female. Sex-role stereotypes are reinforced and promoted at the expense of personal freedom to develop and grow into a whole person.

Many Christian Protestant schools need to examine their practice and philosophy regarding sexism. Answers to the following questions should be honestly sought in view of total biblical teaching: (1) Does God give the gifts of the Spirit according to sex? (2) What is the role of a woman in leadership? (3) What are the God-ordained differences between boys and girls, and between women and men? (4) Are certain courses offered only to boys? Only to girls? If so, why?

PRIVATE SCHOOLS VERSUS PUBLIC SCHOOLS

Private schools. Kienel says, "The Christian school educational environment is not perfect . . . but . . . it is nearer what God would have us provide for our children than is available in the secular educational world, where God and His Word are not welcome" (1974:97).

Proponents of the Christian Protestant schools accept that specific approach to learning for a variety of reasons. Parents feel that the schools really belong to them; religious instruction is an integral part of the learning process; discipline is more precise and more consistently enforced; the basics (reading, writing, and mathematics) are stressed; jointly accepted convictions about social do's and don'ts are enforced and patriotism is taught.

The Christian philosophy of education states that there should be no fundamental differences between what the school and the home and the church are trying to accomplish. All are trying to educate children in the fear of the Lord, which is the essence of wisdom (DeJong, 1977:119).

Parents of students in Christian Protestant schools are willing to pay tuition, accept a limited curriculum, have less alternatives, and forego the benefits of racially integrated education. They believe that God and the Scriptures should be at the center of learning. The following guide on "How to Shop for a Christian School" was prepared by *Eternity Magazine* (1980:9:27).

> Don't ask all these questions at once, but select a few that match your child's unique needs.
> 1. In what ways does the school combine Christianity and learning? (Answers will range from a modest "required chapel" to a quite sophisticated program of seeking God's truth in all subjects.)
> 2. What are the discipline procedures? Under what circumstances would a child be suspended or expelled?
> 3. What is the average number of years the faculty has been teaching? (Look for some seasoned veteran teachers, not a whole staff just out of college.)
> 4. How many present faculty have been here five or more years? (High turnover of staff indicates a problem.)
> 5. Are the teachers required to accept the authority of Scripture or are they merely "Christian" in a general civilized sense?
> 6. What minority groups are enrolled here?
> 7. Must all children come from Christian homes or are some non-Christian homes represented? (Some parents prefer a mix, especially since it may indicate a respect for the academic standards of the school.)
> 8. What rules will my child be expected to follow? Is there a dress code or a student handbook we could look over? (Watch for a wide

variation between home and school, then note if your individual child will respond favorably or unfavorably.)

9. What percentage of last year's students are returning this year?
10. To what colleges have recent high school graduates gone? (Note if any graduates have been accepted in colleges and universities you respect.)
11. How do test scores in basic academic areas compare with other schools in the community? (Most private schools will score higher because of the homes and relative affluence of the parents.)
12. Are there any programs for advanced placement of exceptional students?
13. How many different subjects would a teacher in the upper grades usually teach?
14. What are some of the extra-curricular activities?
15. Who controls the schools? (If a board, who is on the board? If a church, what is it like?)
16. Have there been problems with drugs?
17. Is there a denominational or sectarian emphasis in the religious teaching?
18. Is the school a part of a national association of schools or a state association of secondary schools?
19. Is the school accredited or registered with the state education department?
20. What textbooks would my child be using? How often are they updated?
21. How much involvement are the parents expected to take in the life of the school?
22. Are the teachers certified by the state or working toward it?
23. What contacts are maintained with non-Christian schools, such as athletic competition or debating meets?
24. Can the school supply the names of some parents in my neighborhood with whom I could discuss the school?
25. What led to the founding of the school? (Watch for schools founded to dodge integration or those rooted in church splits.)
26. What standards does the school have for acceptance? (Some schools cater to problem students; others are so selective they would be called "elitist.")
27. How closely have operations come to breaking even financially in the last two years?
28. What experience and academic credentials does the headmaster or principal have?
29. Is the principal also pastor of the church? What role does pastor play in school?
30. What is teacher-student ratio? (1:20, ideal; 1:30, average; 1:35+, high).

Public education. Public schools attempt to socialize children, to teach them what they need to know to support the democratic faith that is the foundation of the country, and to prepare them to become good citizens in a democracy and to practice the values of democratic life. These aids grow out of that body of thought and belief that led to the organization of our country, the construction of our Constitution, and the formation of our government.

The essence of the democratic faith is that the success of the group is measured by the success of each member of the group. Each person is of value to the group and, in that sense, all are equal. However, the worth and dignity of each, and the equality that all share, rest on the ability of the group to provide whatever is required for each one to grow, develop, and mature. For that to happen, there must be a system that provides education for all and the opportunity for all to learn. In our country that system is the public schools.

Education, whether private or public, should strive to meet the following objectives:

1. affirm the worth and dignity of each person
2. declare that all are created equal in that no individual is without value
3. proclaim faith in the ability of each person in society provided each has access to education and to information
4. is based in orderly process within which disagreements and disputes are settled in peaceful ways through adherence to rule and law
5. rest in a basic morality and depend on the people acting justly, humanely, and mercifully
6. provide opportunity for each to act; freedom to act; opportunity to grow; freedom to mature (Young, 1980:1).

SUMMARY

Education is one of the five social institutions. It involves both formal and informal learning settings. Society and individuals are affected by its functions. The organizational structure deals with age levels, the curriculum, and both public and private sponsorship.

DISCUSSION QUESTIONS

1. In what way does education as a social institution reflect society at large?
2. What role do you perceive for the Christian Protestant school?

3. Do you think that the concerns expressed by the Christian school educators are valid? Why?
4. What do you think are the minimum qualities and features that a Christian school should have?
5. From your perspective, how would you rate the public school in your home district, and how would it compare with public schools in, say, New York City?

SUGGESTED READING

Ben Brodinsky, "12 Major Events That Shaped America's Schools," *Phi Delta Kappan* (1976:1:68–77).

"Something Happened: Education in the Seventies," *Phi Delta Kappan* (1979:4:238–41).

H. W. Byrne, *A Christian Approach to Education—A Bibliocentric View* (Grand Rapids: Zondervan, 1961).

James R. Coleman et al., *Parents, Teachers and Children: Prospects for Choice in American Education* (San Francisco: Institute for Contemporary Studies, 1977).

Eternity Magazine special report: "How Wide Is the Spectrum in Christian Schools?" (1980:9:27).

Sterling Fishman, Andreas M. Kazamias, and Herbert M. Kliebard (eds.), *Teacher, Student, and Society* (Boston: Little, Brown, 1974).

Paul A. Kienel (ed.), *The Philosophy of Christian School Education*, 2nd ed. (ACSI-GGS-CHC, 1978).

John Martin Rich, *Challenge and Response: Education in American Culture* (New York: Wiley, 1974).

William Lloyd Turner, "Reasons for Enrollment in Religious Schools: A Case Study of Three Recently Established Fundamentalist Schools in Kentucky and Wisconsin" (unpublished manuscript, University of Wisconsin, 1979).

Rita Warren and Dick Schneider, *Mom, They Won't Let Us Pray* (Old Tappan, N.J.: Revell, 1975).

George P. Young, "The St. Paul Public Schools, An Excellent School System" (unpublished article, St. Paul, Minn., 1980).

_13

RICHARD J. STELLWAY
Northwest Nazarene College,
Idaho

RELIGION

The prospect of applying sociology to the study of religion—
people's beliefs and practices concerning the supernatural—may
at first seem somehow inappropriate. After all if religion, and
Christianity in particular, involves the mysterious workings of a
supernatural God, is not this outside the province of sociology?
Certainly, there are religious phenomena that do not lend themselves to sociological verification. For example, sociology is in no
position to determine the reality of God, or even the validity of
beliefs people may hold about Him.[1] These limitations not-
withstanding, sociology can productively study, first, the body of
people who hold to certain beliefs and the nature of their beliefs
and behavior and, second, the structure of the religious organization that these people establish and the way these organizations
relate to the body of believers and to the larger society in which
they exist. As we proceed to examine the peculiar nature and
practical consequence of the American religious system, our
analysis will comprehend both of these areas.

---

[1]This fact has not prevented Emile Durkheim and other social theorists
from speculating as to the nonsupernatural origins of religion and religious belief.

AMERICA'S RELIGIOUS FREE ENTERPRISE SYSTEM

To appreciate the uniqueness of the religious situation in America is to comprehend the contrast between the emphasis placed on the separation of church and state in this country and the close church-state relationship existing in many other societies. In this latter case an established church enjoys financial and legal support from the state. A share of tax money may be allocated to the maintenance of church property, programs, and personnel. Furthermore, the power of the state may be employed to reward those who support the established church—its rules and its regulations—and to punish or in other ways discriminate against those who do not. This state-church arrangement was, and in some respects remains, operative in many European societies.

The legal separation of church and state was not always operative in American history. Prior to the adoption of the U. S. Constitution, nine of the original thirteen colonies had officially established churches and accorded privileges to members of these churches that were denied to nonmembers. However, when the First Amendment to the Constitution went into effect, this situation changed dramatically. A clause in this amendment specified that "Congress shall make no law respecting an establishment of religion, or prohibiting the free exercise thereof."

In the years since the adoption of the Constitution, the principle of the separation of church and state has gained broad acceptance as has the principle of religious freedom. As far as the government is concerned, people may join any religious group they choose, or they can join none at all! For all intents and purposes, religion in America has taken on the character of a free enterprise system.

FUNCTIONAL CONSEQUENCES OF RELIGIOUS FREE ENTERPRISE

Popularization. Whether this situation has been a good thing for the Christian church at large has become a matter of debate, and the position taken depends largely on the perspective assumed. Sociologist David Martin (1972) sees this from a positive standpoint. Having distinguished between what he terms the pattern of Protestant state churches (Anglican, Lutheran, or Calvinist with or without substantial Protestant dissent) and the pattern of American pluralism, Martin notes that in the former case religion remains permanently allied with an elite culture. According to Martin, this culture becomes increasingly alien to the masses as industrialization and the accompanying transformation of society takes place. Martin views all of this in stark contrast to the pattern of American pluralism which, far from breeding alienation, results in religion's increased popularity.

The fact of different degrees of popularity between these two patterns is particularly evident in organizational participation. While weekly church attendance in nations conforming to a state church pattern currently runs between 3 and 15 percent, weekly church attendance in the United States presently runs around 40 percent. However, with regard to belief, Martin observes that the erosion of organizational participation in Protestant state church patterns is not necessarily accompanied by substantial unbelief.

Organizational differentiation. The second consequence of the free enterprise arrangement, not unrelated to the first, is what sociologists term *organizational differentiation.* Such differentiation refers to the development of new and distinguishing characteristics. With respect to religious organization, it involves a proliferation of religious bodies, each in some respects unique from the others. Religion in American society has undergone organizational differentiation along age lines (e.g., the Jesus People), along racial and ethnic group lines (e.g., the Swedish Baptists), and along class lines (e.g., the snake-handling sects or the Episcopalian church).

The process of differentiation has been praised by some and denounced by others. Its praisers note how difficult it would be for our heterogeneous population to find an equal sense of meaning and belonging in the same (undifferentiated) religious organization. They maintain that the division of religious groups along homogeneous lines has catered to these needs and has thereby fostered significant church growth.

The fact that homogeneous religious groups tend to undergo a more rapid numerical growth than heterogeneous religious groups has been documented by McGavran (1970), who heads up the church growth movement at Fuller Seminary. Out of concern for stimulating such growth, McGavran and his followers have called for the development of religious groups along homogeneous lines.

247

Although McGavran's homogeneity principle is seen to be quite sound by some, it is seen to be quite unsound by others, though for somewhat different reasons. In his now classic book *The Social Sources of Denominationalism*, H. Richard Niebuhr (1957) expresses great concern over what he understands to be predominantly social and economic sources of differentiation. From Niebuhr's standpoint, the increasing religious group differentiation as manifested in what he terms "denominationalism" has occurred at the expense of Christian unity. Rather than transcending socially constructed differences and unifying Christians in the pursuit of a common calling, denominationalism has fractured the church universal.

Opponents of religious organizational differentiation have also expressed concern that the process, when carried to its ultimate conclusion, will result in what has been termed privatization of religion. In such a circumstance each individual selects his belief from the multitude of those presented, constructs his own personal belief system, and practices his religion largely by himself and apart from a fellowship of believers. Such cafeteria theologizing results in a perversion of Christian teaching and a diminution of Christian community as everybody "does their own thing."

Competition. With the disestablishment of religion in America, religious organizations were denied state support and were thereby forced to compete with one another for members— hopefully committed members—who would dedicate their time, talent, and money to the organization. The extent of this competition has been increased by mounting geographic mobility. With the average family moving once every four years, many local churches are hard pressed to complete building programs or other projects, or even to maintain existing ones. Their success depends on their ability to replace departing members with new ones who will be equally willing to lend their support to the church. Yet new migrants to a community are inclined to carefully weigh and compare the programs and services of one local church with those of another. As religious organizations endeavor to survive the rigors of competition, they find themselves catering more and more to the desires and demands of the laity. In the process the laity begins to take on the behavior of discriminating religious consumers.

FREE ENTERPRISE AND CHURCH LEADERSHIP

A religious organization's concern for obtaining and maintaining members places religious leaders, and particularly parish pastors, in an awkward predicament. To fully appreciate their dilemma, it is necessary to comment on two dimensions of Christ's gospel.

Christ was ushered in as the embodiment of good tidings of great joy (Luke 2:10). When He arrived He went about offering help to the sick, rest to the weary, and salvation to the lost (Matt. 11:28). The Comforter had come and many followed Him. This is scarcely surprising since Jesus appeared capable of offering them everything they wanted—health, happiness, even eternal life. But one day as the multitudes were following Him, Jesus turned to them and said, "If anyone comes to me and does not hate his father and mother, his wife and children, his brothers and sisters—yes, even his own life—he cannot be my disciple. And anyone who does not carry his cross and follow me cannot be my disciple" (Luke 14:26–27).

Suddenly a second dimension of the gospel became apparent. Those who dedicated themselves to following Christ could be sure of one thing—life would not be easy. Persecution, personal sacrifice, poverty, conflict, and even family division awaited those who would serve the Lord above all others. Not surprisingly, someone asked, "Lord, are there *just* a few who are being saved?" to which Christ responded, "Strive to enter by the narrow door; for many, I tell you, will seek to enter and will not be able" (Luke 13:23–24, NASB).

Today the masses still prefer Christ the Comforter and are easily turned aside by Christ the Challenger. The fact that both of these messages are integral to the gospel poses a real problem to church leaders, particularly as they engage in the competition for new members. If they preach the gospel of comfort, they stand to add significantly to the fold in terms of numbers but risk accumulating a fair-weather, fainthearted flock in the process. On the other hand, if they preach a gospel of challenge, they may attract but a few and risk losing present members of the flock to "greener" pastures.

Responses to the comfort-challenge dilemma. In interviewing religious leaders, and parish ministers in particular, and in observing how they deal with the comfort-challenge dilemma, four strategies have become apparent. For the purpose of clarification, each strategy is labeled in terms of its basic approach. In the order of consideration that follows, strategy one is that of the confronting challenger; strategy two, the conscientious conformer; strategy three, the impression manager; and strategy four, the peaceful revolutionary.

Strategies one and two involve attempts to maintain or establish consistency between personal conviction and public pronouncement. Strategy three implies a conspicuous inconsistency. Because it includes some holding back of personal convictions, strategy four may be said to involve occasional and moderate inconsistency.

Comparison of Four Response Strategies: Comfort-Challenge Emphasis and Belief-Behavior Consistency

Strategy	Comfort	Challenge	Consistency
Confronting challenger	−	+	+
Sincere conformist	+	−	+
Impression manager	+	−	−
Peaceful revolutionary	+	+	±

1. The leader adopting the approach of the confronting challenger is deeply committed to counting the cost of discipleship and to fulfilling the implications of a Christian commitment. In his ministry he endeavors to establish consistency between his personal convictions and public pronouncements by preaching a gospel of challenge. In calling for commitment, he shuns sugar-coated phrases and avoids pious platitudes while boldly proclaiming the demands of the gospel.

The laity's response to this direct approach will depend on a number of things, most notable of which is the leader's perceived base of authority, the legitimacy of this authority, and the form in which he presents the gospel's demands. However, research reveals that the response can be quite negative and result in diminished giving, diminished attendance, moves for the leader's dismissal, and membership withdrawal (Quinley, 1974).

The confronting challenger, if faced with such a response, may derive some inner satisfaction from faithfully discharging what he understands to be a God-given obligation and possibly from separating the wheat from the chaff. However, church officials as custodians of organizational welfare may regard these same responses with growing alarm and even pressure the confronting challenger to soften his approach or perhaps consider another avenue of ministry (Campbell and Pettigrew, 1959).

2. Unlike the confronting challenger, the user of strategy two (the conscientious conformer) focuses his message almost exclusively on the comfort side of the gospel. Yet if this be the case, he does so sincerely and conscientiously. His neglect of the challenge side of the gospel may stem from his development and internalization of a comfort theology, his conviction that a challenge is circumstantially irrelevant, or possibly his willingness to define his role as that of "comforter" while leaving any challenging to someone else. Like the confronting challenger, his public pronouncements remain consistent with his personal convictions.

In opting to focus almost exclusively on the comfort dimension of the gospel, the leader pursuing strategy two stands to gain a sizable following. And given the incentives and rewards that frequently accrue from numerical growth, this leader may enjoy wide popularity. However, in catering to the comfort dimension, he may err in not sufficiently spurring the laity on to further growth. Furthermore, he may become sidetracked by his very popularity so that he becomes more laity directed than Christ directed.

To avoid these pitfalls, this leader would do well to recall Christ's reference in the parable of the sower to the analogy of seeds sown on rocky ground (Matt. 13:5). To use a descriptive phrase, Christ did not promise a rose garden—at least not in this life. Fair-weather followers may easily turn on their leader or simply turn tail and run at the first signs of adversity. Short of this, by continued exposure to an exclusive comfort theology, a climate of self-indulgence is cultivated. Eventually devotees fall victim to their own lusts, be they wealth, prestige, or even sex.

3. The outward behavior of the user of strategy three (the impression manager) is likely to be quite similar to that of the conscientious conformer. However, unlike both the conscientious conformer and the confronting challenger, the impression manager holds personal convictions and makes public pronouncements that are inconsistent. While remaining quite aware of the gospel's challenge, he has given up all efforts at getting people to take that challenge seriously. Perceiving himself as a realist, he resorts to working within the boundaries of the status quo, giving people what they *want* or *prefer* even when this is inconsistent with what he believes they *need*.

In his book *How to Become a Bishop Without Being Religious,* Charles Merrill Smith asserts the importance of what we have termed impression management. In advocating this approach, he distinguishes between the "religious" leader who insists on publicly expressing deep and abiding convictions, even when it is unpopular to do so, and the "pious" leader who "seems more religious to laymen because he tries very hard to fit the image that laymen conjure up when they think of 'preacher.'" Having made this distinction, Smith states his theses: "You can expect to be a successful clergyman without being religious. But never forget that you cannot be a success unless you are pious" (1965:3–4).

The impression manager's diagnosis of the situation leaves him essentially without a vision. Should he retain his leadership role, this lack of vision may result in his giving a purely perfunctory performance. Such a circumstance is perhaps the most miserable of all unless the minister derives satisfaction from merely being a pleasant leader in society.

Another problem confronting the impression manager stems from the fact that his public performance is at variance with his private conviction. Social psychologists have observed that inconsistency between belief and behavior tends to produce a state of mental dissonance. How the leader deals with this dissonance is critical. If he seeks to resolve it by directing the resulting frustration at his congregation, he risks becoming a thorough-going cynic. If, on the other hand, he seeks to resolve the conflict by tailoring his personal convictions to the preferences and prejudices of the laity, he merely exchanges his present strategy for that of the sincere conformist. This response may be more gradual than instant, and more unconscious than conscious. The leader simply begins internalizing what he has been publicly proclaiming.

4. Like the impression manager and the confronting challenger, the user of strategy four (the peaceful revolutionary) is personally committed to the challenge dimension of the gospel. However, unlike the former, he does not assume that the laity are so committed to their own comfort that they cannot be successfully challenged. Nor does he incorporate the bold uncompromising strategy of the latter. Rather, he opts for a milder go-slow approach. Moreover, when challenging his people, he incorporates a variety of methods, with public proclamation being but one and personal or small-group confrontation being another. Recognizing that spiritual maturity is a matter of degree and that people vary in their mastery of it, he systematically works with those who are ready for greater challenges much as Christ did with His disciples. And with Christ he finds himself saying, "I have many more things to say to you, but you cannot bear *them* now" (John 16:12, NASB).

Insofar as this strategy incorporates both the comfort and challenge dimensions of the gospel, it appears to have definite merit. In presenting these dimensions, the leader attempts to keep both in balance, opening wounds but healing them as well. However, there is one significant pitfall confronting the peaceful revolutionary. Because of the delicacy of the balance, the leader is forever walking a tightrope. On the one hand, there is always the danger of falling off on the comfort side; on the other hand, in struggling to correct his or her balance, the leader may fall off on the challenge side. Furthermore, because lay preferences and perceptions differ, there will be attempts to tip the leader toward one side or the other. Perhaps the key to maintaining the balance lies in realizing the impossibility of pleasing everyone and for all time. Those who would be a person for all seasons may find sustenance in the following warning from Christ to His disciples: "Woe *to you* when all men speak well of you, for in the same way their fathers used to treat the false prophets" (Luke 6:26, NASB).

Factors determining strategy selection. In selecting a strategy for dealing with the comfort-challenge dilemma, a leader's theology will hopefully play a primary role. However, there is evidence to suggest that other considerations frequently take precedence.

These considerations involve the nature of the local congregation and the form of church polity.

1. *The congregation's investment in the status quo* is one factor that affects strategy selection. In 1965 open housing for blacks became a political issue in California. Shortly thereafter Quinley (1974) conducted a survey of ministers in that state. In tabulating the results, he found that 83 percent of those ministers who had openly opposed an antifair housing amendment to the California constitution experienced opposition from their congregations. In writing up his study, Quinley concluded that a congregation may tolerate a minister's stand against civil and social injustice only for as long as the issue does not affect them personally. However, as a study by Dean Hoge (1976) revealed, the minister who expresses concern over, for example, justice for the oppressed and legal representation for the poor is likely to incur the ire of the laypersons who have a vested interest in maintaining the existing state of affairs.

Although this evidence concerns the response of the laity, it does not bear directly on the inclination of religious leaders to challenge them. Of course, given the competition for members that exists in a system of religious free enterprise, religious leaders are likely to view with great alarm the prospect of alienating or aggravating the people in the pews. It should therefore not be too surprising if the mere anticipation of this response is enough to frighten many religious leaders away from taking a prophetic stand on an unpopular moral issue (Hadden and Rymph, 1966). What follows is a review of some evidence concerning the actual behavior of religious leaders when confronted with a controversial moral issue.

In the late 1950s and 1960s discrimination against minority groups became a focal issue in the civil rights movement. In the education sphere much controversy raged over school integration. The inclination of religious leaders to take a stand on a controversial moral issue was put to a real test in the Little Rock school desegregation crisis. Campbell and Pettigrew, two Harvard sociologists, studied the responses of a number of Little Rock ministers to that crisis. In their survey they found that twenty-four of twenty-nine ministers believed that "the removal of legal and artificial barriers to racial contact is morally preferable to the present system" (1959:509–16). However, all of the ministers served congregations with predominantly segregationist sentiments. Not surprising, only eight of the twenty-four integrationist ministers persisted in publicly defending integration on grounds of Christian morality. When faced with the prospect of "turning their people off," the majority apparently chose to pursue the impression-management strategy described above.

The fact that eight ministers opted to challenge their congregations on this issue prompted Campbell and Pettigrew to look further into the situation. Their inquiry yielded a number of observations that are summarized by Pierre Berton:

1. The more popular the denomination in a local area, the less likely are its ministers to defend positions not accepted by local public opinion.
2. A minister is less likely to support desegregation during a crisis if no ministerial figures of high prestige in his denomination lead the way.
3. The minister's support of desegregation is less if his church is engaged in a membership drive, involved in a building program, or fund raising campaign than if it is not so engaged.
4. The more stable the membership of his church, the less likely is the minister to support desegregation during a crisis period.
5. Success (speaking numerically and financially) in the ministry is negatively related to the probability of strong advocacy of unpopular moral imperatives (1965:121–26).

In summary, it appears that the greater the perceived risk seems to be from the standpoint of organizational welfare and stability, the less is the inclination of ministers to challenge their congregations to live up to the moral demands of the gospel.

2. Another factor that affects strategy selection is *construction of polity*. The form of church polity under which a minister serves also has a bearing on that leader's inclination to articulate a gospel of challenge. In most Protestant organizations in the United States, it is possible to distinguish between two forms of polity. In one form, termed *congregational* polity, the minister is given formal authority by the congregation. However, the congregation retains the power to hire and even to fire the minister. While the minister may prefer to derive authority from formal training and ultimately from God, should these sources of authority be a basis for challenging the congregation in areas in which they do not wish to be challenged, the minister may well do so at the expense of being dismissed.

In a second form of organizational polity, the minister's formal authority flows from a body of elders and presbyters. In this *presbyterian* form, this body retains the ultimate right to hire and fire a minister. Should the congregation become unhappy with their minister's proclamation and seek to remove and replace their leader, they must do so through due process by going through the body of elders and presbyters. In practice, then, this body serves as a kind of buffer between a minister and the congregation.

Of the two forms of polity, we might expect that a minister who is personally convinced of the need to challenge the congregation on a controversial moral issue would feel freer to speak out if he were operating within the context of a presbyterian polity. There is some evidence to support this line of reasoning. In his study of twenty-eight religious bodies, James Wood (1970) sought to determine the impact of church structure on the inclination of church leaders to push for strong integrationist policies. After distinguishing between hierarchical and nonhierarchical bodies on the basis of whether the local congregation has the authority to hire and fire the minister, Wood found the integrationist policies of hierarchical organizations to be significantly stronger than those of nonhierarchical ones. Although local ministers did not necessarily have a hand in formulating the organization's integrationist policies, Wood observed that they enjoyed the support of church leaders within the governing hierarchy when publicly affirming these policies.

In the same study Wood also traced the effect of theology on a church organization's position on civil rights. Interesting enough, he found that conservative theology was negatively related to strong support for civil rights. However, upon looking at theologically conservative organizations by themselves, Wood found that the integrationist policies of hierarchical organizations were still stronger than the integrationist policies of nonhierarchical organizations.

Although the presbyterian form of church polity may seem to provide a more favorable setting for a minister to challenge his congregation concerning controversial moral issues, polity alone should not be overestimated. Regardless of polity, church organizations in America remain voluntary associations. This means the laity have options. For example, the laity who view a minister's challenge as meddling may be limited in their efforts to immediately remove their leader under a presbyterian polity, but they can still effectively register their dissatisfaction. As Quinley (1974) observed, they may simply stop attending, stop giving, or transfer their membership elsewhere. Church officials are not inclined to view such actions lightly and may well put pressure on an offending minister to "back off" or possibly consider another avenue of service.

FUNCTIONAL CONSEQUENCES OF COMFORT THEOLOGY

The pressures emanating from the voluntary nature of the church and the competitive nature of the free enterprise religious system are strong enough to push many a religious leader away from the challenge side and toward the comfort side of the gospel. The following paragraphs examine the implications that an emphasis on comfort theology—a theology devoid of challenge—holds for the secularization of our society. This includes both the movement from sect to church and the development of civil religion.

Secularization. Much concern has and continues to be expressed over the secularization of America. We decry the increasing secularization of home, school, and business. We bemoan the fact that, from the vantage point of some, our country has become a vast secular society. In the midst of all this concern, it is fitting to pause and inquire just what secularization represents. The German sociologist Max Weber defined it as "the process by which sectors of society and culture are removed from the domination of religious institutions and symbols" (Berger, 1967:107). When applied to our contemporary society, secularization involves the declining influence of religion—at least vital, authentic religion—in spheres outside the church.

It has become common practice to attribute any declining influence of religion to an increasing respect for science and scientific knowledge. Another explanation offered is that with the increased complexity and diversification of society, religion's role has become narrow or specialized. However, the free enterprise nature of American religion plays no small part in the secularization process. Under our competitive free enterprise system, if people do not like what is preached or taught by one local church, they can easily attend another. Faced with this possibility, local religious leaders are tempted to confine their comments to a narrow spiritual realm lest they open themselves to the charge of meddling. While it is difficult to know how customary this practice is, it is indeed quite frequent, judging from the self-reports of 1,580 Protestant ministers from nine major denominations (Stark et al., 1971). This practice, whether by default or by design, contributes significantly to the secularization process.

Such practice is most disturbing to those of us who are convinced of the potential relevance of Christianity to every facet of human existence and of the need to bring Christianity to bear on every sphere of life.

The movement from sect to church. Whenever sociologists of religion speak of religious change, the twin concepts of church and sect are bound to arise. The idea of the *church-sect* dichotomy was first employed by Max Weber and his student Ernst Troeltsch to describe the forms of religious organization and various religious experience in Europe. According to Troeltsch (1932), sects typically exact a high degree of commitment and involvement from their numbers, seek to model themselves after the New Testament church, minimize the clergy-laity contrast, and draw a sharp contrast between themselves and the world. By way of contrast, Troeltsch described churches as more inclusive in membership, less demanding of members, less biblically focused, and more hierarchical than sects.

In an effort to relate this conceptualization to the American religious situation, H. Richard Niebuhr (1957) employed the concept of *denomination* to connote a middle ground between church and sect. Niebuhr further suggested that because of their inherent stability, sects tended to develop into denominations. Since Niebuhr's early writing, there has been a proliferation of terminology and considerable expansion of the list of phenomena attributed to sects, churches, and denominations. Niebuhr's conceptual scheme has proved quite difficult to apply due to the fact that the many characteristics attributed to sects seldom describe any one organization and fail to change uniformly as sects move along the alleged continuum toward a denomination or church. Consequently, Benton Johnson has suggested that the concepts of church and sect be simplified as follows: "A church is a religious group that accepts the social environment in which it exists. A sect is a religious group that rejects the social environment in which it exists" (1964:542).[2]

Johnson's conceptualization should prove helpful as we assess the role of comfort theology in the movement from sect to church. As we have observed, the American religious system has generated no small amount of proliferation of, and competition between, religious organizations. Out of concern for retaining their supporters, religious leaders have felt pressure to appease their respective constituencies by accepting and even affirming the prevailing social arrangements and cultural practices with which these groups have grown comfortable and concerning which they have a vested interest in maintaining. Insofar as religious leaders have given in to this pressure, they have contributed to the movement from sect to church, as Johnson defines these terms.

In reflecting on the "radical" teachings of Jesus Christ and on His concern that Christians be the salt of the earth, it is difficult to see how authentic religion could ever be used to justify the prevailing status quo. Could it be, as many sociologists have suggested, that religion for the most part has ceased to be an independent variable (prime mover) and is best regarded as a passive, receptive, dependent variable in society?

Civil religion. The practice of vesting prevailing social arrangements and behavior patterns with religious significance, as referred to above, constitutes a limited definition of civil religion. According to Will Herberg, "Civil religion religionizes national values, national heroes, national history, even national ideals" (1973:58). It does so to the extent that these come to be viewed as sacred and above reproach.

Some people have been inclined to herald the advance of civil religion as a means for combating the secularization process by bringing a religious perspective to bear on the affairs of state. However, there are significant problems with this line of reasoning, particularly if one assumes that this practice will somehow result in religion having some significant influence on the affairs

---

[2]As Johnson began to apply this simplified conceptualization to the American scene, he observed that some of the organizations typically classified as sects, by affirming most American values, were actually closer to the church end of the continuum.

of state. In truth, the situation may be quite the contrary.

Cognizant of the fact that most Americans believe in God, national leaders have been quick to legitimize past practices and present policies through liberal references to God and to His divine will. The effectiveness of their efforts prompted sociologist Robert Bellah (1967:14) to propose that civil religion has frequently become the handmaiden of national purposes.

Christian Sen. Mark Hatfield has observed that one of the gravest shortcomings of civil religion is the lack of any reference to personal and, particularly, corporate sin. In the absence of such a consideration, any need for collective repentance is lost sight of. In an article entitled "Repentance, Politics, and Power," Hatfield elaborates on his concern:

> In my opinion, American civil religion has blinded us to our national sin. It has dulled our sensitivity to the need for corporate repentance, because a characteristic of our civil religion is that it has created myths about America as sort of a modern chosen people of God (1977:36).

How does the American system of religious free enterprise relate to civil religion? As we have alleged, the temptation is quite strong for religious leaders in a competitive religious marketplace to attempt to please or appease their followers. Insofar as this manifests itself in attempts to justify or sanctify the social and political status quo, organized religion fosters the kind of civil religion that Hatfield fears. To this situation he sounds a warning: "If we believe in the God of an American civil religion, our faith is in a small and very elusive deity, a loyal spiritual advisor to power and prestige . . . devoid of any moral content" (1977:37).

SUMMARY AND RESPONSE

To return to an earlier theme, the principle of the separation of church and state that emerged early in our nation's history effectively established religion on a free enterprise basis. The proliferation of religious organizations and the voluntary nature of church involvement that emerged established a competitive arrangement. This has had profound implications for the kind of theology espoused by competing organizations. In an effort to attract and retain members, religious leaders have been inclined to emphasize the comfort dimension of the gospel and to neglect the challenge dimension. This has culminated in the emergence and growth of comfort theology—a theology devoid of challenge. This peculiar theology has facilitated the secularization process and the movement from sect to church. It has also had the indirect consequence of affirming prevailing social arrangements and the growth of civil religion.

My own contention is that comfort and challenge are two integral components of Christianity and that the emphasis on either to the neglect of the other results in a gross perversion of the Christian religion. Therefore, although comfort theology may serve to popularize Christianity, it does so at great expense. The practical consequence is an emphasis on "cheap grace" and a tendency toward self-indulgence. Concern for bearing fruit in keeping with repentance and for promoting social justice—particularly as it involves *other* individuals, *other* groups, and *other* nations—all but vanishes. In time Christianity becomes little more than a means for legitimizing a special social status or for justifying the particular preferences and prejudices of its adherents much as religion once did for the Pharisees.

Over half a century ago Max Weber (1958) formulated the argument that religious ideas can serve as a most significant variable in accounting for the activities of men. However, since that time sociologists studying religion have more frequently focused on how religious belief has accommodated the demands of secular society (Johnson, 1964:360; Hadden, 1969:72). This tendency in part reflects the failure of sociologists to find much correspondence between religious ideas and behavioral dependent variables. In other words the consequences of religious ideas have not been evident. It may be, of course, that sociologists have simply not looked hard enough. However, before we jump to this conclusion, we might entertain another thought. Could it be that despite all of our religious salesmanship, these sociologists have reached a valid conclusion? Are they merely witnessing the logical outcome of comfort theology?

Having called attention to the emphasis on comfort theology and to the consequences that befall such an emphasis, it remains to fashion a viable response. A frequent tendency is to hold religious leaders, our spiritual mentors, responsible for any neglect of the challenge aspect of the gospel. Yet in becoming cognizant of the pressures facing these leaders, we are prevented from putting all the blame on them. As members of the church universal, all of us must share the responsibility for bringing the demands of the gospel to bear on our day-to-day world. And there is much we can do. Through research, study, and prayer we can become aware of the problems that the gospel must address. And through personal contact, public prayer, and class instruction, we can make others in our fellowship aware. We can support our leaders by removing some of the risk as they address the challenge dimension of the gospel. Such activities are of utmost importance in insuring that the church will live up to its mandate to be "the salt of the earth" (Matt. 5:13).

DISCUSSION QUESTIONS

1. In your opinion, are there areas with which the church or its leaders probably should not deal in regard to the challenge dimension of the gospel? If so, why not?
2. With which of the significant moral issues of our day would you want to see the church come to terms? Why?
3. In the concluding section of the article, which suggestions have potential concerning things we might do to involve the church in pressing issues and problems facing our world? How would you as an individual or group go about encouraging your congregation to address an issue?
4. Why are church leaders sometimes reluctant to deal with controversial moral and ethical issues? What can prevent such reticence?
5. Concerning the two significant dimensions of the Christian message noted in this chapter, what consequences do you see accompanying a preoccupation with one to the neglect of the other?
6. What themes are frequently reflected in the Sunday morning congregational prayer that addresses the primary concerns of the church? Does it address community or world problems along with local concerns? Does it consider matters of social injustice? Does it ask for assistance in bearing fruit consistent with repentance?

SUGGESTED READING

Peter L. Berger, *The Noise of Solemn Assemblies* (Garden City, N.J.: Doubleday, 1961).

Pierre Berton, *The Comfortable Pew* (New York: Lippincott, 1965).

Orlando E. Costas, *The Church and Its Mission: A Shattering Critique from the Third World* (Wheaton, Ill.: Tyndale, 1974).

Mark Hatfield, *Conflict and Conscience* (Waco: Word Books, 1971). *Between a Rock and a Hard Place* (Waco: Word Books, 1975).

Jeffrey K. Hadden, *The Gathering Storm in the Churches* (New York: Doubleday, 1969).

Dean R. Hoge, *Division in the Protestant House* (Philadelphia: Westminster, 1976).

Donald B. Kraybill, *The Upside-Down Kingdom* (Scottdale, Pa.: Herald, 1978).

David O. Moberg, *Inasmuch* (Grand Rapids: Eerdmans, 1965). *The Great Reversal* (New York: Lippincott, 1977). *The Church and the Older Person* (Grand Rapids: Eerdmans, 1977).

Richard Niebuhr, *The Social Sources of Denominationalism* (New York: Holt, 1929; New York: Median Books, 1957).

Richard Quebedeaux, *The Worldly Evangelicals* (New York: Harper and Row, 1978).

W. Widick Schroeder, Victor Obenhaus, Larry A. Jones, and Thomas Sweetser, *Suburban Religion: Churches and Synagogues in the American Experience* (Chicago: Center for the Scientific Study of Religion, 1974).

Howard A. Snyder, *The Problem of Wineskins: Church Renewal in Technological Age* (Downers Grove, Ill.: Inter-Varsity, 1977).

Rodney Stark and Charles Y. Glock, *American Piety: The Nature of Religious Commitment* (Berkeley: University of California Press, 1970).

Rodney Stark, Bruce D. Foster, Charles Y. Glock, and Harold E. Quinley, *Wayward Shepherds: Prejudice and the Protestant Clergy* (New York: Harper and Row, 1971).

14

ROBERT McCLUSKEY
St. Paul Bible College,
Minnesota

FORMAL ORGANIZATIONS

As with any brief survey of a large field, the following discussion is necessarily restricted in scope. A review of contemporary sociology texts reveals that the subject of "organization" is sometimes included as a subdivision of *groups and group dynamics,* which is an even larger area. Because space is limited, only the concept of organization is included in this essay. The commentary section deals almost exclusively with the *local church* as an organization in order to give the Christian reader a perspective on an area of the subject that will be of particular interest.

OVERVIEW
Under the heading of organizations, the subjects most frequently included in the texts are (1) formal versus informal organizations, (2) bureaucracy, (3) alternative organizations, (4) organizational leadership, and (5) organizational power. An overview of these areas follows.

Organizations—formal versus informal. In the broadest sense an organization is a group whose activities are coordinated for the achievement of specific goals or purposes. In sociology most discussions center in *formal* organizations. What distinguishes formal from informal organizations is the presence of deliberate or explicit coordination of activities. By way of characteristics, a formal organization usually has rules defining each person's duties, organizational charts or a known hierarchy, and a system of rewards and punishments.

Informal structures most often develop to accommodate a short-term or acute need, and they seldom formalize. An example would be a group of neighbors fighting a fire. Such arrangements often emerge, even within formal organizations, as a response to a dislike for the formal structure, as a means of dealing with situations not covered by the formal structure, or simply because things get done better through the informal system. It is not uncommon to find several informal organizations within a single larger formal organization. For instance, an officer of a professional association to which this writer belongs was recently heard to praise a Washington staff member for ability in "cutting through the red tape and getting to the person who can turn the gears that we need to move." Cutting red tape usually means circumventing or cutting across the organizational structure. In order to accomplish this, there must be an informal organization through which things are done.

The bureaucracy. This is perhaps the most common type of formal organization. Indeed, the bureaucratic form is so well known that in attempting to visualize a scheme for organizing people, it is difficult to conceive of any other structure.

Defining a bureaucracy, however, is no easy task, as every observer tends to see it from a slightly different perspective. From one general point of view, a bureaucracy is simply "an administrative system within the social structure of modern, mass society" (Hobbs and Blank, 1975:168). Some other definitions, more or less technical, are: (1) "a hierarchical arrangement between the parts of an organization in which the pyramiding order is based on division of function and authority" (Vander Zanden, 1979:165); (2) "a power-wielding organization with a hierarchy of ranks, the statuses and functions of which are planned in advance and in which the official activities of personnel are supervised by the next higher rank, up to the apex of control" (Green, 1968:325); and (3) "a large-scale formal organization that is designed to coordinate the activities of many individuals in the pursuit of administrative tasks. Bureaucracies are highly differentiated and efficiently organized by means of formal rules and a hierarchical chain of command" (Hobbs and Blank, 1975:485).

Although these definitions reveal some common features of bureaucracy, the complete nature of the structure cannot be understood without examining these commonalities in somewhat greater detail. What follows is a review of Max Weber's bureaucratic model, which is most often cited by scholars and has the following characteristics:

1. Division of labor. People who are specialists are hired for specific functions and held accountable for a standard of excellence in the performance of those functions.
2. Hierarchy of authority. Usually a pyramiding hierarchy in which each individual is responsible for and controls all positions beneath. Subordinates must obey orders from above that are relevant to their duties. Authority, however, is limited to specific sections of the pyramid and the functions thereof.
3. Rules governing behavior. Rules define the relationships between those in the organization and their responsibilities. These rules are attached to the positions, not the personnel, and thus provide consistency even when personnel change.
4. Impersonality. Persons within the structure are impartial and unassuming toward one another. Personal factors do not enter into their relationships.
5. Technical competence. It is assumed that each individual has the special technical competence to perform his or her duties. There is usually some form of testing to insure this.
6. Careers. Persons within a bureaucracy are appointed, not elected. It is assumed they will make a career of their jobs. They are thus freed from political influence.

Although bureaucracy can provide an efficient means of managing large governance and problem-solving functions, it also has some weaknesses. A few are mentioned here by way of example.

First, as a bureaucracy becomes larger, individual areas of specialization become narrower. As a consequence, the duties of each individual within the organization bear less relationship to the objectives or products of the organization as a whole. The hierarchical flow of communication tends to accentuate this situation by minimizing contact across the functions that contribute to the overall objectives or final product. The result is severalfold.

One result is a lack of understanding as to how a specific duty or position relates to the ends of the bureaucracy. This contributes to work that may be inefficient or even irrelevant with regard to those ends. Second, although each duty theoretically contributes directly and importantly to the ends, the individual may find it difficult to discern his contribution, resulting in low morale and lack of motivation.

Third, the existence of well-defined rules and routines for each position tends to produce a preoccupation with them. There also is a tendency of superiors to judge subordinates based on their compliance with "the book," rather than their contribution to the whole.

Another problem common in bureaucracies was recently formulated by Laurence J. Peter and is named for him, in the book *The Peter Principle: Why Things Always Go Wrong* (1969). A brief statement of the Peter Principle is as follows: "In a hierarchy every employee tends to rise to his level of incompetence" (Peter and Hull, 1969:25). In practice, according to the principle, people are promoted up the hierarchy as long as they are competent in the level to which they have attained. The eventual result is that they reach a position for which they are *in*competent. Since it is rare for individuals to be *de*moted in a hierarchy, they will remain in their levels of incompetence.

The corollary follows: "In time, every post tends to be occupied by an employee who is incompetent to carry out its duties," and it is only because "work is accomplished by those employees who have not yet reached their level of incompetence" that the organization can function at all (Peter and Hull, 1969:27).

It should be pointed out, of course, that such brief statements of the Peter Principle provide an oversimplified and, thus, underqualified view of this problem. Competency, for example, is a relative and multifaceted concept. Seldom would an individual be completely incompetent at any position, particularly if he or she was viewed as competent at the immediately subordinate step. It is just as unlikely that one's competency would fail to improve with experience. The Peter Principle does, however, illustrate that hierarchical models, of which bureaucracy is the classic example, have their problems as well as their strengths.

Alternative organizational models. Two influences have set the stage for the emergence of bureaucracy as the dominant organizational type. First, the rise of larger nations has produced the need for formal relationships between larger groups of people over wider areas. Almost simultaneously, the industrial revolution has caused business and industry to seek management methods that will lead to more output with greater efficiency. Over a period of time we have learned that both big business and big government tend to leave people feeling depersonalized. Because impersonality is an explicit characteristic of bureaucracy, it would appear that the bureaucratic nature of business and government is the real villain.

Nevertheless, the affinity of complex groups for bureaucracy cannot be overemphasized. Indeed, it is thought by some that the emergence of the bureaucratic form in larger organizations is inevitable (Blau, 1973). Max Weber wrote, "For the needs of mass administration today, it is completely indispensable" (1947:337). Hobbs and Blank elaborate, saying, "Bureaucracy is the loom upon which modern mass society is woven. Bureaucracy is not simply a way to run government of mass society. In fact, bureaucracy is an administrative system that is used in *any* large organization of mass society" (1975:168).

If it is true that governmental growth and the industrial revolution are the parents of impersonal bureaucracy, the analogous effects of the humanistic counterrevolution now being witnessed in many spheres might be expected to produce interest in *alternative* types of formal organizations. And so it is:

> Recent developments within sociology have expanded the perspective from which formal organizations are studied. Criticisms of the traditional position of Weber and Blau and Schoenherr have surfaced as research and theory have begun to grapple with a series of new issues. . . . Although the critiques have emanated from such diverse sources as symbolic interactionism, ethnomethodology, conflict sociology, Marxism, and social exchange theory, their tendency has been to undermine the conventional approach at the same point—the *production* of organizational reality through the actions of particular people and particular groups of people (Vander Zanden, 1979:171).

In short, most alternative theories of organization emphasize the roles of individuals—the particular skills, characters and values they bring to the group.

An example of such an alternative is the *democratic collectivist* organization. In an excellent contrast of the collectivist with the traditional bureaucratic model, Joyce Rothschild-Whitt (1979) demonstrates that the bureaucracy is not only inappropriate but is opposed to the furtherance of certain types of objectives. Specifically, most types of social action are inconsistent with the notion of depersonalization and, as Rothschild-Whitt points out (1979:509), Weber did not even describe a type of organization for the implementation of social action. He did, however, recognize that "value-rational" authority would require a type of organization with different characteristics from the *instrumentally rational* organization characterized by formal bureaucracy. Quoting Weber (1968), Rothschild-Whitt notes, "A value-rational orientation to social action is marked by a 'belief in the value for its own sake . . . independent of its prospects of success.' It is evidenced by actions that put into practice people's convictions" (1979:509). She further suggests that certain kinds of "church organizations" (1979:509) might fall within the sphere of the collective organization but, as will be pointed out below, the biblically patterned local church seems to be neither the bureaucracy nor the collective.

Organizational leadership. Because of the increasing emphasis on the human aspects of organization, the role of leadership has commanded a larger share of consideration in the study of groups in recent years. This trend has received impetus from the development and application of human behavior principles to group dynamics, especially formal organizational dynamics.

An illustration of this trend is found in a threefold progression involving concepts of people in organizations. Initially, people were seen as *human cogs;* then the focus was on *human relations;* then it was on *human resources.* Implicit in the Weberian model was the notion that people were little more than cogs which, if they were the right size and shape, could be freely interchanged without consequence. As the flush of the industrial revolution was absorbed into unionization and collective bargaining, the humanity and individuality of employees asserted themselves. One result was the onset of human relations—an attempt to recognize that people have needs and ideas as well as brains and muscles.

In practice, however, the predominant thrust of human relations has often been merely that people are cogs that have to be oiled in more ways than one. The individuality of employees is recognized, but it is seen as a set of characteristics that has to be accommodated in order to gain the use of its cogs. In many cases, then, human relations has been little more than a management tool, more acceptable than coercion in molding men and women into standard parts, but having the ultimate intent to smooth the spikes of individuality in the organizational function (Sergiovanni and Starratt, 1971:151–54).

Recently a few sociolpsychologists have proposed that people are far more than intelligent and emotional parts that must be related to; that they are *resources* for production; and that, properly motivated and utilized, the individuality that has often been viewed as a liability can be an organization's greatest asset. Many organizations are now taking steps to unharness the creative and managerial abilities of employees at every level, and the organizations are attaining both productivity and employee satisfaction previously undreamed of (Myers, 1970).

A parallel example of the so-called *new humanism* in organizational leadership philosophy, and one that has several points of contact with the discussion above, is the increasing awareness of, and concern with, the *assumptions* of leadership. To illustrate, Douglas McGregor (1960) has hypothesized a contrast between Theory X and Theory Y assumptions about people at work. He goes on to reasonably posit that management styles based on these respective assumptions will be quite different.

Theory X is based on the assumption that people hate to work, seek to avoid responsibility, and must be coerced into productive activity. Theory Y, on the other hand, views people as creative, desirous of responsibility, and anxious to work at activities that provide nurturance of these characteristics.

It should be obvious that a manager operating under one of these sets of assumptions will have quite a different style from a manager assuming the other. Chris Argyris, in his *Management and Organizational Development* (1971:1–26), labels behavior predicated on Theory X assumptions as Pattern A. Pattern A takes two forms: hard and soft. In general, the hard version is a no-nonsense approach characterized by strong leadership, tight controls, and close supervision. The soft approach relies on buying, persuading, and benevolent paternalism. Both the hard and soft approaches emphasize manipulation and control.

Pattern B is the label used by Argyris for the management style predicated on Theory Y assumptions. Pattern B managers tend toward building identification with, and commitment to, organizational objectives through trust and competency. Argyris writes, "More trust, concern for feelings, and internal commitment; more openness to, and experimenting with, new ideas and feelings, *in such a way that others could do the same*, were recommended if valid information was to be produced and internal commitment to decisions generated" (1971:18). The differences between *hard* Theory X and Theory Y assumptions are quite obvious, but the distinction between the *soft* variety of Theory X and Theory Y are easy to miss. Upon close scrutiny the student of organizational management will discern that soft Theory X is human *relations,* while Theory Y more nearly corresponds to the *human resources* approach.

Organizational power. In sociology the term *power* refers to "the capacity of an individual or group to control or influence the behavior of others, even in the absence of their consent" (Vander Zanden, 1979:502). Thus a discussion of organizational power must include a consideration of the power of the individual within the organization, along with the organization itself within the larger society.

When the persons over whom power is being exercised consent to have their behavior controlled or influenced, the power is said to be "legitimate" and those in possession of the power are said to have "authority" (Rose et al., 1976:161). Authority has been categorized by Weber (1946) as being of three different types:

1. Traditional authority. When people submit to the use of power because certain patterns of empowering have been historically followed, or because particular ways of delegating power are sacred, the authority thus gained is "traditional." Traditional authority can attach to positions, individuals, or both. Examples are familial monarchs and leaders chosen by lot, as in the Bible.

2. Legal-rational authority. This type of authority is vested entirely in the office occupied by a power-wielder. It is usually derived from law or some rule of organization. This is the type of authority most commonly associated with bureaucracy.

3. Charismatic authority. This type of authority is based on the personal qualities of the individual exerting power. Individuals who, because of their personalities, gifts, talents or characters, attract willing followers are said to have charismatic authority.

In recent years a fourth category of organizational authority has emerged—one based on professional norms and skill. Although not widely recognized in sociology texts, an understanding of this category is quite important in view of increasing interest in alternative organizations; in addition, it is essential to adherents of the church, as will be demonstrated later in the essay. Adding this category to those of Weber, we may summarize it as follows:

4. Competency-based authority. The "potential capacity to effect movement toward goal-achievement accruing from knowledge and skill gained through training or experience" (Sergiovanni and Carver, 1973:160).

There are now four categories of authority, and these appear to encompass all possible sources of power legitimation. Robert L. Peabody (1962), under a slightly different scheme, groups the first two categories into "formal" authority and calls the second pair "functional" authority.

As should be apparent, formal authority bases are comprised of "legitimacy, position, and the sanctions inherent in the office," while functional authority bases are comprised of "professional competence, experience, and human relations skills, which support or compete with formal authority" (Peabody, 1962:466–67). This dichotomy reveals a potential morale problem for bureaucracies that may be described as the "ability-authority gap" (Thompson, 1965:6). This situation arises when those with formal authority lack functional authority. Organizations in which ability produces advancement could not experience this problem, because those in positions of power would always be more competent than their subordinates. With the Peter Principle so prevalently at work, however, this ideal is seldom seen. Again, as we shall see, the distinction between formal and functional authority is an especially important one for Christians, whose main organizational identity is with the church.

Large organizations are especially powerful because they can bring the resources of many individuals to bear on selected problems or issues. The best known of these superorganizations are found in business and government.

> Power is often related to control of wealth. In capitalist societies, control over basic industries (steel, oil, and others), large landholdings, and ownership of transportation systems (railroads, airlines) have been primary sources of power. Power enables a group to defend its interests. It gives people the ability to maintain and increase their wealth and prestige. This may be done by influencing government activities (lobbying for protective legislation, winning major government contracts) or by affecting private business (Rose et al., 1976:204).

Light and Keller give a business example:

> The rise in our times of the immensely profitable *multinational corporation,* an organization with productive facilities in several countries. . . . A multinational can move tremendous sums of money around the world to take advantage of favorable—or unfavorable—conditions. And it may, through advertising, create a market in a particular country for merchandise it can no longer sell anywhere else, such as outdated automobiles or television sets (1978:216).

It is perhaps more important for the student to recognize the power of governmental organizations for two reasons. First, although we might largely escape the power of individual business organizations, there is virtually no individual who is not significantly influenced by government.

Second, individuals at the apex of large bureaucracies have tremendous power. In the United States, for example, more and more of the business of governing is being carried out by the administrative branch of government. On the one hand, the judicial and legislative branches are essentially democratic, and a plurality is required for most actions. The administrative branch, on the other hand, is bureaucratic, and the current trend not only places more power in that branch, but places that power into the hands of fewer individuals. In turn, the bureaucratic elements of governing organizations, like business, tend to use their power to gain more power. A comment made by the noted news commentator Howard K. Smith is appropriate here:

> If dictatorship ever comes to America, I am convinced it won't come because of some specific crisis. It will be because our Democracy got so complicated, people couldn't understand it so they asked someone else to do it (*Alert,* National Christian Action Coalition, February, 1980, front page).

In concluding this brief review of some of the important issues in organization, the student should recognize that there are close relationships in the contrasts between traditional bureaucratic organization and alternative types, between human cog and human resource, between Theory X and Theory Y management philosophy, and between formal and functional authority. The contrasts merely provide slightly different perspectives on the evolution of thought regarding people in organizations. At this point the focus of this essay will shift to a specific issue encompassing all of these considerations.

IMPLICATIONS FOR CHRISTIANS

Having reviewed the major subtopics of social organizations, the following discussion will narrow its treatment to a specific organization, the local church. It is important to see the church in its relationship to general organization theory for at least two reasons. First, churches—especially as they grow larger—tend to see themselves as, and pattern themselves after, organizations seen in business, government, education, and industry. As might be expected in view of comments under *Alternative organizational models* above, the church that patterns itself after a traditional secular model must irrevocably find itself tending toward the assumptions, products, and methods of the model that it emulates. The probability is small that such a church organization will conform to biblical norms.

A second problem, perhaps a subproblem of the first, is the tendency of churches to align themselves with the traditional bureaucratic model. Such alignment results in the tendency to treat people as human cogs who must be coerced through the exercise of power or fear (or, at best, human relations) into contributing to the goals of the organization. This is a particularly unbiblical tendency. In view of these problems, a more biblical model of organization will be discussed—that of the church as a body.

The organization of the church. In Scripture two predominant analogies characterize the church—that of a *body* and that of a *building of stones.* Both of these are formal organizations, but not bureaucracies. For purposes of the following discussion, the analogy of the building will be dropped, as it is not intended to describe the characteristics of the church as a functioning organization, but alludes to people in a positional sense only.

The body is a formal organization because it is a group of organs and tissues whose activities are deliberately coordinated for the achievement of specific goals or purposes. It is not a bureaucracy because there is no pyramidal hierarchy. Instead, God teaches us through the apostle Paul that all members of the body are essential and that none is thought to be more important than another (1 Cor. 12:12–27).

On the other hand, the body is not a *collective,* for the members are specialized (1 Cor. 12:28–30). Thus, although organizations of both the bureaucratic and democratic (collective) type may be appropriate for some functions, neither adequately conforms to the biblical model. For a biblical model, we must look to the body.

Diversity versus egalitarianism. As noted above, the rise of humanism has brought traditional bureaucracy to a critical juncture, as the competition for prestige has made the notion of differences (not to mention subordination) socially suspect. The resulting idea that equality means sameness has penetrated deeply into our society, a fact witnessed to by the existence of many liberation movements whose primary objective appears to be erasing distinctions between people. This drive to "do what someone else does best" is an effective method of thwarting God's design, under which each is to do what he or she does best and under which God guarantees his or her uniqueness. The body concept of organization in the New Testament ensures that each is in a special place with a special function and that each will be adequately supported.

Yet for many church members the presence of an organizational chart in the church office is a source of pride; and the higher a person's name is on the chart, the greater is that person's pride. If we are to maintain the biblical pattern, however, it is important for us to understand that an organizational chart of the body can indicate no more than the gifts and callings of individual members, along with the working relationships between them. There is perhaps only one carnal temptation easier to accommodate than the desire to elevate ourselves, and that is our willingness to allow others to elevate us. When confronted with this temptation, the apostle Paul responded, "What, after all, is Apollos? And what is Paul? Only servants, through whom you came to believe. . . . I planted the seed, Apollos watered it, but God made it grow. So neither he who plants nor he who waters is anything, but only God, who makes things grow. . . . For we are God's fellow workers" (1 Cor. 3:5–9). This is the body concept of diversity and equality—fellow workers.

Impartiality versus personality. Weber asserts that emotions have no place in organization. The collectivist replies that emotion is the essence of the human being and hence must have free reign. What are the relative merits of these claims?

In support of the collectivist, there is abundant evidence that the founders of the Judeo-Christian faith allowed emotion to influence their acts and decisions. Further, it is clear that at times Christ displayed emotions. However, God is perfectly rational, and to ascribe misjudgment to Him would be blasphemy. Christians are instructed not to sin in their anger (Eph. 4:26). Does this mean that Christians should seek to be rational and lay their feelings aside when they conduct God's business? Or should they "let it all hang out," trusting that God is always in their emotions? A form of the answer to these questions is found in Tim LaHaye's *Spirit-Controlled Temperament* (1966) and its companion volume, *Transformed Temperaments* (1971). In these books LaHaye points out that God created each of us with a unique set of emotional tendencies and that it is through the transforming power of the Holy Spirit that our temperaments become harnessed for God.

According to LaHaye, "In the revelation of God's will for man found in the Bible, we read the accounts of many spiritual leaders. Several of these characters are classic examples of God's power to transform human temperament" (1971:28). He goes on to examine the lives of four Bible characters and to show that their unique temperaments, as transformed by the Holy Spirit, made immeasurable contributions to the body.

Consider, for example, Peter and Paul, whose conflicting temperaments had the power to bring them into sharp conflict (Gal. 2:11). Yet, within the body they were able to resolve their differences and work together for the edification of the whole (Acts 15:6–18). In fact, the entire record of the relationships between the disciples around the Lord is abundant evidence of not only the tolerance, but also the necessity of varying temperaments in the building of the church.

It is not, then, the destruction or exchanging of the temperament that makes the body work. Instead, it is the transformation that comes from the Spirit's control that permits each individual to contribute to the body through the ministry of his or her particular temperament. The basis for right emotions is spirit control, whereas wrong emotions result from the lack of spirit control.

The pure bureaucrat assumes (Theory X) that the temperaments of employees are under the control of a selfish spirit. Thus he wants emotion left out. The pure democratic collectivist assumes (Theory Y) that emotions are under the control of a benevolent spirit and hence are always beneficial to the organization. The truth, as given in Romans 7, is that all are under the influence of *both* spirits.

It is sadly true that church leaders often operate under Theory X assumptions and use Pattern A management styles, while so-called humanistic managers are Theory Y, Pattern B, people. The absurdity of this situation is that, in the final analysis, only Christians are capable of fulfilling Theory Y assumptions, because without the transforming power of the Holy Spirit, every man and woman is ultimately motivated by selfish desires and the negative qualities of his or her temperament (Rom. 3:10–18). Thus we find a strange world. On the one hand, some church leaders who expect their followers to be lazy, selfish, and difficult to motivate thwart the potential of their constituency to do great things in the Spirit; on the other hand, some secular leaders with the opposite expectations make the most of little human potential and use it to defeat the stewards of the Spirit.

Under the control of the Holy Spirit all emotional tendencies can be transformed; the melancholic, choleric, sanguine, and phlegmatic (LaHaye, 1971) can be modified so as to work together in the body under the headship of Christ. Each will then contribute positively to the work of the body. In contrast, under the control of Satan, love becomes lust, anger becomes retribution, joy becomes pride, sadness becomes guilt, and hatred of sin turns to hatred of sinners.

Is the secret of good organization, then, in bureaucracy, Theory X, and no emotions? Or, is it in democratic collectivism, Theory Y, and all emotion? It is in neither; rather, the secret is "we, who are many . . . one body *in Christ,* and individually members one of another" (Rom. 12:5, NASB, emphasis added).

The Peter Principle and the body. Interestingly, organization according to the body concept will eliminate the Peter Principle. Whereas in a hierarchy workers are placed in positions of responsibility according to seniority, in the body all are placed according to their gifts. The structure of the body is such that there is a place for each gift, and a gift for each place, according to the biblical description.

This is not to say that many local churches do not fall into the Peter Principle; they do. However, they do so only to the extent that they adopt bureaucratic practices instead of biblical ones. Many have heard the following statement in one form or another: "Well, Jones has been a Sunday school teacher longer than anyone else in the church, and he knows the Bible well; so let's make him the Sunday school superintendent." This approach ignores the question of whether Jones has the gift of administration, and it bases his appointment on testimony that he has the gift of teaching and has been steadfast.

A similar syndrome occurs with regard to other positions of leadership. Someone may say, "Smith has shown up at every workday we've had at the church for five years. I'm going to nominate him to the board." Faithfulness, of course, is an important qualification for leadership, but it is by no means the only one. Neither is the possession of manual skills. What should be asked is, Does Smith meet the biblical qualifications for leadership as defined by the church? For example, the leader should be "temperate" (1 Tim. 3:2) and a good manager of his family (v. 4). To adopt one specific quality such as seniority or competence as the criterion for movement to positions of responsibility within the church is to ignore the body principle in favor of the Peter Principle.

A second problem with using the bureaucratic approach in the church is that it reinforces the natural human tendency to regard some positions as more or less important than others. Clearly, this is the basis of the bureaucratic system of incentives; but in the body all members support each other, and the absence of any member causes the body to be incomplete. If, for instance, the gift of serving were to be regarded as less valuable than the gift of teaching (Rom. 12:7), God would have to be declared unfair, as He, through the ministry of the Holy Spirit, "works . . . distributing to each one individually just as He wills" (1 Cor. 12:11, NASB). Honor and reward will be accorded to Christians for time and eternity, not according to the types of gifts received or responsibilities undertaken, but according to the person's motives, quality of work, and the way the gifts were used (1 Cor. 3:12–14; 1 Tim. 5:17). Part of the godly use of gifts is not desiring the gifts of others.

Before concluding this discussion of the body concept of organization, it is important to give a constructive example. There are many church organization alternatives to the bureaucracy. One of the better known alternatives, and one that corresponds fairly well to the body principle, is the *team-centered* approach of Kenneth K. Kilinski and Jerry C. Wofford. Its basic ingredients are:

1. It is an organization in which the basic unit of communication is the group rather than a one-to-one relationship.
2. There is a high amount of mutual influence within each group.
3. Group members manifest their love and acceptance of one another. The group leader is especially warm and accepting of others.
4. The group possesses a high degree of responsibility for decisions and actions within its special area.
5. Communication links are assured among groups within the organization by virtue of overlapping memberships (i.e., individuals are members of more than one group, especially where coordination of efforts is important).
6. The official board of the church has as its membership the leaders of all major groups; therefore, each group has a communication link to the board.
7. The organization sustains a minimum number of organizational layers.
8. Members participate actively in their areas of responsibility (1973:160).

The following diagram by Kilinski and Wofford (1973:163) illustrates the team-centered approach:

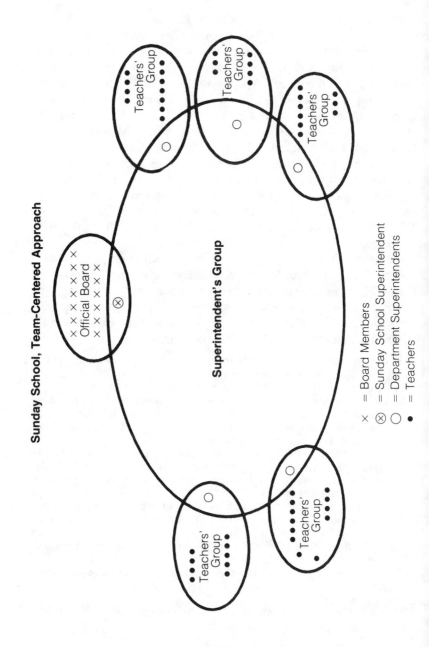

Sunday School, Team-Centered Approach

Teachers' Group

Teachers' Group

Teachers' Group

Official Board

Superintendent's Group

Teachers' Group

Teachers' Group

× = Board Members

⊗ = Sunday School Superintendent

◯ = Department Superintendents

● = Teachers

Note that communication between respective Sunday school teachers and the Sunday school superintendent is not isolated, but is carried on in the context of the whole Sunday school mission. Likewise, individuals are not viewed in an ascending or descending order, but are seen as making their contributions at the same level of importance. When people move within or among the spheres of work, they will do so on the basis of their gifts, and the rewards and honor accorded each one will be determined by the faithfulness with which the gift is exercised, not by the centrality of his or her position.

Clearly, some will occupy positions more central to the determination of the agenda of the church, and there will be movement from the periphery toward the center as spiritual maturity and giftedness obtain. At this point, however, many churches impose a feature of the democratic collectivist organization between the board and the body—the congregational meeting. This is viewed by some as the apostolic church model and ensures that all policy will be that of the general body. This is plainly not a bureaucracy, and it corresponds very closely to the body concept.

Finally, although the biblical model for the church is not a bureaucracy, it also is not a democratic collective. This is apparent from the fact that in the church there is specialization and division of labor, and there are "elders who direct the affairs of the church" (1 Tim. 5:17). These elders are specially called and gifted to communicate and administer the interests of the body. All positions, however, are seen as positions of service and of equal value before God. Selection to any position is according to giftedness, not seniority in some other position. Hence, selection is not based on the Peter Principle.

Power and the body concept. As noted in the introductory section, the exercise of power through the hierarchy to gain more power is a characteristic of a bureaucracy. Because there is no pyramiding within the body, however, there is little opportunity for individuals to accrue power based on the efforts of others.

Within the concept of giftedness, each body member has a unique contribution to make and exercises power to the extent dictated by his or her gifts (1 Cor. 12:12–18). Further, because no member has all of the gifts, no one can appropriately dictate the means of every task. Each is uniquely qualified to determine how his or her job is to be done. The only limitation on the use of gifts is accountability for the edification (building up) of the whole, which rules out using gifts privately to build up oneself.

It is recognized that the gifts of "leadership" (Rom. 12:8) and "administration" (1 Cor. 12:28) at least imply a strong sense of directing. *Young's Analytical Concordance to the Bible,* for example, defines the Greek terms, respectively:

proistēmi: to set or place over or before

kuber; steering, piloting, directing

These are gifts to which legitimate power may attach and, because the power involves the placement of others within the body, it might be viewed as a higher order of power. However, there are some important distinctions between this power and hierarchical power.

First, power in the body does not accrue from position alone, and it does not increase because of movement upward with attendant control over more resources. In fact, this concept of leadership through giftedness provides a classic example of competency-based authority. The body concept of organization requires that qualified members be placed in any position, including those of leadership and administration, only if the giftedness associated with that position is manifest. Thus each member of the body has both formal and functional authority in a designated position, and the ability-authority gap is eliminated.

Second, the leader in the body does not use the power of a spiritual gift to manipulate others for personal benefit or for the exclusive purpose of gaining more personal power. The intent of each gift is to edify the whole, and the organizational structure of the body ensures that this will be the result of the leadership gifts. The structure is such that the overlapping, nonhierarchical relationship of the body organization will tend to transmit the power of each individual to the whole. Likewise, when the gifts are subject to one another, the power of each of the gifts will be transmitted outward, not necessarily *through* the leader, but because of the coordination brought about by the leader's gift. Thus no effort is wasted because of the friction of maintaining subordination. Individuals see themselves as being completely equipped for the organizational role God has given them. This includes leaders who understand that without the other members, their gift would be meaningless and valueless. This is human resources management at its fullest, and the result is increased organizational power without the usually associated concentration of individual power—precisely what God intended.

The church—organization or institution? A distinction made by a secular administrative theoretician could well be studied by church leaders:

> The term "organization" . . . suggests a certain barrenness, a lean, no-nonsense system of consciously co-ordinated activities. It refers to an *expendable tool,* a rational instrument engineered to do a job. An "institution," on the other hand, is more nearly a natural product of social needs and pressures—a responsive, adaptive organism (Selznick, 1957:5).

This distinction, although not a directly biblical one, can help explain why many churches have become more and more efficient but less and less effective in terms of biblical imperatives. First, according to an expanded definition, to institutionalize is "to *infuse with* value beyond the technical requirements of the task at hand. Whenever individuals become attached to an organization or a way of doing things as persons rather than as technicians, the result is a prizing of the device for its own sake" (Selznick, 1957:17).

In other words, an *institution* is an organization that represents more than its products and services. It is somehow good in itself. This goodness derives from some value that has been infused into it, and it would be good to have it around even if it *had* no product or provided no service. Thus "the test of infusion with value is *expendability*" (Selznick, 1957:18). That is, an organization that exists for no purpose other than its product or service will not be missed if its product or service lapses, or if the product or service can be provided more efficiently by another organization. "When value infusion takes place, however, there is a resistance to change" (Selznick, 1957:18).

A frequently seen example of the expendability principle of late is the closing of the neighborhood school. True, the residents who have long been served by the school realize that it is no longer needed, for the diminishing number of neighborhood children are being more efficiently served at the newer school at a new location. Yet the older residents still lament as they pass by the old building, saying, "Seems a shame that the old school is closed. It was such a big part of our lives." The school, as recalled by former students, parents of students, and neighbors who used to drop in, has become infused with value. It has become valuable in a sense separate from its products (students) and services (education).

A second characteristic of an institution is that it tends to maintain itself.

> The transformation of expendable technical organizations into institutions is marked by a concern for *self-maintenance*. A living association blends technical aims and procedures with personal desires and group interests. As a result, various elements in the association have a stake in its continued existence. Moreover, the aims of the organization may require a certain permanence and stability (Selznick, 1957:20).

To summarize, in seeking to maintain itself, the institution recognizes its own value beyond its products and services and it desires to retain those values. The primary duty of the institutional leader is to ensure the continuance of the institution and the preservation of its values. Although the above characterization comes from a secular writer, it overlaps with the Lord's mandate to the church to maintain itself and retain its distinctive purity in the world.

The reader no doubt suspects by now that the following discussion will contend that the church would do well to see itself, in Selznick's terms, as an institution, rather than a mere organization. This distinction is important for three reasons.

First, Christ Himself clearly intended that the body be *present*, if nothing else. The *least* emphatic connotation of His command to "Occupy till I come" (Luke 19:13, KJV) is that His followers should be present in the world until He returns. No doubt He was mindful that salt in any form will do its multifaceted work so long as it remains (Matt. 5:13). His inaugural promise that the gates of hell would not prevail against the church (Matt. 16:18) is divine reassurance that so long as the church remains faithfully on its foundation stone, survival is the worst thing that can happen to it. These are the characteristics of an institution.

Second, the tendency of the modern church is to pattern itself after technical organizations; those who work in the church tend to see themselves as technicians. We find ourselves at a point of social evolution at which productivity is so highly regarded as to constitute virtually the only *raison d'être* for any group. Granted,

God clearly wills the church to do more than exist (John 15:16); but unless it can see beyond its products and services, it will find its existence woefully shallow and frustrating.

Finally, institutional groups require a far different type of leadership than simple organizations. Christians who see themselves merely as organizational managers will be quite inadequate as church leaders. In what follows, each of these areas is considered in a little more detail.

1. One way the church differs from a merely technical institution is that it is not in a state of qualitative change; its values are permanent. As noted above, the body of Christ, the church, *will remain* until His physical reappearance. The church may be distinguished from the human institution, however. For example, Selznick states, "Institutionalization is a *process*" (1957:16), and he reiterates the progressive nature of the process when he remarks that "an organization *acquires* a self" (emphasis added; note the progressive tense) by "the taking on of values, ways of acting and believing" (1957:21).

In contrast, the church is permanently institutionalized. Its eternal values were instantly and immutably infused when God conceived it. The values of a society change and are reflected by slow changes in the values of its institutions over a period of time, but those basic to the church do not.

It is important that those who make up the body be conscious of this relationship between organizational attitude and the preservation of values, because the response of the simple organization to social change is quite different from that of the institution.

For example, a primary function of the technical organization is to respond as quickly and efficiently as possible to the immediate needs and demands of its clientele. The function of the church is to serve its constituency not only by responding to what it asks for, but by seeking to preserve the values that have been established in God's Word, and church tradition. As an institution with eternal and absolute values, the church necessarily must lead its constituency, not follow it as does the technical organization.

If the church decides to act as a mechanistic organization, seeing itself only in terms of productivity, it will tend to quickly set aside any values that seem to impede its efficiency. That is, if its attendance is falling, or contributions are down, it will be vulnerable to suggestions that it no longer offers what people want and should change its image, methods, and message. This tendency is especially strong in our day when more and more churches are accepting productivity as the main standard of success, and traditional biblical values are not always well received. The church must learn once again to see itself as an institution, whose values are more important than its products. Then and only then will it rediscover the promise of Christ that it will prevail.

2. Another way the church differs from a technical institution involves its *values*. What, then, are the values that the church is to maintain? According to Selznick, the values of an institution are "largely a reflection of the unique way in which it fulfills personal or group needs" (1957:17). It would be impossible to find an organization with more effective and permanent methods of fulfilling personal or group needs than the biblical church; hence it is the very embodiment of the notion of institution. That the church must view itself as an institution is, again, especially imperative in the face of the sure knowledge that its values will be less and less acceptable to secular society as time goes by. Perhaps no institution represents values less desirable to the secular world in this day than the body of Christ.

Because of this, churches that value their numbers, budgets, or popularity more than their message may soon be hard pressed to find justification for their self-maintenance. There is ample evidence of attrition among churches that have adopted productivity as their standard of success. It is not unusual to find pastors and church boards adopting numerical or financial goals for themselves, along with the hollow challenge that "if we can't double our congregation (or budget, or facility) in X years, we might as well close the doors!" It is fortunate that Adoniram Judson, who worked for six years to see his first convert (Kane, 1971:146), did not adopt such nonsense; instead, Judson realized that the duty of the institution of the church is to preserve the Word of God and the work of the Spirit is to produce. The memory of men such as Judson should shame the denomination or church that would cease to hold forth the Word in a community just because it is no longer profitable.

Again, there is no intention here to imply that fruitlessness is an acceptable characteristic of the church. On the contrary, such an implication would be counter to the biblical norm. However, it is the function of the church to preserve and convey the values with which it has been infused by Christ; the function of the Holy Spirit is to add the fruit.

3. Still another way the church differs from a technical institution concerns its *leadership*. It is urgent that the body of Christ see itself as more than an organization, because the type of leadership required by an institution is quite different from that required by a simple organization.

> The design and maintenance of organizations is often a straightforward engineering proposition. When the goals of the organization are clear-cut, and when most choices can be made on the basis of known and objective technical criteria, the engineer rather than the leader is called for.
>
> From the engineering perspective, the organization is made up of standardized building blocks. His ultimate ideal is complete rationality, and this assumes that each member of the organization, and each constituent unit, can be made to adhere faithfully to an assigned, engineered role (Selznick, 1957:137–38).

Of course, there are many ways in which the church goes beyond this description; hence the church must go beyond mere engineering. The biblical concept of discernment (Heb. 5:14), for example, belies any notion that most decisions and choices of church leadership can in Selznick's words above, "be made on the basis of known and objective technical criteria"; church members are by no means "standardized building blocks," and their goal is not "complete rationality." The apostle Paul cogently informs us that the product of the church is in the eyes of the world "foolishness" (1 Cor. 1:18). Finally, as mentioned above and in Scripture, the church is not "standardized" as an organization; instead, Christians are a "peculiar people" (1 Peter 2:9, KJV), that is, they belong to God.

The church must have the kind of leadership that looks beyond the technical aspects of organization. Concerning such leadership, Selznick says:

> The limits of organization engineering become apparent when we must create a structure *uniquely adapted to the mission and role of the enterprise.* This adaptation goes beyond a tailored combination of uniform elements; it is an adaptation in depth, affecting the nature of the parts themselves. . . . In this way the organization as a technical instrument

> takes on values. As a vehicle of group integrity it becomes in some degree an end in itself. This process of becoming infused with value is part of what we mean by institutionalization. As this occurs, *organization management* becomes *institutional leadership*. The latter's main responsibility is not so much technical administrative management as the maintenance of institutional integrity (1957:138).

Perhaps it is because church leaders have fallen into the practice of viewing the organizations they lead as "a tailored combination of uniform elements" that we so seldom see "an adaptation in depth, affecting the nature of the parts [of the body] themselves." Perhaps it is because church leaders have come to view themselves as engineers rather than hearts that churches often see themselves as machines rather than bodies.

> The integrity of an enterprise goes beyond efficiency, beyond organization forms and procedures, even beyond group cohesion. Integrity combines organization and policy. It is the unity which emerges when a particular orientation becomes so firmly a part of group life that it colors and directs a wide variety of attitudes, decisions, and forms of organization, and does so at many levels of experience. The building of integrity is part of . . . the "institutional embodiment of purpose" and its protection is a major function of leadership (Selznick, 1957:138).

Should the church provide this type of unity? Should it color and direct attitudes, decisions, and even forms of organization? If so, the organizational form must not be allowed to dictate the values, means, and ends of the body. All too often, though, this is what happens when churches are patterned after the forms or organization found in management texts or in successful businesses.

Certainly, the church leader must maintain the organization as a going concern within the boundaries of institutional mission and philosophy, as must any other institutional leader. These boundaries are delineated by Scripture, but Scripture permits, and *requires*, that the unique giftedness and needs of the constituency be accounted for and developed by the leader. It is noteworthy that Selznick describes the institution as an "organism" (1957:5) and a "living association" (1957:21). It is precisely this characterization that Christ had in mind when He chose the analogy of the body for the church. The church is not merely a mechanized group of human cogs that turns out saved souls or social good, or a hierarchical circuit of components assembled for the purpose of pro-

ducing spoken, written, recorded, printed, and projected testimony. Instead, the church is a living, growing, feeling organism
that loves, rejoices, and reproduces; in short, a body.

DISCUSSION QUESTIONS

1. To what extent is the church you attend a formal organization?
2. Is there any bureaucracy in that church? Is this good or bad?
3. Which type of leadership would be most effective in a local
   church—Theory X or Y? Why?
4. Which of the four categories of authority presented in this
   chapter should a pastor exercise? Why?
5. To what extent should a local church utilize theories and research in formal organizations? Why?

SUGGESTED READING

Ted. W. Engstrom and Edward R. Dayton, *The Art of Management for
Christian Leaders* (Waco: Word Books, 1976), and Ted W. Engstrom, *The
Making of a Christian Leader* (Grand Rapids: Zondervan, 1976). These
books are cited as examples of an approach to organization and leadership that tends to be in contrast with the institutional philosophy set
out in this essay. Engstrom tends toward the technical organizational
model, although some consideration is given to a team approach in the
latter volume.

Kenneth K. Kilinski and Jerry C. Wofford, *Organization and Leadership in
the Local Church* (Grand Rapids: Zondervan, 1973). An excellent example of the application of the "body concept" to the organization of the
local church. Outlines the application of leadership principles consistent with biblical objectives.

Francis A. Schaeffer, *The Church at the End of the 20th Century* (Downers
Grove, Ill.: Inter-Varsity, 1978). This book brings into sharp focus the
need to militantly preserve the traditional biblical mission of the
church. A forceful demonstration of the attrition of Christian values.

Philip Selznick, *Leadership in Administration: A Sociological Interpretation*
(New York: Harper and Row, 1957). The classic treatment of the distinction between technical organizations and institutions. A secular
text that has tremendous implications for local church administration.

Thomas J. Sergiovanni and Robert J. Starratt, *Emerging Patterns of Supervision: Human Perspectives* (New York: McGraw-Hill, 1971). A secular
examination of modern leadership techniques. Although written predominantly for school administrators, the concepts are applicable to the
church, which is in large part an educational institution.

15

RICHARD PERKINS
Houghton College,
New York

MINORITY-MAJORITY RELATIONS

Certain scarce goods are divided unequally in all societies. These goods are routinely distributed to groups within each society, with some groups receiving more and others less. Of course, the specific types of goods vary from society to society, or even with respect to various groups within the same society. Even so, all scarce goods fall into one or more of three very general categories—wealth, control, and honor—that sometimes are referred to as privilege, power, and prestige (see chap. 6).

One aspect of stratification relevant to most modern societies concerns the unequal distribution of these goods to groups identified on the basis of certain inherited, or ascriptive characteristics. These characteristics may be inherited socially (e.g., a distinctive language or religion) and/or genetically (e.g., distinctive facial features or skin color). The ethnic and racial groups that typically receive a less-than-proportionate share of the goods in a given society are called minority groups, even though these groups may constitute a numerical majority (as in the case of blacks in the Republic of South Africa). Majority groups are those that receive a greater-than-proportionate share. Majority groups are therefore defined primarily in terms of power, as those with or the capability to establish an institutionalized system of action that favors its own members in the distribution of scarce goods. It is necessary therefore to recognize that majority and minority groups are always involved in some form of competition whereby one group benefits at the expense of another. However, overt competition is typically institutionalized and thus taken for granted—at least by members of the majority group. Only rarely is there a violent revolt against this system of unequal distribution. For example in the United States, major revolts involving minority groups have been infrequent, the last being the urban disturbances in the middle and late 1960s. But just because a system is calm and normal does not mean that conflict has been eliminated; it has only been transformed into a routine competitive system.

THE PROBLEM OF RECOGNITION

There are several facets of minority-majority group stratification that must be grasped clearly by the Christian hoping to integrate faith with learning in this area of sociological analysis. The first concerns the routine nature of the unequal distribution system.

If it can be agreed that Christianity should foster a spirit of benevolence and equality—values supported by Scripture passages such as Luke 3:7–11—then the subject of minority-majority relations can be approached in this light.[1]

Also, starting with this Christian value perspective, there are certain topics ordinarily found within sociological analyses of

---

[1]However, this is not the same thing as inquiring into the general subject of stratification; Christ seems to have been rather ambivalent about inequality in general—a subject addressed in chapter 6. Therefore the problems of inequality will be examined, not simply as the process whereby some people are wealthier or more powerful than others, but also in terms of the question of injustice. The Bible does not say that stratification per se is wrong, but it does say injustice is wrong and that it should be eliminated. Needless to say, the difference between inequality and injustice is not always apparent. For one thing, inequality is a term that relates to an empirical (i.e., observable) phenomenon whereas injustice suggests a value. While I do not wish to overlook the qualitative differences between these two phenomena, I also do not wish to ignore the important relationship between them.

minority-majority relations about which this essay will have little to say. For example, racial or ethnic prejudice (the stereotyped belief that members of "out groups" are inferior to one's own group) is clearly contradictory to these Christian values. Therefore, instead of discussing these rather blatant violations of Christian teachings, this chapter will concentrate on more subtle processes: in particular, the process whereby certain aspects of a minority-majority stratification system tend to be overlooked by otherwise sincere Christians.

Thus, in considering these issues from a Christian perspective, one finds that the Bible teaches Christians to have a concern for other persons and to demonstrate a spirit of benevolent equality to other Christians (Phil. 2:1–4; 1 Cor. 13:1–7).

Adopting this general moral perspective would immediately predispose a Christian to question any system that routinely favors one group over another (that is, a system that discriminates positively and negatively) on the basis of ascriptive traits such as skin color, ethnicity, etc. However, many Christians may never have raised such questions. This chapter will inquire into the reasons why this is often the case.

First of all, many persons may not be aware of the situation. This may be a bit hard to believe at first glance; after all, it is fairly obvious that American blacks are more likely to be poor than whites. Even so, given the nature of residential segregation in the United States, many white students may have personally known very few blacks or members of other minority groups. Furthermore, if perchance a middle-class white person *is* acquainted with some black persons, the latter may not be representative of blacks in general. Because our society is also divided along class lines, a middle-class white is likely to typically interact with middle-class blacks. As a result, their conclusions about blacks in general will be based on a very small and nonrepresentative sample.

America has, in a sense, hidden its problems of racism and poverty, causing many to lose sight of these issues. Moreover, even if we commonly experience interracial situations, we may not be familiar with the scope of the problem of inequality. For example, few Americans realize that the average black dies approximately six years younger than the average white, or that black infant mortality has historically been nearly double that of white infants.[2] Even though evidence like this of widespread discrimination is shocking and regrettable in the light of Christian values, a Christian may simply not have known about statistics like these before.

Sometimes it takes a very careful analysis to reveal facts like these—facts that are not at all obvious to the average person. Yet this discussion leads to the second reason why many Christians fail to even raise certain questions about our system of racial and ethnic inequality. The unequal distribution of goods is typically a routine and therefore taken-for-granted aspect of the American social system. Most persons have devised satisfactory ready-made explanations for events they observe that otherwise might be troubling. For example, it may be recognized that blacks are more likely to be poor than whites. However, many persons also have internalized an ideology (or a set of assumptions and values that constitute an argument as to why a system of unequal distribution is either desirable in itself or at least the best of a number of alternative systems) based on capitalistic values. One aspect of this system is the tendency to see inequality of private property as justified on the basis of what could be called the *equal opportunity myth*. Proponents of this ideology—and this includes most middle-class persons (especially Christians, who tend to be politically conservative)—argue that poverty is the justified result of some personal or collective defect such as laziness.[3] Like all ideologies, this explanation of poverty may be partially accurate. Nevertheless, the massive weight of sociological evidence demonstrates the mythlike nature of these assumptions. The idea that all

[2]The example of black-white relations in contemporary America is used throughout this chapter for two reasons. First, it is illustrative of most aspects of the general subject we are studying; the general analytical conclusions reached from a study of black and white relations apply also to Indian and white relations in America, to Protestant and Catholic relations in Northern Ireland, and so on. (Of course, this does not deny that there are also important differences between each case.) Secondly, black-white relations is the most salient example of minority-majority group relations for most persons reading this text.

[3]The voluminous literature on religious conservatism and economic ideology is summarized in Wuthnow (1973:129–32). Also, see chapter 10 on "Economics" in this volume. It is interesting too to note that true capitalism calls for equal opportunity and fair competition.

Americans have an equal chance to succeed in terms of occupational and income mobility is contradicted by the findings of contemporary research (Jencks, 1979). Even so, these findings are not widely known. Even if they were, the ideology would undoubtedly still appeal to many persons who otherwise would be hard put to explain certain features of normal daily life.

Ideologies have the capability to subtly remove from consideration issues that otherwise would perplex people. Christians ought to be especially sensitive to this tendency since ideologies are often based on religious truths. For example, the political values on which the American republic was founded have consistently appealed to religious sources.[4] Whenever America has been threatened by internal or external strife, the tendency of leaders has been to seize once again the mighty patriotic phrases and public ceremonies that seem to shore up the people against any tendency to falter in the face of a crisis. (One has only to consider the fact that the playing of the national anthem before all major sporting events had its origin during the early stages of the Cold War.)

Perhaps the clearest illustration of how religion is linked to the justification of a social system relates directly to the subject of minority-majority relations. This subject will be analyzed in some detail since it played such a dramatic role in our national history. It also amply illustrates how the central moral message of religious tradition can be radically altered by an ideology that seemingly contradicts it.

RACISM, SLAVERY, AND CHRISTIANITY

Slavery existed in North America for more than two hundred years. Before being abolished by the Thirteenth Amendment in 1865, slavery had grown to become the dominant factor in the Southern economy. Although the majority of whites never owned any slaves and only a very small percentage of those who did owned a large number of slaves, the justification of white dominance was accepted by the vast majority of all Southern whites. In

---

[4]For example, the Declaration of Independence contains references to "Nature's God," and on our dollar bill can be found the phrase *annuit coeptis,* which loosely translates as "God has blessed our undertakings."

short, racism, the ideology that maintains that a group should be subordinated due to their alleged genetic or cultural inferiority, became a major part of the Southern way of life. At the same time, religion—in particular, fundamentalist Protestant Christianity—played an unusually predominant role throughout the South, especially when slavery was a dominant institution (Reed, 1972: chap. 6).

American slavery has been referred to as "a peculiar institution" due largely to the extensive ideology of racism used to defend American slavery. The greatest threats to slavery were generated by abolitionists, "free-soil" critics, and in general by the democratic ideology that asserted that "all men are created equal." The defenders of slavery reasoned that if all men were indeed created equal, then it must be concluded that blacks are not human since slaves (that is, blacks) could not be equal in any way to whites.

Slaves were defined as chattel (property) and not as humans, and they were treated as such. For example, no slave could be legally taught to read and write. Slave marriages were not considered legal, nor were they binding in any way on the master. He could sell the slave parents from each other, or the children from the parents, if he found altering the present arrangement to be more profitable (as was often the case). These and other customs had no parallel in other slave societies in the Old or New World—a point that will be discussed below.

The American ideology of racism defined the black as a subhuman species, inferior to whites in every respect. As has been seen, this definition of superiority was necessary in order for the supporters of slavery to defend their considerable economic, political, and social interests against the very real threats that were constantly being raised against them.

From the racist's point of view, it became necessary to prove that God not only approved of slavery, but that He originally ordained the inferiority of blacks. If this case could be made, then slavery could be said to be a divinely ordained institution that was perfectly suited to these "inferior beings." Rather than being sinful, as the abolitionists maintained, slavery—based on white supremacy—could be viewed by its supporters as a wholly legitimate institution. Even more, the abolitionists could now be seen as not only wrong, but heretical as well.

With all this riding on the merits of the proslavery case, it is no wonder that the Bible received their considerable attention. What the advocates of slavery came up with is quite interesting.

First, they discovered that the Old Testament apparently condones the basic institutional arrangement of slavery. For example, God's message for Israel in Leviticus 25:44–46 was as follows: "Your male and female slaves are to come from the nations around you; from them you may buy slaves. . . . You can will them to your children as inherited property and can make them slaves for life."

The New Testament is silent on the issue, however. Even so, silence was taken by the advocates of slavery as a sign of divine approval. They theorized, for example, that if God had changed His mind about slavery, Christ would have said so when He healed the Roman centurian's slave (Luke 7:7–10). Instead, He only commented on the great faith of the slave owner. Neither did Paul denounce slavery but instead repeatedly advised the slave and master to fulfill their mutual obligations. There is no direct statement in the Bible that slavery is contrary to God's will; rather, the unloving treatment of the slave is denounced (Eph. 6:5–9; Col. 3:22).

This point is also emphasized in the Book of Philemon. Philemon, a member of the church at Colosse and a slave owner, was receiving back a runaway slave, Onesimus, who had fled to Rome. Onesimus had become a Christian while being ministered to by Paul, who was in prison. Paul concentrates on the loving relationship that should exist between fellow Christians rather than on the issue of slavery: "Perhaps the reason he was separated from you for a little while was that you might have him back for good—no longer as a slave, but better than a slave, as a dear brother. He is very dear to me but even dearer to you, both as man and as a brother in the Lord" (Philem. 15–16).

The conclusion seems clear that slavery per se could not be refuted on the basis of the Scriptures. However, this example points out the importance of grappling with such issues in terms of "relative relativism" (see chap. 3). In this perspective we recognize that the Holy Bible is God's divine revelation encapsulated, as it were, in a cultural form. Slavery was part of the culture of the people in both Old and New Testament times. But does this mean it is applicable to people in the 1980s—or was to their ancestors in the 1780s? The question cannot be given a certain answer, but it is clear that the issue goes further than the conclusions reached by the advocates of slavery.

Even though contained within cultural packages, the relevant biblical passages nevertheless speak very clearly about certain issues, namely, the relationships that should exist between slaves and masters, especially in cases where one or both are Christians. The explicit Christian message lying beneath the cultural form is that differences cease in Christ; in Him believers are equal—whatever else may divide them. Paul reminded the Galatians of this, saying, "You are all sons of God through faith in Christ Jesus, for all of you who were baptized into Christ have been clothed with Christ. There is neither Jew nor Greek, slave nor free, male nor female, for you are all one in Christ Jesus" (3:26–27).

This spiritual equality does not contradict slavery, for Paul is not saying that males and females, or slaves and masters, do not in fact exist—only that Christians are to regard each other as equals before God. However, this message *does* contradict the basis of American slavery, namely, the ideology of racism.

As has been pointed out, American slavery was buttressed by a unique ideology. Due to several factors not found in other slave colonies, there emerged a set of values that defined whites and blacks as belonging to different biological species. The latter group was defined as wholly inferior to the former. Hence white racism sought to not only defend slavery and thus the bondage of the black but, more importantly, it sought to deprive blacks of any sense of humanity. But such a notion would be foreign to an Old Testament Hebrew and to a New Testament Greek. This does not mean that ethnocentrism was nonexistent. The tendency to evaluate other groups as strange and culturally inferior was an important characteristic of both the Jews and Greeks. Nor does this mean that slavery was nonexistent, for both the Jews and the Greeks (as well as most other ethnic peoples) were at least familiar with slavery. Ethnocentrism and slavery existed, but racism did not; thus slaves were seen as people who happened to be unfortunate enough to be slaves. They may have been captured in wars, or they had been sold into slavery for any one of a number of reasons. But the inferior status of the slave in no way reflected on the slave himself as a person. Thus slave and master could be equal members in the same Christian church in ancient Rome, whereas such a condition could never have been tolerated in the American South.[5]

This difference constitutes the crucial analytical distinction. It is one thing to acknowledge the inferiority of the status of a slave; it is quite another to define the slave as a nonperson—for even if the slave becomes a free person, the stigma of permanent inferiority would stay with him or her.

Thus it is the American ideology of racism and its relationship to religious values that serves as our illustration as how ideologies and religion can be cojoined. Understanding the dynamics of this relationship is crucial for the Christian for there is no guarantee that other contemporary ideologies—equally unchristian in their definitions of reality—do not usurp the basic message of Christ.

RACISM AND THE BIBLE

As we have seen, racism was developed as a defense of North American slavery, but it is a peculiar defense—one that was invented under rather unique social circumstances and found in its most visible form in the American South. American racism—quite apart from the specific issue of slavery—was justified on biblical grounds. Rather than ponder the meaning of the passages already cited that indicate slaves and masters are equal before God, Southern apologists seized on the story of Noah as their basis for the claim that blacks were inherently inferior to whites.

This story, given in Genesis 9:18–27, was called "The Curse of Ham"; it became the theological basis of Southern racism. Noah and his three sons, Shem, Ham, and Japheth, survived the Flood when the ark landed on Mount Ararat. Noah made wine from grapes he had planted, became drunk, and retired to his tent naked. His son Ham saw his nakedness and told his brothers. The sacred record states, "When Noah awoke from his wine and found out what his youngest son had done to him, he said, 'Cursed be

---

[5]Converted Roman slaves were often renamed, with a number being substituted in place of their former names. Thus Paul acknowledges Quartus ("number four slave") as a brother in Christ (Rom. 16:23, KJV). It was Tertius ("number three slave") to whom Paul dictated the epistle of Romans (vv. 22–23).

Canaan! The lowest of slaves will he be to his brothers'" (Gen. 9:24–25). It is apparent that what became known as "The Curse of Ham" really began with a curse on Noah's grandson (and Ham's son), Canaan.[6] Canaan, meaning "to be low," was the ancestor of the Canaanites, the traditional enemy of the Hebrews. In this respect, then, the curse apparently has nothing to do with Africa or the African slave trade, but rather refers to the long-lasting enmity between Israel and the dwellers of the lowlands, that is, the Philistines.

The interpretation of the passage has been seen as controversial by some scholars, but the point is that the apologists for slavery did *not* regard the passage as controversial. For them its meaning was clear. Rev. Alexander McCarne, a prominent Methodist clergyman of the nineteenth century reflected this certainty when he stated that Noah "spoke under the impulse and dictation of Heaven. His words were the words of God himself, and by them was slavery ordained. This was an early arrangement of the Almighty, to be perpetrated through all time" (1842:148). Such men argued that slavery was ordained by God and that blacks were created as inferior beings designated specifically for slavery. According to them persons who objected to slavery—and more importantly to the racist ideology whereby black inferiority was defined—were in opposition not only to the Southern way of life but also to God Himself.

However, all of this put the proslavery Christians in somewhat of a bind. For one thing, they had to regard the slave as an inferior species set apart, or else recognize the inconsistency between

---

[6]The problem of interpretation was compounded by the fact that the King James Version (the only version the slaveholders had) translates *beno hakatan* in verse 24 as "younger son." The word is the superlative form and is typically translated "youngest son." But is Ham the youngest son of Noah? He is always listed as the middle son (Gen. 5:32; 6:10; 1 Chron. 1:4). Since the curse falls on Canaan, Noah apparently meant "grandson." The issue is important because Ham's sons included Cush (translated as "black"), a word associated with Ethiopia and hence Africa. Thus if —as the Southerners claimed—the curse was in fact placed on Ham (meaning "hot" and perceived as another link with Africa), it would extend to Cush, the first African, and hence to his descendants enslaved by Southern whites. But Canaan was Ham's son and the curse is placed on him. The fulfillment of this curse is seen in Joshua 16:10.

democratic and Christian values on the one hand and racism and slavery on the other. Even so, they would ordinarily wish for the religious conversion of the slave, thus making him a brother in Christ. However, conversion would produce literacy as well, for a Christian would ordinarily be given the Scriptures to read. But teaching a slave to read was a criminal offense in all slave states, for it was thought that literacy would lead to rebellion. (In this respect it is interesting to note that the major slave revolts were led by black itinerant lay preachers, all of whom were literate as a result of their training.)

It was difficult for the slaveholders to resolve these tensions but it was attempted nonetheless. For example, the Virginia House of Burgesses rejected an English request for laws facilitating black conversions by responding that their "weakness and shallowness of minds renders it in a manner impossible to attain any progress in their conversion" (Jordan, 1968:184).

There were, of course, very different conclusions drawn by other contemporary and equally sincere Christians. The point, however, is that the degree of sincerity apparently had little to do with whether or not a person supported both racism and slavery. Rather, the key variable was a social factor: where did the Christian live, with which reference groups did he or she identify, and what were his or her economic and political interests? Testimony to this fact is borne by the existence of Southern Methodists, Southern Presbyterians, and Southern Baptists as separate denominations that originally split with their Northern counterparts over the issue of slavery.

How could millions of persons sincerely claim a personal relationship with Jesus Christ while supporting an institution that routinely exploited, humiliated, and dehumanized millions of other persons, many of whom also professed to be their brothers and sisters in Christ? The question is an important one, for it reveals an unsettling sociological insight that is equally applicable to Christians today.

INTERESTS, IDEOLOGIES, AND LIFESTYLES

This issue can be examined on two levels of analysis. The more obvious of these concerns the link between interests and interpretations of reality. It is commonly recognized that people's goals and aims (in short, their interests) will have an effect on how they define what is—or ought to be—happening around them. It is for this reason that there are conflict-of-interest laws; one would not want a man who owned an interest in, say, a coal mine to be a governmental inspector of mines. His interest in doing his job well (e.g., closing down unsafe mines) could likely conflict with his financial interests.

This same point is also made many times in Scripture: "Do not store up for yourselves treasures on earth. . . . For where your treasure is, there your heart will be also" (Matt. 6:18–21). Christians are constantly reminded in the Bible that the desire for material riches can pull them in a direction in which they ought not to go. This is illustrated, for example, in the case of a rich young man (Matt. 19:16–22). Christ commented on this saying, "I tell you the truth, it is hard for a rich man to enter the kingdom of heaven" (v. 23). The Lord taught that the rich are spiritually handicapped. They have greater barriers to overcome—namely, their interests in their considerable material possessions—than do people from less affluent segments of society. Wealth itself is not a barrier, but inordinate love for it, and dependence on it, can keep a person from God.

The application of this insight to the issue of Southern slavery is straightforward. Whatever the merits of either the proslavery, or antislavery/racism argument, it is interesting to note one rather clear relationship: those who attempted to support white supremacy on a scriptural basis were much more likely to come from geographical areas in which slavery was a vital economic factor.

Historical evidence thus indicates that financial interests can distort Christian values. Furthermore, there is no reason to believe that this process has ceased simply because slavery has been abolished. Other contemporary interests such as the values of individualism and materialism are quite evident today and have the same effect.[7]

A second and more subtle analysis explains how religious values can be thwarted by ideological positions that run counter to

---

[7]On the subject of individualism and its effect on the church, see Snyder (1977). On the subject of materialism and the church, see White (1979).

these values. Not only can religious values be distorted by economic or political interests—as has been noted above—but ironically certain aspects of a religious perspective can distort certain aspects of its own values. Again, we will use the example of race relations in the American South to illustrate this point.

Both during and after slavery, the South developed a rigid racial caste system in which blacks were put in a position of extreme economic dependence. Whether as slaves in 1830 or sharecroppers in 1930, blacks were dependent on whites for their basic livelihood. Whites used extreme measures to keep the blacks in their traditional place. Needless to say, the mechanisms were often harsh and cruel. For example, the efforts to subordinate blacks by fear included an annual average (between 1890–1915) of over one hundred lynchings that, of course, were illegal; but these acts were typically ignored by the whites who controlled the local police and judicial functions.[8] Thus there was operating in the South for centuries a routine system of exploitation, cruelty, and inhumanity in opposition to the most basic Christian values. Yet almost no Christians publicly opposed this system. Why?

It is quite likely that many Christians did not publicly oppose the system of race relations because to do so would have meant ostracism at best and death at worst. But another reason why Southern Christians did not raise a protest was that their peculiar Christian perspective defined public ethical questions as non-religious issues. Instead of such public matters, they concentrated on private moral affairs.

The dominant religious orientation in the South has historically been Protestant fundamentalism. Whether in the North or in the South, fundamentalism sponsors a rather unique conception of sin. The fundamentalist conception of sin is typically restricted to acts and thoughts that concern only the individual or his immediate personal relations with others. For example, private acts like drinking alcohol, smoking, swearing, card playing, dancing, and various forms of sexual immorality constitute its domain of sin. Whatever else can be said about this catalog of offenses, it embraces essentially private acts. Moreover, when attention *is*

---

[8]A biographical account of racial violence and injustice written by a black Christian can be found in Perkins (1976).

given to public matters, issues that represent public extensions of private sin are typically singled out—for example, pornography or gambling.

The functional nature of this private conception of sin is apparent. Peter Berger observes:

> The limitations to private wrongdoing . . . has obvious functions in a society whose central social arrangements are dubious, to say the least, when confronted with certain teachings of the New Testament. . . . Protestant fundamentalism's private concept of morality thus concentrated attention on those areas of conduct that are irrelevant to the maintenance of the social system, and diverts attention from those areas where ethical inspection would create tensions for the smooth operation of the system. In other words, Protestant fundamentalism is ideologically functional in maintaining the social system of the American South (1963:113–14).

Due to the operation of this religious world view, a Christian man could avoid adultery or swearing and be honest in his financial dealings, but at the same time he could exploit black slaves or sharecroppers on his land and still think of himself as a good Christian.

The point should be obvious that it is one thing to obey the law and act normally by avoiding deviant behavior, but it is often quite another thing to act in a way consistent with Christian values. It is likely that this is at least partially what is meant when Christians are admonished to be "a peculiar people" (1 Peter 2:9; Titus 2:14, KJV).

It may be concluded that Christian values such as the teachings on love and equality can be blunted by ideologies based on financial or political interests. In addition, it is apparent that the moral force of Christianity can be diverted by a limited conception of sin restricted to certain private issues. Thus in both respects a potentially radical Christianity can be neutralized. In fact, Christianity can be (and has been) refashioned into a religious ethos that actually supports a system standing in many ways in opposition to its basic teachings.

History's warning to Christians should be clear. The main tenets of Christianity have been neutralized on a massive scale in the past, and it is reasonable to assume that aspects of this same process are operating in our contemporary society.

INSTITUTIONALIZED EVIL

At one time America had a caste system maintained by means of racially discriminatory laws: slavery was legal, and such persons could not marry legally or even control the destinies of their own children. Moreover, after slavery was abolished, laws were passed in many states forbidding most blacks to vote, assemble together for political reasons, or even to travel freely. Other laws were specifically designed to emphasize the perceived inferiority of blacks. For example, segregation laws excluded blacks from the use of certain public facilities, drinking fountains, and rest rooms.

This de jure discriminatory system has largely been eliminated by means of recent federal court decisions and executive orders. Even so, the effects of several hundred years of massive legal discrimination cannot be eliminated simply by writing new laws. Thus, even though the direct source of discrimination has largely been neutralized, a de facto institutionalized system that produces racially discriminatory effects still operates in many respects. For example, blacks typically die sooner than whites. But how do they die? If there was in America an explicit policy to exterminate members of minority groups, everyone would be horrified. In that case the public would insist that those who perpetrated such a policy should be punished. If these people were operating legally (as in Hitler's persecution of the Jews), public opinion would demand that the laws be changed immediately.

But blacks do not typically die younger than whites because someone deliberately kills them. This result is the product of social forces that are much more subtle, unintended, and often unrecognized. If the results are evil, they are caused by nothing more sinister than normal people going about their normal affairs.

For example, it is typical for poor people to live in areas where rents are relatively cheap and available.[9] For many people this

---

[9]This would be an issue of stratification and not minority-majority relations were it not for the fact that blacks and other minorities are more likely to be poorer than majority group members. For example, in 1980 the average black earned about 65 percent of the average white worker's income. Also, the black unemployment rate was twice that of whites, and the black unemployed worker was more likely to be out of work for a longer time than the unemployed white worker. These conditions continue largely unchanged today.

means that they must live in the urban area known as the inner city, or ghetto. These are areas historically characterized by high rates of social instability—crime, separation and divorce, illegitimacy, delinquency, and so forth. People who grow up in such areas go to local schools supported by the tax base of that local area (see chap. 10). As a result poor neighborhoods generally have poor schools (e.g., high student-teacher ratios, high teacher turnover, and poor facilities). Poor schools have high dropout rates and produce students who typically have low average academic performances. Such schools typically turn out students who are generally unlikely to do well occupationally. As a result they will be poor and, like their parents, will live in ghetto areas. Thus the cycle repeats itself across generations.

This rather bleak scenario has been called *the cycle of poverty* because it operates in a vicious circle. Of course, some talented and/or fortunate individuals escape from this cycle; but most do not. Various state and federal programs are being tried (at huge expense and rather disappointing and frustrating results) to intercept this cycle. Unfortunately, most of these programs are guaranteed to fail.[10] They usually operate on the twin assumptions that large amounts of money will solve the problem and that the specific problem (e.g., poverty) exists in isolation from the system that surrounds it. Neither assumption is valid. Thus billions of dollars have been spent to improve ghetto education—an effort that has not produced the desired results. Furthermore, even if something wonderful happened and every ghetto student graduated with a doctor of philosophy degree, there would not be enough jobs for these people. Education cannot solve the problem of poverty when the latter reoccurs as a routine (though undesirable) feature of our economic system. As long as the poverty cycle is in operation, no amount of adjustment in the educational system is going to solve the problem.

Many people realize this, but many of the same ineffective remedial programs are funded each year for several very important

---

[10]The typical remedial effort involves upgrading the school system in various ways, usually by improving the physical plant. Unfortunately, there isn't the slightest bit of research evidence that indicates improved physical environments will improve scholastic performances (Coleman, 1966).

reasons. First, the antipoverty programs are very effective in doing something they were not specifically designed to do; namely, they supply many thousands of middle-class social workers with well-paid jobs.[11] Second, the real cause of poverty, the economic system, is unlikely to be changed (at least for the first reason cited); so people content themselves with "realistic" but ineffective programs. The American voters have never demonstrated their willingness to vote for political candidates who promise to push for the kind of changes that would reduce or eliminate poverty. This is because many voters (at least *white* voters) perceive the cure as worse than the disease itself.

What is left is a huge and complicated institutionalized system that routinely distributes scarce goods unequally and has many unintended and, from a Christian perspective, evil results. For example, it is unquestionably evil that black residents of the urban ghetto die at a rate three times higher than that found in white residential areas for the urban working class. Of course, the real causes of situations like this are largely economic. Poor white people will die at about the same rate as poor black people, but the higher proportion of blacks who live in ghetto areas makes it also a racial problem.

As stated above, no one is officially in charge of exterminating lower-class blacks. This is neither a desirable policy, to say the least, nor is it necessary. Rather, the typical conditions of the ghetto produce this result whether anyone likes it or not. Poor housing, unsafe heating systems, malnutrition and poor diet, inadequate or nonexistent playgrounds (and hence unsafe recreational activities), crime victimization, inadequate health care, unhealthy working conditions—all these and others are typical

---

[11]Many of my students who want to "work with people" are headed for these jobs when they graduate. To say the least, they would be very disappointed if these jobs were eliminated. They wouldn't be the only ones, as the following quote reveals: "While government figures show that $11.4 billions would raise all the poor above the officially defined poverty level, in fact more than $30 billion are spent on programs to get people out of poverty, and there are still more than 5 million families below the poverty level. Clearly most of the money spent on the poor does not reach the poor, but is absorbed by the salaries of officials, staffs, consultants, and by other expenses of the anti-poverty organizations" (Sowell, 1975:195–96).

features of the urban ghetto that combine to reduce the probability of a normal life span (Furfey, 1978).

A CHRISTIAN RESPONSE

How are Christians to respond to all this? First, it must be realized that ignorance is not bliss, at least not for the people who are adversely affected by this system; and these are the people Christians are commanded by Christ to care for. Believers must face squarely the inescapable fact that to do nothing about the system and its unintended consequences is to perpetuate its consequences. A person who does nothing either through lack of care or through ignorance actually helps to perpetuate the evil results. It must be remembered that people like us *are* the system: that is, normal people doing normal things that have certain evil—if unintended—results.

This implies that it is the institutionalized system that Christians must change. The Bible commands Christians—as individuals—to feed the hungry and care for the sick. But would it not also be wise to root out the social causes of hunger and sickness? If so, Christians should expect to face very real problems; whereas it is relatively simple to feed hungry people, it is much more difficult and complex to attack the institutional sources of hunger and sickness—poverty and crime (see Sider, 1977 and chap. 10 in this volume).

Rather than causing us as Christians to become apathetic and passive, the complexity of the task ahead ought to generate at least two responses. First, it should cause us to diligently study the social sciences as a way of increasing our intellectual ability in order to comprehend the workings of our system. The person least likely to take action is the one who does not even know there is a problem. Furthermore, the person who becomes only superficially aware of the problem lacks the capacity for understanding. Without understanding the complex dynamics of the system, groups often attempt ineffective programs that sometimes make the situation worse. Christians are needed who not only are concerned but also have unusual analytical capabilities. Christian concern and zealous action are never enough; Christians are needed who are guided by sophisticated understanding. Anything less is likely to make the situation worse—or, if nothing else, to bring about the frustrated "burn out" of those who "get involved" but do not comprehend the scope of what they are involved with.

Second, Christians must recognize that they need each other and that they need to be organized as Christians if they hope to extend their influence significantly. The tasks before Christians are too great for "Lone Ranger" action. The isolated individual—no matter how dedicated and capable—is unlikely to bring about changes in the institutionalized patterns discussed here. To make necessary changes in voting patterns, school board policies, zoning regulations, housing codes, and school attendance boundaries takes effective organization.

Many contemporary Christians argue that it is not the proper role of the organized local church to promote social programs designed to bring about structural changes in our society. I sympathize with this viewpoint only because the local church typically is an ineffective agent of direct social change. There are many other single-purpose organizations that are designed specifically to promote needed social changes. These organizations typically welcome the participation of interested citizens whose personal motivations may be quite varied. Membership in these organizations provides not only an opportunity for Christian service but an excellent witnessing opportunity as well—demonstrating to non-Christian colleagues that contemporary Christians are prepared to join in "secular" efforts to promote causes compatible with (and in fact demanded by) Christian values.

The Christian is called to demonstrate concern for those in need. Love for others must not remain only an abstraction. Nor is faith enough. James says that "faith without deeds is dead" (James 2:26). However, these deeds must be sponsored by keen insights and motivated by sincere belief. Knowing that Christ first loved us, we Christians must sacrifice ourselves in love for each other. The words of 1 John summarize these thoughts effectively:

> This is how we know what love is: Jesus Christ laid down his life for us. And we ought to lay down our lives for our brothers. If anyone has material possessions and sees his brother in need but has no pity on him, how can the love of God be in him? Dear children, let us not love with words or tongue but with actions and in truth (3:16–18).

What is true of material possessions must also be true of knowledge. Once the dimensions of the problems facing others are understood, we are called, as it were, from darkness into light. Thus Christians have an obligation to act where possible to change the situation so that the problem is effectively reduced. If Christians then turn their backs on the problem once they are aware of it, they are doubly condemned. Therefore knowledge brings with it a responsibility that should give believers a new orientation toward their calling as Christians.

DISCUSSION QUESTIONS

1. Do you believe everyone in America has an equal opportunity to succeed, or is discrimination built into the system? Why? What evidence do you have?
2. The author of this essay has argued that ideologies can thwart certain basic Christian imperatives. For example, certain widespread interests in maintaining white supremacy resulted in the reinterpretation of New Testament commands to treat each other as equals under God's grace. Do you think this is a convincing example and that the argument is valid? Does it apply—perhaps in a variant form—today to Christians you know?
3. Do you believe the active promotion of social equality is a biblical concept? What is the basis for your belief?
4. Assuming that you agree with the author's argument regarding "institutionalized evil," can you suggest realistic goals for change which could be bought by Christians like yourself?

SUGGESTED READING

John Dolland, *Caste and Class in a Southern Town* (New York: Anchor, 3rd ed., 1957). Southern caste relations in the 1930s are carefully examined by an American psychologist.

Nathan Glazer, *Affirmative Discrimination: Ethnic Inequality and Public Policy* (New York: Basic Books, 1975). The attempt to undo the system of de jure discrimination has led to a federally enforced policy that now does what it is trying to eliminate: racially discriminate. This review uncovers the dilemmas involved in recent Supreme Court decisions regarding such matters as busing, affirmative action in employment, and open housing.

Lewis Killian, *The Impossible Revolution, Phase 2: Black Power and the American Dream* (New York: Random, 1975). Killian argues that the American political system is incapable of bringing about changes that could defuse contemporary racial tensions. An excellent overview of United States political history, black-white relations, and the expected black revolution that cannot succeed.

John Perkins, *Let Justice Roll Down* (Glendale: Regal, 1976). Written by a Southern black, this book tells of his experiences of being raised in the South. It also tells of a ministry he has begun called the Voice of Calvary. This book illustrates how Christians can work to overcome structural injustice in the name of Christ. It shows how social concern can be an integral part of evangelism.

Thomas Sowell, *Race and Economics* (New York: McKay, 1975). The complex relationships between race, ethnicity, and state-capitalism are explored, including a historical overview of slavery as an economic institution, a comparison of race and economics in South and North America, and the process of industrialization and immigration. A key feature of the book is the comparative analysis of various American minority groups in terms of economic mobility.

William Wilson, *Power, Racism and Privilege: Race Relations in Theoretical and Sociohistorical Perspective* (New York: Free Press, 1973). An excellent overview of the main theoretical perspectives in contemporary sociology. The major theoretical concepts in this book are power and ideology. The perspective is usefully employed to compare contemporary and historical race relations in America and in South Africa.

__16

STANLEY A. CLARK
Tabor College,
Kansas

COLLECTIVE BEHAVIOR
AND SOCIAL MOVEMENTS

The front edge of the flood knifed out of the Middle Fork around 8:00 a.m. During its seventeen-mile plunge down the hollow, the flood . . . pulverized everything caught in its path. The wreckage of hundreds of homes and other buildings was strewn all over the landscape. The survivors were huddled together all over the hillsides, numb with shock, afraid to move. But soon people began to drift around in slow dazed circles, looking for missing relatives, seeking shelter, . . . and trying to comprehend the sheer enormity of what had happened. A man of seventy . . . tried to convey the futility of that afternoon:

"We just milled around to see what we could find. Just drifted around. Nobody knowed what to do or what they was lookin' for" (Erickson, 1977:40–41).

The flood described above destroyed Buffalo Creek, West Virginia, in 1972. Perhaps the old man's statement, with all its grammatical difficulties, best captures the essence of what sociologists call *collective behavior:* what, indeed, *is* someone supposed to do when there are suddenly no rules to guide his or her action? This fascinating question led scholars early in this century to develop a substantive field of study that has since grown to the point where it includes phenomena ranging from concert audi-

311

ences to race riots to the gay rights movement. In the light of this diversity, we should not be surprised to find that our grasp of the subject is only tentative!

This chapter will attempt to accomplish two things. First, it will offer a summary of the field of collective behavior, as it has traditionally been described by sociologists and others. Second, and more importantly, it will present and deal with a number of significant issues that Christians must address if they hope to integrate this topic with biblical insights on the human condition. Clearly the reasons why people engage in the activities described below involve both who they are as God's creation and, especially, how they relate to their Creator. No simple answer will be provided; the challenge will be in the struggle to define these issues in a way that is consistent with one's own beliefs.

COLLECTIVE BEHAVIOR: A DEFINITION

In its purest form, collective behavior occurs in unstructured or ambiguous situations—those in which the rules specifying appropriate behavior are either inadequate, have broken down, or are nonexistent. This involves those types of human activity that occur *outside* conventional social institutions. It is not what would normally be considered *group* behavior, in that a "collectivity" is only loosely and informally structured and is subject to sudden shifts in focus, leadership, and communication. By nature the behavior of collectivities tends to be unexpected and temporary, arising more or less spontaneously from unstable situations for which the people involved are poorly prepared.

Unfortunately, sociologists can only account for a limited number of behaviors from the above definition. Primarily, those would be *panic, disaster reactions, hysteria,* and *unplanned crowds.* There are numerous other more conventionalized collective actions that are also included in most definitions of the field. For example, much crowd activity is predictable in nature (consider, for example, the behavior of people at a professional sports event). Social movements are another case in point: they could hardly be said to be temporary or spontaneous in nature, and yet they are routinely studied under the general rubric of collective behavior. Neither would one be likely to view fashion-related behavior as unexpected or unstructured. What sociologists are trying to say is that the presence of preexisting norms (and lasting social structure) does in fact characterize much of the behavior included in this field of study. There are certain definitional problems involved here that are too complex to develop fully; hence it will be necessary to accept the fact that a single classificational scheme, no matter how ingenious, will be inadequate to include all the forms of human behavior that have traditionally been labeled "collective."

HISTORICAL AND THEORETICAL BACKGROUND

Collective behavior as a field of study does not have a long or particularly illustrious history. Its earliest input came from the writings of French sociologists near the beginning of this century (LeBon, 1896; Tarde, 1903). Strands of relevant thought can also be identified in the works of Sigmund Freud (1921), who was influenced by LeBon. The term itself was coined by Park and Burgess (1921) at the University of Chicago. From that point there has been a relatively continuous progression of writers working "in descent"; that is, as students of earlier scholars in the field. For example, Herbert Blumer (1951), who attempted to systematize the area, was a student of Park; Turner and Killian (1972), whose textbook (first written in 1957) remains the standard in the field, were students of Blumer; and many recent sociologists have either studied under or been influenced by Turner and Killian. The recency of organization in the field is even more dramatic; it was only in 1978 that an official section on collective behavior and social movements was established with the American Sociological Association, although initial interest had been expressed as far back as 1974.

One would expect such a relatively new field to be short on coherent theory, and that *has* been the case for the most part. The parameters are simply too broad to enable comprehensive theory construction to succeed. Historically, the French writers (particularly LeBon) were convinced that crowd behavior was pathological or at least primitive in nature rather than civilized. A "crowd mind" was said to take over individuals in a collectivity, so that they were no longer themselves but rather like barbarians. This idea of a mental unity and power was shared by other early scholars (Ross, 1908; Simmel [tr.] 1950), who seemed to fear crowds as

313

being irrational and dangerous. Modern theorists have insistently pointed out the fallacy of this perspective; for example, Killian (1974) emphasizes the crucial role of *reason* at work in crowd behavior; emotion is not nearly as significant as cognition in explaining how people act in collectivities. It has also been observed that imputing irrationality to crowds represents the bias of people who were essentially antidemocratic in philosophy.

Probably the most well-known theoretical formulation was developed by Neil Smelser (1962) as a "social action" model of collective behavior. Briefly, his approach is that such behavior is guided by various kinds of shared beliefs, each of which focuses on some element of the social order that has broken down and needs to be repaired or reconstituted. It may be a value, a norm, human motivation, or some material aspect of culture. Whatever the form, collective behavior will not occur unless three conditions exist: (1) a strain in a system, that is, the elements somehow fail to operate harmoniously; (2) a belief is developed to identify the source or cause of that strain; and (3) some event occurs that triggers action by giving concrete substance to the belief. Smelser's theory postulates that a more or less definite series of stages must occur in the natural history of an event before collective behavior will actually take place.

Consider, for example, what Smelser calls the "hostile outburst" (riot). It may occur when the mechanisms for rewarding people fail to operate fairly and thus create *strain*. Those who feel discriminated against may develop a *belief* that there are certain groups or policies responsible for their troubles (thus they try to locate the source of strain in order to *reconstitute* that particular element). Given the proper context and flow of events, a *triggering event* may set off a minor disturbance or even a full-fledged riot. Its outcome will be greatly affected by the response of the *control agents* (for example, police or national guardsmen).

The social action theory is a complex one that has its share of critics. It has achieved fame as the first systematic attempt to frame a comprehensive theory for the field, and it has sparked considerable research activity by those interested in testing its many propositions.

Another fairly well-developed perspective in collective behavior is that of the systems theorists, particularly Klapp (1972). According to this theory, a society is usually balanced with respect to providing enough safety valves to release or offset any tensions in the system. Games, gambling, sports, and carnivals are all examples of such mechanisms. If the tension-management devices are less than effective, the tension side of the balance can become overloaded. The result is "spillover"—collective behavior, rumors, deviance, and so on—as shown in the following diagram adapted from Klapp (1972:201):

A Systems View of Collective Behavior

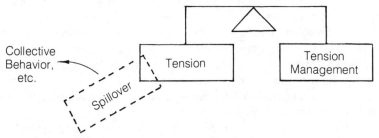

Both of these explanations have, of course, their own strengths and weaknesses. At this point in the field's development, it is probably more helpful to look for useful ideas from each of the various perspectives than to cast full support behind any one of them.

TYPES OF COLLECTIVE BEHAVIOR

Following the lead of most textbooks in the field, seven major categories of collective behavior will be identified. The intent is to briefly review these phenomena rather than to study them in detail. Consequently, much will be implied rather than stated, so there will be ample time to deal with issues of relevance to the Christian studying the field. Most introductory textbooks devote a chapter or more to collective behavior, and they should be consulted for further elaboration.

Crowds. The most common form of collective behavior is the crowd; it is in fact the prototype in the field. Crowds are frequent and varied in form, primarily characterized by a common focus of attention; a rudimentary and fleeting sense of membership, power, and solidarity; and the spread of moods and emotions by means of close physical contact and "contagion." Following the classic lead of Blumer (1951), sociologists have identified four types of crowds. These are the *casual* crowd, which is short-lived and relatively insignificant (for example, people waiting for a bus); the *conventional* crowd, which is preannounced and clearly focused (for example, an audience); the *expressive* crowd, whose object is simply to release emotion (for example, orgies or victory celebrations); and *acting* crowds, which act out of anger toward an object of attention (for example, urban riots). This typology is a dynamic one, for the crowd can change form very suddenly—as when an expressive crowd begins to act, or a conventional crowd becomes expressive.

Mass contagion. This broad term brings to mind several related types of collective behavior, and it appears under many different names in introductory textbooks. The chief characteristic of all these phenomena is the combination of high suggestibility/gullibility and some kind of energetic and frenzied activity. There are three major subtypes.

Hysterical contagion is one major subtype of mass contagion. In certain situations—usually involving stress or exhaustion—people in a collectivity come to sense some mysterious and threatening force in their surroundings. It can range from an unseen insect in a textile mill (Kerckhoff and Back, 1968:3–18) to imaginary gas being sprayed in the air by a phantom intruder (Johnson, 1945:175–86). If, instead of actively dealing with their fear together, group members choose instead to respond inwardly and individually, an hysterical fear can be rapidly developed and disseminated to others. Usually some physical symptoms accompany this hysteria, such as fainting, rash, shortness of breath, and dizziness. The duration of this contagion is typically quite short, following definite contagion patterns from person to person (Kerckhoff and Back, 1968:35ff.). Two cautionary observations are necessary: first, not everyone falls prey to the fear (in most cases only a minority of persons exhibit any symptoms); second, the fear is not necessarily always imaginary, and there may indeed be legitimate forces at work (e.g., viruses or insects), particularly among those first affected. However, scientists have rarely been able to identify objective causal agents in those studies that have been conducted.

Another major subtype of mass contagion is *mass delusion*. Although the same general pattern of stress and contagion may be observed with this second subtype, the fear is *non*hysterical in nature. A belief becomes widespread in a collectivity that something extraordinary is happening: for example, people may believe the Virgin Mary has been seen by someone (Tumin and Feldman, 1955:124--39); or perhaps people believe their windshields are being pockmarked by atomic fallout particles (Medalia and Larsen, 1958:221–32). The word "delusion" must be used with care; its definition implies that the belief is a false one, when in fact there is always the possibility that it may be accurate and legitimate. After all, the delusions of thousands of persons who have observed unidentified flying objects (UFOs) in the past few decades should at least be given passing thoughts of plausibility due to the sheer numbers involved. We must be careful not to judge this behavior as irrational by definition.

Mania is a third major subtype of mass contagion. There are many examples in modern society of a rush toward some desired goal—a collective obsession that leads people to personal sacrifice, speculation of their resources, and possible economic disaster. The Klondike gold rush of 1897 is a case in point, as are the various land-selling schemes in Florida, Arizona, and elsewhere during this century and even the recent silver boom. These ventures are speculative frenzies in which products are bought and resold in a spiraling process, or boom, that ultimately ends in collapse and lost fortunes. It could be argued that these actions are nothing more than intense institutional activity; nevertheless, there is certainly an element of the noninstitutional at work as well.

Collective violence and civil disorder. Protests and rioting are phenomena to which everyone has become accustomed; they are fairly common as ways of collective expression in the late twentieth century. However, there are a variety of possibilities within this general category, and each one will be dealt with briefly.

When a collectivity gathers to express a shared grievance and to marshal public sympathy for its cause, the gathering has the ingredients of *protest activity*. We shall assume that this activity is nonviolent in nature and that the focal point of protest is demonstration in a grievance context. The members of the gathering may threaten the institutional order by warning, for example, that a strike is imminent or that they are about to take over some building; they may engage in symbolic behavior such as burning draft cards or effigies; or they may simply appeal for the support of others. Protests often occupy a transitional status in human collective behavior. They frequently develop from casual or conventional crowds, and often they are transformed into still other forms of action (rioting, for example).

Shared grievances, as has been suggested, may produce *collective violence* under certain conditions. By *violence* is meant aggressive and injurious or damaging actions of individuals against perceived enemies or enemy property. This includes such phenomena as strikes, general rioting, spontaneous acts of war, and vigilante actions; it excludes violent crimes committed by single individuals (e.g., assault, rape, or murder), unless those crimes are perpetrated as part of crowd action. The two most often studied forms of collective violence are the *mob* and the *riot*.

Mob action is aggression by a crowd that is directed against a single object of attention (for example, a person, building, or border crossing). Perhaps the crowd is attacking an embassy or a bank building, or looking for an alleged rapist to punish or lynch. Often the object of wrath is symbolic, representing a larger enemy in some way. Further, the victim is often scapegoated—simply taken as the first of the enemy "species" to appear on the scene at a critical moment.

The behavior is called a *riot* when the target of aggression is general rather than specific and when the destruction is random instead of focused. One often reads of the "riot era" in the United States in the late 1960s, when universities and ghettos alike were embroiled in collective violence. Actually, rioting varies along a continuum of violent behavior; some riots are relatively free of violence. Also, rioting may be more or less organized. This type of collective behavior tends to be impulsive and primarily emotional in nature; in fact, some major riots—perhaps the majority (Methvin, 1970)—are planned by those who want them to occur.

Disaster behavior. Natural and man-made disasters (e.g., hurricanes, floods, and explosions) are fairly commonplace on a world-wide basis. Theorists have alerted us to the fact that these events by themselves are not sufficient to cause collective behavior. The key factor is that of system *overload*. The event must be one that radically affects the social order of a region (e.g., authority and control patterns, or norms), its system of meaning (values, definitions of reality, and the like), or survival itself (shelter, health, and subsistence). Under these sorts of breakdown, people are left to construct or rebuild on their own an orderly social bond. The amount of advanced preparation certainly has a profound impact on the collective response to disaster events; in those communities, for example, where fire or tornado drills are routinely practiced, collective behavior in actual disaster is much less likely.

Panic. To understand the nature of panic, it is necessary to introduce the idea of the "individualistic crowd." *Most* crowd behavior is truly collective in nature: members cooperate to achieve some sort of common goal. However, individuals in a state of panic do not cooperate with each other. The goal of individual survival or well-being takes over the collectivity. According to Turner and Killian,

> The norms that permit people to live together in a relatively peaceful, harmonious state require that the individual forego some of his own gratifications. He does so with faith that others are also adhering to these norms and making their own sacrifices. Evidence that other members of the collectivity are disregarding these norms and, instead of being punished as deviants, are gaining an advantage in the pursuit of a scarce object releases the individual from the moral obligation to observe the norms. A new norm arises: collective support for untrammeled pursuit of individual survival or gain, and the behavior of the crowd becomes individualistic and competitive (1972:87).

Panic, then, involves the simultaneous flight of people on the basis of some specific and immediate fear. Theoretically, not every such situation will produce panic. There has to be a combination of certain elements, including partial entrapment with limited escape routes; poor communication within the collectivity; and a perceived threat that is so immediate that the only viable option is to try to escape. People trapped in a plummeting airplane, or in a collapsed coal mine, would probably not panic because there is no escape. Where there is the possibility that some people will be able to survive or succeed—but *only* some—it is not difficult to imagine the intensity with which avenues of behavior will be pursued.

Diffuse collectivities. An oversimplified definition of this type of behavior will have to suffice. We define diffuse collectivities as those that have all the characteristics of collective behavior except for a common location. In other words diffuse crowds exist *across* instead of within space. There is some sort of common focus, or common response; and, most crucially, there is a sense of awareness that others are similarly engaged. These collectivities "constitute an imagined audience from which the individual derives a perspective or frame of reference" (Turner and Killian, 1972:118). Communication is obviously vital to the appearance and continuation of these "crowds." Standard lists of behaviors include several items in this category.

A *scandal* occurs when an individual in a responsible position is suspected of acting immorally or irresponsibly. In this situation there is what amounts to a *diffuse acting crowd* whose members express their outrage and take steps to remove the offender from office, or otherwise punish the person. It is here that we see the raw operation of the social mores; and the news media during the past few years have certainly had their share of scandalous stories to relate.

Fashion, fads, and *crazes* are related phenomena that share in common a display of self in awareness of others. *Fashion,* by far the most fundamental of the three, refers to the variations in expression of style that characterize a given culture. It may be in reference to clothing, language, hair style, or other anchors; its occurrence is highly conventionalized (it supports an industry) and is fairly regularized (it occurs in crude cycles). Fashion provides both relief from boredom and prestige, as well as a chance to express one's identity. *Fads* are fashion-like in nature, but represent more short-lived innovations that are less conventionalized and usually rather trivial in content (e.g., youth jargon, hula hoops). A *craze* is simply a fad that requires zealous dedication and sacrifice by those involved. Crazes are highly competitive and obsessive, resembling mania (described earlier in this chapter). Their focus can be trivial (flagpole sitting, marathon dancing) or serious (war crazes). The term *public* refers to a group of people with a common interest. All those who are interested in, and divided over, an issue of any kind form a public. At any point in time there are as many publics as there are current issues, and memberships tend to overlap as a consequence. Publics define, shape, and alter the various matters of current debate; their opinions are highly valued by politicians, manufacturers, and others who draw their livelihood from meeting the interests and needs of the population. A great deal has been written about publics regarding their role in policy formation and their relationship to the major institutions.

Social movements. Depending on one's perspective, social movements may or may not be placed in the same category as the other forms of behavior discussed above. Realistically, there is little in the definition of collective behavior that overlaps. A social movement is the long-lasting and organized effort of individuals working together to affect some aspect of their society—typically, to either defend, restore, or change the status quo. They tend to be spawned from the broad trends of social history (Blumer, 1951:167–222; Roberts and Kloss, 1979) on the basis of such general concerns as civil rights, pacifism, suffrage, opposition to technology, the environment, and so on. Movements develop when the routines of daily life are broken and when general unrest and uneasiness begin to be collectively articulated against an existing social arrangement. They draw from the ranks of the dissatisfied or the marginal. Sometimes they are oriented toward a return to the past, or they may rally around the present. Some are revolutionary in nature, seeking to overthrow the established order; others are visionary, and still others are isolationist or retreatist. Some appear again and again throughout history, while others come and go in response to specific historical events and then vanish.

Some writers maintain that social movements are nothing more than long-lasting collective behavior. However, this view is rejected by other writers as being much too dim or light-hearted, and they see movements rather as serious, organized attempts to alter significant aspects of a social system in manifestly political ways. Whatever the persuasion, much has been written about social movements. We know that they are a common feature of the contemporary social map; and that their ebb and flow depends largely on their appeals for membership, the urgency of the problems they address, and the response of control agents in the larger environment.

ISSUES FOR THE CHRISTIAN

Daily media reports present clear evidence that humans can be powerfully swayed by their social and natural environment. Some of the more extreme examples include stampedes at rock concerts, ritual suicides of cult members, and destructive rioting in the streets. Then there is the multimillion dollar fashion industry, the massive political campaign advertising, and other examples of less dramatic but equally potent forms of external collective influence. Collective behavior cannot be understood apart from this tendency to be pressured toward action by one's milieu. Further, Christians must not be naïve about the fact that they are just as likely as others to be confronted by influences from outside themselves; susceptibility is part of the human condition.

There is however a fundamental reality for all people in the face of this situation, namely, *choice*. People have the capacity to choose at nearly every juncture of their daily lives. Consider the following as theoretical choice components of any social situation: (1) *initial involvement*—do we participate or not? (2) *role*—do we attempt to influence the course of events, that is, do we exercise leadership? (3) *acceptable behavior*—where do we establish boundaries beyond which we refuse to proceed? (4) *disassociation* —do we remain with a group (or, involved in an activity) that violates our self-imposed limits?

As a general rule each of the above choice elements can be found in any instance of collective behavior—ranging from pep rallies to social movements. Through them all, the issue of volition is clear. Christians do have choices that they exercise regularly in the collectivities with which they become involved. The situation of the Christian is also far from being mechanical, for two believers in a crowd setting may arrive at different decisions regarding involvement, even after following the same process of deliberation and consultation with God's Word. The important ingredient is for each one to submit to God's leading in all decisions to be made.

For the Christian, then, at least three major issues must be considered. The first is *identity*: to whom do I look for standards of self and behavior? The second issue is *responsibility*: to whom am I accountable for my behavior? Under what conditions? Finally, there is the issue of *stewardship:* how should I best spend time, energy, and resources? In the discussion that follows we will grapple with each of these questions in an attempt to chart a path toward Christian understanding of collective behavior. The first task, however, will be to discuss some episodes of collective behavior that are recorded in Scripture and to offer some assessment of what the Bible teaches on this subject.

Collective behavior in the Bible. The Scriptures record in detail numerous examples of collective behavior. This is not surprising since, after all, the Old Testament tells the story of a mobile nation that was confronted by enemies and that experienced divine intervention at every turn. Also, the New Testament portrays the story of the incarnate God directly challenging a zealously guarded religious institution. These settings are ripe for the outbreak of noninstitutionalized collective action. What is particularly intriguing about the scriptural accounts, however, is their universal focus around the battle of good and evil.

Human wickedness and divine judgment constitute the first of two major ways in which we see the expression of the battle between good and evil. Throughout the Bible, God is shown as responding to instances of unrighteousness or sacrilege with destruction and chaos. He uses either the natural environment or humans (both believers and nonbelievers) to execute His wrath, in both cases using disasters to accomplish that purpose. Consider the following: (1) the destruction of Sodom and Gomorrah by brimstone and fire (Gen. 19); (2) the ten plagues in Egypt that culminated with the Passover (Exod. 7–12); (3) Samson destroying the Philistine temple and many of the people (Judg. 16); and (4) the plague and panic in the city of Ashdod following its sacrilege of the ark (1 Sam. 5).

Response to God's Word, the second major context within which the theme of good and evil develops, pertains to the Word of God provoking or inciting impassioned responses from masses of people. The Gospels record a great deal of crowd behavior in connection with Jesus' ministry on earth, while the Book of Acts records reactions of crowds to the preaching of early church leaders such as Peter, Paul, and Barnabas. The responses of crowds to what they heard and saw covers the entire range of human emotions, as the following list indicates:

1. *Anger and indignation.* We read of the crowd's rage at Jesus for claiming deity (John 8:58–59), of the stoning of Stephen (Acts 7:57–58), and of the riots in Ephesus and Jerusalem surrounding Paul (Acts 19:23–41; 21:27–22:24).
2. *Terror and remorse.* The response of those at Golgotha following the death of Christ illustrates this emotion (Luke 23:44–48).
3. *Awe.* Those who saw Jesus healing the sick repeatedly experienced a sense of amazement at what they saw. Consider the paralytic of Luke 5:25–26, the demon-possessed boy of Luke 9:42–43, and the crippled woman of Luke 13:12–13.
4. *Worship and joy.* The response of the Israelites when the ark was brought into Jerusalem (2 Sam. 6:5) was paralleled by the reception of Jesus on His triumphal entry into the same city (John 12:12–13).
5. *Audience-like attentiveness.* The crowds quietly received instruction in some cases, as when Jesus taught in Bethsaida and ministered to the five thousand (Luke 9:10–17), or when Peter preached in Jerusalem (Acts 2:14–41).

Thus it is apparent that Christ's own claims of deity, as well as the claims of His followers concerning their faith in Him, illustrate that a strong collective response occurs when the Word of God is proclaimed to those who do not believe. Today when the Bible is preached, the revelation of God still incites the masses to action, just as was true when Christ was on earth.

It may be argued that the instances of collective behavior in the Bible all represent the outcome either of God's wrath against unrighteousness, or the proclamation of His Word to the unredeemed. However, the interpretation of this behavior must be done with caution. For example, religious beliefs of *all* kinds are capable of evoking intense collective activity, as is true of all leaders with charisma and all disasters regardless of their perceived or actual source. That recorded biblical instances all seem to revolve around wickedness and faith may simply result from the fact that the Bible focuses on those very themes. After all, people have stoned others for political as well as religious beliefs, and crowds have become enraged at soccer games as well as at claims of deity. Consequently, it would not be wise to conclude from these accounts that *all* collective behavior somehow at root reflects a struggle between wickedness and righteousness, or the mind of Christ versus the mind of unbelief.

At the same time, however, it is important to have a deeper vision about the hand of God in human history. The very impulses that motivate much collective behavior—such as greed and lust—are, after all, hallmarks of sinful rebellion against the Creator. If people were slaves to good rather than evil, would there be rioting, panic, or a rush for recognition? Perhaps the accounts of collective behavior in the Bible represent a microcosm of the human condition apart from God. At that level there is much to learn from the scriptural accounts that are designed to instruct people in understanding the realities of God and His creation.

Identity. One of the remarkable things about human nature is its strong sense of *other-directedness*—the tendency to look to other people to find out who or what they are and how they should behave. Social psychologists have long recognized the fact that one's definitions of self come through interaction with others. People possess a *social* self that manifests itself in many ways, including the collective behavior in which they engage. People seem to be, as Klapp (1969:38–46) pointed out cogently, on a "collective search for identity" that has led them into such avenues as hero-worship, cults, and fashion changes. Indeed, it is difficult to conceive of fashion apart from the desire to achieve the recognition of others. The same could be said for the more bizarre expressions of fashion—the fad and the craze. According to Klapp, the purpose of these involvements is to attract attention ("Look at me!") while at the same time identifying the real "me."

In the midst of this search for self, the important issue of identity emerges. Before someone can become willing to take part in collective behavior, there must be some kind of identification with the others who are involved. For example, if I were to be suddenly confronted by a large and noisy crowd that waved a Norwegian flag and chanted in the Norwegian language, it is highly unlikely that I would feel strongly compelled to join in the chorus. Probably the only response I would feel would be curiosity—hardly the same as anger, desperation, disgust, or some other motivating human response. There must be, in other words, some significant overlap between how I view myself and how I perceive the others before any sort of commonality—and hence willingness to become involved—can emerge.

For the Christian, the self-concept is derived from Scripture as well as through socialization and personal experience. This means that in addition to all other elements of self-definition, Christians must see themselves as sinners who are redeemed, made in the image of God, and being used to bear His truth. Such a self-view means that Christians do not need to search for an identity, for they already have one (1 Peter 2:9–10). The process of identification—of saying to another person or group that "we are one"—is ultimately based on our common redemptive experience with other believers. There are, naturally, other bases for our sense of commonality with others. For one thing Christians possess incredibly complex personalities, and they are likely to find something they share in common with almost anyone they would meet. And, of course, we are instructed time after time in the Scriptures to identify with those who are poor, oppressed, and lonely—even when our own estimations might lead us to conclude that we have *nothing* in common with them. However, the single most fundamental consideration (the master role) for the Christian is to be a follower of Christ, and other allegiances are risky at best. Christians are told in 1 John 2:15–17 that nothing in the evil world system comes from the Father, and love of the world casts them as the enemy of God (James 4:4). Since Christian standards have their source in the revelation from God, it is improper for believers to look around horizontally to a fallen world for their standards; for them to do so would be to deny the essence of their status as new creatures and sojourners in this life.

The point made here is that the involvement of Christians in collective behavior, be it fad, fashion, riot, or social movement, is fundamentally rooted in their willingness and ability to see in others around them something with which they can identify and therefore act on jointly. That such activities arise from a world that does not bow to Christ as Lord must give Christians pause as they consider what sorts of involvements are acceptable. More will be said on this point shortly. Each believer must act thoughtfully and responsibly in all matters. Certainly the typical responses of a child of God should not include identifying with a crowd whose activities border on illegality, or whose demeanor exhibits loss of self-control. Moreover, the believer should not engage in behavior whose sole purpose is to draw attention to oneself.

Responsibility. The notion of responsibility in collective behavior is a broad one, including the phenomena of self-control, accountability, and rationality. The following paragraphs will discuss those topics of most direct relevance to the Christian who is trying to identify a biblical basis for involvement in collective behavior.

Probably the most immediate concern arises over the issue of self-control. One common characteristic of crowd behavior is the loss or weakening of this quality. Consider behavior in panic or that of an angry mob as cases in point. Of course, most events in daily collective life are less extreme, but the process of becoming suggestible can be found even in simple crowd behavior. Situations involving the absence or weakness of norms present individuals with an invitation to behave in ways they otherwise would not even consider. It should be understood that people never totally abandon their sense of being that has been cultivated over the years through socialization. There are several factors that work to limit the range of acceptable behavior in a crowd, including the mores of members, the suggestions of the leaders, and the activities of control agents. However, at the very least, it can be said that incentives to "let loose" in such settings are quite strong. It is not difficult to stretch at least some of the constraints that keep us behaving properly in established social life. Thus people in collectivities can become overly raucous, or violent; or they can become exceedingly afraid, or upset.

There are few qualities of the Christian life that receive more attention in the Bible than this notion of self-control. For example, 1 Peter cautions several times that believers must have a clear mind and have full control over the emotions and proclivities of the flesh (1:13; 4:3–7; 5:8). The same theme is stated explicitly in other places as well (1 Thess. 4:4–6; Titus 2:2–6). Although these texts do not spell out precisely how this is to be accomplished, or what is to be subdued, even a casual reading of a passage describing the fruit of the Spirit (Gal. 5:22–23) offers clear evidence of pleasing Christian character.

What, then, is the relevance of these directives to the student of collective behavior? First, note those passages that provide direct commands against giving free rein to one's emotions. These include uncontrolled anger (James 1:19–20); orgies, carousing, drunkenness, and brawling (1 Peter 4:3–5; Gal. 5:16–26; Rom. 13:12–14); intense fear (1 John 4:16–18; 2 Tim. 1:7); and rumor, gossip, and slander (Rom. 1:29–32; Eph. 4:29–31; Col. 3:8; James 4:1–12; 2 Tim. 2:16; Titus 3:1–2). These actions are part of the sinful nature that Christians have forsaken in their rebirth; and they must bring all of their thoughts into the captivity of a Spirit-directed life (2 Cor. 10:5).

Self-control as described above is not a burden. It is in fact the key to freedom in the daily Christian walk. Christians have the power to disassociate themselves from actions that they know are not pleasing to God. They can resist an ugly crowd scene; they can overcome exaggerated hysterical fears with the calmness and assurance befitting those whose steps are ordered by the Lord (Ps. 37:23). They are enabled to behave in a way that models Christ, no matter what the setting or circumstance.

This, of course, is a two-edged sword. Having possession of the tools, Christians need to resist these situations; they are consequently accountable for the outcomes of the paths they elect to follow. One of the most common rationalizations for misbehavior of any kind is to cast blame on the general environment in which that behavior occurred. This type of thinking produces laments that center around "uncontrollable impulses" and "peer pressure." Those involved say crowds "make" them do things and contagious anger is "inevitable," given certain provocations. But such thinking for Christians is clearly in error. God has given believers powerful and rational minds, and no residue of impulse is beyond the control of the indwelling Holy Spirit. Not only is this true, but Christians have the ability to think *critically* in even the most ambiguous or threatening situations. The Christian knows when he or she is with a group that is growing increasingly unruly, or is likely to crumble under the strain of an unidentifiable fear. The real issue is the decision, not the social pressures. Christians are capable of studying God's Word, obeying the Holy Spirit, and making reasoned moral decisions. The time to *train* our impulses and thoughts is before the crisis develops. A believer does not learn the kind of self-control that pleases God instantly in the frenzy of a collapsing building or rioting crowd. Wisdom and discipline are the product of years of patience and sacrifice; no better analogy can be found than that in Jesus' story of the foolish builder who experienced tragic consequences due to his failure to implement the Word of God *before* the storm (Matt. 7:24–27).

Up to this point the discussion of self-control has been largely confined to the types of behavior characterized by the absence of norms. Earlier it was noted that many other activities also fall under the heading of collective behavior, and the ground rules for involvement by Christians may not always be couched in terms of resisting the temptations to participate. For example, willingness by a Christian leader to speak out collectively against social injustices may require considerable self-control, particularly when the consequences of such actions would be great. More broadly, for *any* situation in which biblically ordered behavior contradicts what the secular world views as acceptable behavior, there may be no choice for a Christian but to become deeply involved; and in these cases, it is of utmost importance that the believer have a clear and controlled mind if the message of the gospel is to be heard.

However, even this issue can be a complex one. A careful reading of 1 Peter reveals that the body of Christians was being encouraged by the apostle not to protest against government (2:13–15). They were to resist the worldly fashions of the day (3:3–6), including unruly behavior (4:3–5), and also to accept harsh and evil slavery if that was to be their lot (2:18–21). Peter's point seems to be that suffering abuse and persecution was a part of the price to be paid for being God's distinct and chosen people. There are then no simple answers to the question of self-control; yet this discipline must be mastered if we are to design a Christian lifestyle that pleases God.

Stewardship. One interesting fact about collective behavior is the enormous range of significance that is attached to it. General social movements such as those for civil rights or protection of the environment are profound; so are open insurrections against established governments. Yet there are also seemingly trivial forms of collective action. Consider the craze: it can marshal as much, if not more, energy and attention as the most revolutionary outburst, and yet it can center on something as modest as tulip bulbs or goldfish. Obviously any form of human behavior requires at least *some* fraction of the available resources of time, energy, talent, and possessions. And this raises the final major issue for the Christian: what constitutes the wise and godly use of those resources? What are the criteria for determining whether the efforts required to engage in collective behavior are worth the cost? This final section will highlight some of the basic forms of collective behavior and raise, rather than answer, some of the appropriate questions.

One form of collective behavior is *expressive crowd behavior,* or letting off steam. This involves the use of a release mechanism that is beneficial to a society as well as to the individuals who comprise it. It is important that any social system channel tensions into acceptable outlets—one of which, typically, is the expressive crowd. Victory celebrations, annual festivals, and raucous parties all serve this function in some respects. Are these activities acceptable for the Christian? If so, what are the limits? Is it wise to expend energy in nonproductive ways? Are there alternatives to these mechanisms? Can discretion be exercised in the midst of a noisy crowd? The release of energy is certainly not wrong in itself; the significant factors are the context and general purposes that motivate and direct this release. Screaming for joy after a sports victory, for example, seems to be qualitatively different from screaming in anger at the effigy of a group enemy.

Another form of collective behavior is *diffuse collectivities* (fashion, fads, crazes, manias, rushes). The true origin of fashion is a topic of debate among scholars, but its link with status and display of self are matters of empirical record. Our lives are encased in fashion and its change, be it in terms of clothing, language, demeanor, or any other aspect of style. Should the Christian be involved in keeping up with styles? How does participation in the fashion process contribute to godly character? Does a good steward spend money on the items in fashion around him or her? Consider the more intense phenomena of fads and crazes. Do world record attempts in marathon dancing constitute a wise use of time and energy? Does an obsession with *any*thing worldly, collective or otherwise, symbolize maturity in the Christian life? Chasing elusive dreams of quick wealth may be universal in human nature, but does that fact give Christians a standard that pleases God? In this discussion I am not arguing for the rejection of all fashion or fad-related behavior but am simply raising questions that press for defensible answers.

Social movements are a third form of collective behavior. These movements vary widely in the amount of involvement required of members. Some demand total allegiance and self-sacrifice; at the other extreme are those in which membership and participation involve completely individual decisions (e.g., the health foods movement). It is safe to say that one's identification at *any* level with the goals or programs of a social movement will imply the commitment of time and energy. In what sorts of movements is involvement justifiable or reasonable? Does the Christian's investment of self in a movement impact on the appearances (witness) given off as followers of Christ? Finally, several writers have stated that social movements originate in unrest and dissatisfaction with the status quo. If such an assessment is correct, is that a proper motivation for a Christian to get involved? Are there other ways to initiate desired social change or express dissatisfaction?

Civil disorder (riots and protest) is another form of collective behavior. Continuing the line of investigation that is being pursued, let us inquire as to what sorts of protest activity are acceptable. How does the Christian express grievance? Does the threat or use of violence affect a believer's views about involvement? Christians have long disagreed on these questions, and it is by no means suggested that the issues can be reduced to binary choices. These are complex and troubling debates, particularly in an era of frequent outbreaks of civil disorder. The point is that to fail to deal with all these issues is inexcusable; indeed, failure to act in some way to resolve them is tantamount to being a choice in itself, with many implications that have to be faced.

CONCLUSIONS AND APPLICATIONS

This has been a very brief treatment of the issues that are relevant to the phenomenon of collective behavior. Hopefully, it has been made clear that such behavior reveals a great deal about oneself as well as God. What appears as chaos and breakdown is not an abiding trait of social life; the Creator is too orderly to have formed such a world. What seems chaotic is not really the absence of order, but rather the emergence of order. Humans cannot function in an environment without rules, and so they have learned to construct new norms when the existing ones are weak, inadequate, or overthrown.

The study of collective behavior ultimately reveals the nature of the human condition: man's suggestibility; creativity; other-directedness; need for identity, order, and meaning; and response to crisis. Most importantly, it provides a glimpse of elemental social action—the raw ingredients of human behavior. Fear, hope, greed, violence, elation, sacrifice, and other such basic responses surface and come to life in the behavior of collectivities. There is much instructive value in studying these elements, particularly when that analysis is conformed to God's Word. To conclude this section, we must now identify some of the fundamental biblical truths that relate to the Christian's involvement in collective behavior.

God's standard of conduct for Christians has a relevance to collective behavior. Passages enjoining the Christian to refrain from anger, rage, and brawling (e.g., Eph. 4:29–31 and James 1:20) were dealt with above. This emphasizes the Christian's involvement in crowds, mobs, and rioting. The Bible specifically speaks against drunkenness, orgies, and debauchery (Rom. 13:12–14). It commands submission to, and respect for, the authority of established rulers (Rom. 13:1–2; Heb. 13:17; Titus 3:1–2; 1 Peter 2:13–17). Although this may not necessarily deny the possibility of Christians ever becoming involved in protest activities or social movements of rebellion, it does call for careful reflection on the part of the believer who is inclined to become involved. Probably the ultimate yardstick against which to measure participation in collective behavior is found in the biblical directives to do all in the name of Jesus (Col. 3:17) and to the glory of God (1 Cor. 10:31). The Holy Spirit, working within the believer, can direct decisions that literally fulfill this awesome obligation.

God enables Christians to be strong in the events that surround them. Christians are offered the wisdom of God as a gift (James 1:5), and they are exhorted to have the mind of Christ (Phil. 2:5) and to submit all thoughts to Him (2 Cor. 10:5). Consequently there is within Christians the power to withstand the temptation to do wrong; believers need not focus on self or on what others think. God has empowered them to be able to move through life in the peace and love that come through fixing their thoughts on Him (Isa. 26:3; 1 John 4:13–18). Not only is it possible to resist the all-encompassing environmental pressures, but it is possible to overcome them through the greater power within (1 John 4:4).

This means enjoying liberation from such things as runaway emotions, desires for revenge, selfish impulses, loss of hope, frantic searches for identity, and other expressions of the sinful nature in people who live apart from God.

Christians are allowed to choose a responsible course of action for themselves. As long as there is conscious submission of the will to biblical teaching, Christians are free to develop their own perspectives on these phenomena—including whether or not to participate. One person may decide to attend a demonstration or join in a fad, and another may not. But this freedom of choice is clearly constrained by their accountability to God and to each other. Time, energy, and resources are precious commodities that call for diligent stewardship. There is a place for commitment to the social causes, but that commitment must not hinder fellowship with God. There is a place for triviality in the believer's life, but it must never occupy a position of prominence. Similarly the release of emotion, or expression of political dissent, must be undertaken with great care. However harmless such involvements in collective behavior may appear, if they offend other Christians or cause them to question their own faith, the involvements must be curtailed for the larger good.

The discussion above has been clearly restrictive in nature. This may evoke in the reader images of an archaic and unrealistic view of contemporary social life. But the mark of maturity in the Christian life has always been found in one's discernment of—and willingness to pursue—the deep truth found within Scripture. If this means an abandonment of what may at times appear to be natural or harmless, then so be it. Christians are called to be salt and light to a dying world, and that requires sacrifice. The writer of Hebrews presents a challenge to take much more seriously what it means to live a righteous life. In concluding a discussion on Jesus as High Priest, the author writes:

> We have much to say about this, but it is hard to explain because you are slow to learn. In fact, though by this time you ought to be teachers, you need someone to teach you the elementary truths of God's word all over again. You need milk, not solid food! Anyone who lives on milk, being still an infant, is not acquainted with the teaching about righteousness. But solid food is for the mature, who by constant use have trained themselves to distinguish good from evil. Therefore let us leave the elementary teachings about Christ and go on to maturity (5:11–6:1).

DISCUSSION QUESTIONS

1. Was the first-century church a social movement? Why? Why not?
2. What do you believe are the limits for Christian participation in expressive crowd behavior?
3. What should be the Christian response to such social phenomena as fashion, fads, and crazes? Why?
4. Should a Christian become involved in a social movement? Why?
5. Is a Christian ever justified in being involved in civil disorder or civil disobedience? Why?

SUGGESTED READING

Kai T. Erikson, *Everything in Its Path: Destruction of Community in the Buffalo Creek Flood* (New York: Simon and Schuster, 1977). One of the many books written on specific examples of collective behavior; this one is both informative and illustrative of research in the field. It deals with mass contagion.

Robert R. Evans (ed.), *Social Movements: A Reader and Sourcebook*, 1973; *Readings in Collective Behavior*, 2nd ed., (Chicago: Rand McNally, 1975). The best source available for readings. Both provide good overviews and lively readings on the various types of behavior discussed in this chapter.

Irving L. Horowitz and W. H. Friedland, *The Knowledge Factory: Student Power and Academic Politics in America* (Chicago: Aldine, 1970). The annotation for the Erikson book above applies, except that this book deals with protest/disorder.

Alan C. Kerckhoff and Kurt W. Back, *The June Bug: A Study of Hysterical Contagion* (New York: Appleton-Century-Crofts, 1968). The annotation for the Erikson book above applies, except that this book deals with mass contagion.

Orrin E. Klapp, *Currents of Unrest: An Introduction to Collective Behavior* (New York: Holt, Rinehart and Winston, 1972). A comprehensive text written from the symbolic interaction perspective.

Eugene H. Methvin, *The Riot Makers* (New Rochelle, N.Y.: Arlington House, 1970).

Joseph P. Perry, Jr., and M. D. Pugh, *Collective Behavior: Response to Social Stress* (St. Paul: West, 1978). A comprehensive text from the more eclectic approach.

Ron E. Roberts and Robert M. Kloss, *Social Movements: Between the Balcony and the Barricade*, 2nd ed. (St. Louis: C. V. Mosby, 1979).

Melvin M. Tumin and Arnold S. Feldman, "The Miracle at Sabana Grande." (*Public Opinion Quarterly* 19, 1955), pp. 124–39.

Ralph Turner and Lewis Killian, *Collective Behavior*, 2nd ed. (Englewood Cliffs, N.J.: Prentice-Hall, 1972). The truly classic textbook in the field of collective behavior.

—— 17

DONALD L. CONRAD
Bethel College,
Indiana

DEMOGRAPHY, POPULATION, AND ECOLOGY

When Christ met with His disciples after His resurrection, He commanded, "Go ye into all the world, and preach the gospel to every creature" (Mark 16:15, KJV). How big was that first-century mission field?

The best estimate that demographers can give to that question is that the world then had about the same population size as does the United States and Canada today—250 million. It wasn't until about the time the Pilgrims came to Jamestown in 1620 that the total world population doubled to reach 500 million, and it was not until a few years before the Civil War that it doubled again to reach the first billion. But in just eighty years (about the time many of your parents were born in the 1930s), another one billion gain in population was added!

Suddenly, in just one lifetime—that of your parents—look what has happened. By 1965 another billion gain had occurred, and most of the readers of this book were part of it. By 1976, in just eleven years, another billion increase brought the world population to four billion. (That is 4000 million or 4,000,000,000 persons.) In 1980 the figure passed 4.5 billion, and each year the world's population increases by more than the total population of France.

Such statistics stagger our comprehension. It is hard to grasp even 100,000 people watching the Super Bowl in the Memorial Coliseum in Los Angeles; try to conceive of ten of those at once in the same town and you have one million. If you could imagine 220 cities in the United States, each with ten coliseums filled at once, you could put in those 2,200 coliseums all the population of the United States. But since the United States has only 5 percent of the world's population, twenty times that many would be required, or 44,000 coliseums, to seat everyone in the world. Furthermore, we would need to build four new Astrodomes every day to care for the population growth of five million a month. Of course, the Great Commission is not to build coliseums, but to witness to *each one* about the gospel.

DEMOGRAPHY AND POPULATION

The study of the size, growth, and characteristics of population is known as *demography*. Specialists in many different disciplines are demographers, not just sociologists. The census is a major source of information. Nations have been taking censuses for many thousands of years, as did the Hebrews in the days of the Exodus, and the Romans in the year Christ was born. Demographers do much more than count people, however; they study the structural aspects of populations—their size, rate of growth, geographic distribution, composition in terms of sex, race, occupation, education, and language—and they also study the population processes of fertility, mortality, migration, and occupational mobility (McGee, 1980:278).

In the last few decades the mushrooming population growth, or explosion, along with the deterioration of the environment and approaching exhaustion of unrenewable resources, has made the study of demography and human ecology urgent concerns to scientists, policy makers, and the general public. In 1798 Thomas Malthus, a British clergyman-economist, wrote the first major study of population. His gloomy prediction that population would grow geometrically while food could increase only arithmetically, bringing famine, disease, and war, provoked great controversy and criticism. Certainly the founding fathers of our country, poised on the edge of a vast frontier, would have found his cry of doom unrealistic in 1800. But a few generations later, neo-Malthusians like Paul Ehrlich (1968) would be writing of *The Population Bomb* that could explode during the next two decades, bringing the death of the ocean and the end of mankind. If Osborn's or Petersen's scenario of a crowded earth with bodies packed solid over every inch did not dramatize our plight enough, Rachel Carson's *Silent Spring* (1962) did. Environmental awareness, ecosystems, ecology, and "earth days" became a part of most everyone's consciousness and vocabulary, and at least one chapter on population or ecology appears in almost every biology, economics, and sociology text or social problems reader.

I am aware that many people do not like statistics, but it is difficult to study population growth without them. There are three main types of statistical data that demographers generate: data on population distribution, population composition, and dynamic population processes.

Population distribution. More than 80 percent of the earth's surface is not hospitable to humankind and consists of deserts, frozen arctic, rugged mountains, steaming rain forests, and oceans. If the population of the United States were equally distributed over the fifty states, we would have about 60 persons in every square mile. But in Nevada, with 11,000 square miles, there are only 500,000 persons, or 4.7 per square mile. On the other hand, Tom Skinner recently described Harlem where he grew up:

> I was born and raised in a community called Harlem which is located in the northern tip of Manhattan in New York City. It's a 2½ square mile area with a population of one million people. The social statisticians say that if I took the entire population in the United States (all 200 million Americans) and you forced them to live somewhere in New York, it still would not get as congested as Harlem is right now. On the block where I lived (125 yards North to South, 55 yards East to West) there were 4,000 people (appeal letter: March, 1980).

Population density is "population size per unit of land area" (Phillips, 1979:405). India, with 1.3 million square miles of land, has nearly 600 million population, or more than ten times the density of the United States. Bangladesh has crowded nearly 80 million people into an area about the size of Minnesota. If all of the United States were that crowded, we would have nearly three billion people! Yet Hong Kong and Calcutta are much more

Demography, Population, and Ecology

crowded than is Bangladesh (Hartley, 1972:96–97). Density also refers to potential for social contacts as McGee so graphically notes:

> if we assumed an average density of one person per square mile for the U.S. in 1500, there would have been 314 persons within any circular area with a ten-mile radius. If there are 8,000 persons per square mile for the average central city in 1970, the number of persons within the same circular area would be 2,512,000. Finally, Manhattan Island, with a density of approximately 75,000 persons per square mile has 23,550,000 potential contacts within a circle having a ten-mile radius! . . . When too many people are concentrated in relatively small areas, they lack the resources to satisfy their collective expectations regarding human welfare (1980:271–72).

One of the striking facts that emerges as population density figures are compared is that density is increasing much more rapidly in the underdeveloped nations. Many of them now have nearly twice the density that is found in the developed nations, and it appears that in another twenty years this will increase to three times as dense due to their much more rapid rate of population growth (Perrucci et al., 1977:524). Some underdeveloped nations, however, think they are still underpopulated, and so they have strong pronatalist policies to increase their population and to settle their sparsely populated frontiers.

A second dramatic statistic provided by demographers is the extent to which the American people—in fact, almost the whole world—have literally moved to town. *Urbanization* is a worldwide phenomenon of this century. If all of human history could be reduced to a twenty-four-hour day, until a few minutes ago nearly everyone lived in the country. Then suddenly, as if by a hundred thousand magnets, millions of people were drawn to the towns and cities. As late as 1800 only 3 percent of the world's people lived in communities of 5000 or more. It has passed 40 percent now, and by the year 2000 more than half of all the living will be in towns, most of them in large cities. Kenkel (1980:477) estimates that at the time of Christ probably fewer than .5 percent of the 250 million persons on earth lived in cities of 20,000 or more. Agricultural technology, the industrial revolution, medical and military science, and much more combined to make large cities possible and essential.

The next chapter will explore this topic in much greater detail. It is interesting to note in passing, however, that in the United States back in 1790, there were only two towns of over 25,000 population. Less than 4 percent of our people were urban. One hundred years later, in 1890, there were 160 towns of 25,000 or over, and 35 percent of the country was urban. The 1990 census is expected to find that in just two hundred years the United States will have moved from an almost totally rural society to one in which more than 85 percent of us will be urban. My ninety-nine-year-old grandfather saw the country go from 28 percent urban to 76 percent; I may see it go from 50 percent to 90 percent; yet urban areas comprise only about 1.5 percent of the land area (Dressler, 1976:464). Because many urban residents have moved back to the suburbs or to surrounding smaller towns, cities have been reaching out by annexation to include more people in their tax base. Population counts are increasingly being based on Standard Metropolitan Statistical Areas, which is a name given to concentrations of population around central cities of 50,000 or more (Perrucci et al, 1977:528). Some of these concentrations have reached out along the major radial highways to overlap adjacent cities and create supercities known as *megalopoli*. Within five of these densely settled areas (Boston-Washington, Buffalo-Chicago, San Francisco-Los Angeles, etc.), nearly half of the American people are now located according to U.S. Census Bureau projections, and it may increase to 60 percent by the year 2000.

Population composition. Within a community, or within a nation, it is important to know *who* lives there as well as how many reside there. Most sociology texts will include charts showing such facts as sex ratios, age pyramids, occupational distributions, racial and marital categories, and socioeconomic factors. Because of space limitations, these are omitted here. It is important, however, to understand the principle of the *age pyramid,* for it graphically shows the percentage of the population, divided by sex, that is in each age category. In a country like Honduras with a high birth rate but a low life expectancy, 51 percent of the population is clustered in the young categories at the bottom, gradually diminishing to small fractions at the top and creating a graph that looks like a Christmas tree or Egyptian pyramid. However, if an epidemic would strike only youngsters, the pyramid might resemble a top. If a tribe experienced a raid in which most of the females were captured, or the males were killed, the pyramid would be lopsided in those age brackets.

Since 1900 considerable progress in medicine and public health has added nearly twenty years to average life expectancy, so that many more Americans are now living past sixty-five. In the past twenty years the United States also has had a significant decrease in the birth rate. This means that more public services will be needed for the increasing block of older citizens, and less will be invested in schools and other services for the young. In a few more years America will have a smaller segment in the center of the age pyramid, but there will need to be supporting services for rather large groups on both ends of the age spectrum. If Americans continue to have small families and to prolong the lives of older people, the senior *dependency ratio* will be high, requiring greater contributions to Social Security, Medicaid, and similar programs (McGee, 1980:273–77).

A second aspect of population composition is the *gender ratio*. At birth in this country there are about 104 male babies born for every 100 females. By the teen years, due to higher mortality rates for males, the ratio is about even. By age 65 there are only 70 males for every 100 females, and by age 85 the ratio has dropped to 62. Senior citizen facilities, retirement communities, and geriatric wards in hospitals are filled primarily with females, for they outlive men on the average by about eight years. In the USSR the ratio starts with 104 as in the United States, but by age 65 the ratio has dropped to 44. In a few countries this pattern is almost reversed. In the region of India the ratio starts at 107, but by age 65 it is still 105 males for every 100 females (McGee, 1980:275). Thus it is known that the ratio is not to be explained strictly by biological differences but is a population characteristic that is also affected by culture and social mobility. In Alaska, for example, there is a shortage of females at all ages, whereas in Washington, D.C., there has been a surplus of females. Employment opportunities in the government bureaucracy led many thousands of single girls to migrate to the capital; the jobs and opportunities on the Alaskan frontier were much more appealing to males.

The make-up of the population is very important to those concerned about product marketing today or planning for future social needs. Whether the need is greatest for diapers, elementary teachers, geriatric nurses, motorcycles, high-rise apartments, or slim jeans depends a lot on the age, sex, and ethnic distribution of a population, along with their income, marital status, and education. Most marketing surveys, political polls, and research studies have a section called demographic data, for the composition of a population has been found to have considerable bearing on their needs, wants, and attitudes. Certainly the strategy of evangelism and church ministry must take into account the composition of the population to be reached. For instance, churches today focus not only on teen-age ministries, but are also beginning to develop programs for the over-sixty-five "Keen-agers."

Population processes. Demography goes beyond mere description of distribution and composition. Knowledge that enables prediction is the goal of most sciences. There are three main population processes that enable us to make projections: births, deaths, and migration. These are called fertility, mortality, and mobility. The *crude birth rate* is the number of babies born in one year in a population of 1000 persons. The *death rate* is the number of deaths in one year per 1000 persons. *Immigration* measures the number who move into the designated area, and *emigration* refers to those who leave. The *natural increase* is the number of births, less the number of deaths, plus the number of immigrants, less those who have left (Spencer, 1979:496). The following example may make this clearer. Suppose Gilligan's Island were inhabited with 1000 persons the day before the *S.S. Minnow* was marooned there. During the year, 60 persons were born and 20 died. The Skipper and his passengers immigrated, adding seven, and only the professor succeeded in getting off the island. Gilligan's Island's natural increase would be computed this way: 1000 + (60−20) + (7−1) = 1,046. The growth rate would be 4.6 percent that year—very high. If the same rate prevailed each year, the *doubling time* until there would be 2000 on the island would be less than twenty years.

Not much data is available on population patterns on this continent for the millennia before the first settlers came from Europe to this country. In 1500 there were probably one million or more Native Americans already here. When the first decennial census was taken in 1790, the population was recorded at about four million, but no effort was made to count the inhabitants outside of the thirteen colonies. Only in the last one hundred years have most countries developed systematic records; and in some of the underdeveloped nations, vital statistics are still educated guesses. For example, Mao Tse Tung is reported to have denied just before his death that mainland China's population had passed the projected 850 million, saying they had probably not yet reached 800 million, perhaps not even 700 million. If the projection involving China is that inaccurate, world population projections may need to be revised considerably. The United States also still has some inaccuracies in the reporting of population statistics. The 1970 census may have undercounted by nearly five million (due mostly to minorities who do not have a regular residence). However, the U.S. Census Bureau has developed a variety of methods to correct such errors, and the 1980 census endeavored to make the most comprehensive and accurate projection of any ever undertaken in history.

One can project the growth of population in the United States on the basis of registered vital statistics that at present note a birth rate of about fifteen per thousand and a death rate of about nine. This net gain of six per thousand, when multiplied by the 225 million in the country, gives an increase of approximately 1,300,000 for 1981. To this must be added the net migration gain of more than 400,000. Thus *if past rates continue,* the United States will gain nearly two million in population this year. This is an important point. We can project from past rates, but we cannot predict with certainty how many people will die, be born, or migrate in the future. What we do know is that if the death rate remains fairly constant and if couples average three children per family for the next fifty years, the population in the United States will exceed 475 million by the year 2020 and 950 million in less than ninety years from now (Robertson, 1977:483).

It is also known that the fertility rate for the past several years has been considerably less than that. In fact, at the current rates, 1000 women during childbearing years will produce only 1,900 offspring, or less than it takes to replace the 2000 parents. If this lower-than-Zero Population Growth pattern continues, the population of the United States can be expected to stabilize at only a little above 250 million in the next generation.

The sudden turnaround in the number of live births is also apparent in the following vital statistics reported by Kenkel (1980:445). It was not until 1954 that Americans registered four million births in one year. In 1957 the number peaked at 4,308,000, which was a crude birth rate of 25.3 based on our population then of 165 million. It was a fertility rate of 122.9. By 1964 the number of births had dropped below four million as the postwar baby boom ended. Environmental consciousness grew, marriages were postponed, contraception became common, and abortions were much more prevalent. By 1977 only a little more than three million births were recorded, resulting in a crude birth rate of 15.3 and a fertility rate of 67.4. No one, certainly not the neo-Malthusians, was predicting such a precipitous change in family values and birth data in the short span of twenty years.

One pattern that has almost become predictable on the world demographic scene is what has been called the *demographic transition*. In almost every society that has become more technologically developed, improved medicine and nutrition have brought a radical drop in the rate of infant mortality and the loss of mothers in childbirth. The life expectancy of the older population has also been extended by slowing the mortality rate. In agrarian, hunting, and pastoral economies, children are deemed valuable for maintaining the subsistence economy and for providing security in old age and an heir to preserve the land and herds. When 50 percent of the children perish in the first two years and many more fail to outlive their parents, cultural values toward large families become deeply ingrained and persist even when they are no longer functional.

In the first stage of the demographic transition when both the death rate and birth rate are high, the population remains quite stable, perhaps for millennia. When the death rate drops but the birth rate remains high, the natural increase suddenly jumps and a population explosion occurs, as has been true over much of the world in the past one hundred years. Gradually, as has occurred in Europe and is now happening in the United States the average family size drops. Improved education and effective contraception drop the birth rate down close to the lowered death rate, and the population again stabilizes. Unfortunately, in the process of this stabilization, which is still only beginning in many of the populous underdeveloped nations, three or four billion people have been added to the "spaceship earth." The impact of those additional billions on the ecosystem is the major concern of what is called *human ecology,* and it is to that topic that much attention has been turned.

HUMAN ECOLOGY AND THE ENVIRONMENT

"Ecology refers to the mutual relations between organisms and their environment—in brief, to the total web of life wherein all plant and animal species (including human) *reciprocally* interact with one another and with the physical features of their habitat" (Vander Zanden, 1979:587). Robertson calls attention to the fact that "life on earth exists only in the biosphere, a thin film of soil, air, and water at or near the surface of the planet. Within this biosphere all living organisms are interdependent, existing in a delicate balance with one another and with the environmental resources that support them . . . in an *ecosystem*" (1977:487).

Jonathan Turner rather concisely shows how ecology relates to human societies and our future:

> The details of the complexity of interrelationships traced out in ecological study is not easily explained or understood. However, it is evident that life forms are closely dependent upon one another. No single species escapes its dependency on other life forms and the environment. Therefore, the capacity for life within the ecological community is reduced when the chains, cycles, and flows of nature are interrupted or out of balance. Advanced technologies "create great demand for energy resources and cause the discharge of waste residues. These are dumped into the basic renewable resources—air, soil and water—upon which all life depends. As these renewable resources receive waste residues, the basic cycles, flows and chains that rejuvenate (them) are disrupted. . . . For example, the life that produces 80% of our oxygen— the ocean's phytoplankton—is being invaded by chemicals that are running off into the oceans. The soil upon which we depend is becoming saturated with chemical fertilizers and pesticides." . . . The ecosystem upon which the human species, and other life forms, depends is disrupted and jeopardized (1978:525).

If any fact has been forcefully brought to peoples' consciousness, it is that no man is an island in ecological matters. All are dependent on each other; we are our brothers' keepers. Metta Spencer points out that "the world is a single ecological system. DDT or mercury dumped into the Great Lakes may eventually kill birds in the South Seas or the Mediterranean. . . . If the polar ice caps melt, the penguins won't be the only ones to notice. We may exploit one another in the short run, but in the long run nobody comes out ahead" (1979:512).

There is little serious question but that the earth's supply of natural resources is limited, especially of some of the fossil fuels and other unrenewable minerals. Advanced economies such as that of the United States use a major share of many of these resources even though they have only a small percentage of the world's population. As other and larger countries such as China and India become more industrialized and energy consuming, the increased drain will quickly exhaust the limited resources. Robertson suggests:

> To bring everyone up to our economic level would require, for example, that we extract 75 times as much iron, 100 times as much copper, 200 times as much lead, 75 times as much zinc, and 250 times as much tin as we now do every year (Erlich and Erlich, 1972). Yet, there is evidence that even at present rates of extraction, known supplies of several of these minerals may be exhausted within the next quarter century [before 2000] (1977:281).

McGee brings the reality of this home when he notes:

> Problems of population growth are not, however, limited to developing nations. The U.S., for example, has the highest per capita standard of living in the world and is the world's leading food exporter. But many of the problems facing it today are directly or indirectly a consequence of population size. The "Baby Boom" after World War II produced a tidal wave of children. Elementary school buildings had to be dramatically enlarged . . . it overwhelmed the colleges . . . energy shortage, deterioration of the national park system, unemployment, pollution, and water shortages. . . . The U.S. now has too many people to maintain the standard of living that became conventional in the 1940's and 1950's. Today's American college students probably cannot expect in maturity to enjoy the affluence to which most became accustomed in childhood (1980:333).

Even water, which long has been thought to be free and inexhaustible, is becoming polluted, scarce, and costly. In the United States, 6000 gallons of water are consumed per person each month (McGee, 1980:280). A long drought in 1980 covered twenty-four states and placed impossible demands on wells and reservoirs. Uncontrollable fires raged through tinder-dry suburban hillsides, crops perished, water was rationed, and dust storms were produced by winds blowing one hundred miles an hour; discomfort, frustration, and anger were the inevitable results. Rains finally came to rescue areas that were right at the brink of disaster. If Americans continue to remove the forests, disturb the ecological balance of land and sea, double the usage of water, and pollute the resources, nothing can prevent the occurrence of some major disaster in the highly populated arid zones such as Los Angeles County.

By now most people have experienced or read about the stinging, unhealthy smog caused by air inversions, have seen areas of national parks become crowded and slumlike, and have learned of the dead or dying Great Lakes. The public is familiar with nuclear reactor malfunctions, energy brownouts, and oil spills. All these and more are constantly reminding us of the fact that "it can happen here."

David Dressler has summarized a number of other consequences of rapid population growth beyond the impact on the ecological environment:

1. Economic advances lost through greater population growth, especially in underdeveloped countries. If GNP grew at 1% and population at 3%, the per capita income and wealth would decline. Living now at the edge of starvation, continued growth in population worsens the situation.
2. Unemployment and underemployment if population grows faster than the economic base. To keep people busy, they often are employed in labor intensive, drudgery-type tasks which lowers productivity.
3. Political instability—frustrations from unemployment, low income, crowding, low quality of life leads to willingness to follow revolutionary movements which often result in military, totalitarian regimes.
4. High proportion of youthful members in the society. In some fast growing countries, approximately half the population is under 16 (in the U.S., the average age is now 30), placing considerable strains on the economy and the family to provide facilities and training.
5. High mobility toward the cities as presumed "meccas" of opportunity; creating shack towns, unemployment, ghettos, and impossible demands upon city budgets (1976:441–43).

There is a growing awareness among Christians that these matters have great significance for our lives and implications for

Christian ministry. David McKenna, a respected evangelical educator and spokesman, recently was interviewed by the *United Evangelical Action* staff of the National Association of Evangelicals (NAE) concerning his views on issues that face the church in the world of the 1980s. Devoting considerable attention to ecological issues, McKenna stated that stewardship of resources will be a crucial issue for the church. He explained:

> One futurist predicted that by the middle 1980's, there would be food riots in the streets of New York. That sounded far-fetched at first. But, much of our food is tied to petroleum, and when Philadelphia had gasoline riots in mid 1979, I suddenly saw the reality of that man's prediction . . . for us who are used to having all, to have a little less and to be forced to shift from abundance to a mildly competitive posture of first come, first served, brings out the animal in us.
>
> It seems to me that if we need a prophetic voice in the '80s, it is the unpopular voice that the church is going to have to live with less. And that seems contrary to everything Christians believe in. Our mindset is "if you expand your ministry, God will provide the cattle on a thousand hills." Well, there is truth in that, of course, but there is also a certain reality of accountability which God calls us to, particularly in a time of decreasing resources . . . if you take what the futurists are saying, the question between the haves and the havenots in the '80s may be one of the most crucial areas within the church (UEA, spring, 1980:10–13).

Social psychological research shows that when laboratory animals become overcrowded, they experience restless anxiety, violent aggression, and a "behavioral sink." When human groups continue to crowd together in a "concrete city" the result may be neurosis, alcoholism, illness, crime, and violence despite our social and spiritual programs to prevent and treat them. Larger and more densely populated nations often try to expand their territorial boundaries at the expense of smaller, less densely populated ones to gain *Lebensraum,* as has been illustrated by German and Japanese aggression in World War II, recent Chinese movements into Russia and India, and extended conflict in Indochina. McKenna thinks that we must either solve the problems of limited resources in an equitable manner or face the threat of war. He concludes: "The rest of the century is going to be a running skirmish with social issues that represent a shifting back and forth among the economic powers of the world, in my opinion. There never was a war fought that was not fought over resources. Consequently . . . unless we resolve the energy question we will have war over resources" (UEA, 1980:12).

Paul Erlich cautioned back in 1968, "As more and more people have less and less, as the rich get richer and the poor poorer, the probability of war increases. The poor of the world know what we have, and they want it" (Hartley, 1972:287). That same year Eisenhower said, "I have come to believe that the population explosion is the world's most critical problem" (Hartley, 1972:293). In the 1980s this may well be doubly true.

WORLD HUNGER

World hunger, a second major area of concern to Christians, is related to, but goes beyond, the problems of the struggle for living space and fair distribution of material goods and essential natural resources. Estimates by the United Nations and the President's Panel on Food Supply have placed the number of malnourished persons living on inadequate diets at nearly one-third of the world's population, or between one and two billion. And the world adds a net of about two hundred thousand stomachs a day. If population growth can be slowed and further advances in food technology and agronomy can be made, we might be able to lessen this hunger figure. Unfortunately, the "Green Revolution" of increased food supply through advanced technology, new seed strains, and high-powered fertilizers has had some negative effects on the environment. It is also apparent that political considerations often determine whether the achieved gain in food will actually get to the hungry. Human compassion has often responded to urgent appeals to save those starving from some natural or political disaster, only to have the food denied distribution for internal political reasons.

Furthermore, as Horton and Hunt point out,

> world population might not stabilize; a massive die-off is a distinct possibility. There might not be enough fertile cropland left to feed such a population. Deforestation, soil erosion and desert expansion are proceeding at record rates. It has all happened before. The North African breadbasket of the Roman Empire is now mostly wasteland (1980:418).

Some climatologists are predicting major weather fluctuations, a cold century, or a new ice age. Any very radical shift in temperature, rainfall, or atmosphere would quickly jeopardize not only millions of lives, but much of civilization as we know it.

If the weather remains favorable, enough food may be grown to hold starvation down from massive proportions, but if a drought should hit the major grain-producing areas again, as it has recently, and last for "seven years of famine" such as Egypt faced in the days of Joseph (Gen. 41:54), multiplied millions would undoubtedly perish. The apocalyptic horseman of famine foretold in Revelation could quickly be with us, as well as the horsemen of war, conquest, and death (6:1–8).

Emile Bonoit, in the "First Steps to Survival," warns:

> Hunger, true hunger—*serious* long continued undernourishment—is probably the source of more human misery than anything else in the world. And the problem is getting worse all the time. Hunger is actually a sort of dull torture which in time destroys bodies and spirits, and may even prevent human beings from developing properly. This condition may affect 10–20% of the world's population. The Technological approach faces overwhelming difficulties due to energy shortages and adverse ecological effects. The Redistributionist approach has been followed with billions of food aid being given by the U.S. and other countries, plus aid in development, and much private charity—yet we have more poor and hungry than ever before (Perrucci et al., 1977:536–39).

This does not mean that Christians should not support world relief. It does suggest to donors that more is involved than their going without a meal so others need not starve. Spencer states:

> Scarcity is not unavoidable. It is created by people, either on purpose or as an unintended result of other decisions. Much more food could be produced, but agribusiness and governments control production to keep prices up, or to help balance of payments deficits. Nearly three fourths of the world's agricultural land is controlled by 2.5% of the landholders. Nearly one-half of all by just .2%! The U.S. exports much grain and meat, but mostly to industrial nations, not India or Africa. In fact, we import from less developed countries more food than we send them. The hungriest people on earth may be the ones who are sending us our dinners (1979:517).

Furthermore, Robertson cautions us that

> in Asia, life expectancy is fifty-six years and the per capita GNP is $450; in Africa, life expectancy is forty-five years and per capita GNP is $340. In Europe and North America, by contrast, life expectancy is seventy-one years, while per capita gross national product is $3,680 in Europe and $6,580 in North America . . . but even if all the food in the world

were equally distributed, there would not be enough to go around—we would *all* be malnourished. And if the entire food supply in the world were distributed at the dietary level that we take for granted in the U.S., it would feed only one-third of the current world population (1977:476).

If grain that is fed to livestock to be consumed as meat in the United States were used instead as cereals, it would feed one billion people. Christians *could* make a difference by changing their accustomed lifestyle, but instead they consume more meat each year.

POPULATION CONTROL AND SANCTITY OF LIFE

Most of the literature in this field of demography, environment, and ecology takes the perspective that population growth must be slowed, fertility must be controlled, and fewer babies must be born. Nearly two-thirds of the governments are now pursuing antinatalist policies, and population specialists warn that these policies must motivate and reward people for small families. Without these results, they warn, the ecological forces of disease, insect predators, war, infanticide, primitive contraception, and abortion will again keep populations in balance as they did until the past few centuries. Robertson (1977:486) states that if all societies had continued to rely on hunting and gathering for their subsistence, the world population would have leveled off at around ten million people. Throughout human history, mothers have given birth to large numbers of children, most of whom died at birth or before adulthood. Even today, in many of the less developed areas of the world, nearly half of all children born alive die before they are five years old; and many more are stillborn.

Although everyone is against mortality, the issue often is not whether babies will die; instead, it is whether they will die as fetuses by abortions before they gain personality and social identity, or in the months and years after birth because the world cannot or will not provide them with a chance to live. In this generation on a world-wide basis, abortion has been the most practiced and effective means to limit population. Sterilization may well become the most frequent and effective means of the next generation. Many Christians believe that neither of these two methods can be fitted into a biblical view of the dignity and sanc-

Christian Perspectives on Sociology

tity of life and responsibility of parenthood, nor with Jesus' express command, "Let the little children come to me, and do not hinder them, for the kingdom of heaven belongs to such as these" (Matt. 19:14). It is significant to note that, according to Francis Schaeffer (1979), the current secular expression regarding population control stresses the "quality" rather than the "sanctity" of life. This, then, provides a basis for eliminating those humans who reduce the overall quality of human life.

It is appropriate that we as Christians take our stand on the sanctity of life and the right of the potential child, once conceived, to be nurtured, protected, and brought to birth. But if the effort stops here, and we neglect those millions who must then exist in filth, hunger, abuse, crippling malnourishment, and hopeless crowding, how hypocritical and inadequate has been our righteous posturing about the right to life. Perhaps Jesus would commend Christians for their conscience against abortions, but rebuke them for missing the larger issue of making life possible for the living. "[This] ought ye to have done, and not to leave the other undone. [It is easy to] strain at a gnat, and swallow a camel" (Matt. 23:23–24, KJV).

Can there be any reasonable doubt that God is prolife? But that is not to say that the sanctity given to human life and nature is the same as God's own sacredness. God is both holy and just, and He requires a price for sin. Thus from God's viewpoint human life *is* violable under certain conditions (Exod. 21:22–23). Christians must increasingly grapple with issues that confront them concerning the meaning of life: capital punishment, war, abortion, hunger, and euthanasia. Several observations may be helpful. First, to regain and preserve the quality of life and break the power of death, Christ *gave* His life as a ransom; He came and died that we might have more abundant life and eternal life (John 10:10). Jesus also said, "Whoever loses his life for me and for the gospel will save it" (Mark 8:35). Second, God took life. In Old Testament times animal sacrifices were required to atone for sin. Furthermore, written into the Levitical legal and moral code was the principle of restricting retribution to an "eye for eye" (Deut. 19:21), but it did require capital punishment, national judgment, and visiting iniquity to the third and fourth generations. Third, God denied potential life by forbidding an Israelite to marry a Gentile

352

even if no other was available. It is obvious that the command "Be fruitful . . . fill" an empty earth (Gen. 1:28) was a long-range goal, not a personal mission and universal obligation.[1] Though our first ancestors lived many generations, and some had numerous children, the Book of Genesis records a significant shortening of the human life span. Sometimes God permitted barren marriages, and He even called some to celibacy.

Finally, and perhaps most importantly, God established a surplus life capacity, using the principle of the survival of a few to maintain the balance of nature in the earth's ecosphere. Fish, birds, and mammals normally can and do produce much more than is necessary to reproduce the parent. The law of the jungle destroys the excess and keeps all the species in balance. Human males and females also have a natural fecundity, but it is not reasonable to believe a moral God intended for most human offspring to die in an animal-type struggle for the survival of the fittest. This makes the matter of how many children, and when, a matter of Christian stewardship, choice, and responsibility (Ps. 127:3–5).[2]

From the onset of puberty to her menopause—a period of about forty years—a normal human female will release from her ovaries nearly five hundred eggs; each egg will have life, but will require union with a male life cell to survive and trigger the growth of division that is in the master plan of the universe. In practice most of the eggs die because a natural or human decision is made that prevents conception. It is possible for a woman to bear up to thirty children in a lifetime; the *Guinness Book of World Records* cites a mother in Russia who in the eighteenth century had sixty-nine! In America a generation ago, families of twelve to eighteen children were quite common. Hutterites still average ten to twelve children and double their population every sixteen years. In a century they have grown from a few hundred to many thousands to become the fastest growing population group in America.

During pregnancy, and usually during lactation, ovulation is

---

[1]The unfolding of human history must not only be understood in the light of God's providential dealings but also the effects of sin in the human race must be taken into account.

[2]The theological issues are too complex to explore in this essay, but readers will find Hulme (1962) and Theilicke (1964) helpful.

suppressed naturally. It may also be suppressed by taking the hormonal birth-control pill, by tying the Fallopian tubes, or by the surgical removal of the ovaries. Once an ovum is released, and possibly fertilized, "ovacide" is accomplished by denying it the life-sustaining habitat of the uterus through use of the "morning-after" estrogen pill, or use of an intrauterine device which, in some not fully understood process, apparently spontaneously aborts any fertilized egg before it is harbored in the placental shield. Many people do not equate either of these acts with having an abortion, even though newly conceived life is not preserved. Many others, however, including Schaeffer and Koop (1979) would emphatically insist that abortions occur in both cases.

Much greater fecundity is built into the male's reproductive capacity. One normal ejaculation contains 150 million or more living sperm cells, most of which could unite with an egg and complete the genetic code and stimulus to create a new human being. An average male over a period of fifty or more sexually active years would probably release more than 400 billion sperm cells! One man's seed would be more than enough to create all the persons who have ever lived on earth many times over. God did not intend that more than a very few should ever bear fruit. The death of the rest is "spermacide." Sexual partners accomplish the destruction of sperm cells by using contraceptive measures such as condoms, foams, douches, and coital interruption; and masturbation is also an artificial way to destroy sperm cells. Many Christians believe that the union of a sperm and ovum should be a planned and prayerful event, not an accidental consequence of the marvelous fecundity with which God has equipped us, or a matter of "just having as many as God gives us."

Serious differences arise among sincere Christians, however, when wrestling with what to do about unplanned, and sometimes undesired, pregnancies. For example, how should a thirteen-year-old girl from a fine Christian home be counseled after being influenced into a sexual experience that resulted in a pregnancy? Should she be helped to obtain an abortion? Should she be advised to finish the pregnancy and then adopt out her firstborn child? Should she keep and raise the child herself? Should the father be located and told he should marry her? Each of these options may have bad consequences for all the parties involved.

Likewise, what response should be given to the fifty-year-old grandmother whose children are all married and who, as she is entering menopause, unexpectedly finds herself pregnant. She will probably not even consider adopting the baby out, but should she accept the risk to herself and the child to complete the pregnancy and with her husband try to raise another child at their age? These examples, like those infrequent pregnancies that result from rape or incest, are not common. Much more frequent and central to the point of this chapter are those decisions faced by younger married couples who experience contraceptive failures that bring pregnancies sooner or more often than they had planned. In weighing the rights of the unborn against those already living, should the unborn child always (or ever) be sacrificed to save the life of the mother? Should the child ever be sacrificed to perserve the quality of life of other children already born, as has been done frequently throughout history around the world? Or should the child be saved when the parents know a pitiful existence of illness, hunger, and squalor may be ahead? If we affirm for life, how great is the responsibility that rests on us not to "offend one of these little ones" (Matt. 18:6, KJV), but to nurture each of them in life and faith to the fullest extent that careful stewardship can make possible. In grappling with the questions posed above, it is incumbent on the Christian to submit to the standards of God's Word regardless of conflicts with the socially approved solutions of the world. The conclusions reached by secularists may not be relevant to Christians, who function on a different set of assumptions.[3]

CHRISTIAN RESPONSIBILITY FOR THE EARTH

Genesis teaches that when the Lord God made the universe, "no

---

[3]However, this does not mean we can ignore these questions. If we are going to hold to a prolife position, these questions must still be answered but from a different perspective. We must address the consequences to the mothers and children involved if we are to be morally responsible. At a minimum those holding a prolife position need to advocate and support programs that will meet the psychological, physical, and spiritual needs of all the parties involved. It must also be recognized that not all sincere Christians will interpret the Scriptures in the same way and come to the same conclusions concerning abortion. As this important issue is debated in Christian circles, it needs to be done in Christian love and understanding. Unfortunately this often has not been the case.

shrub of the field had yet appeared on the earth and no plant of the field had yet sprung up; the LORD God had not sent rain on the earth and there was no man to work the ground. . . . Now the LORD God had planted a garden in the east, in Eden. . . . And the LORD God made all kinds of trees grow out of the ground—trees that were pleasing to the eye and good for food. . . . The LORD God took the man and put him in the Garden of Eden to work it and take care of it" (Gen. 2:5, 8–9, 15). Thus the first man was intended to be a guardian of the Lord's earth!

When the psalmist lifted his heart in worship, he exclaimed, "The earth is the LORD's, and everything in it, the world, and all who live in it" (Ps. 24:1). Western cultures are more prone to believe and act as though the earth and everything in it is theirs to control and utilize, even to exploit, exhaust, pollute, and destroy. Lynn White claims that Christianity has become the most person-centered religion the world has ever seen. It not only has established a dualistic view of people and nature, but also insists that it is God's will that people utilize nature for their own ends. White believes we will continue to have a worsening ecological crisis until we reject the thought that nature has no purpose for existence save to serve people (Folsom, 1971:17–19).

In primitive and many Eastern societies, people are seen as a part of the natural world, which they respect as "mother earth." Industrialized Western societies see the human species as conquerors and lords of nature, which they freely exploit to advance their own affluence and comfort. And when they are finished with the materials they have carelessly torn from the earth, they frequently just as carelessly dump them in and around their "garden-nest" with little regard for the destruction of the ecological balance that sustains all life, including theirs. Robert Hutchins is said to have declared that the issue now is how to make the earth a decent habitat for mankind. The real test may be whether mankind can be made decent enough to inhabit the earth.

Some scientists can foresee nothing but the collapse of the whole industrial society. They anticipate radical drops in the living standard and population, very high death rates, and mass starvation—all in much less than one hundred years. This fate, they argue, can be averted only by stabilizing the population quickly and adopting an antigrowth attitude toward technology and industrialism now. Although irresponsibility and greed cause much of the earth's destruction, it is impossible, as Robertson points out, to reduce the problem to a simple conflict between the "good guys" and the "bad guys." He says, "All of us are presumably in favor of protecting the environment, yet, all of us are guilty of practices that worsen the problem" (1977:489). As someone once quipped, some nature lovers, to preserve the vanishing whooping crane, would gladly sacrifice a considerable number of people—*other* people, of course. The grim reality is that one of the most endangered species is our own children and grandchildren. The issue is larger than amount of affluence, altered lifestyle, or quality of life; it is the threat to all life itself, lest the earth become as barren as the moon, Mars, or Venus.

To clean up the environment will require years and multiplied billions of dollars. It will also demand considerable control of individuals and industry by regulation. It is debatable whether or not Americans are willing to pay those costs in dollars and loss of affluence and personal freedom. Thus the big issue is whether consistent, long-range enforcement is possible. Folsom sees this as a Christian challenge:

> As a result of this ecological crisis we are only now seeing a whole new area of moral responsibility. The conscience of the Christian must be awakened to the moral implications in ecology. If the ecologists are correct, our very survival on this planet is at stake. We must help form the Christian conscience and point out all the areas of life where the Christian presence is necessary. Today there is no doubt that a Christian must be involved in saving the earth (1971:21).

God commanded, "Do not defile the land where you live and where I dwell" (Num. 35:34); yet Isaiah later laments, "The earth is defiled by its people" (24:5); and Amos warns, "And thou shalt die in a polluted land" (7:17, KJV). To destroy the earth is to attack its Creator and Sustainer (John 1:3, Col. 1:16–17); to despoil the Eden we are commanded to dress and keep is to engage in willful rebellion and to move toward short-sighted self-destruction. The selfish and sinful injustices of fallen mankind in Noah's day brought divine judgment in the form of the destruction of the environment; and most of earth's people, animals, and vegetation perished in the judgment. Through natural processes, God prepared a new Eden for the sons of Noah; and now it again has been polluted by the sinfulness and carelessness of people. In the last days, as described in Revelation, human sin will once again bring the disruption of natural processes and ecological upheavals; the result will be the fiery destruction of God's judgment. Ultimately God will create a new heaven and a new earth in which dwells a new social order characterized by righteousness; sin will not enter to mar this eternal home (2 Peter 3:13). Surely creation awaits its new home with eager longing (Rom. 8:19–22; Eph. 1:10).

It is apparent that if Christians take seriously their God-given commission to restore and be stewards of the earth, they must not only be concerned with redemption for the world that is to come, but also realize that church ministry includes concern for this life and this world. Where such concern is evident Christians will join, and probably lead, major efforts for resource management, preservation of unrenewable materials and threatened species. Moreover, Christians will personally and collectively work to reduce the pollution of air, water, soil, sound, and sight, as well as assist groups and nations that experience hunger, want, illness, and fear to help themselves to self-sufficiency and a decent quality of life. They will surely want to oppose discrimination and exploitation, knowing these evils widen the gulf between those who have little and those who have much. The practical Christian response to many of these issues was the concern that led Ron Sider to publish *Rich Christians in an Age of Hunger: A Biblical Study* (1977), a stimulating and action-provoking bestseller that everyone should read. A test of America's sense of justice and the love and compassion of Christians may well be shaping up as we are "invaded" by hundreds of thousands of boatlift people, "wetbacks," and other non-European, nonwhite, non-Protestant refugees at a time when we are facing a declining economy, unemployment, shrinking space, vanishing resources, and inflationary government spending. What attitude would Jesus want us to have as we face these multitudes (Matt. 9:36–38)?

The crowding, misery, and hunger found in cities like Calcutta, Bombay, Hong Kong, Nairobi, Cairo, Mexico City, and San Juan stagger the imagination. Missionaries have tried to tell the story, but their inability to describe or alleviate it is matched by people's inability to comprehend what it is really like. How can these teeming millions be reached for Christ and an abundant life of faith and service when so many of them just exist in daily human misery, fear, and angry despair?

One practical response for a young person relates to Christian vocation. It is obvious that there will be a great need for many to enter the people-helping professions and ministries of all kinds. As employment opportunity shifts more from industrial production to service occupations, should not many young people seek to serve Christ in areas of service that help to meet human needs? Urban planning, agronomy, health and medicine, basic scientific research, social service, church-related ministries, world relief, counseling, and economic development are just some of many examples of need. The study of basic social science disciplines such as sociology, economics, political science, geography, anthropology, and psychology are needed to provide a foundation for specialization in the applied areas.

Ritzer et al. (1979:208) gives the important reminder that there is a danger in overemphasizing the "doomsday" inevitability of ecological problems. If people feel the situation is hopeless, motivation to rise to meet a serious problem could well become lost in a fatalistic resignation to impending disaster. Joyce Blackburn (1972:60) asks, "Is the environment outside the province of Redemption? Is that why it ranks low on the list of 'Christian' priorities?" (Note: My own research among scores of ministers and their wives, and many college students, has consistently found environmental issues very low on a fairly lengthy list of moral and social issues that should engage the consciences of Christians and the witness and mission of the church.) Mark Hatfield has said, "We must find viable means to relate the Good News to the turmoil of our era." Blackburn asks:

> Who more than a Christian should care about NOW? There are folk who testify that their hearts are in heaven already, where their treasure is. But their feet are on the same earth my feet are on. And, so long as we are HERE, we must affirm God's gifts to man through individual and collective witness . . . we must include the habitat in which He placed mankind. I can no longer quote glibly the psalmist's line, "The earth is the Lord's and all the fullness thereof . . ." The earth is the LORD'S? . . . The earth IS the Lord's. . . .
>
> I am convinced that the Christian . . . is the NATURAL one to tackle environmental crisis. We are the ones who can bring balance to the issue. We are the ones who can combine moral adventure with the

wisdom of caution (Matt. 10:16b), fully *aware* that Eden was not a final creation . . . we dare not relate ourselves only to depravity and decay. Ours is the vision of potential restoration, or *redemption*. . . . What man ruins, God wants to make whole again. That is love in perpetual motion. Love is "continuing creation" in defiance of brutal, destructive power. It is for me to decide whether I will or will not "do in little what God can do in large" (1972:60, 68).

DISCUSSION QUESTIONS

1. Do you believe use of an intrauterine device or "morning-after" pill constitutes abortion? Why?
2. How would you advise the thirteen-year-old pregnant girl described in this chapter? Why? Do you believe there are any circumstances under which abortion should be permitted? Why?
3. As the number of older people in this country doubles, how can we make their lives more secure and meaningful?
4. What do you see as the Christian's responsibility toward environmental quality and depletion of resources? Why?
5. What do you see as the Christian's responsibility toward hunger and starvation in other countries and in our own? How can one person have any effect on such a vast problem?

SUGGESTED READING

Michael E. Adelstein and Jean G. Pival (eds.), *Ecocide and Population* (New York: St. Martin's Press, 1972). Though secular and becoming dated, this small collection of essays states the environmental problem, discusses several controversies relative to ecology, and suggests solutions, strategies, and sources of further study.

Joyce Blackburn, *The Earth Is the Lord's?* (Waco: Word, 1972). A Christian writer describes how the threat to the Georgia tideland marshes near her home awakened her to ecological issues. She found that strategic efforts by informed citizens can be politically effective. This is an interesting account and useful handbook for individuals, church groups, and faith-at-work organizations seeking to actively relate the Christian perspective on ecology to political decision-makers.

Paul Folsom, *And Thou Shalt Die in a Polluted Land, An Approach to Christian Ecology,* (Liguori, Mo.: Liguorian Pamphlets and Books, 1971). This one-hundred-page paperback was written by a Catholic priest. It raises many issues for those who seek to examine the Bible, faith, and responsibility in ecology from a Christian perspective.

Shirley Foster Hartley, *Population: Quantity Vs. Quality* (Englewood Cliffs, N.J.: Prentice-Hall, 1972). A sociological examination of the causes and consequences of the population explosion; it is more humanist than Christian in orientation. Her thesis is that concern for the quality of human life requires giving attention to the impact of growing population quantity, and she forcefully develops her belief. The approach highlights differences between developed and less developed nations, and she writes in a style that college students can easily follow.

Francis A. Schaeffer and C. Everett Koop, *Whatever Happened to the Human Race* (Old Tappan, N.J.: Revell, 1979). A forceful presentation of the dehumanizing trends in society by two renowned authorities in their field. Schaeffer, a Christian philosopher, and Koop, surgeon-in-chief of Philadelphia's Children's Hospital, address such topics as abortion, euthanasia, and infanticide from a biblical perspective. This book, along with the film series that accompanies it, is strongly recommended to the student.

═ 18

KENNETH GOWDY
Bethel College,
Minnesota

COMMUNITIES AND URBANIZATION

Community is one of those common words in our vocabulary that
is used in many different ways. We use it to refer to such different
phenomena as ethnic groups, towns, people with some common
characteristics who may not even know each other, and, of course,
the church as the community of believers. We even speak of experiencing community—having an experience that evokes warm
feelings within us. Community seems to be at the very heart of our
lives as human beings.

It should come as no surprise therefore that the term community
has been one of the major concepts in the discipline of sociology.
Early sociologists recognized that they were living through a
period in history in which the nature and form of human communities were undergoing fundamental changes. Although the
changes encompassed virtually all aspects of social life, they were
most apparent in the rise of the industrial city.

URBANIZATION

Cities existed long before industrialization began in England in
the 1700s. They were present in Mesopotamia, the Nile Valley, and
other places as early as 3000 B.C. However, this *first urban revolution*

did not result in cities as we experience them today in the United States. The early cities were much smaller both in area and population. They were "walking cities" in the sense that they were small enough so that a person could walk from side to side in one day. The population rarely rose above ten thousand, and less than 10 percent of any population ever lived in cities prior to industrialization.

The *second urban revolution* began in the eighteenth century with improved agricultural techniques and the beginning of industrialization. However, the industrial revolution really took hold only in the nineteenth century. In 1800 only 2 percent of the world's population lived in cities of twenty thousand or more. By 1900 the figure had grown to 9 percent and by 1950, to 21 percent (Cousins and Nagpaul, 1979:6).

Six percent of the population of the United States lived in cities of twenty-five hundred or more in 1800. One hundred years later, 40 percent lived in such cities, with most of the growth occurring in the second half of the nineteenth century. By 1970 almost three-fourths of all United States residents lived in settlements of twenty-five hundred or more people (Gist and Fava, 1974:61, 66).

Recent urbanization trends have also included a trend toward larger urban centers. The table below based on Schnore (1973:95) provides a perspective on both the growth of cities in general relative to total population growth, and the relative growth of different sized cities. It shows that the most rapid growth in cities since 1850 has been in the large cities of over 100,000 inhabitants.

Growth Rates in Three Periods for Cities of Different Sizes

Period	Total World	Percent Increase in Population of: Cities 5000 plus	Cities 20,000 plus	Cities 100,000 plus
1800-1850	29	175	132	76
1850-1900	37	192	194	222
1900-1950	49	228	240	254

One other important trend in the urbanization process must be mentioned. Although there has been a growing concentration of population throughout the world, in recent decades there has also been a decentralization of people within those concentrations, particularly in the United States. This process is more commonly referred to as suburbanization. It involves the location of residences outside the political boundaries of a major city. This has resulted in large urbanized areas that are socioeconomically integrated with a central city even though they are not within the legal boundaries of that city. (The U.S. Census Bureau refers to these integrated areas as SMSAs or Standard Metropolitan Statistical Areas.) Suburban areas held almost 70 percent of the population of the United States in 1970. Within these areas, by the same date, more people lived in the suburbs than lived in the central cities (Cousins and Nagpaul, 1979:284).

COMMUNITY: THEORETICAL PERSPECTIVES

The foregoing summary of urbanization trends merely describes some of the population changes that have been occurring, especially in Western societies, for the past two centuries. The emergence of the industrial city represented a new type of social order, a new form of human community. Sociologists have sought to understand and explain this new social pattern. Although many different views have been taken, most of them may be summarized within three general theoretical perspectives: the typological, ecological, and community-society perspectives.

The typological perspective. Contrasting types is one of the major techniques that sociologists have used in their efforts to analyze and explain industrialization and its impact on communities. They have contrasted the passing with the present, or developing, social order. The list that follows was adapted from McKinney and Loomis (1970) and Reisman (1964:123) and presents some of the typologies in sociology, along with the authors of those typologies:

Contrasting Types of Social Order

Spencer:	Military	Industrial
Tonnies:	Gemeinschaft	Gesellschaft
Durkheim:	Mechanical solidarity	Organic solidarity
Weber:	Traditional	Rational
Redfield:	Folk	Urban
Becker	Sacred	Secular
Sorokin:	Familistic	Contractual

The classical sociologists are best represented on the subject of community by Ferdinand Tonnies (1940) whose German terminology continues to be used by American sociologists today. Tonnies spoke of the two types of society as gemeinschaft (usually translated "community" if translated at all) and gesellschaft (usually translated "association" if translated at all).

Tonnies asserted that the gemeinschaft type of social order was based on consensus and harmony. In other words its members shared a common view of life. The prototype of the gemeinschaft social order was the family; but this type of social order was also present in the neighborhood, the village, and the town (based on common land), and it was present in friendships and in the church (based on a consensus of beliefs and values).

In contrast, the gesellschaft type of social order was based not on harmony and consensus, but on rational agreements in the form of contracts and laws. Its prototype was the commercial and industrial city. Tonnies (1940:264) saw this type of social order spreading until the "entire 'world' begins to resemble one large city." The spread of gesellschaft in turn meant the decline of gemeinschaft (although Tonnies [1940:18] asserted that "the essence of both Gemeinschaft and Gesellschaft is found interwoven in all kinds of associations"), a trend that he did not favor. Tonnies clearly believed that the rise and spread of an urban way of life was accompanied by a loss of community, a social order based on physical proximity and a consensus of beliefs and values. Except for Tonnies' evaluation of the trends, it is fair to say that his contrasting types are typical of most of the sociologists who have used typologies to clarify the change accompanying urbanization.

Two later essays on the city may be used to further clarify the view of the city commonly held by those using the typological approach to the study of urban community. Neither of the authors, Georg Simmel (1950) and Louis Wirth (1938), explicitly developed a typology, but the contrast of urban with rural or small town life is clearly implicit in their essays.

Simmel described the metropolitan person as highly rational and matter-of-fact in dealing with things and with people. This is the inevitable result of being in a social setting where the stimuli confronting humans are more than we can handle without ignoring some of them. This selective response to people who are the source of the stimuli results in an impersonal, blasé attitude. In addition the city is characterized by a high division of labor that calls for specialization by its work force. This results in people having differing interests and values. Therefore they relate to one another without emotion in a calculated matter-of-fact way. On the other hand, this provides urbanites with a degree of individual freedom not possible in small town life.

Wirth approached urban life in a somewhat different manner. He asserted that the city is characterized minimally by three factors: population size, population density, and heterogeneity. On the basis of these characteristics, Wirth went on to deduce a series of propositions that he felt were descriptions of urban life. These included the following qualities:

1. Individual variation or differentiation
2. Spatial segregation ("a mosaic of social worlds")
3. Formal social controls
4. Secondary relationships
5. Specialization
6. Complex social organization
7. Rapid group turnover
8. Land-use based on the greatest economic return
9. Spirit of competition and mutual exploitation
10. Depersonalization

Both Simmel and Wirth describe a social order that is in sharp contrast to Tonnies' gemeinschaft (community) in which there is a strong sense of solidarity within a locality based on a relatively clear social structure and a strong moral order. In contrast, the city is a place of complexity, impersonal individuality, contractual and utilitarian relationships based on competition, and individual freedom. In this typological approach, community and urbanization are seen as antithetical to each other.

If the typological perspective is an accurate one, it raises serious questions for Christians. Does God intend for people to live in societies in which they relate to one another as objects, as means to ends? Are the biblical qualities of love, compassion, forgiveness, personal worth, and justice compatible with urban (gesellschaft) life? It would appear that Christians should oppose urbanization if the view of cities by the typologists is accurate.

The ecological perspective. The apparently antithetical nature of community and urbanization could be used as an argument for defining community in a different way, and that is what the ecological perspective does. Ecological sociologists have restricted the use of the term community to refer to a localized population. The other relational characteristics (collective identity and common culture) are then viewed as variables that may or may not be present within that population.

The ecological approach to community had its classical expression in the work of Robert Park (1952), Ernest Burgess (1925), and their students at the University of Chicago. Borrowing from a biological model, these early human ecologists asserted that the basic process in human relationships is competition (within a larger context of basic cooperation), particularly competition for space or the use of land. This (cooperative) competition produces communities or areas of land use with their "own peculiar traditions, customs, conventions, standards of deviancy and propriety, and if not a language of its own, at least a universe of discourse, in which words and acts have a meaning which is appreciably different for each local community" (Park, 1952:201).

The ecological perspective on urban communities is probably best known in Burgess's concentric zone theory. Burgess drew concentric circles to represent differing uses of land resulting from economic competition. For example, the innermost circle represented the central business district where land was used largely for commerical purposes. The outermost circle represented land used for residences, residences of the wealthy who could afford to commute to the heart of the city. Burgess (1925:50) asserted that his chart represented "an ideal construction of the tendencies of any town or city to expand radially from its central business district."

Subsequent empirical research has shown that the concentric zone theory must, at best, be modified. The attempt by the early human ecologists to ignore cultural factors and use only "natural" competitive factors to *explain* land use has proven to be an oversimplification. Nevertheless, the many empirical studies of land use and population characteristics carried out by human ecologists have provided us with a wealth of descriptive information. Some of the findings have particular significance for an understanding of community in urbanized areas.

First, the ecologists have rather convincingly demonstrated that urban areas, including metropolitan areas, are socioeconomically interdependent. Each urban area as a whole is therefore a community in the sense that each is a localized, interdependent population that forms a socioeconomic entity. The significance of this finding is best seen when the political structure of a metropolitan area is compared to this socioeconomic reality. In other words a metropolitan community is virtually always made up of many political units such as a central city and its surrounding suburbs, not to mention the counties, school districts, and other units of government. Therefore, although people within the metropolitan area are interdependent in many aspects of their social life, there is no single political structure to oversee and integrate the various parts.

A second type of finding that human ecologists have demonstrated through their research is the segregated use of space in cities. Two types of segregation are of importance here. One is the specialized economic use of land wherein economic activities tend to cluster together and be physically separated from residences. Even within the areas given over to economic activities, a measure of specialized use of land takes place. Heavy industry is usually separated from commercial sections of a city, and there may even be specialized commercial areas such as an automobile dealers "row" or a clothing area, depending on the size of the city.

A second type of segregation is that of people. Residential areas tend to become differentiated from one another in terms of such characteristics as socioeconomic status, race, ethnicity, and even the presence or absence of children in the household. Both the segregation of activities and the segregation of types of people represent the specialized use of land that Park and Burgess tried to chart in Chicago. Although the specific pattern varies from city to city, the process of segregation always seems to be present. This fact, coupled with the foregoing finding of interdependence throughout the urban area, again raises the question of just where community is and what that term means, especially in large urban areas.

If the ecological perspective is an accurate one, it also raises serious questions for Christians. For example, does not the work of Christ result in the breaking down of barriers between people?

It would appear that Christians ought to exemplify a countertrend to the segregation patterns found in urban settings.

Furthermore, if the whole urban area is an interdependent whole, should not Christians, above all others, demonstrate a *united* concern for the *whole* metropolitan area and not just for their own neighborhoods?

The community-society perspective. In this section a very wide range of approaches to the study of communities is brought together. However, all of them have tried to treat the community as a social whole in itself as it is related to the larger society of which it is a part; also, all have seen the local community as affected by changes taking place throughout society.

Maurice Stein (1960) brought together a number of discrete community case studies in an attempt to develop a theory of community in America. Stein found that these studies, when viewed collectively, clearly indicate that the American community has been greatly affected by three major processes of social change: urbanization, industrialization, and bureaucratization. Stein concluded that these processes have resulted in local communities losing much of their local autonomy and experiencing social disorganization. In other words community is being eclipsed in the United States. Although Stein did not define what he meant by community, it is quite clear that he was referring to a *quality* of life, not merely a localized population.

Roland Warren (1978) also used case studies as the empirical basis for developing a theory of community in America. Using a structural-functional framework, Warren identified five types of essential social structures in communities: a company, a public school, a local government unit, a church, and a voluntary health association. He analyzed the extent to which each was influenced by local community activities and concerns, and also to what extent by extra-community ties. He concluded that "the 'great change' in community living includes the increasing orientation of local community units towards extra-community systems of which they are a part, with a corresponding decline in community cohesion and autonomy" (Warren, 1978:52).

Warren therefore came to much the same conclusion as Stein, although his meaning of community (as a *social system*) was more precise. However, Warren's communities were all rather small (the

369

largest was under fifty thousand). Furthermore, one was a suburb in a metropolitan area and hardly qualified as a social system.

One student of urbanization who has addressed himself to the large city is Scott Greer (1962). In Greer's view the city can be adequately understood only in its relationship to the wider society of which it is a part. The process of urbanization is a manifestation of a larger societal process often referred to as an increase in social scale. This dynamic of increase in social scale is most succinctly expressed as a decrease in the space-time ratio wherein it takes less time to send goods, messages, and people over or through space.

This increase in social scale has resulted in widening the range of social interdependence and, at the same time, the range of social control. For localities it has meant the loss of autonomy, exposure to conflicting norms, and the fragmentation of a consensus-based moral order. Our society has become increasingly dominated by large organizations (bureaucracies) whose headquarters exist in the large metropolitan areas. Decisions made in these headquarters reach out and influence the economic and political patterns in cities throughout the nation.

At the same time, Greer asserts that individuals within a city enjoy a great degree of freedom, including freedom from involvement with people in one's locality. This makes "primary community" impossible. In highly urban parts of the city, according to Greer, "the local area is not a community in any sense"; at best, "it is a community 'of limited liability' in the suburbs" (1962:103). By the phrase "of limited liability" (not original with Greer), reference is made to the fact that individuals invest relatively little in the life of their local communities and may withdraw even that involvement when they feel that the returns are too small.

In addition, Greer points to the "violent disjuncture" between the political city and the socioeconomic city in the metropolitan area. This is the problem referred to earlier in the discussion of the ecological approach to the city—the lack of a single integrating government for the metropolitan area even though it is a single socioeconomic unit. Furthermore, Greer says the many governments that do exist are not very effective. The central cities are actually run by bureaucracies that are becoming increasingly autonomous, and the suburban governments are bogged down in trivia because of their powerlessness to deal with the significant factors in their lives (due to the dependence on the large extra-community bureaucracies referred to above). Greer concludes that "it is likely that increase in scale is eventually inimical to the democratic local polity" (1962:208).

Thus Greer comes to essentially the same conclusion as do Stein and Warren. All three agree on the decline of autonomy and integration on the local level. To put it differently, they agree that urbanization has resulted in a decline of gemeinschaft.

This third perspective raises further questions for Christians. If urbanization results in the loss of local control over our lives, can we as Christians support it? On the other hand, does the growing social scale provide a situation wherein Christ can break down barriers to unity such as time and space? Are those who control the large bureaucratic organizations (private and public) to be viewed as potential reconciling agents, or are they symptoms of the growing concentration of evil power, the power to coerce and control?

URBAN COMMUNITY RESEARCH FINDINGS

Since the form of community today in the United States (and increasingly throughout the world) is urban, what has recent research found concerning the way in which the increasing size of community affects humans as they relate to one another?

A recent review of such studies (Fischer, 1976) provides us with a concise summary of their findings. Some of these overlap or repeat ideas already presented, but their repetition here in a systematic summary will be preparatory to a discussion of the nature and significance of community in urban America for Christians.

First, size has been found to be related to certain physical conditions. One of these has already been noted as a major finding of the ecological sociologists: land use tends to be specialized and segmented. This is true of economic activities, but it is also true of residential neighborhoods that are segmented (sometimes even segregated) on the basis of social class, type of household (single, married without children, families with children), and/or race and ethnicity. In addition, size is related to the density of housing. Apartment buildings, even apartment building complexes, are a common sight in large cities. Finally, size is positively related to the presence of a variety of facilities and services. The larger the city, the greater the number and variety of services.

A second major factor related to urbanization is social composition. As Wirth (1938) theorized (see above), cities are characterized by heterogeneity of people in terms of their ethnicity, race, religion, social class, and lifestyle. Cities are truly communities of diverse kinds of people. It therefore follows that people tend to encounter more people who appear different, or strange, in the city. It also is true that people are more likely to relate to others in the city as *categories* rather than as *persons* because they are not acquainted on a personal basis.

However, this does *not* mean that most urbanites are lonely people without intimate relationships. In fact, research clearly indicates that city dwellers are as likely to be members of intimate groups as are rural people. However, those relationships are likely to be more specialized in their functions (that is, centered in one or two activities) and not related to locality. In other words social relationships (groups) in the city are based primarily on common interests, not on physical proximity such as neighborhood. This means that cities are not only heterogeneous in terms of individuals, but they are also diverse in terms of social groups (groups that are based on shared interests, *not* on locality). This represents a third major factor related to urbanization, namely, social groupings.

Suburbanites are somewhat more localized than central city residents in their relationships, but a given suburb also tends to be less heterogeneous in its social composition. Nevertheless, even in suburbs we do not approximate community in terms of Tonnies' gemeinschaft.

Another aspect of social groupings in the city is the greater presence of unconventional (often viewed as deviant) people. Apparently one of the characteristic qualities of size is that as it increases it provides the "critical mass" (Fischer, 1976) necessary for the emergence of groups of people with unconventional lifestyles. Generally speaking (there are definite exceptions), people who differ significantly in their lifestyle from the majority have difficulty finding others of like-mindedness in small towns and even in most suburbs. As an area's size grows the number (not necessarily the percentage) of such people increases, and as they locate one another they form groups with distinctive subcultures (lifestyles).

This vital third factor of social grouping may be summarized by observing that urbanites do not appear to be more lonely or socially isolated than nonurbanites, but their relationships are based much more on shared interests than on shared locality. Even family relationships remain strong in cities, although relatives are not very likely to live in the same neighborhoods.

One other finding that should be included here is that community size is negatively related to community cohesiveness, a sense of community wholeness, and community-wide moral order. Relatively few people in large cities feel a sense of responsibility and attachment to the city as a whole or even to their own neighborhood. In addition, the presence of significantly different subcultures within the city results in a lack of agreement on values and morality.

Nevertheless, the limited available research concerning the impact of urbanization on individuals indicates that urbanites are not any less mentally and emotionally healthy than nonurbanites. There is some evidence that dwellers of large cities are somewhat less happy than rural people. There is clear evidence that higher population density areas are disliked, perhaps because crime and disease rates are higher in such areas. In addition, people in cities are proportionately more impersonal than in small towns; but this is undoubtedly the result of social situations in which strangers meet, a common occurrence in a city and one in which personal intimacy is considered to be inappropriate. In other situations, as has been noted above, urbanites are commonly intimate. Overall, then, as Fischer observes, "the urban state of mind seems none the worse for its urban experience" (1976:177). "Healthy personalities . . . are bred in intimate personal groups. Those groups flourish in small and large communities alike" (1976:203).

THE PROBLEM OF DEFINING COMMUNITY

The foregoing research findings help us to appreciate the problems with which sociologists have been struggling in their attempt to understand the nature of community in our urbanized society. It is clear that community in the city is not the same as community in the preindustrial Europe of Tonnies or even in small-town

America. Nevertheless, Fischer (1976:240) concludes his review of urban research by suggesting that it is inaccurate to contrast *rural community* with *urban individualism*. He suggests instead that the *unity* of a rural community and the *multiplicity* of communities within a single urban area (community) be contrasted. Even if that is a better way of conceptualizing the contrast between nonurban and urban communities, it must be carefully noted that the *communities* within the urban setting, in contrast to rural communities, *are not based on locality but rather on common interests.*

If the reader feels a little confused at this point, then I am having a measure of success in communicating the problem of defining this common concept of community. As one sociologist has put it, "It is doubtful whether the concept of 'community' refers to a useful abstraction. Certainly confusion continues to reign over the uses of the terms" (Stacey, 1969:134).

As long ago as 1955, George Hillery studied ninety-four definitions of community and found basic agreement on only three variables: social interaction, a common geographical area, and one or more other types of common ties. Even then he had to exclude some human ecologists from that consensus. The term community has been used to refer to such wide-ranging relationships as those based on common interest, shared locality, a common occupation, special purposes (such as a prison), and even a region of the earth (such as the community of the Organization of Petroleum Exporting Countries [OPEC]).

Perhaps we can begin to bring some clarity to the use of the concept of community if we understand it as potentially having three major dimensions that vary both in the use of the concept as well as in social reality. *Territoriality,* the first of these dimensions, is the most common. Community can refer to a locality where people relate to one another on a recurring basis. The size of territorial communities can vary from very small (such as a neighborhood of a few blocks or a village) to very large (such as the New York metropolitan area). This is the dimension that human ecologists emphasize.

The second dimension is the *organizational patterns of a population,* the social relationships of the people sharing a common territory. It is commonly linked to the first dimension above because it requires locality of some type. Nevertheless, we find it worthwhile to speak of this second dimension separately because it can vary from locality to locality. This dimension is of particular concern to those sociologists who use a system perspective in viewing the life of a local population holistically. They are interested in the extent to which the people in a locality are interdependent on one another and independent of people outside the locality in their daily living. They are also interested in the kind of grouping (organizations) that are found in a given local community and the patterned ways in which the people meet their needs and concerns. They often ask this question: To what extent is a community an integrated whole and relatively independent of extracommunity forces?

The third dimension of community is the *psychocultural* dimension (Poplin, 1972:21–22). This is probably the most difficult dimension to research, and it is one that many sociologists believe should no longer be included in the concept (Schnore, 1973:69). However, it refers to the heart of gemeinschaft: the commonly held beliefs, values, and goals; the shared way of life; and a sense of social solidarity, that is, a sense of belonging, of oneness. *Consciousness of kind* is a phrase that captures much of the meaning here. It is a quality that is subjectively experienced by community members who share a sense of "weness" among themselves as contrasted with a sense of "theyness" when thinking about or relating to people who are not a part of their own community.

In Tonnies' gemeinschaft the above three dimensions of community are joined together. The preindustrial village or town was a relatively self-sufficient and self-governing population that lived interdependently in a locality and shared a common way of life and a strong sense of oneness—or so Tonnies believed.

A modern metropolitan urban area is also a population living in a locality, but the other two dimensions of community must now be qualified. For one thing the population may be interdependent in some ways but fragmented and dependent in other ways. We have seen that a metropolitan area may be a socioeconomically interdependent unit, but it is rarely a single political unit. Furthermore, any given city is greatly dependent on, and influenced by, extracommunity social organizations and processes for many of its basic internal social processes.

375

In addition, locality within the American metropolis is of less consequence for social relationships than is kin, lifestyle, and social class. Most urbanites have neither a sense of identity with nor an involvement in their cities. Therefore the psychocultural dimension of community is even less tied to locality than the organizational dimension.

These changes in the interrelatedness of territory, organization, and psychocultural unity have accompanied the recent changes in transportation and communication. Technological efficiency has radically reduced the space-time ratio for moving people, goods, and messages, which together form the heart of social life. This has resulted in space (locality) becoming less important for social life. It has also resulted in an increase in the scale of social life to the point where it is not uncommon to speak of the imminent appearance of the global village, the idea being that most of the people on the earth will be linked together as one interdependent unit. This unit will be dominated (controlled) by giant multinational corporations located in the major metropolises of the world. Tonnies seemed to see this change quite accurately:

> During the period of Gemeinschaft this younger principle of space (social organization in space: village, town, neighborhood), remains bound to the other principle of time (family, tribe, people: connected with past and future generations). In the period of Gesellschaft they become disconnected, and from this disconnection results the city. It is the exaggeration of the principle of space in its urban form. In this exaggeration, the urban form becomes sharply contrasted with the rural form of the same principle, for the village remains essentially and almost necessarily bound to both principles. . . . That is, from a certain point on, the towns by their influence and importance achieve, in the nation, predominance over the rural organization (1940:272).

However, as was seen in the review of the research on urban life, urbanites continue to have intimate relationships (psychocultural community) even though the scale of social life has grown. In fact, there is evidence to indicate that the psychocultural dimension of community has been enlarged (Gusfield, 1975) and intensified (Fischer, 1976) by the growing scale.

What, then, is community in urbanized society? For most sociologists today, the psychocultural dimension has been dropped and the locality dimension has been loosely joined to the organizational dimension. Schnore, a representative of this trend, defines a community as a "localized population which is interdependent on a daily basis, and which carries on a highly generalized series of activities in and through a set of institutions which provides on a day-to-day basis the full range of goods and services necessary for its continuity as a social and economic entity" (1973:75)

However, the psychocultural dimension continues to be too important to be ignored. There are indications that this dimension may be reconceptualized as "social network," emphasizing the flexibility of ties that people have with one another, each person not only seeing himself or herself at the center of those ties but also as part of a large network of people of the "same type" (Gusfield, 1975:45–52; see also Bell and Newby, 1972:52–53). For the moment there seems to be "a dichotomy in community studies between those which focus, to put it crudely, on the people, and those which focus on the territory" (Bell and Newby, 1972:32).

These complications and disagreements make the task of integrating sociology and the Christian faith even more difficult than usual (it is often difficult enough under the best conditions). However, before attempting the integration, we must analyze what community means to Christians.

COMMUNITY IN CHRISTIAN THOUGHT AND LIFE

Although the word *community* itself is not found in most Bible concordances, dictionaries, or theological wordbooks, community has always been an important idea among Christians. We frequently refer to ourselves as a community of believers. John Dillenberger and Claude Welch assert that Protestantism is a "historical community of faith" that views "itself as a part of that total community which is the Christian church" (1954:309).

In what sense is the Christian church a community? First of all, it is a *God*-created people even as was Israel in the Old Testament (1 Peter 2:9–10). The church is not the product of natural processes such as gregariousness or kinship. It is the result of the saving work of God. Because the church is the people of God, it is made up of people who do not normally form a community. Instead, God's power overcomes common social barriers and binds together people who come from social categories that would normally divide them (1 Cor. 12:13; Eph. 2:14–15; Col. 3:9–11).

Second, this new creation is marked by a bond of love and a

sense of oneness. Its members share their joys, sorrows, burdens, and even material resources. In fact, they are referred to as the body of Christ, which is a living organism (Eph. 1:22–23). This image of unity also highlights the interdependency of the various members of the church on one another. It also depicts the dependency of the whole body on its Head, Jesus Christ (1 Cor. 12:12–27). The various members are given gifts by their Head, and the members are to use their gifts for the common good of the whole. Thus the church is a fellowship, a community (1 Cor. 1:2, 9).

Those who have participated in and observed local churches at work recognize that on the practical level the Christian community falls far short (to put it kindly) of perfection. The qualities described above reflect more of what the community of believers ought to be or should aspire to become than what believers generally practice.

Here we find another (a fourth) dimension or use of community. It is what Gusfield (1975) refers to as the utopian use. Community here represents an ideal, a hope, a goal. Is this New Testament ideal merely a utopian dream, or is there some relationship to the actual life of Christians?

The New Testament writers clearly related the ideal to real people. Only about 20 percent of the time is *ecclesia* (the Greek word translated "church") used without any specific geographical limitation. More than eighty times it refers to Christians in a house, city, region, or some other type of territory. It is therefore obvious that "the Church in the early days of Christianity was conscious of being a community called by God to salvation and uniquely bound together by the bonds of a love that was more than human, one indeed which had its source in God" (Richardson, 1938:55). Nevertheless, it is also clear that New Testament writers recognized many discrepancies between the actual churches and the ideal church.

Those discrepancies resulted from the fact that the early Christians were not sinless saints but rather, like Christians today, were sinners experiencing the first fruits of God's redemptive work in their lives while they continued to live in an evil age. Their (and our) situation was even further complicated by their understanding of the mission of the church. They were to be "in the world"

(John 17:11) proclaiming the good news concerning Jesus, but they were also to be "not of the world" (v. 16). Their work as witnesses could only be carried out within the social life of host communities that were "of the world." Their own Christian community life was therefore lived within the context of sinful social life and it inevitably reflected that sinfulness.

This tension between the ideal and the actual life of the Christian church, already present in the New Testament, has continued to confront Christian communities in every place and every age. It has, however, been handled differently. One common view has emphasized the responsibility of the church to influence as many people and as much of their life as possible because of the sovereign rule of God over all of life. This has resulted in a willingness to accept a significant discrepancy between the ideal and the actual, to let the wheat and the tares grow together in this age, making sure that the church's "leavening" influence is as great as possible. At times this has resulted in Christian communities in which little or no difference existed between them and their host societies (or cities).

Another common view has emphasized the need for the church to order its life according to the ideal community described in the New Testament. This view has stressed the need for purity in the church and the importance of a distinctive community life. At times this has resulted in a church that was isolated, or at least insulated, from its society and that lacked the ability to effectively relate to it.

There is every reason to believe that *neither* of these approaches has resulted in the establishment of urban Christian communities that are clearly unusual and the product of a nonhuman power at work in the city. In a review of community studies done before the late sixties, Whitley (1969) concluded that the churches in the United States were essentially a reflection (mirror) of their communities. The studies indicated that local congregations reflected the stratification systems in their communities instead of cutting across them. In other words Whitley thought the churches were not unnatural, God-created social groups made up of people who would not normally associate together. Although a decade has passed since Whitley's review, and although virtually every generalization has its exceptions, there is no good evidence to

379

indicate that the seventies produced any significant change in the earlier pattern.

Nevertheless, recent decades have seen a renewed interest in the church as a community. This has probably resulted in part from the fact that industrialization and urbanization (modernization) have been accompanied by a decline in the influence that the formal organized church has been able to directly exercise over society. Whatever the reasons, recent thought has combined aspects of the two earlier views of the church described above.

On the one hand, there has been a call for the internal life of the church to exemplify the impact of Christ on human relationships. In the words of Williams, it should transcend "old tribalism (colors, caste, class barriers) and break through the limitations of our national communities" (1968:46). "Its life is expected to reveal certain characteristics that will distinguish it from other human communities" (1968:83). In its internal life the church is to be a demonstration community, a city set on a hill.

But on the other hand, the church is also to be a place where people are trained to "take the servant presence of its Lord" into the structures of the world (Williams, 1968:89). In its external life the church is to be yeast that transforms the world's structures from within, as well as salt that preserves the world from decay by bringing out its intended qualities—order, peace, justice, and health. The internal distinctive life and the external mission are to coexist. One must not be sacrificed for the other. The church must live in a "creative tension" with the world.

The foregoing theology arose out of discussions among mainline denominational representatives under the auspices of the World Council of Churches. Evangelical leaders, while appreciative of the renewed concern for the church and its mission in the world, have found the World Council statements lacking in commitment to evangelism. In turn, the World Council representatives have been critical of the failure of evangelicals to give evidence of a commitment to changing the inhuman social conditions found in our cities. However, the decade of the seventies has seen renewed concern (see Kerr, 1974, for a review of earlier evangelical involvement in urban social ministries) among evangelicals for a more balanced ministry, particularly in urban communities (see also Ellison, 1974; Greenway, 1979). These trends would seem to indicate that the concept of community in all of its dimensions is of growing concern to most Christians today. (Catholic Christians have also been reassessing their views. See Conn, 1979b.)

A concern for community in an urban setting must begin with a theology of the city. How does God view and relate to cities? To what extent are Christians called to witness to and/or seek to expand the church's ministry in cities? Conn (1979a) indicates that Christians have held virtually every conceivable position on these questions. There is not space here to argue the case, but this writer believes the Scriptures clearly indicate that God is Lord of *all* creation, including the city, and that Jesus died for the whole world, including urbanites, in order to overcome evil forces that separate people. The church's task is to bear witness everywhere to these facts in *deed* and *word*, including in the cities. Part of that witness will include demonstrating a life of uncommon love both within the community of believers and beyond it to those who are part of the larger urban community and its diverse subcommunities.

Such a theology in turn calls for an understanding of the impact of urbanization on community. Earlier in this chapter a summary of related research findings was presented. Here we can only remind the reader of those urban characteristics that are especially important for our current concern.

First, let us notice that the urban community is a community in only a single sense, namely, in terms of territory. Urban areas are neither single organizational nor single psychocultural communities.

This leads to a second finding: an urban community (territory) is really communities (organizationally); that is, most urban areas are fractured politically and have no single integrative political structure that is concerned with the whole.

In addition the city provides us with considerable freedom to choose intimate friends. This results in friendship groups that are based on common interests, not on locality (such as a neighborhood or municipality). These groups tend to be quite specialized in their social functions, that is, people meet their needs for social intimacy in groups that exist almost exclusively for that purpose. This specialization of relationships is a quality that pervades the city. Business, political, educational, medical, recreational, and even religious groups tend to be quite limited in their scope.

Urban communities are also places with great social diversity. Ethnic and religious groups are greater in number and diversity in cities than in nonurban areas. Social classes are somewhat more distinct and cohesive. Furthermore, cities are places with more unconventional (deviant) people. Nevertheless, urbanites tend to keep to their own kind; that is, the poor and oppressed are seldom in the presence of the wealthy and powerful.

Finally, cities are characterized by situations of anonymity where people relate to one another on the basis of categories.

As Christians we must ask to what extent the separation of the organizational and psychocultural dimensions from the territorial dimension of community is important. To what extent is our current form of community a distortion of God's intention for humans?

There can be no doubt that Paul saw the incarnation, death, and resurrection of Jesus as the pivotal event in human history because through this event God was demonstrating His willingness and power to overcome the effects of sin that divide people and destroy community. Jesus came to restore community. This is good news especially to those who suffer the most when sin fractures community—the poor, the prisoners, the physically and socially handicapped. The modern city is certainly the most glaring picture of a fractured community.

The modern urban community is therefore in need of God's liberating, healing, and re-creating power that He manifested in raising Jesus from the dead. It is the task of Christians to bear witness to the good news of God's power. But how? Many Christians certainly have not effectively fulfilled their mission to date. How do we allow God to reveal His revolutionary power within Christian communities? In addition, how can we effectively witness to God's compassion and transforming power within urban communities?

Obviously, Christians must put themselves in situations where God can do *His* work. So long as Christians avoid associating with people who are significantly different from them, they will not experience God's power to unite people who do not naturally unite. In other words, so long as churches are socially homogeneous in terms of ethnicity, race, social class, and lifestyle, the only reconciling work they are in a position to experience is that of resolving personality conflicts.

In like manner if Christians are not involved in the social structures and processes of the city, or if their witness is only to what God can do for individuals, then their witness to God's judgment and redemption of the city will not make contact with the problems of urban community. These problems need to be seen as more than just the sum of individuals living in sin. For example, the politically fractured urban locality has resulted in central cities and suburbs competing with one another for power and control to be used by the holder for its own good. This is a structural problem. If Christians in an urban area could see themselves as one community united in Christ, they could do much to witness to the unity of the urban area. Evangelicals have tended to see sin as a purely individual matter and have therefore focused only on personal vices such as alcoholism and prostitution. The result has been a failure to witness to social sins such as economic inequality and monopoly that are so much a part of urban life. Humans need to repent as individuals, to be sure, but they also need to repent and change their ways collectively. Urban Christian communities should lead the way.

Happily, there is evidence today not only of concern but also of action among Christians in various walks of life. Young adults are at a particularly important decision-making stage. It is encouraging to see an increasing number of them with a heightened desire to both experience and witness to authentic Christian community within the urban setting.

DISCUSSION QUESTIONS

1. What is your reaction to the urbanization trend in America and the world? Is it good, bad, or neither good nor bad?
2. Does urban life have to be impersonal? Why?
3. Is the church you attend a community? Why?
4. Should a Christian community seek to be socially homogeneous or heterogeneous? Why?
5. What is your reaction to the concept of collective sin given in this chapter? Several chapters in this collection have referred to structural evil. Do you believe there is such a thing? Why?

SUGGESTED READING

Colin Bell and Howard Newby, *Community Studies* (New York: Praeger, 1972). A quite readable review of community theory and research with a format and perspective that is different from the books by Bernard Poplin listed below: includes both American and European studies.

Jessie Bernard, *The Sociology of Community* (Glenview, Ill.: Scott, Foresman, 1973). Another quite readable review of community theory and research; format and perspective are different from that of Poplin. The author's thesis is that the sociology of community is in crisis and needs a new approach.

Craig Ellison (ed.), *The Urban Mission* (Grand Rapids: Eerdmans, 1974). An excellent collection of essays on the mission of the church in the urban setting. Ellison is more practical than Greenway, author of a similar text listed below.

Jacques Ellul, *The Meaning of the City* (Grand Rapids: Eerdmans, 1970). The now classical biblical study of the city by a French social scientist and Reformed church layman.

Roger S. Greenway (ed.), *Discipling the City* (Grand Rapids: Baker, 1979). See description for Ellison's book above. Greenway is more substantive.

Dennis E. Poplin, *Communities: A Survey of Theories and Methods of Research* (New York: Macmillan, 1972). Still another quite readable review of community theory and research. The book is a review and synthesis of American works.

Leo F. Schnore, "Community: Theory and research on structure and change." Pp. 67–125 in Neil J. Smelser (ed.), *Sociology: An Introduction* (New York: Wiley, 1973). An excellent essay representing the newer ecological perspective on urban community.

Roland L. Warren, *The Community in America* (3rd ed.) (Chicago: Rand McNally, 1978). A theoretically clear and consistent analysis of the impact of modernization on American communities.

19

RONALD BURWELL
The King's College,
New York

SOCIAL CHANGE

The study of social change has deep and pervasive roots in sociology. Earlier thinkers who contributed to the rise of sociology as a discipline were preoccupied with questions about the development and the future of society. Therefore, one of the values for the student of sociology in studying social change is to gain greater insight into the nature of the discipline itself. Furthermore, by understanding some of the sociological thought regarding social change, students are better equipped to interpret the phenomenon of change as it confronts them in the modern world.

To the reader who may be wondering if there is a need to study social change, we might pose the following question: Have you ever heard a Christian leader say that we live in a society that is in moral and spiritual decline? There is a great likelihood that most readers have heard such statements. A number of questions immediately leap to our mind. Have values and attitudes in America been changing? Do such things have a relationship to the decline of a society? Do societies decline? These and many other possible questions demonstrate the need to apply sociology to the study of change. Although this essay will not directly examine change in American society, hopefully some of its general points may be applied to the United States in the 1980s.

The concept of *social change* may be distinguished from the idea of *culture change* in several ways. On the simplest level it is probably the case that sociologists use the phrase social change while anthropologists use culture change. This, however, points to a more fundamental difference. Over the past several decades a growing consensus has emerged that sees *society* or *social system* and *culture* as two analytically different approaches to the same phenomenon. The term society has come to refer to the patterns or systems of relationships that govern the interaction between individuals and collectivities. The term culture has become more narrowly restricted to refer to the content and patterns of values, ideas, and systems that shape the behavior of people and the patterns of their artifacts (Kroeber and Parsons, 1956:583).

Using this approach, the term culture change on the one hand refers more appropriately to change in the areas of values, norms, and ideas—to the whole cognitive realm. On the other hand, the term social change refers to transformations in patterns of social organization and the interaction among people and groups. This distinction between culture change and social change is important because it reflects a more precise use than what is common in everyday speech. However, it should be noted that in many cases even social scientists use the terms interchangeably. This chapter will deal with change in a broad sense and thus will have reference to both cultural and social change. For the sake of clarity, the phrase social change will be used unless it is absolutely necessary to use the phrase culture change in its specialized sense.

The organization of the chapter reflects the twin goals of summarizing sociological thought on social change and evaluating and applying that thought from an explicitly Christian perspective. The following sections will examine the approaches used by sociologists in dealing with the idea of social change. First, however, it is necessary to establish a historical appreciation for the close ties between sociology and the study of social change.

HISTORICAL CONTEXT

In many ways sociology is a child of the Enlightenment. Thinkers during this eighteenth-century period stressed the use of reason and tended to question traditional beliefs and values. There was a strong belief in the idea of universal human progress. Evidences of the passing of old ways and the establishment of new patterns of life were constantly available to the observer. The social philosophers who laid the groundwork for the development of sociology were confident that society was moving progressively upward to more complex and superior forms. Nevertheless, there were also countervailing thoughts about *Paradise Lost* when man lived more simply in a state of nature unhindered by societal restraints.

The Enlightenment stress on human progress was reflected in virtually all the classical writers in sociology. Frequently this took the form of some sort of evolutionary sequence that explained the past and gave some logic for the future. We could cite the ideas of Auguste Comte, who saw mankind passing through three grand epochs, including the theological/military epoch, the metaphysical/judicial epoch, and the epoch of science and industry. These epochs emerged because of a fundamental law governing the natural progress of civilization. Herbert Spencer's view of sociology included a heavy stress on the parallels between society and living organisms.

A number of early sociologists were impressed by the rise of industrial society and the consequent reduction of the rural community and its way of life. Many were convinced that the change was good although there was some trepidation about the loss of certain traditional values. The movement from rural to urban is well illustrated by Tonnies' dichotomy of gemeinschaft and gesellschaft (see chap. 18). Similar themes are found in the depiction by Maine of societies that are based on status as opposed to societies that are based on contract. Finally, Durkheim's polar types of mechanical and organic solidarity are also rooted in an evolutionary movement evident to those living in a period of industrialization and urbanization. It should be stressed that contemporary sociological thought about social change bears clear affinities to some of the ideas of these early classical writers, for example, in the study of modernization.

THEORETICAL PROBLEMS

In discussing the key theoretical problems in sociology, William Skidmore places first on his list the problem of how to conceptualize social *order* and the related concept of social *change*

(1975:18). He says order and change are mirror images of the same problem. The assumption that change will take place implies that there must be some order that is undergoing modification. The sociological interest in the problem of order is seen as a central theme that has endured over the years from the earliest stages of sociological thought to the present. By juxtaposing order and change, a basic problem for anyone interested in studying social change can be introduced. This problem has been the subject of a lively debate in sociology concerning the possibility of using one theoretical focus to study both order and change. On the one hand, it would seem that some approaches in sociology are best suited to an analysis of order; on the other hand, it appears that different approaches are useful in revealing process and change. In a subsequent section the major types of social change theories will be discussed; it will be evident that these approaches vary in their degree of success in dealing with order or change. It is sufficient at this point to merely refer to the debate and to note that some theorists, including Skidmore, believe that any truly adequate sociological theory must be able to account for both order and change (1975:24).

Another problem confronting the student of social change is to decide on the level of analysis to be used. Much of the classical sociological thinking about social change resulted in elegant, grand conceptual schemes. While this macrosociological theorizing was extremely provocative and stimulating, there was virtually no way to test it empirically. The approach of most contemporary studies of social change has been at the microsociological level. This concentration on specific, observable, short-term changes in society has made it possible to generate a great deal of empirical data. An example of this latter approach might be the analysis of how a specific technological innovation has affected social relationships (e.g., for the growing use of snowmobiles in the arctic, see Pelto, 1973). It would seem that in studying social change we are forced to choose between macro-level or micro-level analysis with certain consequences for operationalizing and evaluating the theories that are set forth.

A fundamental disagreement in sociology has separated those who see a causative role for ideas and values in the shaping of human behavior from those who root human behavior in noncognitive, materialistic bases. In fact, there is a fundamental polarity that transcends sociology and finds expression in a number of social sciences such as anthropology and psychology. As applied to social change, however, the disagreement means that some theorists believe that societal change can be brought about by changes in the ideas and values that people hold. The most celebrated theory reflecting this approach might be Max Weber's Protestant ethic hypothesis in which he argues for a shift in moral, ethical, and religious values as having a role to play in the rise of modern industrial capitalistic society (Weber, 1930). Theorists on the other side of the disagreement over values and attitudes in social change would argue that all cognitive phenomena are themselves controlled by more basic materialistic factors. In other words, values and attitudes undergo change themselves and do not precipitate social change. The classic representative of this viewpoint might be Karl Marx (1964), who stressed the concept of cognitive phenomena as being projections or superstructures that arise out of an economic base composed of the relationships of production. As there were changes in the economic base, so there followed consequent changes in the realm of ideas.

Over the years sociologists have spent a great deal of time and energy trying to resolve the debate represented by Weber and Marx regarding the nature of social change. One approach, implicitly recognized by both Marx and Weber, is to argue that social change is a complex process that involves a multitude of factors—both cognitive and noncognitive. The truth may be that there is a dialectic with the material realm creating change in the ideological realm, and vice versa.

Ultimately, the most difficult problem to be solved in relation to social change is to discover the actual causes or sources of change. At the simplest level the issue revolves around whether or not the causes for change are external or internal to the society. Some conclude that society changes primarily in response to externally induced crises, for example, changes in climate or availability of natural resources. Others see society as guided by an inner dynamic that is relatively unhindered by external factors, for example, an inevitable movement to greater specialization and differentiation. As might be guessed some have gone beyond this dichotomy to assert that both types of causes operate but in different contexts at different points in time. Claude Levi-Strauss has suggested a contrast between "hot" and "cold" societies in that the former type changes because of internal factors, while the latter type of society changes largely in response to external factors. Levi-Strauss identifies modern, complex, urban society as being "hot," while traditional, so-called primitive society is seen as being "cold" (Charbonnier, 1969).

MAJOR THEORIES

The major theories of social change that have been formulated over the years were guided to a great extent by attempts to deal with the problems we have just outlined. These theories could be categorized a number of different ways. Recently, however, Richard Appelbaum (1970) has created a particularly helpful categorization of theories of social change, and it has been widely used. Applebaum finds four major types of social change theories: evolutionary theory, equilibrium theory, conflict theory, and rise-and-fall theories. Before briefly summarizing what these theories involve, it might be well to show how these theories differ regarding certain assumptions about social change.

The four types of theory logically arise in response to two basic questions that may be asked. The first question is, What is the extent of stability inherent to society itself? In other words this question asks *how stable* society is on the basis of its intrinsic nature. The two obvious responses that seem evident to this question are (1) either society is inherently stable, or (2) it is inherently unstable. Furthermore, given the assumption that society is inherently stable, there are two further options. These are (1) either society is stable in the sense that little if any change occurs within society itself, or (2) society is stable in that change is smooth and gradual without disturbing the overall balance of society.

The second of the two basic questions that give rise to social change theories can be stated this way: Is there any direction or predictability for the changes that are occurring? Again, the two possible responses are rather simple: (1) yes, there are uniformities and predictable elements that help us see where change is going; or (2) no, there is a lack of uniformity—change is essentially unpredictable.

Using the answers to these two questions, it is possible to construct a diagram that reveals the basic differences in the various social change theories:

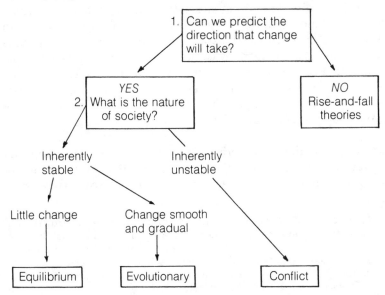

The significance of these differing assumptions about society and change will be more evident after we briefly describe the various characteristics of the four types of theory.

Evolutionary. Historically, evolutionary theory has enjoyed the longest period of popularity. The earliest views of how society changes were probably based on some sort of evolutionary theory. We have noted some early sociologists and social philosophers who incorporated evolutionary ideas into their theories. One of the best-known examples of early evolutionary theorists is Lewis Henry Morgan, whose views are outlined in *Ancient Society* (1877). Morgan set forth a comprehensive scenario for the social and material technological evolution of human soceity. He saw all societies moving through roughly the same (unilineal) sequence of seven stages. For a time his ideas were very influential, but critics noted the difficulty of charting a common path of development that holds true for all societies. Contemporary evolutionary theories reject a simple course of development for all societies and argue instead for reoccurring patterns. For example, the views of Marion Levy (1966) on modernization focus on general processes like specialization, interdependency, centralization, differentiation, bureaucratization, and universalization that can be seen in various forms in a number of societies. In other words the process transcends society, but the actual form is unique to each case. Much contemporary thinking about social change as evolutionary stresses the adaptive mechanisms whereby a society interacts with its environment. New forms of social structure and behavior are like mutations that may or may not have adaptive advantages for their society.

Equilibrium. In some ways equilibrium theories are closely related to evolutionary theories. Both make use of the notion that society is analogous to a living organism. Both use the idea of society interacting with its environment. In fact Appelbaum states clearly:

> The difference between evolutionary theories and equilibrium theories, as mentioned previously, is largely one of emphasis; the latter focus on social mechanisms that tend to restore equilibrium in the face of (generally exogenous) disturbances, while the former focus on the process of change itself. These are two sides of the same coin, and the difference is more analytic than real (1970:127)

In a sense one is forced to consider a fundamental question of sociological theory, namely, Is it possible to construct a sociological theory that adequately deals with both structure (stasis) and process? Evolution and equilibrium are two components in a comprehensive scheme used by certain theorists to accommodate both structure and process (Moore, 1974).

Equilibrium theories are well suited for analysis of society as a smoothly functioning system that ought not to change except for external difficulties. The sociological theories known as structural functionalism are exemplars of equilibrium theories of change. Talcott Parsons, probably more than any other sociologist, is identified with structural functionalism. Interestingly, Parsons wrote a number of books and articles that sought to explain social change. At times he used an equilibrium approach, while at other times he developed evolutionary themes (Parsons, 1951; 1964). This shifting back and forth between these two approaches to change lends additional support to the statement quoted above by

Applebaum. Basically, equilibrium theorists see societies as seeking some sort of harmonious balance between component parts and the environment. This balance (homeostasis) may be distributed by external factors (e.g., changes in the environment) or by internal factors (e.g., inherent strains and tensions). The disturbance or crisis evokes a response that takes the form of society trying to regain balance. This means that society tries to return as much as possible to the state in which it was prior to the disturbances. Frequently, this is not possible and so the society changes in whatever manner is needed to regain its balance. The idea, however, is that society changes only in response to crisis and only as much as necessary to regain equilibrium.

Conflict. Conflict theories take the position that society is inherently unstable and that change is precipitated by factors within the structure of society. Frequently, conflict theories are based on the work of Karl Marx. Marx regarded society as composed of elements that virtually guaranteed the eventual occurrence of a violent, sudden massive revolution. As long as society was characterized by inequality and exploitation of some members of the society, change would take place. Although conflict theorists differ from evolutionary and equilibrium theorists about the nature of change, proponents of all three views believe that they can detect some of the contours of the direction that change will take.

Rise and fall. This approach stands in contrast to the three positions just outlined. Rise-and-fall theorists argue that the direction of social change is never completely predictable. Instead, society may be conceived of as shifting among several different forms; at any point in time society can change in more than one direction. An example of this might be Max Weber's ideas regarding types of authority. After presenting the ideal types of traditional, charismatic, and bureaucratic authority, Weber notes that there is not a clear-cut line of progression. On one occasion traditional authority might be replaced by charismatic authority, while on another occasion it may be succeeded by bureaucratic authority. Other examples of rise-and-fall approaches to social change might be philosophies of history that trace a sequence of rise and fall for civilization or that see the form of society as a recurring cycle. Before concluding our summary of the four major theories, we should point out that many sociologists believe it is possible to use more than one of the approaches in their work.

In addition to these four general types of change theory, there are a number of more specialized theories of change. One such specialized theory would be *modernization* theory, which has had an increasingly visible place in recent study of social change. Students of modernization are primarily concerned about understanding how certain societies are moving toward a particular pattern of life characterized by an increasing scale of social relationships, development of bureaucracies, industrialization, and urbanization. Although not strictly parallel, modernization involves a society becoming more and more like the highly complex societies found in North America and Western Europe. A number of modernization theories have developed to deal with this kind of change. Most, however, have as their basic motif strong evolutionary characteristics. A number of factors are selected and societies depicted as moving at different points on continua that are constructed for each of these factors, for example, specialization and centralization. It is not surprising that this is the case since evolutionary theories are suitable to deal with gradual, progressive change that seems to characterize much modernization. Some other approaches also are feasible and find their exponents.

INTEGRATIVE APPROACHES

Christians who study sociology have several options when it comes to thinking through the implications of their faith for the discipline of sociology. An extreme view might be that it is totally illegitimate to mix considerations about Christianity with those of sociology. Proponents might believe that these two realms belong in distinct categories and any attempt to link them is an error. A slightly less extreme view might be to regard sociology with a great deal of suspicion. These suspicions would arise primarily from a belief that sociology by its very nature is anti-Christian and therefore worthy of hostility and rejection. The contributors to this collection reject both of these positions. Instead, they reflect a commitment to some model of integration of a Christian world view and sociology.

Integration may take several forms. At the simplest level it may simply involve applying the insights of a field of study to problems that confront a Christian; conversely, it may involve applying Christian moral principles to the conduct of the discipline. At a slightly more complex level integration may involve a systematic attempt to resolve problems that are posed for the Christian faith by the branch of study. For example, Christian students of sociology are often bothered by the determinism found in much of the sociological literature. One type of integration might involve trying to show how sociological determinism can be accommodated within a Chrsitian view of humanity. At its most sophisticated level, however, integration must involve an ongoing process where sociological data and theories are evaluated by using aspects of one's Christian world view as a set of control beliefs. Conversely, the Christian must allow the truth found in sociology to bring about necessary changes in his world view. Such integration can best be conceived of as a dialectical process of ongoing interaction between one's Christian world view and sociology. All three forms of integration are important and useful for Christians. In the paragraphs that follow an attempt will be made to develop some preliminary relationships between Christianity and sociological thought regarding social change.

INTEGRATIVE ISSUES

Some time was spent above outlining various problems and theories related to social change. Initially, it might be asked whether or not any of the four basic approaches to social change are more likely to be adopted by the Christian sociologist. In order to answer that question, it must be determined whether or not the biblical materials provide any insight into the basic questions guiding these theories. For example, does the Bible depict society as inherently stable or inherently unstable? Does the Bible reflect the view that we can predict the direction that social change will take? Perhaps depending upon one's views of the last days (eschatology), a person might be inclined to argue that the Bible gives us some indication of where a certain society is going. Many Christians have interpreted the Bible to say that society will inevitably deteriorate or decline. While there may be merit in this view we must remember that there is a degree of disagreement among Christians as to what the Bible actually asserts in its eschatological teachings. Furthermore the prophetic statements of the Bible are more likely to refer to a number of societies over a significant period of time than the course of change in only one society over a limited span of time. Nevertheless, most of the orthodox biblically based eschatologies would not easily be fitted with any view of social change that proposed an inevitable movement toward a more perfect society. Some evolutionary social change theories might tend toward a greater stress on *progress*. These theories would be less feasible for the Christian to hold. Apart from this qualification, it would seem that several options are available to the Christian. In fact, like his non-Christian counterpart, the Christian who studies social change may find that, depending on the setting, more than one basic theory is necessary to adequately comprehend the data. It would seem that a Christian could still opt for any of the four major types of social change theory as long as this was done within the limits of a biblical world view. Given this latitude, decisions regarding which theory or theories to use will probably be determined on other grounds, for example, empirical adequacy or personal relevance.

One of the purposes that has traditionally guided the study of social change has been a desire to understand the processes in order to control them. In some cases the intention has been to guide the future direction of one's own society. In this regard social change has been seen as having links with futurology. In other cases, the intention has been to understand social change in order to bring about change in contexts other than one's own society. A wide range of change agents from revolutionaries to missionaries have looked at the study of social change for help in their projects. In this connection a critical ethical issue arises in the form of the following question: Is it ever right to seek to introduce change in someone else's society? In some ways this question is linked to the issue of cultural relativism (see chap. 3). Generally, those who hold to a strong philosophical cultural relativism are critical of attempts to change another society.

Even for those who reject philosophical cultural relativism and allow for some absolutes, there are serious concerns. Depending on the view one has of social change, the process of introducing change may be fraught with danger. One of the most famous case studies of induced culture change is Laurston Sharp's "Steel Axes for Stone Age Australians" (1952). This widely reprinted study illustrates some of the possible dysfunctional results of a simple technological innovation introduced by well-intentioned missionaries. The study fits especially well with an equilibrium model of change where change is essentially external to the social system. Unfortunately, in this case a new equilibrium was difficult to achieve after the change occurred.

This problem of whether or not we can be agents of social change is particularly acute for Christians who are missionaries in cultures different from their own. Sometimes this problem is referred to under the term *contextualization*. Certain questions (suggestive of guiding principles) would seem to be necessary to decide a course of action for anyone in this situation:

1. Is this change based on biblical principles? (Are these supercultural and absolute, or is this change only a reflection of the change agent's ethnocentrism?)
2. What are the likely latent and manifest consequences of this change? (Are there parallels from other cases that might give guidance?)
3. Can the change be introduced more effectively by change agents drawn from members of the target culture itself? Can they suggest possible consequences?

Anyone contemplating the introduction of change in society would do well to consider the high possibility that the change will have implications that are unanticipated and maybe even prove negative. Hence one should proceed with caution so that change is introduced carefully and only when deemed absolutely necessary.

Earlier in this chapter the fundamental debate between Marx and Weber regarding the role of ideas in social change was introduced. This issue illustrates a point at which the Christian might wish to consider the applicability of a biblical world view. Although it seems true that there is an interaction between the sociocultural context of people and their environment, a thoroughly deterministic perspective must be questioned. One value of Weber's view over that of Marx is that by allowing the realm of ideas to have a role in social change, Weber respects the rationality and agency of persons. The biblical view is that man is a creature who reasons, wills, acts, and chooses—in short, human conduct is not totally determined by socioeconomic factors.

The person who pursues a Weberian view of social change finds that there are a number of interesting implications that may be drawn to help understand contemporary society. For example, Weber's theory of the Protestant ethic can help us understand the process of secularization, a phenomenon that raises critical problems for the Christian in contemporary society. According to Weber, one of the unintended consequences of the set of ideas launched in the Protestant Reformation was a progressive disenchantment of the world. On the one hand this disenchantment led to people seeing their world as a place no longer permeated by the supernatural. For some this meant that the supernatural was no longer relevant to their lives. For others the disenchantment of the world meant that the natural world became a place where certain laws operated that were discoverable. The world then was characterized by a rationality that made a study of its principles possible. Stated in the simplest possible way, we are saying that Weber's stress on the implications of ideas for change led to a particular theory that elucidates both the process of secularization and something about the rise of modern science.

Having suggested how Weber's ideas on social change might relate to some concerns of Christians, it is necessary to note that the same may be said of Marx's formulations. While Marx's theory of human nature may not fit as nicely with Christianity as we would like, Marx offers some profound insights into the nature of society. For example, Marx explains how various aspects of culture, including religion, can be used to hinder social change. Drawing on this notion makes it easier for us to understand why Christian churches may resist attempts to change society. Economic and political facts may counteract moral and ethical considerations when Christian groups are called on to engage in social action to change society. At that point we can often turn to Marx for convincing reasons for this occurrence.

Another well-known idea in the area of sociocultural change is William F. Ogburn's concept of "culture lag." This theory illustrates yet another facet of the problematic relationship between the tangible material aspects of a society and the abstract conceptual realm. Simply stated, Ogburn proposed that the economic and technical aspects of a society, which he included in the term "material culture," change through a complex interaction with the external environment. The nonmaterial aspects, or "adaptive culture," can change only when and if there is a change in the material culture. This creates a potential for problems if the adaptive culture lags behind changes in the material culture. In fact, Ogburn believed that this happened quite frequently. An example of culture lag might be the rise of modern factories, with norms governing labor relations being based on small cottage industries.

In some ways Ogburn seems to be arguing that Marx was right and that the material, economic, and technical realms lead the way in social change. Nevertheless, his basic point that there may be different rates of change for different aspects of society can be accepted without the additional idea of economic determinism. When the idea of differential rates of change is studied, it provides some interesting implications—one of which is directly relevant to Christian missions.

Missionaries frequently combine the provision of economic and technical assistance with the propagation of the gospel. While there are good reasons for this, there can be a problem. Given the concept of cultural lag, it is not surprising that missionaries are often able to introduce new economic and technical advances to the people they are working with, for example, in the provision of medical care. However, they may find that the abstract realm of religious belief is strangely resistant to change. What has occurred is a change in one part of the culture but not an accompanying change in the other parts of the culture. In some cases the culture lag is overcome only after a period of tension and turmoil.

Although detailed studies of social change have been avoided and specific applications of these ideas to a biblical world view have only been suggested, it is hoped that some contours of the field have been made more visible to the reader. By studying social change we can better understand the nature of society itself. Social change is intimately tied to basic considerations about the nature of society and the nature of persons. If we can understand something of social change, this may mean that we have some potential to control the future; and this in turn raises troublesome questions about the propriety of actually controlling social change, particularly in another culture. As the rate of social change accelerates in more and more of the societies of the world, the study of social change will become increasingly important.

DISCUSSION QUESTIONS

1. Is social change good or bad? Why?
2. Can we accept social or cultural evolution while rejecting biological evolution? Why?
3. Can we accept Marx's theory of social change without compromising a biblical world view? Why?
4. Which of the four theoretical perspectives on social change do you believe is most adequate? Why?
5. What ethical considerations should be involved in any attempt to control social change?

SUGGESTED READING

Richard Appelbaum, *Theories of Social Change* (Chicago: Markham, 1970). A good overview of the grand theories of social change. Links ideas about social change with sociological theory.

Amitai Etzioni and Eva Etzioni-Halevy, *Social Change: Sources, Patterns and Consequences* (New York: Basic Books, 1973). A widely used collection of readings on the topic of social change. Provides both theoretical and empirical studies of the process of social change.

Clifford Geertz, *Agricultural Involution* (Berkeley: University of California Press, 1968). Geertz is a well-known anthropologist who has written extensively about culture change. This study examines change in Indonesia—particularly from the perspective of interaction between the society and its environment. There is also a provocative comparison of the process of change in Indonesia and Japan.

Wilbert Moore, *Social Change* (2nd ed.) (Englewood Cliffs, N.J.: Prentice-Hall, 1974). A frequently cited introduction to the study of social change. The approach is basically equilibrium with some attempt to accommodate criticisms usually leveled at that position.

Arthur H. Niehoff, *A Casebook of Social Change* (Chicago: Aldine, 1966). A helpful collection of almost two dozen case studies of attempts to introduce change in the five major developing areas of the world. Especially useful for anyone considering the role of a change agent.

Louise S. Spindler, *Culture Change and Modernization: Mini-Models and Case Studies* (New York: Holt, Rinehart and Winston, 1977). Written from an anthropological perspective, this book presents six basic middle-range theories of culture change. It also has four interesting case studies that illustrate the theories.

20

STEPHEN A. GRUNLAN
St. Paul Bible College,
Minnesota

SOCIOLOGY AND THE CHRISTIAN

As we read the other chapters in this volume, two questions come to mind. First, what does the discipline of sociology have to contribute to the Christian's involvement in this world? Second, what does the discipline of sociology have to contribute to the Christian's understanding of God and His activity in this world? This chapter will examine these two questions.

SOCIAL INVOLVEMENT

While praying for His disciples, Jesus said, "My prayer is not that you take them out of the world but that you protect them. . . . They are not of the world, even as I am not of it. . . . As you sent me into the world, I have sent them into the world" (John 17:15–18).

Robert Webber suggests in his latest book that there are three approaches the Christian can take toward the world. He calls the first approach the "separational model" (1979:75–103). According to this approach, the Christian is to have as little as possible to do with the world. Webber explains:

> The separatist maintains that the two (the world and the kingdom of God) are so different that one can live in one or the other but not both at the same time . . . (the separatist) assumes that sin has permeated every area of the world to such an extent that the true Christian cannot traffic with the world without compromising with sin and becoming contaminated by it.

Webber calls the second approach the "identificational model" (1979:105–33). According to this approach, the Christian brings the kingdom of God into the world rather than separating it from the world. While the kingdom of God is brought into the world, it is not of the world. This model represents a dualistic approach. It is exemplified by Jesus' words, "Give to Caesar what is Caesar's and to God what is God's" (Matt. 22:21). The Christian lives in two realms and has responsibilities to each. Since God is the Creator of this world and ultimately controls it, the Christian is free to participate in the world. When the two realms come into conflict, the Christian's first loyalty is to the kingdom of God.

The third approach Webber discusses is the "transformational model." According to this approach the kingdom of God comes into the world to transform the world. Webber sees four basic tenets to this model:

1. The central conviction of the transformational model is that the structures of life can be converted and changed.
2. The transformational model presupposes the radical effect of sin on all structures of life. (It affects all creation.)
3. The transformational model presupposes the cosmic nature of Christ's redemption. (It extends to all creation.)
4. The transformational model sees the church as that social context in which the redeemed reality is to be modeled (1979:163–64).

In his book Webber critiques each of these models. While finding value in each of the models, he appears to lean toward the transformational model. Early in his book he states, "Thus the activity of the Christian in culture should be to unfold God's creation according to the purposes of God, so that every area of culture reflects Christian values" (1979:18). Even a cursory reading of the other chapters in this volume would lead us to the conclusion that most, if not all, of the contributors would be most comfortable with the transformational model.

If Christians are to be involved in the world, then what does the discipline of sociology have to contribute to that involvement? In chapter 1 of this volume, Reimer briefly alludes to some contributions. It will be suggested here that there are at least three major contributions that the discipline of sociology can make to the Christian's (and the church's) ministry of reconciliation and transformation.

UNDERSTANDING SOCIETY

If we are going to minister in and to society, we must understand society. Sociology can supply the Christian with the tools and concepts necessary for a better understanding of society. Before beginning to minister to society and its members, the Christian needs to understand the society, the individuals that make it up, and the dynamic relationship between the two. Society has structure; it consists of social institutions (see chaps. 9–13), formal organizations (see chap. 14), and less formal groups (see chap. 8). However, societies are not static structures but dynamic organisms in constant change (see chap. 19). The structuralist perspective is like a photograph in that it catches the essence of the society at any given moment. The dynamic perspective is like a moving picture in that it catches the process of society in change. Both perspectives are important in understanding the nature of society.

By way of example, sociology offers a basis of understanding to the one who is concerned about indications of racially prejudiced attitudes among members of his or her church. An understanding of the processes involved in socialization (see chap. 4) supplies a framework for evaluating the societal contribution to attitude formation. Thus the study of sociology enables us to learn how individuals acquire the attitudes and prejudices of the society, and particularly the subculture, in which they live. It is difficult to attempt to correct attitudes and prejudices until the processes by which they are acquired are adequately understood.

Another example of how an understanding of society is essential to effective ministry involves local church outreach. A church may sense a need to reach out to the community in which it is located. It then gives to its governing board, Christian education committee, or some other group the responsibility to formulate a plan or program for this outreach. The panel involved will usually entertain a number of ideas, discuss them, and finally settle on the one that seems most effective. Unfortunately, however, the original goal is often forgotten; instead of an outreach program, the program that usually is seen as most effective is the one that best suits the church. All too often a committee neglects to seriously consider the nature and needs of the community. For example, the demographics of the community are rarely considered (see chap. 17). Most public libraries have census data readily available, or they can easily obtain it. This data will give the committee information on the breakdown of the community's population by age groups, sex, marital status, income, as well as births and deaths.

A review of the census data can provide a church with valuable information. For example, if the data shows that a significant portion of the population is aged sixty-five and over, then a church might consider some sort of senior-citizen program. On the other hand, if the data reveals a significant number of young married couples in the lower middle-income brackets, other ministries might need to be considered. In that case the church might think in terms of a day-care center and/or a preschool program. The point is that if a church wants to reach a community, its programs must meet the needs of that community. Sociology provides tools and concepts for ascertaining those needs.

EVALUATING COURSES OF ACTION

When a problem or need has been discovered and understood, what is the most effective approach to solve the problem or meet the need? Again, a sociological perspective may contribute to the process of evaluating the options available. Such a perspective can throw light on which course of action would have the greatest possibility of achieving the desired ends.

For example, let us assume that a Christian is part of a formal organization and believes that injustices are taking place. If that Christian believes that he or she should attempt to redress those injustices, several possible approaches might be considered. How would the person determine the approach that might be most effective? A knowledge of formal organizations, bureaucracy, and styles of leadership (see chap. 14) would provide a basis for evaluating both the problem and the possible solutions. Without an understanding of the dynamics of an organization, it is very difficult to bring about change in that organization.

As another example of how a sociological perspective can aid in evaluating various courses of action, let us think of committee assignments in a local church. If the church has a task that should be done and determines that it ought to be handled by a committee, then how does the church decide how many and which persons should be on the committee? An understanding of the structure and dynamics of groups (see chap. 8) would be most useful in determining group membership. For example, it would help a church to know what happens to a group's efficiency as its size is changed. Sociological research (Davis, 1969:35–54) indicates that efficiency decreases as group size increases. For example, if a task can be accomplished by one person in fifty hours it may take two persons thirty hours, three persons twenty-five hours, and four persons twenty hours. Then two persons require sixty person-hours to do the task, three persons require seventy-five person-hours, while four persons require eighty person-hours. Although the four-person group is least efficient, it also takes the shortest elapsed time to complete the task.

With the amount of work that is done by committees in most churches, an understanding of the structure and dynamics of groups is vital for maximum effectiveness. Decisions on the size and composition of groups as well as the type of leadership and structure that is best for each specific task may be made more wisely with the aid of a sociological understanding of groups. Sociology is a valuable tool for both individuals and churches as they make decisions about the most effective course of action for accomplishing a particular ministry.

RESEARCH TECHNIQUES

The third contribution that sociology can make to the ministry of individuals and churches is to provide tools for research (see chap. 2). Both Samuel Southard (1976) and James Engle (1977) discuss the important and useful sociological research techniques available to individuals and the church. Between them they suggest four basic techniques.

Documentary research. Much data has already been collected by other researchers. If the data the researcher needs has already been collected by others, then his task simply involves going to the documents where it is recorded and recovering the data. Much information that would be of great value to individuals and churches in making decisions concerning ministry has already been collected. Census data has already been mentioned. Other sources of data include court records, the *Congressional Record,* and various reports and statistics produced by different units of federal, state, and local government. Governmental units on every level research and publish findings on every imaginable topic. Under the recent Freedom of Information Act, almost all of this data is available to the public.

There are many other types of documents that may prove useful to local churches. Often churches have kept many years of records on attendance, giving, etc. Frequently this data has never been analyzed. This type of data can provide useful information. It can be used to spot trends, pinpoint problem areas, and reveal areas of strengths and weaknesses. Also, most denominations compile many different types of data and statistics. They often also carry out various types of research projects. Although the obvious place to begin is with the data available within one's own denomination, data collected by other denominations may prove extremely valuable. A local church may be considering a certain type of community outreach. If churches of another denomination have already attempted that type of program, it would seem to be only logical to examine their data and results.

Documentary research can be a valuable tool for individuals and churches. Sociologists have developed methods for researching documents and organizing the data into statistically useful forms (for example, see Thomlinson, 1965:43–44; Phillips, 1971; 147–58). These sociological methodologies permit the use of research and data of others for one's own purposes.

Surveys. This technique involves methods of gathering data. The two major survey methods are questionnaires and interviews. Although both methods involve asking subjects to supply data, the distinction is that questionnaires are self-administered while interviews are administered by a researcher. A questionnaire involves supplying the subject with a series of printed questions asking for the desired data. The advantage of a questionnaire is that it can be administered to many persons in various locations at the same time. Some disadvantages of questionnaires are that subjects may misinterpret questions, leave some questions unanswered, supply undecipherable answers, or not even return the questionnaires.

When interviewing, the researcher and/or research assistants personally ask the questions of each subject and record the answers themselves. Interviewing usually results in more complete data than questionnaires. This is because misunderstood questions can be explained, the subject can be encouraged to answer all the questions, and vague answers can be clarified. Then, too, since the interviewer records the answers, he or she has the data in hand. Some disadvantages of interviewing are that it requires much more time than questionnaires; and if the subjects are spread out over any distance, it can become very expensive.

Observation. This is one of the most readily available and least-used research techniques. Sociological observation involves more than just looking at something or someone. It involves observing a situation from a specific perspective with identifiable criteria in mind.

By way of example, suppose a pastor wanted to evaluate the effectiveness of various committees in his church. First, he would need to establish criteria for evaluation. These might include the type of leadership, interpersonal dynamics, the type of decision making, and group product. Next, he would need to establish categories for each area, that is, types of leadership. The sociological literature on groups (see chap. 8) would provide these. When the pastor had specific criteria and categories for recording his observations, he would be ready to observe.

The two basic types of observation are participant and nonparticipant. In participant observation the observer is a participant in the activity being observed. Returning to the example above, if the pastor were a member of the committees he was observing, he would be engaged in participant observation. In nonparticipant observation the researcher observes as an outsider. Returning to the example of the pastor desiring to evaluate church committees, he would be engaged in nonparticipant observation if he attended the meetings of committees of which he was not a member and did not participate in any way but merely observed as unobtrusively as possible.

Experiments. The fourth technique, experiments, may be the least useful for individuals and churches. However, there are some situations in which it may prove valuable. An experiment involves changing one thing (called the independent variable) in a situation while attempting to hold everything else constant. If something else changes (called the dependent variable), we may conclude that the change in the dependent variable was brought about by changes in the independent variable.

An example of a situation in which an experiment might be an appropriate research tool would involve the examination of various options for collecting tithes and offerings in a church. Suppose a group of individuals in a church advocates having offering plates at the church exits rather than passing the plates during the service. Another group might argue that this would lead to a decrease in giving and income for the church. How might the church determine if the second group is correct or not? If a search of the literature uncovers no data on churches that have tried both methods, the church will need to conduct an experiment. The church could check the records for the past five years and try to find two months that have historically produced equal income. If two such months can be found, then one method of collecting offerings could be used one month and the other method used the other month and the amount of income compared. For the purposes of the experiment, as many factors as possible in the services for both months should be held constant. No other innovations of any type should be permitted. Although a study of this type would not meet the strict requirements of an experiment, it would use a basic experimental design. If the difference in income was significant and if the experiment were conducted a second time (called replication) with the same results, you could draw some fairly firm conclusions.

All of the research methods discussed above may be useful tools for enabling individuals and churches to have more effective ministries. In choosing a research technique, the situation and the type of data needed should dictate the appropriate one. A basic understanding of sociology can better enable the Christian to understand society and minister more effectively to it.

SOCIOLOGY AND THEOLOGY

In chapter 1 of this volume, Reimer has defined sociology as a discipline that "deals with society and social interaction, and that relies on the scientific method to pursue its goals." James Buswell defines theology as follows: "The word '*theology*,' which combines *theos*, 'God,' and *logos*, 'rational expression,' and which literally means 'the rationale which treats of God,' may be defined as the study which treats directly of God and His relationship to the world and to man" (Buswell, 1962:13). What relationship, if any, exists between sociology and theology? I would like to suggest that the two disciplines have a common goal and therefore have much to contribute to each other. Their common goal is the search for truth, and all truth is God's truth.[1]

Contributions of theology to sociology. Theology has some important contributions to make to the discipline of sociology. While some of these have been alluded to in chapters 1 and 2 of this volume, they will be made explicit here. Humans are the focus of sociological study; and so an understanding of human origins and the essence of human nature are critical for understanding society. Theology can provide sociology with a biblical, and therefore true, understanding of the origin and essence of humanity.

Theology points to the fact that humans are created beings.[2] One of the biblical passages dealing with the creation of humans is Genesis 2:7: "And the LORD God formed man from the dust of the ground and breathed into his nostrils the breath of life, and man became a living being." Several theologians have suggested that "dust" symbolizes the material aspect of humanity, while "breath" symbolizes the immaterial aspects of humanity (Babbage, 1957:10; Brunner, 1947:108; Verduin, 1970:22–24).

Genesis 1:26–27 teaches that humans are created in the image of God. This most likely does not refer to the material or physical dimensions of humans because God is a spirit-type Being (John 4:24). On their physical side humans resemble the animal creation. They share many of the same biological characteristics as animals. Ronaly Kotesky, a professor at Asbury College, points out that to understand the essence of human nature, we must take into account the similarities between humans and animals (1980:120).

---

[1] It is recognized that although most sociologists would agree that sociology as a science is concerned with the search for truth, many would deny it is God's truth. However, their denial does not change reality.

[2] It is not the purpose of this essay to discuss either the nature of creation or its time reference.

While humans are similar to animals in some ways, they are qualitatively distinct from them in other ways. This qualitative distinction results from humans being made "in the image of God" (Gen. 1:27). While many of the church fathers distinguish between the "image" of God and the "likeness" of God (Gen. 1:26), today most evangelical theologians see these terms as parallel and as meaning the same thing. Also, these theologians are generally agreed that the reference to "man" in verse 26 refers to humanity, not just to males. This view is supported by verse 27, which speaks of male and female as being created in God's image.

Most theologians agree that the image of God refers to humanity's ability to relate to God as beings that in some limited way share aspects of His essence. What is that aspect of God in us that allows us to relate to Him and each other? Theologians suggest that self-consciousness, reason or rationality, and responsibility are involved. Francis Schaeffer sums up these characteristics in the term "personality" (1968:87).

Evangelical theologians generally believe that the central aspects of human personality are reason and responsibility. God created humans with the ability to reason so as to be able to relate to God. As a rational Being Himself, God wanted to relate to rational beings. Responsibility grows out of reason. Humans are responsible to their Creator. God has created them with the capability to respond to Him and they are responsible to do so.

While humans were created in the image of God so as to be able to relate to Him, that relationship was affected by their rebellion against God. God's relationship with humans was not completely severed because of the Fall, but it was drastically altered. All humans no longer had direct access to God. Most had come to God through mediators. Thus priests spoke to God for them, and prophets spoke to them for God. Sacrifices were necessary to atone for acts of rebellion (sins). God's relationship with His people was, for the most part, formal and at a distance.

While several of the church fathers, as well as some contemporary theologians, have seen the Fall as completely destroying the image of God in humanity, most evangelical theologians have seen the image as marred rather than destroyed. It is interesting to note that humans have not lost their power to dominate creation, although the Fall has made it more difficult for them to do so. Humans have not lost their ability to distinguish right from wrong. They have not lost their ability to hear and respond to God. The teaching of Genesis 3:14–19 is that all creation fell with humanity, and Romans 8:18–22 speaks of the effects of the Fall on nature. Yet in spite of the Fall, the apostle Paul could say that God could be seen in nature (Rom. 1:20). It is also true that the image of God survives in humanity.

Sin and the Fall have had consequences for all humans, with each one of us being affected. Emil Brunner, a Reformed theologian, sees the direct consequence of the Fall and human sin as being a distortion in humanity's sense of direction. He argues that God had set the direction for humans, but they sought to become gods themselves and to set their own direction. Because of the Fall the human tendency is now to look to humanity and the world for direction rather than to God (1952:125–28). This, then, becomes the basis of modern humanism.

There was nothing fallen humans could do about the power of sin over their lives or do to be reconciled to God. However, God was able to make a way of reconciliation. The apostle Paul tells us,

> Therefore, if anyone is in Christ, he is a new creation; the old has gone, the new has come! All this is from God, who reconciled us to himself through Christ and gave us the ministry of reconciliation: that God was reconciling the world to himself in Christ, not counting men's sins against them. And he has committed to us the message of reconciliation. We are therefore Christ's ambassadors, as though God were making his appeal through us. We implore you on Christ's behalf: be reconciled to God. God made him who had no sin to be sin for us, so that in him we might become the righteousness of God (2 Cor. 5:17–21).

These verses reveal that humans may be reconciled to God through Christ. The old creation was marred by sin; so humans have the potential to be recreated or, in Paul's words, to become a "new creation." Humans can be accepted by God, not because they deserve to be, but because Christ took their sins on Himself. The basis of the reconciliation of humans is grace, God's unmerited favor toward them (Eph. 2:8–9). Reconciliation is a free gift.

Any approach to sociology that ignores the biblical account of the origin of humans and its implications, as well as the effects of the fall and the potential of redemption, will always come short of the full truth. An understanding of the scriptural view of human nature is essential for a valid sociology.[3]

Contributions of sociology to theology. Not only can theology contribute to sociology, but sociology also has some valuable contributions to make to theology. Charles Kraft (1977), a professor of anthropology at Fuller Theological Seminary, has suggested a number of contributions that anthropology can make to theology. Several of these also relate to the contributions that a sociological perspective can make to theology. Three of these contributions will be explained below.

The first contribution that sociology makes is in drawing a sharp distinction between the data and the interpretations of the data. A researcher may have done a thorough piece of research and produced extremely accurate data; however, the quality of the data does not necessarily guarantee the accuracy of the interpretation of that data.[4] Theologians can learn from sociologists the importance of separating their data from their interpretations.

The basic data base for theologians is the Scriptures. Evangelical theologians recognize that their data is sacred. The Bible is the inspired, infallible Word of God. However, the fact that the data of theologians is sacred does not mean their interpretations are sacred, inspired, or infallible. The doctrine of inspiration and infallibility only extends to the documents, not to the interpretations.[5] The theologian, as well as the sociologist, must recognize and account for the presuppositions brought by the research to the data.

A second contribution that sociology makes to theology is helping to make theology relevant by supplying data.

Paul Tillich points out, "Theology, as a function of the Christian church, must serve the needs of the church. A theological system is supposed to satisfy two basic needs: the statement of the truth of the Christian message and the interpretation of this truth for every new generation" (1951:3).

---

[3]Although not all Christian sociologists might agree with this statement, this is the firm conviction of myself and of the coeditor of this volume.

[4]However, it is obvious that poor data will never yield a good interpretation.

[5]This is not meant to deny the role of the Holy Spirit in enabling believers to understand God's Word, but is a recognition of human fallibility.

Tillich then goes on to point out that most theological systems fail to keep these two points in balance. He says, "Most of them either sacrifice elements of the truth or are not able to speak to the situation." Tillich, then, and with some justification, accuses evangelicals of being so preoccupied with the "truth" that their theology is often irrelevant to the needs of the average Christian (1951:3–6).

Kraft sees this problem arising because theologians don't "start from questions that concern ordinary people, rather than from those that are of vital concern only to academicians" (1977:183). Kraft goes on to point out that theologians

> belong to particular subcultures that have perfectly valid needs and interests. But as in all subcultures a great many of these needs and interests are specific to the kinds of life experience peculiar to that subculture alone. If, therefore, theologizing is done only by academicians, it will continue to relate rather specifically to their concerns, rather than those of the members of other subcultures unless it is done by academicians who learn to study other groups of people where they are and to deal theologically with their concerns as well (1977:183).

Sociology can provide theologians with literature, research, and tools for a better understanding where the ordinary person hurts and needs answers. Also, theologians basically deal with issues on a philosophical level, whereas lay persons deal with issues on a behavioral level. Sociology can help theologians bridge that gap.

The third area in which a sociological perspective can contribute to theology is in distinguishing between form and meaning. This contribution grows out of the sociological concept of cultural relativity as it is applied to the absolute truths of Scripture (see chap. 3). The ability to distinguish between cultural forms and their meanings is critical to the task of making theology relevant to various subcultures. Theologians need to recognize that cultural forms are important because of their meaning to particular people rather than in and of themselves. As Grunlan and Mayers point out,

> Cultural forms derive their meanings from their cultural context and can only be fully understood in that context. A cultural form retains its meaning only in its own culture; once it is transferred to another culture, it takes on another meaning.
>
> The cultural forms in the Scriptures must be understood in the context of their own culture. Cultural forms found in the Scriptures are not sacred; it is their meanings that are sacred (1979:278).

Sociological insight can aid the theologian in distinguishing between the culture of the Bible and the eternal truths in the Bible. For example, God never meant to absolutize kissing as the standard greeting between Christians (1 Cor. 16:20; 2 Cor. 13:12; 1 Thess. 5:26); rather, He utilized the cultural form of greeting that was standard in that culture to teach that believers should warmly greet each other. In North American culture that truth is embodied in a handshake. In Latin American an *embrazo*, or hug, would embody the same truth.

Sociology and theology have much to contribute to each other as they seek to understand God and His revelation and creation. Sociology also has significant contributions to make to the ministry of believers in the world. Where sociological insight can further one's walk with the Lord, those insights should be welcomed.

DISCUSSION QUESTIONS

1. In what ways do you believe a sociological perspective can aid in your Christian walk?
2. How might sociological research methods help various ministries in your church to be more effective?
3. How important do you believe a proper understanding of human origins and the essence of human nature is to a proper understanding of sociology? Why?
4. Does sociology need to take into account the Fall and its consequences? Why? Why not?
5. Do you believe sociology can aid the task of theology? Why?

SUGGESTED READING

Earle E. Cairns, *The Christian in Society* (Chicago: Moody, 1973). This is a classic work on Christian social involvement. According to Cairns, Christian involvement in social change is an imperative, not an option.

James Engel, *How Can I Get Them to Listen?* (Grand Rapids: Zondervan, 1977). A handbook on social research for Christian organizations.

Samuel Southard, *Religious Inquiry* (Nashville: Abingdon, 1976). A good introduction on the why and how of social research for Christian ministry.

Robert E. Webber, *The Secular Saint* (Grand Rapids: Zondervan, 1979). The author presents three basic models for the relationship between the Christian and society. He critiques each of the models and then gives some ideas on Christian social action.

REFERENCES

Accrediting Association of Bible Colleges Manual.
  1975   Wheaton, Illinois.
Akers, Ronald L.
  1977   Deviant Behavior: A Social Learning Approach. Belmont, Calif: Wadsworth.
Albini, Joseph L.
  1971   The American Mafia: Genesis of a Legend. New York: Appleton-Century-Crofts.
Alexander, John
  1978   "The economics of Jesus." The Other Side 14:14–18.
Appelbaum, Richard
  1970   Theories of Social Change. Chicago: Markham.
Argyris, Chris
  1971   Management and Organizational Development. New York: McGraw-Hill.
Asch, Solomon E.
  1956   "Studies of independence and submission to group pressure." Psychological Monographs 70:9.

Babbage, Stuart B.
   1977   Man in Nature and Grace. Grand Rapids: Eerdmans.
Babbie, E. R.
   1977   Society by Agreement: An Introduction to Sociology. Belmont, Calif.: Wadsworth.
Bales, R. F.
   1950   Interaction Process Analysis. Cambridge, Mass.: Addison-Wesley.
   1970a   Personality and Interpersonal Behavior. New York: Holt, Rinehart and Winston.
   1970b   SYMLOG: System for the Multiple Level Observation of Groups. New York: Free Press.
Bales, R. F. and Stodtbeck
   1951   "Phases in group problem solving." Journal of Abnormal and Social Psychology 46:485–96.
Balkan, Sheila, Ronald J. Berger, and Janet Schmidt
   1980   Crime and Deviance in America: A Critical Approach. Belmont, Calif.: Wadsworth.
Bandura, Albert
   1973   Aggression, A Social Learning Analysis. Englewood Cliffs, N.J.: Prentice-Hall.
Bane, Mary Jo
   1976   Here to Stay: American Families in the Twentieth Century. New York: Basic Books.
Banfield, Edward C.
   1974   The Unheavenly City Revisited. Boston: Little, Brown.
Becker, Ernest
   1975   Escape From Evil. New York: Free Press.
Becker, Howard S.
   1963   Outsiders: Studies in the Sociology of Deviance. New York: Free Press.
Bee, Helen
   1978   The Developing Child. New York: Harper and Row.
Bell, Colin and Howard Newby
   1972   Community Studies. New York: Praeger.
Bell, Daniel
   1959   The End of Ideology. New York: Free Press.
Bellah, Robert N.
   1967   "Civil religion in America." Daedalus 96:1–21.

Bennis and Shepherd
   1976   "Theory of group development." Graham S. Gibbord
           and Hartman, eds., Analysis of Groups: Contributions
           to Theory, Research, and Practice. San Francisco:
           Jossey-Bass.

Bensman, Joseph and Bernard Rosenberg
   1963   Mass, Class and Bureaucracy. Englewood Cliffs, N.J.:
           Prentice-Hall.

Berelson, Bernard and Gary A. Steiner
   1964   Human Behavior: An Inventory of Scientific Findings.
           New York: Harcourt, Brace and World.

Berger, Peter L.
   1963   Invitation to Sociology. Garden City, N.Y.: Doubleday.
   1967   The Sacred Canopy. New York: Doubleday.
   1977   Facing Up to Modernity. New York: Basic Books.

Berkhof, Louis
   1950   Principles of Biblical Interpretation. Grand Rapids:
           Baker.

Berton, Pierre
   1965   The Comfortable Pew. New York: Lippincott.

Bete, Channing L.
   1980   Educating Handicapped Children. Greenfield, Mass.:
           Bete.

Bierstedt, Robert
   1970   The Social Order. New York: McGraw-Hill.

Blackburn, Joyce
   1972   The Earth Is the Lord's? Waco: Word Publishers.

Blau, Peter
   1973   The Organization of Academic Work. New York: Wiley.

Blood, Bob and Margaret Blood
   1978   Marriage (3rd ed.). New York: Free Press.

Blummer, Herbert
   1951   "Collective behavior." In A.M. Lee (ed.), New Outline of
           the Principles of Sociology. New York: Barnes and Noble.

Bonger, William
   1916   Criminality and Economic Conditions. Boston: Little,
           Brown.

Boughey, William
   1978   The Insights of Sociology. Boston: Allyn and Bacon.

Bowlby, J.
1969   Attachment and Loss, Vol. 1. New York: Basic Books.

Bredemeier, Harry C. and Richard M. Stephenson
1962   The Analysis of Social Systems. New York: Holt, Rinehart and Winston.

Briar, Scott and Irvin Piliavin
1965   "Delinquency, situational inducements and commitment to conformity." Social Problems 13:35–45.

Brodinsky, Ben
1976   "12 major events that shaped America's schools." Phi Delta Kappan 1:68–77.
1977   "Back to the basics: the movement and its meaning." Phi Delta Kappan 7:522–27.
1979   "Something happened: education in the seventies." Phi Delta Kappan 4:238–41.

Broom, Leonard and Philip Selznick
1977   Sociology: A Text With Adapted Readings (6th ed.). New York: Harper and Row.

Brunner, Emil
1947   Man in Revolt. Philadelphia: Westminster.
1952   The Christian Doctrine of Creation and Redemption. Dogmatics, Vol. 2. Philadelphia: Westminster.

Burgess, Ernest W.
1925   "The growth of the city: An introduction to a research project." Pages 47–62 in Robert E. Park et al., The City. Chicago: University of Chicago Press.

Buswell, James Oliver
1962   A Systematic Theology of the Christian Religion, Vol. 1. Grand Rapids: Zondervan.

Byrne, H. W.
1961   A Christian Approach to Education—A Bibliocentric View. Grand Rapids: Zondervan.

Campbell, Ernest Q. and Thomas F. Pettigrew
1959   Christians in Racial Crisis: A Study of Little Rock's Ministry. Washington: Public Affairs Press.

Carson, Rachel
1962   Silent Spring. Boston: Houghton Mifflin.

Carwardine, William H.
  1894   The Pullman Strike. Chicago: Kerr.
Charbonnier, George
  1969   Conversations With Claude Levi-Strauss. London: Jonathan Cape.
Clarke, Alfred C.
  1972   "An examination of the operation of residential propinquity as a factor in mate selection." American Sociological Review 17:17–22.
Clinard, Marshall B. (ed.)
  1964   Anomie and Deviant Behavior. New York: Free Press.
Clinard, Marshall B. and Robert F. Meyer
  1979   Sociology of Deviant Behavior (5th ed.). New York: Holt, Rinehart and Winston.
Cloward, Richard and Lloyd Ohlin
  1966   Delinquency and Opportunity. Glencoe, Ill.: Free Press.
Cobb, Stephen G.
  1979   "Toward a Christian sociology." Unpublished paper used for teaching.
  1979a   "Christian socialism now and then: Carwardine and the Pullman strike." Paper presented to the Mid-West Sociological Society.
Cohen, Albert K.
  1955   Delinquent Boys. Glencoe, Ill.: Free Press.
Cole, George F.
  1979   The American System of Criminal Justice (2nd ed.). North Scituate, Mass.: Duxbury Press.
Coleman, James S.
  1966   Equality of Educational Opportunity. Washington: U.S. Government Printing Office.
Comte, Auguste
  1854
  (1896) The Positive Philosophy of Auguste Comte. Translated by H. Martineau. London: Bell.
Conn, Harvie M.
  1979   "The kingdom of God and the city of man: A history of the city/church dialogue." Pages 9–59 in Roger S. Greenway (ed.), "Christ and the city: biblical themes for

building urban theology models." Discipling the City. Grand Rapids: Baker.

Cooley, Charles H.
1909   Social Organization. New York: Scribner's.
1949   "Primary groups." Logan Wilson and William Kolb (eds.). Sociological Analysis. New York: Harcourt, Brace and World, pp. 352–355.

Coon, D.
1980   Introductory Psychology. St. Paul: West.

Coser, Lewis and Bernard Rosenberg
1976   Sociological Theory. New York: Macmillan.

Cosgrove, Mark P.
1977   The Essence of Human Nature. Grand Rapids: Zondervan.

Cosgrove, Mark P. and James D. Mallory, Jr.
1977   Mental Health: A Christian Approach. Grand Rapids: Zondervan.

Coulson, C. A.
1958   Science and Christian Belief. New York: Fontana Books.

Cousins, Albert N. and Hans Nagpaul
1979   Urban Life: The Sociology of Cities and Urban Society. New York: Wiley.

Cressey, Donald R.
1953   Other People's Money. Glencoe, Ill.: Free Press.
1969   Theft of a Nation. New York: Harper and Row.

Davis, J. D. (ed.)
1972   Davis' Dictionary of the Bible. Old Tappan, N.J.: Revell.

Davis, James H.
1969   Group Performance. Reading, Mass.: Addison-Wesley.

Davis, Kingsley
1948   Human Society. New York: Macmillan.

Davis, Kingsley and Willbert E. Moore
1945   "Some principles of social stratification." American Sociological Review 10:242–49.

DeFleur, Lois B., John C. Ball, and Richard W. Snarr
1969   "The long-term social correlates of opiate addiction." Social Problems 17:225–33.

DeJong, Norman
　1977　Education in the Truth. Nutley, N.J.: Presbyterian and Reformed.

DeJong, Peter and Donald R. Wilson
　1979　Husband and Wife: The Sexes in Scripture and Society. Grand Rapids: Zondervan.

Denisoff, R. Serge and Ralph Wahrman
　1979　An Introduction to Sociology. New York: Macmillan.

Dillenberger, John and Claude Welch
　1954　Protestant Christianity: Interpreted Through Its Development. New York: Scribner's Sons.

Dolbeare, Kenneth M. and Murray J. Edelman
　1971　American Politics: Policies, Power, and Change. Lexington: Heath.

Doll, Ronald
　1974　Curriculum Improvement: Decision Making and Process. Boston: Allyn and Bacon.

Dombrowski, James
　1966　The Early Days of Christian Socialism in America. New York: Octagon.

Domhoff, G. William
　1967　Who Rules America? Englewood Cliffs, N.J.: Prentice-Hall.
　1971　The Higher Circles: The Governing Class in America. New York: Vintage Books.

Dressel, Paul L.
　1963　The Undergraduate Curriculum in Higher Education. Washington, D.C.: Center for Applied Research.

Dressler, David and William M. Willis, Jr.
　1976　Sociology: The Study of Human Interaction (3rd ed.). New York: Knopf.

Duberman, Lucile and Clayton A. Hartjen
　1979　Sociology: Focus on Society. Glenview, Ill.: Scott, Foresman.

Dunphy, Dexter
　1972　The Primary Group. New York: Appleton-Century-Crofts.

Durkheim, Emile
  1893
  (1933) The Division of Labor. Translated by George Simpson.
         New York: Macmillan.
  1962   "The normal and the pathological" in The Sociology of
         Crime and Delinquency. New York: Wiley.

Ehrlich, Paul R.
  1968   The Population Bomb. New York: McGraw-Hill.
Ellis, Robert L. and Marcie J. Lipetz
  1979   Essential Sociology. Glenview, Ill.: Scott, Foresman.
Ellison, Craig (ed.)
  1974   The Urban Mission. Grand Rapids: Eerdmans.
Ellul, Jacques
  1964   The Technological Society. New York: Knopf.
Ember, Carol R. and Melvin Ember
  1973   Cultural Anthropology. New York: Appleton-Century-
         Croft.
Engel, James F.
  1977   How Can I Get Them to Listen? Grand Rapids: Zonder-
         van.
Engel, James F. and H. Wilbert Norton
  1975   What's Gone Wrong With the Harvest? Grand Rapids:
         Zondervan.
Erikson, Kai T.
  1977   Everything in Its Path: Destruction of Community in the
         Buffalo Creek Flood. New York: Simon and Schuster.
Eternity Magazine
  1980   "How wide is the spectrum in Christian schools?" 9:27.

Fantini, Mario D.
  1973   "Alternatives within public schools." Phi Delta Kappan
         7:444–48.
Farrell, Michael
  1979   "Phases of group development." Paper presented at
         Fourth Annual Scientific Meeting of A. K. Rice Institute,
         Houston.
Federico, Ronald C.
  1979   Sociology. Reading, Mass.: Addison-Wesley.

Festinger, Leon, Stanley S. Schachter, and Kurt Back
  1950   Social Pressures in Informal Groups: A Study in Human
          Factors in Housing. New York: Harper.
Fischer, Claude S.
  1976   The Urban Experience. New York: Harcourt, Brace,
          Jovanovich.
Fischer, Robert B.
  1971   Science, Man and Society. Philadelphia: Saunders.
Fletcher, Joseph
  1966   Situation Ethics: The New Morality. Philadelphia:
          Westminster.
Folsom, Paul
  1971   And Thou Shalt Die in a Polluted Land, An Approach to
          Christian Ecology. Liguori, Mo.: Liguorian Pamphlets
          and Books.
Fontana, Vincent
  1973   Somewhere a Child Is Crying. New York: Macmillan.
Freud, Sigmund
  1960   Group Psychology and the Analysis of the Ego. New
          York: Bantam Books.
  1949   Group Psychology and Analysis of the Ego. New York:
          Liverwright.
Friedrichs, Robert W.
  1970   A Sociology of Sociology. New York: Free Press.
Furfey, Paul
  1978   "Solving our poverty problem." The Other Side 14:
          19–23.

Gans, Herbert J.
  1975   "The uses of poverty: the poor pay all." Pages 219–24 in
          Paul B. Horton and Gerald R. Leslie (eds.), Readings in
          the Sociology of Social Problems. Englewood Cliffs,
          N.J.: Prentice-Hall.
Geiger, H.J.
  1971   "Health and social change: the urban crisis." Pages
          241–48 in J. K. Hadden et al. (eds.), Metropolis in Crisis.
          Itasca, Ill: Peacock.
Geis, Gilbert
  1967   "White collar crime: the heavy electrical antitrust cases

of 1961." Pages 139–50 in M. Clinard and R. Quinney (eds.), Criminal Behavior Systems: A Typology. New York: Holt, Rinehart and Winston.

Gibbons, Don C.
1977   Society, Crime and Criminal Careers: An Introduction to Criminology. Englewood Cliffs, N.J.: Prentice-Hall.

Gist, Noel P. and Sylvia Fleis Fava
1974   Urban Society. New York: Crowell.

Glaser, Daniel
1978   Crime in Our Changing Society. New York: Holt, Rinehart and Winston.

Goldthorpe, J. E.
1968   An Introduction to Sociology. London: Cambridge University Press.

Goodlad, John I.
1975   The Dynamics of Educational Change. New York: McGraw-Hill.
1977   "Alternative schooling: language and meaning." Today's Education 1:84–86.

Gordon, L. and Patricia Harvey
1978   Sociology and American Social Issues. Boston: Houghton Mifflin.

Gove, Walter (ed.)
1975   The Labeling of Deviance: Evaluating a Perspective. New York: Wiley.

Graham, Patricia Albjerg
1974   "America's unsystematic education system." American Education 6:12–19.

Green, Arnold W.
1968   Sociology: An Analysis of Life in Modern Society. (5th ed). New York: McGraw-Hill.
1972   Sociology: An Analysis of Life in Modern Society. (6th ed.). New York: McGraw-Hill.

Green, Ernest J.
1978   Personal Relationships: An Approach to Marriage and the Family. New York: McGraw-Hill.

Greenway, Roger S. (ed.)
1979   Discipling the City. Grand Rapids: Baker.

Greer, Scott
 1962   The Emerging City. New York: Free Press.

Gromacki, Robert G.
 1974   New Testament Survey. Grand Rapids: Baker.

Grunlan, Stephen A. and Marvin K. Mayers
 1979   Cultural Anthropology: A Christian Perspective. Grand Rapids: Zondervan.

Gulley, Halbert E.
 1968   Discussion, Conference, and Group Process. New York: Holt, Rinehart and Winston.

Gundry, Patricia
 1977   Woman Be Free! Grand Rapids: Zondervan.

Gusfield, Joseph R.
 1975   Community: A Critical Response. New York: Harper and Row.

Hadden, Jeffrey K.
 1969   The Gathering Storm in the Churches. Garden City, N.Y.: Doubleday.

Hadden, Jeffrey and Raymond C. Rymph
 1966   "Social structure and civil rights involvement: a case study of Protestant ministers." Social Forces 9:51–61.

Hakes, J. Edward (ed.)
 1964   An Introduction to Evangelical Christian Education. Chicago: Moody Press.

Hall, Richard S.
 1977   Organizations: Structure and Process. Englewood Cliffs N.J.: Prentice-Hall.

Hansen, Donald A. and Joel E. Gerstl
 1967   On Education: Sociological Perspectives. New York: Wiley.

Hare, Alexander P.
 1976   Handbook of Small Group Research. New York: Free Press.

Harrington, Michael
 1969   The Other America: Poverty in the United States. Baltimore: Penguin.

Harris, Michael
1979 "No more teachers' dirty looks." Mother Jones, April.
Harrison, E.
1964 Introduction to the New Testament. Grand Rapids: Eerdmans.
Harris, William H. and Judith S. Levey (eds.)
1975 The New Columbia Encyclopedia. New York: Columbia University Press.
Hartley, Shirley Foster
1972 Population: Quantity Vs. Quality. Englewood Cliffs, N.J.: Prentice-Hall.
Hatfield, Mark
1977 "Repentance, politics, and power." Sojourners 6:35–38.
Hawley, A. H.
1971 Urban Society: An Ecological Approach. New York: Wiley.
Herberg, Will
1973 "Religion in the U.S.—where it's headed." U.S. News and World Report (June 4):54–60.
Hess, E. H.
1970 Ethology and Developmental Psychology. In P. H. Mussen (ed.), Carmichael's Manual of Child Psychology. New York: Wiley.
Hestenes, Roberta and Lois Curley
1979 Women and the Ministries. Pasadena, Calif.: Fuller Theological Seminary.
Hillery, George A., Jr.
1955 "Definitions of community: areas of agreement." Rural Sociology 20:111–23.
Hirschi, Travis
1969 Causes of Delinquency. Berkeley and Los Angeles: University of California Press.
Hobbs, Donald A. and Stuart J. Blank
1975 Sociology and the Human Experience. New York: Wiley.
Hoge, Dean R.
1976 Division in the Protestant House: The Basic Reasons Behind Intra-Church Conflicts. Philadelphia: Westminster.

Holland, Morris K.
  1978   Psychology: An Introduction to Human Behavior. Lexington: Heath.
Holmes, Arthur F.
  1977   All Truth Is God's Truth. Grand Rapids: Eerdmans.
Homans, G. C.
  1950   The Human Group. New York: Harcourt and Brace.
Hoover, Kenneth R.
  1976   The Elements of Social Scientific Thinking. New York: St. Martin.
Horton, Paul B. and Chester L. Hunt
  1976   Sociology. (4th ed.). New York: McGraw-Hill.
  1980   Sociology. (5th ed.). New York: McGraw-Hill.
Horton, P. B. and G. R. Leslie
  1974   The Sociology of Social Problems. Englewood Cliffs, N.J.: Prentice-Hall.
Huber, Joan
  1980   "Ransacking mobility tables." Contemporary Sociology 9:5–8.
Huff, Darrell
  1954   How to Live With Statistics. New York: Norton.
Hulme, William
  1962   The Pastoral Care of Families: Its Theology and Practice. New York: Abingdon.
Huxley, Aldous
  1937   Ends and Means. London: Chatto and Windus.

Inlow, Gail M.
  1973   The Emergent in Curriculum. New York: Wiley.

Jeeves, Malcolm A.
  1976   Psychology and Christianity. Downers Grove, Ill.: Inter-Varsity.
Jencks, Christopher
  1979   "Why students aren't learning." The Center Magazine 4:12–14.
Jensen, I. L.
  1978   Jensen's Survey of the Old Testament. Chicago: Moody.

Johnson, Alan
  1976 "History and culture in New Testament interpretation." In S. J. Schultz and M. A. Inch (eds.), Interpreting the Word of God. Chicago: Moody.
Johnson, Benton
  1964 "Ascetic Protestantism and political preference in the Deep South." American Journal of Sociology 69:359–66.
  1975 Functionalism in Modern Sociology: Understanding Talcott Parsons. Morristown, N.J.: General Learning.
Johnson, Donald M.
  1945 "The 'phantom anesthetist' of Mattoon: a field study of mass hysteria." Journal of Abnormal and Social Psychology 40:175–86.
Johnson, Harry
  1960 Sociology: A Systematic Introduction. New York: Harcourt, Brace.
Johnstone, Ronald L.
  1975 Religion and Society in Interaction: The Sociology of Religion. Englewood Cliffs, N.J.: Prentice-Hall.
Jones, Peter
  1968 The Christian Socialist Revival, 1877–1914: Religion, Class, and Social Conscience in Late Victorian Britain. Princeton: Princeton University Press.
Jordan, Winthrop
  1968 White Over Black: American Attitudes Toward the Negroes. 1550–1812. Baltimore: Penguin.

Kane, J. Herbert
  1971 A Global View of Christian Missions. Grand Rapids: Baker.
Karp, David A., Gregory P. Stone, and William C. Yoels
  1976 Being Urban. Lexington: Heath.
Kelley, Robert K.
  1979 Courtship, Marriage, and the Family. New York: Harcourt, Brace, Jovanovich.
Kenkel, William F.
  1980 Society in Action: Introduction to Sociology. New York: Harper and Row.

Kerckhoff, Alan C. and Kurt W. Back
  1968   The June Bug: A Study of Hysterical Contagion. New York: Appleton-Century-Crofts.

Kerr, William Nigel
  1974   "Historical evangelical involvement in the city." In Craig Ellison (ed.), The Urban Mission. Grand Rapids: Eerdmans.

Kienel, Paul A.
  1974   The Christian School: Why It Is Right for Your Child. Wheaton, Ill.: Victor Books.
  1978   (ed.) The Philosophy of Christian School Education. Whittier, Calif.: ACSI-GGS-CHC.

Kilinski, Kenneth K. and Jerry C. Wofford
  1973   Organization and Leadership in the Local Church. Grand Rapids: Zondervan.

Killian, Lewis M.
  1974   "Laying the ghost of LeBon: cognitive themes in theory of collective behavior." Paper presented at sixty-ninth meeting of American Sociological Association.

Klapp, Orrin E.
  1969   Collective Search for Identity. New York: Holt, Rinehart and Winston.
  1972   Currents of Unrest: An Introduction to Collective Behavior. New York: Holt, Rinehart and Winston.

Kloss, Robert M., Ron E. Roberts, and Dean S. Dorn
  1976   Sociology With a Human Face. St. Louis: Mosby.

Kotesky, Ronald L.
  1980   Psychology From a Christian Perspective. Nashville: Abingdon.

Kraft, Charles
  1977   "Can anthropological insight assist evangelical theology?" Christian Scholar's Review 7:165–202.
  1979   Christianity in Culture. Mary Knoll, N.Y.: Orbis.

Kroeber, A. L. and T. Parsons
  1956   "The concepts of culture and of social system." American Sociological Review 21:582–83.

Kuhn, Thomas S.
  1962   The Structure of Scientific Revolutions. Chicago: University of Chicago Press.

Ladd, George Eldon
  1966   The New Testament and Criticism. Grand Rapids: Eerdmans.

LaHaye, Tim
  1966   Spirit-Controlled Temperament. Wheaton, Ill.: Tyndale.
  1971   Transformed Temperaments. Wheaton, Ill.: Tyndale.

Lazarsfeld, P. F. and R. K. Merton
  1954   "Friendship as a social process," in Freedom and Control in Modern Society. eds. M. M. Berger, T. Abel, and C. Page. New York: Van Nostrand. 18–66.

LeBon, Gustav
  1896   The Crowd: A Study of the Popular Mind. London: Ernest Benn.

Leeper, Sarah Hammond, Dora Sikes Skipper, and Ralph L. Witherspoon
  1979   Good Schools for Young Children. New York: Macmillan.

Leslie, Gerald R., Richard F. Larson, and Benjamin L. Gorman
  1980   Introductory Sociology, Order and Change in Society. New York: Oxford University Press.

Levy, Marion
  1966   Modernization and the Structure of Society. Princeton, N.J.: Princeton University Press.

Lewis, Oscar
  1968   A Study in Slum Culture. New York: Random.

Lickona, Thomas
  1977   "How to encourage moral development." Learning 7:37–40, 42–43.

Light, Donald, Jr. and Suzanne Keller
  1978   Sociology. New York: Knopf.

Lindsell, Harold
  1976   The Battle for the Bible. Grand Rapids: Zondervan.

Linton, Ralph
  1936   The Study of Man. New York: D. Appleton-Century.

Lovelace, Richard
  1979   The Dynamics of Spiritual Life. Downers Grove: InterVarsity.

Lowry, Ritchie P. and Robert P. Rankin
  1977   Sociology, Social Science and Social Concern. Lexington: Heath.

Ludwig, Tom and David Myers
  1980   "Poortalk." An interview in The Other Side 16:10–16.
Lundberg, George A.
  1947   Can Science Save Us? New York: Longmans.
Lyon, David
  1976   Christians and Sociology. Downers Grove, Ill.: Inter-
          Varsity.

Maccob, Eleanor and John C. Masters
  1970   "Attachment and dependency." In P. H. Mussen (ed.),
          Carmichael's Manual of Child Psychology (Vol. 2). New
          York: Wiley.
McCarne, Alexander
  1842   "Slavery defended from scripture against the attacks of
          the abolitionists." In H. Sheldon Smith, In His Image,
          But . . . Racism in Southern Religion 1780:19–20.
          Durham: Duke University Press.
McGavran, Donald A.
  1970   Understanding Church Growth. Grand Rapids: Eerd-
          mans.
McGee, Reece
  1980   Sociology: An Introduction (2nd ed.). Chicago: Holt,
          Rinehart and Winston.
McGregor, Douglas
  1960   The Human Side of Enterprise. New York: McGraw-
          Hill.
MacIver, Robert
  1970   "The golden rule." In Robert MacIver, On Community,
          Society, and Power. Chicago: University of Chicago
          Press.
McKinney, John C. and Charles P. Loomis
  1970   "The typological tradition." In Albert N. Cousins and
          Hans Nagpaul (eds.), Urban Man and Society. New
          York: Knopf.
McMurray, Martha
  1978   "Religion and women's sex role traditionalism."
          Sociological Focus 11:81–95.

Mann, Richard
  1967   Interpersonal Styles and Group Development. New
          York: Wiley.
Marrett, Cora Bagley
  1980   "The precariousness of social class in black America."
          Contemporary Sociology 9:16–19.
Martin, David
  1972   "Great Britain, England." In Hans Mol (ed.), Western
          Religion. The Hague, Netherlands: Mouton.
Marx, Karl
  1964   Selected Writings in Sociology and Social Philosophy.
          Translated by Thomas Bottomore. London: McGraw-
          Hill.
Mason, Harold Carlton
  1964   "The History of Christian Education." Pages 25–36 in J.
          Edward Hakes (ed.), An Introduction to Evangelical
          Christian Education. Chicago: Moody.
Mayers, Marvin K.
  1974   Christianity Confronts Culture. Grand Rapids: Zonder-
          van.
Mazur, Allan
  1968   "The littlest science." The American Sociologist 3:195–
          200.
Mead, George Herbert
  1934   Mind, Self and Society, part 3. Chicago: University of
          Chicago Press.
Medalia, Nahum Z. and Otto N. Larsen
  1958   "Diffusion and belief in a collective delusion: the Seattle
          windshield pitting epidemic." American Sociological
          Review 23:221–32.
Meninger, Karl
  1973   Whatever Became of Sin? New York: Hawthorne Books.
Merton, Robert K.
  1938   "Social structure and anomie." American Sociological
          Review 3:672–82.
  1952   "The bureaucratic personality." Robert Merton et al.
          (eds.), Reader in Bureaucracy. Glencoe, Ill.: Free Press.
Methuin, Eugene H.
  1970   The Riot Makers. New Rochelle, N.Y.: Arlington House.

Meyer, William J. and Jerome B. Dusek
    1979   Child Psychology. Lexington: Heath.
Mickelsen, Anton Berkeley
    1963   Interpreting the Bible. Grand Rapids: Eerdmans.
Michels, Robert
    1960   Political Parties: A Sociological Study of the Oligarchical Tendencies of Modern Democracy. Magnolia, Mass.: Peter Smith.
Milgram, Stanley
    1963   "Behavioral study of obedience." Journal of Abnormal and Social Psychology 67:371–78.
Mills, C. Wright
    1956   The Power Elite. New York: Oxford University Press.
Mills, T. M.
    1964   Group Transformation. Englewood Cliffs, N.J.: Prentice-Hall.
    1967   The Sociology of Small Groups. Englewood Cliffs, N.J.: Prentice-Hall.
Moberg, David
    1970   "The manipulation of human behavior." Journal of the American Scientific Affiliation (March):14–17.
Moore, Wilbert
    1974   Social Change. Englewood Cliffs, N.J.: Prentice-Hall.
Morgan, C. T. and R. A. King
    1966   Introduction to Psychology. New York: McGraw-Hill.
Morgan, Lewis H.
    1877   Ancient Society. New York: World.
The Morning Advertiser
    1894   The great strike of 1894 and its features: organized labor's demands, as formulated by President Debs, A.R.U., General Master Workman Sovereign, Governor Altgeld and the Federation of Labor; also the opinions of the press of the country on the late strike and its significance. New York.
Muson, Howard
    1979   "Moral thinking." Psychology Today 9:48–49, 51, 53–54, 57–58, 67–68, 92.
Myers, David G.
    1978   The Human Puzzle. New York: Harper and Row.

Myers, M. Scott
  1970   Every Employee a Manager. New York: McGraw-Hill.

National Association of Evangelicals
  N.D.   Unity in Action. Wheaton, Ill.: NAE.
Neubeck, Kenneth J.
  1979   Social Problems: A Critical Approach. Glenview, Ill.:
          Scott, Foresman.
The New Columbia Encyclopedia. New York: Columbia University Press.
  1975
Nida, Eugene A.
  1954   Customs and Cultures. Pasadena: William Carey.
Niebuhr, H. Richard
  1957   The Social Sources of Denominationalism. New York:
          Median Books.
Nye, F. Ivan
  1958   Family Relationships and Delinquent Behavior. New
          York: Wiley.
Nixon, Howard
  1978   The Small Group. Englewood Cliffs, N.J.: Prentice-Hall.

Ogburn, William F.
  1922   Social Change With Respect to Culture and Original
          Nature. New York: Viking.
Ohio vs. Whisner
  1976   351 N.E. 2nd 750, Ohio.
Olson, J.
  1974   "Us or them: a short look at a sociological debate." The
          Other Side 6:54–59.
Other Side, The
  1979   "Let 'em eat air." The Other Side 15:12–36.
Otterbein, K. F.
  1977   Comparative Cultural Analysis. New York: Holt,
          Rinehart and Winston.

Park, Robert Ezra
  1952   Human Communities. Glencoe, Ill.: Free Press.

Park, Robert E. and E. W. Burgess
    1921   Introduction to the Science of Sociology. Chicago: University of Chicago Press.

Parsons, Talcott
    1951   The Social System. Glencoe, Ill.: Free Press.
    1964   "Evolutionary universals in society." American Sociological Review 3:339–57.

Parsons, Talcott and Robert F. Bales, in collaboration with James Olds and others
    1955   Family, Socialization and Interaction Process. Glencoe, Ill.: Free Press.

Parsons, Talcott, Robert F. Bales, and Edward A. Shils
    1953   Working Papers in the Theory of Action. Glencoe, Ill.: Free Press.

Peabody, Robert L.
    1962   "Perception of organizational authority: a comparative analysis." Administrative Science Quarterly 6:463–82.

Pelto, P. J.
    1973   The Snowmobile Revolution: Technology and Social Change in the Arctic. Menlo Park, Calif.: Cummings.

Perkins, John
    1976   Let Justice Roll Down. Glendale, Calif.: Regal Books.

Perry, John and Erma Perry
    1979   The Social Web: An Introduction to Sociology. New York: Harper and Row.

Perrucci, R., D. D. Knudsen, and R. R. Hamby
    1977   Sociology: Basic Structures and Processes. Dubuque: Brown.

Peter, Laurence J., and Raymond Hull
    1969   The Peter Principle. New York: Morrow.

Phillips, Bernard S.
    1971   Social Research: Strategy and Tactics. New York: Macmillan.
    1979   Sociology: From Concepts to Practice. New York: McGraw-Hill.

Poplin, Dennis E.
    1972   Communities: A Survey of Theories and Methods of Research. New York: Macmillan.

Postman, Neil
   1979   "Order in the classroom." Teaching as a Conserving Activity. New York: Dell.
Preble, Edward and John J. Casey, Jr.
   1969   "Taking care of business—the heroin user's life on the street." International Journal of the Addictions 4:1–24.
President's Commission on Law Enforcement and Administration of Justice
   1967   Task Force Report: Crime and its impact: an assessment. Washington, D.C.: U.S. Government Printing Office.

Quebedeaux, Richard
   1974   The Young Evangelicals. New York: Harper and Row.
Queen, Stuart A. and Robert W. Habenstein
   1974   The Family in Various Cultures. Philadelphia: Lippencott.
Quinley, Harold E.
   1974   "The dilemma of an activist church." Journal for the Scientific Study of Religion 23:1–21.
Quinney, Richard
   1979   Criminology. Boston: Little, Brown.

Ramm, Bernard
   1956   Protestant Biblical Interpretation (rev. ed.). Boston: Wilde.
Rappoport, L.
   1972   Personality Development: The Chronology of Experience. Glenview, Ill.: Scott, Foresman.
Ravitch, Diane
   1979   "Color-blind or color-conscious?" The New Republic 18:15–18, 20.
Reed, John Sheldon
   1972   The Enduring South: Subcultural Persistence in Mass Society. Lexington: Heath.
Rieman, Jeffrey H.
   1979   The Rich Get Richer and the Poor Get Prison: Ideology, Class and Criminal Justice. New York: Wiley.
Reissman, Leonard
   1964   The Urban Process. New York: Free Press.

Rich, John Martin
    1974   Challenge and Response: Education in American Culture. New York: Wiley.
Richards, L. O.
    1970   A New Face for the Church. Grand Rapids: Zondervan.
Richardson, C. C.
    1938   The Church Through the Centuries. New York: Scribner's Sons.
Ritzer, George
    1975   Sociology: A Multiple Paradigm Science. Boston: Allyn and Bacon.
Ritzer, George, Kenneth C. W. Kammeyer, and Norman R. Yetman
    1979   Sociology: Experiencing a Changing Society. Boston: Allyn and Bacon.
Roberts, Ron E. and Robert M. Klass
    1979   Social Movements: Between the Balcony and the Barricade. St. Louis: C. V. Mosby.
Robertson, Ian
    1977   Sociology. New York: Worth.
Robin, Gerald D.
    1980   Introduction to the Criminal Justice System. New York: Harper and Row.
Roethlisberger, F. J., W. J. Dickson, and G. C. Homans
    1950   Citations in the Human Group. New York: Harcourt and Brace.
Rose, Jerry D.
    1976   Introduction to Sociology. Chicago: Rand McNally.
Rose, Peter I., Myron Glazer, and Penina Middal Glazer
    1976   Sociology: Inquiring into Society. New York: Harper and Row.
    1977   Sociology: Inquiring into Society. San Francisco: Canfield Press (Harper and Row imprint).
Ross, E. A.
    1908   Social Psychology. New York: Macmillan.
Rothschild-Whitt, Joyce
    1979   "The collectivist organization: an alternative to rational-bureaucratic models." American Sociological Review 44:509–27.

Rushdoony, Rousas J.
  1976   Intellectual Schizophrenia. Philadelphia: Presbyterian and Reformed.

Sadku, Myra
  1979   A student guide to title IX. Resource center on sex roles in education, National Foundation for the Improvement of Education, 8–13.
Saint Paul Bible College
  1978   Catalog 1978–1980. Bible College, Minn.: St. Paul Bible College.
Saint-Simon, Henri De (ed. and trans. by Felix Markham)
  1964   Social Organization, the Science of Man and Other Writings. New York: Harper and Row.
Samuel, Vinay and Chris Sugden
  1979   "A solicited comment on 'The contextualization continuum'." Gospel in context 2:17–19.
Sarason, Seymour and John Doris
  1977   "Mainstreaming: dilemmas, opposition, opportunities." The Exceptional Parent. August, 1977.
Scanzoni, John
  1972   "Sociology" in Robert W. Smith (ed.), Christ and the Modern Mind. Downers Grove, Ill.: Inter-Varsity.
Scanzoni, Letha and Nancy Hardesty
  1974   All We're Meant to Be. Waco: Word.
Scanzoni, Letha and John Scanzoni
  1975   Men, Women and Change, A Sociology of Marriage and the Family. New York: McGraw-Hill.
Schaeffer, Francis A.
  1968   The God Who Is There. Downers Grove, Ill.: Inter-Varsity.
  1976   How Should We Then Live? Old Tappan, N.J.: Revell.
Schaeffer, Francis A. and C. Koop
  1979   Whatever Happened to the Human Race? Old Tappan, N.J.: Revell.
Scharf, Peter (ed.)
  1978   Readings in Moral Education. Minneapolis: Winston.
Schmalleger, Frank
  1979   "World of the career criminal." Human Nature 2:50–56.

Schnore, Leo F.
1973   "Community: theory and research on structure and change." Neil J. Smelser (ed.), Sociology: An Introduction. New York: Wiley.
Schur, Edwin M.
1973   Radical Nonintervention: Rethinking the Delinquency Problem. Englewood Cliffs, N.J.: Prentice-Hall.
Scrivens, Robert
1979   "The big chick." Today's Education. November/December, 1979.
Selznick, Philip
1957   Leadership in Administration: A Sociological Interpretation. New York: Harper and Row.
Sergiovanni, Thomas J. and Fred D. Carver
1973   The New School Executive: A Theory of Administration. New York: Dodd, Mead.
Sergiovanni, Thomas J. and Robert J. Starratt
1971   Emerging Patterns of Supervision: Human Perspectives. New York: McGraw-Hill.
Sharp, Laurston
1952   "Steel axes for stone age Australians." In E. H. Spicer (ed.), Exploring Human Problems in Technological Change: A Casebook. New York: Russell Sage Foundation.
Shaw, Marvin E.
1976   Group Dynamics. New York: McGraw-Hill.
Sider, R. J.
1977   Rich Christians in an Age of Hunger: A Biblical Study. Downers Grove, Ill.: Inter-Varsity.
Silberman, Charles E.
1970   Crisis in the Classroom. New York: Random House.
Simmel, Georg
1950   "The metropolis and mental life." Kurt H. Wolff (ed. and trans.), The Sociology of Georg Simmel. New York: Free Press.
1950a   The Sociology of Georg Simmel. Kurt H. Wolf (trans.), New York: Free Press.
Skidmore, William
1975   Theoretical Thinking in Sociology. Cambridge: Cambridge University Press.

Skinner, Burris F.
   1971   Beyond Freedom and Dignity. New York: Knopf.
Skinner, Tom
   1980   An appeal letter mailed in March.
Slade, Margot
   1979   "The legacy of malnutrition." Psychology Today 6:164,
           170.
Small, Dwight H.
   1959   Design for Christian Marriage. Westwood, N.J.: Revell.
Smart, Laura S. and Mollie S. Smart
   1980   Families: Developing Relationships (2nd ed.). New
           York: Macmillan.
Smelser, Neil J.
   1962   Theory of Collective Behavior. New York: Free Press.
   1965   (ed.) Readings on Economic Sociology. Englewood
           Cliffs, N.J.: Prentice-Hall.
   1973   (ed.) Sociology: An Introduction (2nd ed.). New York:
           Wiley.
Smith, Charles Merrill
   1965   How to Become a Bishop Without Being Religious. Gar-
           den City, N.Y.: Doubleday.
Smith, Richard A.
   1962   "The incredible electrical conspiracy." Pages 357–72 in
           M. Wolfgang, Z. Savitz, and N. Johnson (eds.), The
           Sociology of Crime and Delinquency. New York:
           Wiley.
Snyder, Howard A.
   1977   The Problem of Wineskins: Church Renewal in
           Technological Age. Downers Grove, Ill.: Inter-Varsity.
   1979   Community of the King. Downers Grove, Ill.: Inter-
           Varsity.
Sorokin, Pitirim
   1950   Altruistic Love: A Study of American Good Neighbors
           and Christian Saints. Boston: Beacon.
Southard, Samuel
   1976   Religious Inquiry. Nashville: Abingdon.
Sowell, Thomas
   1975   Race and Economics. New York: McKay.

Spencer, Herbert
1873
(1961)   The Study of Sociology. Ann Arbor: The University of
         Michigan Press.
Spencer, Metta (with editorial collaboration of Alex Inkeles)
   1976   Foundations of Modern Sociology (2nd ed.). Englewood
          Cliffs, N.J.: Prentice-Hall.
Stacey, Margaret
   1969   "The myth of community studies." British Journal of
          Sociology 20:134–47.
Stampp, Kenneth
   1956   The Peculiar Institution. New York: Knopf.
Stark, Rodney, Bruce D. Foster, Charles Y. Glock, and Harold E.
Quinley
   1971   Wayward Shepherds: Prejudice and the Protestant
          Clergy. New York: Harper and Row.
State of North Carolina vs. Columbus Christian Academy et al.
   1978   78-OVS-1678.
Stein, Maurice
   1960   The Eclipse of Community. Princeton: Princeton Uni-
          versity Press.
Storer, Norman W.
   1980   Focus on Society. Reading, Mass.: Addison-Wesley.
Suchman, Edward A.
   1968   "The hang-loose ethic and the spirit of drug use." Jour-
          nal of Health and Social Behavior 9:146–55.
Sumner, William Graham
   1906   Folkways. Boston: Ginn.
Sutherland, Edwin H.
   1937   The Professional Thief. Chicago: University of Chicago
          Press.
   1947   Principles of Crimonology (4th ed.). Philadelphia: Lip-
          pincott.
   1949   White Collar Crime. New York: Holt, Rinehart and
          Winston.

Tabb, B.
   1979   "The demise of our free enterprise system." The Other
          Side 12:44–49.

Tannenbaum, Frank
  1946   Slave and Citizen: The Negro in the Americas. New York: Vantage.

Tarde, Gabriel
  1903   The Laws of Imitation. New York: Holt, Rinehart and Winston.

Tayler, F. W.
  1903   "Group management." Transaction of the American Society of Mechanical Engineers 24:1337–480.

Tenney, Merrill C.
  1961   New Testament Survey (rev. ed.). Grand Rapids: Eerdmans.
  1968   (ed.) Zondervan Pictorial Bible Dictionary. Grand Rapids: Zondervan.

Theilicke, Helmut
  1964   The Ethics of Sex. Grand Rapids: Baker.

Thibaut, John W. and Harold H. Kelley
  1959   The Social Psychology of Groups. New York: Wiley.

Thio, Alex
  1978   Deviant Behavior. Boston: Houghton Mifflin.

Thomas, William I. and Florian Znaniecki
  1927   The Polish Peasant in Europe and America, Vol. 1. New York: Knopf.

Thomlinson, Ralph
  1965   Sociological Concepts and Research. New York: Random.

Thompson, Victor
  1965   Modern Organizations. New York: Knopf.

Thorsell, Bernard A. and Lloyd W. Klemke
  1972   "The labeling process: reinforcement or deterrent?" Law and Society Review 6:393–403.

Throckmorton, Burton H.
  1959   The New Testament and Mythology. Philadelphia: Westminster.

Tillich, Paul
  1951   Systematic Thology, Vol. 1. Chicago: University of Chicago Press.

Time
  1978   Learning to excel in school. July 10.

Timmons, Tim
  1976   Maximum Marriage. Old Tappan, N.J.: Revell.

Toffler, Alvin
  1970   Future Shock. New York: Random House.

Tonnies, Ferdinand
  1940   Fundamental Concepts of Sociology. Charles P. Loomis
          (trans). New York: American Book.

Triplett, N.
  1898   "The dynamogenic factors in pacemaking and compe-
          tition." American Journal of Psychology 9:507–33.

Troeltsch, Ernst
  1932   The Social Teaching of the Christian Churches, Vols.
          1–2. Olive Wyon (trans.). New York: Macmillan.

Trueblood, Elton,
  1967   The Incendiary Fellowship. New York: Harper and Row.

Tubbs, Stewart L.
  1978   A Systems Approach to Small Group Interaction. Read-
          ing, Mass.: Addison-Wesley.

Tuckman, B. W.
  1965   "Developmental sequence in small groups." Psycho-
          logical Bulletin 63:384–99.

Tumin, Melvin M. and Arnold S. Feldman
  1955   "The miracle at Sabana Grande." Public Opinion Quar-
          terly 19:124–39.

Turner, Jonathan H.
  1978   Sociology: Studying the Human System. Santa Monica:
          Goodyear.

Turner, Ralph H. and Lewis M. Killian
  1972   Collective Behavior (2nd ed.). Englewood Cliffs, N.J.:
          Prentice-Hall.

Turner, William L.
  1979   "Reasons for enrollment in religious schools: a case
          study of three recently established fundamentalist
          schools in Kentucky and Wisconsin." Unpublished
          manuscript, University of Wisconsin.

Tylor, Edward B.
  1871   Primitive Culture. London: J. Murray.

United Evangelical Action
  1980   United Evangelical Action.
U.S. News and World Report
  1979   "Give us better schools" 11:31–32.

Vander Zanden, James Wilfrid
  1979   Sociology (4th ed.). New York: Wiley.
Verduin, Leonard
  1970   Somewhat Less Than God. Grand Rapids: Eerdmans.
Vermont vs. Lebarge
  1976   134 Vt. 276.

Warren, Roland
  1978   The Community in America (3rd ed.). Chicago: Rand
          McNally.
Webber, Robert E.
  1979   The Secular Saint. Grand Rapids: Zondervan.
Weber, Max
  1930   The Protestant Ethic and the Spirit of Capitalism. Talcott
          Parsons (trans.). New York: Scribner's Sons.
  1958   From Max Weber: Essays in Sociology. Fairlawn, N.J.:
          Oxford University Press.
  1947   The Theory of Social and Economic Organization. Glen-
          coe, Ill.: Free Press.
  1968   Economy and Society. New York: Bedminster Press.
  1977   The Protestant Ethic and the Spirit of Capitalism. Talcott
          Parsons (trans.). New York: Scribner's Sons.
Weitzman, L.
  1975   Sex-Role Socialization, in J. Freeman, ed., Warren: A
          Feminist Perspective. Palo Alto, Calif.: Mayfield, pp.
          106–44.
Weston, Louise
  1977   The Study of Society. Guilford, Conn.: Dushkin.
White, John
  1979   The Golden Cow. Downers Grove, Ill.: Inter-Varsity.
Whiting, John W. and Irvin L. Child
  1953   Child Training and Personality: Cross Cultural Study.
          New Haven: Yale University Press.

Whitley, Oliver Reed
1969   The Church: Mirror or Window? St. Louis: Bethany.

Whyte, William F.
1955   Street Corner Society. Chicago: University of Chicago Press.

Williams, Colin W.
1968   The Church. New Directions in Theology Today, Vol. 4. Philadelphia: Westminster.

Williams, Don
1977   The Apostle Paul and Women in the Church. Glendale, Calif: Regal.

Willowbank Consultation on Gospel and Culture
1978   The Willowbank Report—Gospel and Culture. Wheaton: Lausanne Committee for World Evangelism.

Wirth, Louis
1938   "Urbanism as a way of life." American Journal of Sociology 44:14—16.

Witmer, S. A.
1964   "The Bible Institute and College Movement." Pages 379—91 in J. Edward Hakes (ed.), An Introduction to Evangelical Christian Education. Chicago: Moody.

1970   Education With Dimensions. Fort Wayne, Ind.: The Accrediting Association of Bible Colleges (reprint).

Wogaman, J. Philip
1977   The Great Economic Debate: An Ethical Analysis. Philadelphia: Westminster.

Wolfgang, Marvin E. and Franco Ferracuti
1967   The Subculture of Violence: Towards an Integrated Theory in Criminology. London: Tavistock.

Wood, James
1970   "Authority and controversial policy: the churches and civil rights." American Sociological Review 35:1057—069.

Woods, L. B.
1979   "Is academic freedom dead in public schools?" Phi Delta Kappan 2:104—106.

Wuthnow, Robert
1973   "Religious commitment and conservatism: in search of an illusive relationship." In Charles Glock (ed.), Religion in Sociological Perspective. Belmont: Wadsworth.

Young, Edward
   1958   An Introduction to the Old Testament (rev. ed.). Grand
           Rapids: Eerdmans.
Young, George P.
   1980   "The St. Paul public school system." Unpublished
           manuscript, St. Paul Public Schools.

INDEXES

AUTHOR INDEX

SUBJECT INDEX

Index

DATE DUE

AGT '84			
MAY 1 '89			
GAYLORD			PRINTED IN U.S.A.